INITIATING THE MILLENNIUM

Initiating the Millennium

THE AVIGNON SOCIETY AND ILLUMINISM
IN EUROPE

Robert Collis

Natalie Bayer

OXFORD
UNIVERSITY PRESS

OXFORD
UNIVERSITY PRESS

Oxford University Press is a department of the University of Oxford. It furthers
the University's objective of excellence in research, scholarship, and education
by publishing worldwide. Oxford is a registered trade mark of Oxford University
Press in the UK and certain other countries.

Published in the United States of America by Oxford University Press
198 Madison Avenue, New York, NY 10016, United States of America.

Library of Congress Cataloging-in-Publication Data
ISBN 978–0–19–090337–4

9 8 7 6 5 4 3 2 1

Printed by Integrated Books International, United States of America

*To George and Teddy, our rays of illumination,
and to the memory of Gennadii Iur'evich Magakov.*

Contents

Acknowledgements

THE TOPIC OF this study is pan-European in scope, and we were fortunate enough to receive considerable help in the preparation of this work across Europe (and beyond). This good fortune, moreover, came about without any prior consultations with oracular authorities in Iowa (or elsewhere). The support we received was thus based on a generosity of spirit rather than any *spirit* of generosity. In Russia, we were greatly assisted by Iurii Kondakov, who helped us secure a second batch of crucial documents from the Russian State Historical Archive in St. Petersburg. We are also grateful to Iurii Khalturin and Andrei Serkov. In Sweden, we were kindly aided by Ulf Åsén, the archivist of the Swedish Order of Freemasons in Stockholm. Kjell Lekeby also gave up his time to transcribe the shoddy handwriting of Gustaf Reuterholm, for which we are very grateful. We would also like to thank Henrik Bogdan for giving us the chance to write this book, and Andreas Önnerfors for first fostering our interest in the Illuminés d'Avignon in Sheffield.

It has been a great pleasure and privilege to correspond with Antoine Faivre in France for a number of years. We benefitted enormously from his unrivalled knowledge of the field, not only in commenting on drafts of our chapters, but also in directing us to invaluable source material in various archives scattered throughout Europe. We would also like to thank Pierre-Yves Beàurepaire and Thierry Zarcone for sharing both archival material and their own work, as well as Michel Chazottes in Avignon. We would also like to thank Simon Perrotin for his help in translating some suitably cryptic letters and prophecies by Madame Bouche.

We were also fortunate to receive a tremendous amount of help from scholars in the United States. First, we are truly indebted to the generosity of Clorinda Donato of

California State University, who translated several extremely difficult letters and notes written in Italian by Ottavio Cappelli. Without her aid, we would have been deprived of an invaluable source for our work. We are also grateful to Alexander Martin for sharing his collection of material related to Barbara von Krüdener, and to the late Jane Williams-Hogan for providing information on the Swedenborgians. At various points throughout this project, we also obtained valuable nuggets of information from Marsha Keith Schuchard. Thanks also to Kris Mogle, Head of Interlibrary Loans at Drake University, for always promptly supplying us with the rather obscure texts we regularly required. Thanks, too, to Christine Elizabeth Jacobson, Assistant Curator of Modern Books and Manuscripts at Houghton Library, Harvard University, who kindly supplied us with details about an alchemical manuscript housed at her institution. We would also like to thank Kaley Wresch, for her assistance in preparing the final draft of the manuscript; Kenneth Loiselle; and Cynthia Read, for her help throughout. We are both extremely lucky to have wonderful colleagues at the Department of History at Drake University and are especially grateful to the chair, Karen Leroux, for her support.

In England, Katariina Nara-Zanotti aided us in the translation of some French manuscripts, and at various points we were generously helped by Susan Snell and Martin Cherry, librarians at the Museum of Freemasonry in London. We would also like to thank the following scholars for their help: Reinhard Markner in Innsbruck, Jan Snoek in Heidelberg, Peter Forshaw and Wouter Hanegraaff in Amsterdam, and Peter Lineham in Palmerston North in New Zealand. Thanks are also due to Karin Borgkvist of the Riksarkivet in Stockholm, Jac Piepenbrock of the Prince Fredrik Masonic Centre in The Hague, and Paola Ferraris of the Archivio di Stato di Roma for ensuring that we had access to important source material. We would also like to acknowledge the support of the University of Sheffield, the Helsinki Collegium for Advanced Studies, and Drake University over the past seven years. This project was made possible by a generous grant from the Center for the Humanities and the College of Arts and Sciences at Drake. The Leverhulme Trust also provided us with a substantial travel grant that facilitated a great deal of our archival research in Moscow and St. Petersburg in 2012.

Last, but certainly not least, we have received the unwavering support of our families, in both practical and emotional ways. Svetlana Magakova spent countless evenings transcribing Russian texts, when she was not looking after her grandchildren. Graham Collis undertook a research trip to the British Library, which was of great help, and also did his fair share of looking after the grandkids. Christina Collis has been an enormous support during the entire project and put in a wonderfully helpful stint with her grandchildren when we were in the final stages of writing the manuscript. Thanks also to Liz Collis, Katya Sotnikova, and Sergei Sotnikov for their love and support.

Abbreviations

ACSD	Academic Collection of Swedenborg Documents (Bryn Athyn)
ACV	Archives cantonales vaudoises (Chavannes-près-Renens, Switzerland)
AdBBAdW	Archiv der Berlin-Brandenburgischen Akademie der Wissenschaften (Berlin)
ADC	Archives départementales de la Charente (Angouleme)
ADdlD	Archives départementales de la Drôme (Valence)
ADdV	Archives départementales de Vaucluse (Avignon)
ADHM	Archives départementales de la Haute Marne (Chaumont-Choignes)
AdP	Archives de Paris (Paris)
AdSdR	Archivio di Stato di Roma (Rome)
AGA	Archives Georges Alphandéry, Château de Grignan (Avignon)
AMAE	Archives du ministère des Affaires étrangères (La Courneuve)
AN	Archives Nationales (Paris)
BIdlA	Bibliothèque interuniversitaire de la Sorbonne (Paris)
BL	British Library (London)
BMdA	Bibliothèque Municipale d'Avignon (Avignon)
BMdL	Bibliothèque Municipale de Lyon (Lyon)
BMdG	Bibliothèque Municipale de Grenoble (Grenoble)
BNCdR	Biblioteca Nazionale Centrale di Roma (Rome)
BNdF	Bibliothèque Nationale de France (Paris)
BNUdS	Bibliothèque Nationale et Universitaire de Strasbourg (Strasbourg)
CMCPF	Cultureel Maçonniek Centrum Prins Frederik (The Hague)

DWL	Doctor Williams's Library (London)
HHStA	Haus,- Hof- und Staatsarchiv (Vienna)
HLHU	Houghton Library, Harvard University (Cambridge, MA)
HSAS	Hauptstaatsarchiv Stuttgart (Stuttgart)
HSD	Hessisches Staatsarchiv Darmstadt (Darmstadt)
HSP	Historical Society of Pennsylvania (Philadelphia)
KB	Kungliga Biblioteket (Stockholm)
KCUP	Kislak Center for Special Collections, Rare Books and Manuscripts, University of Pennsylvania (Philadelphia)
MC	Médiathèque Ceccano (Avignon)
MPA	Musée Paul Arbaud (Aix-en-Provence)
NA	The National Archives (Kew)
NAS	The National Archives of Scotland (Edinburgh)
NCCL	New Church Conference Library (London)
RA	Riksarkivet (Stockholm)
RGB	Rossiiskaia gosudarstvennaia biblioteka (Moscow)
RGIA	Rossiiskii gosudarstvennyi istoricheskii arkhiv (St. Petersburg)
RNB	Rossiiskaia natsional'naia biblioteka (St. Petersburg)
SFOA	Svenska Frimuare Ordens Arkiv (Stockholm)
SPF IRI	Sankt-Peterburgskii filial Instituta rossiiskoi istorii RAN (St. Petersburg)
TsGIA SPB	Tsentral'nyi gosudarstvennyi istoricheskii arkhiv Sankt-Peterburg (St. Petersburg)
UUB	Uppsala universitetsbibliotek (Uppsala)
ZBZ	Zentralbibliothek Zürich (Zürich)

Introduction

∽

ON THE EVE of the French Revolution the Marquis de Luchet published a lengthy broadside, entitled *Essai sur la secte des illuminés*, against what he viewed as a pernicious influence that was spreading throughout Europe.[1] His target was not the Bavarian Order of Illuminati, which between 1776 and 1785 advanced a rational vision of human perfectibility within the structure of a secret society.[2] Rather, in his introduction, Luchet states clearly that his sight was aimed at an amorphous, yet dangerous, sect whose "mystical machinations" and "fanatical eagerness" were fanned by "anything that carries the livery of Swedenborg or Schroepffer."[3] In other words, he envisaged his essay as a clarion call against those who espoused the theosophical doctrine of Emanuel Swedenborg and the necromantic esotericism of Johann Georg Schrepfer.[4] The pejorative label *illuminés* was a recent term used to categorise those who embraced interrelated strands of thought that included Christian theosophy, Cabala, alchemy, high-degree Freemasonry, and Rosicrucianism. An air of charlatanism was also connected to *illuminés*, as is evident in the Comte de Mirabeau's early denunciation in 1786, in which he proclaims that "the Rosicrucians, the Cabalists, the *Illuminés* and the Alchemists" were guilty of "monstrous follies that have bloodied and dishonoured the earth" and directly links them to the notorious adventurer Cagliostro.[5] Thus the illumination sought by *illuminés* was not the clear-eyed, luminous variant that is still largely associated with the Age of Enlightenment. Both Mirabeau and Luchet utilised the term *illuminé* to denigrate those who championed strands of what in recent decades we have come to call Western esotericism.[6]

Who were these *illuminés* to whom both Mirabeau and Luchet were so vehemently opposed? In 1786, Mirabeau asserted that they could be found in Berlin, where they received the protection and favour of Friedrich II.[7] However, according to Luchet, writing three years later, their baleful influence was being felt across Europe. He is thankful

Initiating the Millennium. Robert Collis, and Natalie Bayer, Oxford University Press (2020) © Oxford University Press.
DOI: 10.1093/oso/9780190903374.001.0001

that the French court had not been seduced by "the elements of theosophy" and posits that the labouring bourgeoisie were fortunately still too uneducated to be hoodwinked. Nonetheless, he asserts that "there are a host of small anti-philosophical parties composed of learned women, priest theologians and some pretended sages." Luchet claims that the "petits princes" at German courts "indulge themselves in the sweet incense that intoxicates the Priests of the *Illuminés*." He adds that the *illuminés* have succeeded in securing many proselytes to the east, in Poland and Russia, where "religion lends itself to mystical systems." To his horror, even England was "not entirely free from these shameful beliefs."[8] Luchet's principal concern about the proliferation of *illuminés* is centred squarely on their dangerous enthusiasm. For Luchet, this danger was not politically oriented; instead, it follows in the Voltairian tradition of railing against the harmful effects of religious fanaticism and superstition. A misogynistic strain also seems to run through his criticism of "learned women."

Luchet offers no concrete information about either the precise composition or location of these *illuminés*. Despite this obfuscation, the author provided enough clues in his account for readers familiar with the cultural and religious landscape of Europe to be able to identify the sect that was in the line of fire. At the time, only one "sect" of *illuminés* included "learned women, priest theologians and pretended sages" *and* had pan-European ambitions: this society was based in Avignon. However, the "sect" had been established in Berlin, in 1779, by a triumvirate of individuals—Tadeusz Grabianka (1740–1807), Antoine-Joseph Pernety (1716–1796), and Louis-Joseph-Bernard-Philibert Guyton de Morveau (known as "Brumore"; 1738–1787)—who combined to form a distinctive initiatic society. Pernety and Brumore were lapsed priests, and Grabianka qualified as a "pretended sage." Further, from its genesis, the group had included the very "*femmes Savantes*" ridiculed by Luchet. By 1789, this charismatic and dynamic trio had succeeded in forging an extraordinary religious society that attracted prospective candidates from across Europe.

Luchet's reticence to fully expose the *illuminé* hydra may have stemmed from a sense of practical necessity. At the time he was writing, he was, after all, an attaché to Prince Heinrich of Prussia, who had been initiated into this very sect of *illuminés* in 1780 by none other than Brumore, Luchet's direct predecessor at the royal court in Rheinsberg.[9] It seems highly improbable that Luchet was unaware of what Mirabeau blasted as the "monstrous follies" being championed by *les illuminés* at the Prussian court. Luchet may have been misguided in his estimation of the danger posed by *les illuminés*, given the myriad other threats faced by the Ancien Régime in 1789. Nevertheless, his salvo reflects the sense of fear that was rising among the proponents of secularity in France in the 1780s vis-à-vis the spread of the "insipid" dogma of the *illuminés* in their homeland and across Europe.[10] The strident language adopted by Luchet testifies to the changed social, cultural, and political landscape in 1789. Only six years had passed since L.-S. Mercier had first drawn attention to *illuminés* as a distinctive sect. Yet Mercier's account contains none of Luchet's vitriolic tone. On the contrary, in Mercier's eyes, "these visionaries," whom he refers to as "Martinists," in reference to Louis-Claude de Saint-Martin, "are the gentlest of men, calm and moderate."[11]

In the 230 years that have passed since Luchet wrote his essay, a number of historians have examined, in varying depths, the Illuminés d'Avignon, who were the principal target of his polemic. The earliest commentary on the society was published by Abbé Augustin Barruel, in 1797, in his conspiratorial narrative of the French Revolution. In this influential work, Barruel firmly located the epicentre of the "denomination of theosophical *illuminés*" in Avignon, although they had spread their "abominable mysteries" throughout France.[12] According to Barruel, the society in Avignon were devotees of Swedenborg, whose writings he brands as "a labyrinth of impiety and imposture."[13] Barruel pronounces that, far from being the passive, quietist-like enthusiasts described by Mercier, they had formed "the most secret and most monstrous of lodges" in order to "form the most terrible tribunal for Kings." If this was not damning enough, Barruel added that "was there ever such atrocious ferocity shown" by the ringleaders of this society, who "sharpened the dagger" of the assassin of sovereigns.[14] By conflating the theosophical *illuminés* with the "atheistic" *illuminati*, Barruel created a conspiratorial myth that has proven to be extremely resilient.

In 1814, Henri Grégoire included a brief account of what he referred to as the "fanatics of Avignon" in his history of religious sects.[15] Despite being framed in negative terms, Grégoire's description is, on the whole, balanced and accurate. Thereafter, however, the society does not seem to have interested French historians for the remainder of the nineteenth century. One notable exception is a serialised article on alchemy published in 1863 by the poet Thalès Bernard.[16] He was privy to a seemingly lost collection of manuscripts related to the *illuminés* in Avignon, albeit largely unaware of the significance of the documents and more generally of the "société hermétique" he describes.

Besides Bernard's non-historical piece, a lengthy lacuna of nearly a century was to pass before Marc de Vissac published an article, in 1906, dedicated to the Illuminés d'Avignon.[17] This work merits praise, as Vissac was the first historian to devote attention to an invaluable manuscript that recorded the consultations of members of the society of *illuminés* with an oracle named Sainte Parole (Holy Word) between 1779 and 1785.[18] Several French historians have made extensive use of this manuscript in order to elaborate on Vissac's groundbreaking work. Yet, though Vissac deserves to be lauded for bringing this manuscript to our attention, his article is also littered with wholly uncorroborated assertions. Notably, he seems to have unconditionally accepted a claim, dating back to 1841, which posited that Pernety directed the activities of the *illuminés* from "Mont Thabor," that is, the country estate of the Marquis de Vaucroze in the village of Bédarrides.[19] This unsubstantiated narrative, which accentuates Pernety's pre-eminence within the society, has subsequently been perpetuated by numerous historians, whose analysis, moreover, was somewhat blinkered and over-reliant on the single nugget of true gold unearthed by Vissac.[20]

A distinctly different emphasis is found in Russian and Polish accounts of the society, which largely highlight the role of Grabianka. This focus is unsurprising, given that Grabianka was a Polish nobleman from Podolia who was technically a subject of the Russian Empire for the last fourteen years of his life. Crucially, historians in Russia and Poland were also able to draw on the substantial trove of archival material drawn from Grabianka's personal manuscripts. These documents were confiscated by the Russian authorities in St. Petersburg in 1807, after Grabianka, who had been living in the Russian capital since 1805, was arrested and imprisoned.[21]

Mikhail Longinov was the first historian to utilise this material, in 1860, when he published an article on Grabianka's involvement with the illuministic society between 1779 and 1807.[22] Yet Longinov neither provided any references nor indicated the provenance of his information. The same tendency is evident in a short study of the Avignon Society by A. N. Pypin in his broader survey of Freemasonry in Russia. Pypin draws heavily on Longinov, but also includes fresh material related to the ritual practices of the group in Russia. Once again, however, no reference is made to the provenance of the material being discussed.[23] Remarkably, it was over 150 years before this treasure trove of documents was identified and utilised in a scholarly manner by Iu. E. Kondakov, as part of a monograph on broader illuminist currents in early nineteenth-century Russia.[24]

In the wake of Longinov's article, the Polish historian A. J. Rolle produced the first extended biographical account of Grabianka.[25] Rolle relied heavily on Longinov's unreferenced article. However, he did embellish his work with valuable material drawn from archives in Podolia, from where both he and his subject hailed, material that has since been destroyed. Subsequent studies by Polish historians have, in large measure, combined the prior work of Longinov and Rolle, as well as that of the published French sources.[26]

A notable exception is an English-language article published in 1968 by Maria Danilewicz, who emigrated from Poland to Britain during World War II. As a prominent librarian, she was able to use her access to published sources in Britain to broaden our understanding of the links between Grabianka and Swedenborgians in London. Moreover, she also first drew attention to how Grabianka's acquaintance with Swedenborgians in London led to direct English involvement in the society in Avignon. This dimension was expanded by Clarke Garrett in 1975, in his monograph on millenarians in France and England at the time of the French Revolution. He devoted a chapter (entitled "The Mystical International") to the group, focusing, in the main, on its cosmopolitan complexion.[27] Garrett's emphasis on the pan-European aspect of the Avignon Society also incorporated an Italian perspective, based on the research of Renzo de Felice. In 1960, Felice published a seminal work on illuminism and mysticism in Rome between 1789 and 1800, which included a chapter on the supposed prophet Ottavio Cappelli (1736–1800) and his consequential involvement with the Avignon Society.[28] More recently, Andreas Önnerfors has analysed the participation of two Swedish noblemen in the society in the late 1780s.[29] In so doing he has considerably elaborated upon earlier fleeting references to these two Swedes in connection with the Avignon Society.[30]

Yet to this day, our knowledge and comprehension of the society remains fragmentary at best, with glaring gaps and a surfeit of erroneous claims. The present work seeks to redress this neglect. In so doing, it represents the first book-length study of the Avignon Society in English. Our overarching aim is to shine an exacting light on the many obscure facets of the society that is most commonly referred to as either the Illuminés d'Avignon or the Avignon Society. Even here, there is a need for clarification. During its twenty-eight-year existence, between 1779 and 1807, the group of *illuminés*, who first came together in Berlin, went by several names. Indeed, the society does not appear to have given itself a name at all until it was effectively re-established in the papal enclave of Avignon, in 1787. Thereafter members simply referred to the "society at Avignon" or, more commonly, "the Union." Moreover, in its last incarnation in St. Petersburg, the group was known as the New Israel Society (NIS) or the People of God.

. The society's emergence in 1779 occurred at a time when illuminist thought had already begun to exert a profound hold on the imagination of a significant segment of the European nobility. Since the 1750s, the notorious adventures Giacomo Casanova and Comte de Saint-Germain had beguiled the courts of Europe, with their self-fashioned auras of mystery and ancient wisdom.[31] Both men unashamedly tapped into the latent reservoir of early modern occult philosophy to assume the roles of sage adepts seeped in alchemical and cabalistic wisdom. Their legacy was continued by Count Cagliostro from the late 1770s.[32] Furthermore, the 1770s witnessed the development of high-degree Freemasonry in a variety of guises across Europe. The dizzying profusion of such rites, from St. Petersburg in the east to London in the west, all drew from the same common reservoir of occult philosophy as had the likes of Casanova and Saint-Germain. However, whilst the earlier adventurers had plied solitary careers, the establishment of high-degree rites created a framework in which esoteric symbolism as well as active pursuits that drew on older alchemical and cabalistic thought penetrated into the associational culture of Freemasonry.[33] This emergent form of Freemasonry proved to be highly enticing to many, combining, as it did, lavish initiation rites with strong fraternal bonds. Not to be outdone, Cagliostro adapted to this new dynamic by forging his own brand of esoteric Freemasonry.[34]

In recent years a number of important studies have been published that highlight the prevalence of illuminism in European society during this era.[35] As Christine Bergé notes, illuminism at this time was a "complex intellectual and spiritual movement" whose practitioners "were adventurers of thought."[36] The term *illuminisme* has been commonly used by French scholars since at least the 1920s, when August Viatte published his seminal two-volume work *Les sources occultes du romantisme*. The English variant will be used in this work too, as its etymological root links it to the broader Enlightenment in a more positive way (though it is necessary to remember that *illuminés* was initially a pejorative label). Those who embraced enlightenment principles and those who expressed illuminist sentiment were the children of the same age, though they were seeking divergent paths to knowledge and differed greatly.[37] This tallies with Dan Edelstein's assertion that

" 'hermetic' and 'ordinary' philosophers often shared an identical epistemological framework."[38] Antoine Faivre has also noted the "contrary yet complementary faces" of "the Enlightenment and the light of the illuminists."[39]

It was within this cultural and social context that Grabianka, Pernety, and Brumore founded a formal initiatic society in Berlin. They, too, were children of their time. Grabianka, in particular, comported himself in a manner befitting an eighteenth-century adventurer. To a lesser extent, Brumore also adopted such a guise, whereas Pernety fulfilled the role of learned sage. The influence of high-degree Freemasonry is also undeniable. Yet it is significant that this founding triumvirate had very little direct involvement with the fraternity. We know that Pernety was a Freemason, as his name was recorded in 1782 on the register of members of La loge Royale d'York de l'Amitié, in Berlin.[40] Nonetheless, he does not seem to have played an active role in the life of this lodge, nor has any evidence come to light of his involvement in Freemasonry in France. Those who have credited Pernety with creating his own high-degree rite in Avignon in the 1760s have thus done so without any corroborating evidence.[41] What is more, there are no documents that point to Grabianka and Brumore being Freemasons.

From its inception in 1779, Grabianka, Brumore, and Pernety, who were all Catholics and conversed in French, developed a number of distinctive features within the society.[42] Consultations with the Holy Word were to remain a critical feature of the society for many years. Initiation into the society provided individuals with a means to consult with the divine, with Brumore acting as the oracle, about a myriad of issues, some relatively trivial and some life-changing. An elaborate nine-day consecration ritual was enacted from the very beginning of the society's activities in Berlin. This theurgical rite may not have been entirely original, as it was predated by the three-day ceremonial used by Élus Coëns in the 1760s under the initial supervision of Martinez de Pasqually. However, it outdid its Martinist forerunner, not only in terms of the length of the consecration rite, but also in its lavish liturgical practices.

Women and children were consecrated from the very beginning of the society's existence. In this way, the group was much more of an inclusive religious sect than an exclusive fraternity that barred candidates because of their gender or age. The family-oriented nature of the society was based on the millenarian doctrine that played a fundamental part in the society's raison d'être. Consecration into the society signalled that a candidate had become one of the elect and would attain salvation. Thus any family members who were not consecrated would be counted among the damned when the imminent millennium began. The family-centred nature of this initiatic society was highly distinctive and remained a core feature of the group until its demise.

One other noteworthy feature of the society throughout its existence was its inclusion of a variety of Christian denominations and having a multinational colouring. The three Catholic founders actively encouraged Protestant candidates of various denominations, as well as Orthodox Christians, to join their fold (at least until 1790). Moreover, by 1790 the society included initiates from France, Poland, Russia, Sweden, the Italian peninsula,

England, Scotland, Ireland, Switzerland, and the German states. This pan-European dimension is also evident in the various locations in which the society was active during its existence, which included Berlin, Rheinsberg, Podolia, Valence, Avignon, Paris, London, Rome, and St. Petersburg. Garrett labelled the society a "mystical international," though a cosmopolitan congregation of *illuminés* might be a more fitting name for the time period.

Yet in many ways, the society became a victim of its own success. By 1790, when the group was arguably at its peak, the sheer range of Christian denominations represented from across Europe created a volatile confessional mix in which it became increasingly difficult to maintain harmony. The society was also accessible to all classes of European society, although the nobility were undoubtedly in a majority. Initiates ranged from Prince Heinrich of Prussia (the king's brother) to the English carpenter John Wright. A significant number of physicians and merchants were associated with the society, in Avignon in particular; in St. Petersburg, the members attracted to the group were overwhelmingly from the upper nobility.

In 1780 the society became noticeably more millenarian in nature. The pronouncements of the Holy Word began to contain increasingly stark prophecies about imminent tribulations. These oracular warnings came to be combined with direct contact with purported prophets. The first was a Polish gentleman named Rohoziński, who was acquainted with Grabianka, whose predictions were disseminated well beyond the small circle of initiates of the Berlin society. Thereafter prophets came to play a crucial role in fuelling the millenarian expectancy of the society. Some, such as Samuel Best in London and Suzette Labrousse in Paris, never formally joined the society but had close links to individuals in the group. Others, however, such as Ottavio Cappelli and Thérèse Bouche, were consecrated into the Avignon Society and went on to exert a profound influence on the group itself and at the court of Emperor Alexander I of Russia respectively.

Since the 1970s a wealth of literature has appeared vis-à-vis the prevalence of millenarian sentiment and a distinct upsurge in supposed prophets and prophetesses in Europe during the age of revolution.[43] In Britain, one can point to the aforementioned Samuel Best and to Dorothy Gott and Elspeth Buchan in England and Scotland in the 1780s, as well as to Richard Brothers and Joanna Southcott in the 1790s, to name but the most well-known.[44] In France, the likes of Jacqueline-Aimé Brohon, Jean-Baptiste Ruer, Labrousse, and Catherine Théot also gained considerable notoriety in the 1780s and 1790s.[45] The participation of the Avignon Society within this broader millenarian climate has not been ignored; however, the unique role it played in promoting this culture has not been fully appreciated. A number of crucial factors were enticing in this regard: the allure of the elaborate initiatic rites, redolent of high-degree Freemasonry, and of being included in a millenarian community of members from across Europe that promoted a highly distinct form of sociability.

All these distinctive features—the central role of the Holy Word, family participation, the elaborate nine-day consecration ceremony, and, most significantly, the all-pervading culture of millenarianism—long remained intrinsic elements of the Avignon Society during its various phases. This is not to say that the society did not adjust and change amid the various vicissitudes that beset both the society and Europe as a whole between the 1780s and early nineteenth century. We will explore how the society's early embrace of Swedenborgian doctrine, for example, was dramatically repudiated by the end of 1788, to be replaced by a pronounced veneration of the Virgin Mary. The turn to Marianism also marked an increased emphasis, advocated by Cappelli, on the need to conform to Roman Catholic dogma, at the expense of the more ecumenical spirit that had reigned in the society during its first decade. We will also examine how Grabianka instigated a number of reforms from the late 1790s, including the utilisation of a dedicated temple and the introduction of hierarchical degrees (akin to Freemasonry). We will demonstrate how he reconfigured the nine-day consecration ritual along much more modest lines, in keeping with the changed circumstances of the society during its time in St. Petersburg in the first decade of the nineteenth century.

The scope of this study covers nearly half a century, between 1779 and 1822, encompassing one of the most tumultuous epochs in European history. The study will proceed in a chronological fashion. This allows us to chart the changing circumstances and fortunes of the society as it developed from a small circle of alchemical adepts in 1779 into a multinational and multi-confessional society a decade later. A chronological presentation also offers us the best means to portray and evaluate how the society as a whole, as well as the individual members, reacted to the tumult of a revolution and a war in quick succession that rent the European continent at the time.

The first three chapters chart the initial decade of the society's existence, between 1779 and 1789. Chapter 1 concentrates on the group's activities in Berlin, Rheinsberg, and Podolia. Chapter 2 focuses on Grabianka's year-long residence in London in 1785–1786. Chapter 3 incorporates what was arguably the society's golden era, between 1787 and early 1790, when it was based in Avignon. The history of Ottavio Cappelli's involvement in the society in Rome between late 1789 and his execution in 1800 is the subject of chapter 4. Chapter 5 moves back to Avignon and assesses how Grabianka navigated the revolutionary turbulence in the city and ensured the continued presence of the society in the 1790s, albeit in diminished form. In chapter 6, our attention shifts to Galicia, Podolia, and St. Petersburg between 1802 and 1807. This period of renewed activity by Grabianka culminated in 1807 with his arrest by the Russian authorities in February and death in the notorious Peter and Paul Fortress in October. The final two chapters reflect on the legacy of the NIS. Chapter 7 concentrates on how Russian initiates continued to espouse and promote the millenarian doctrine that had played such a pivotal role in Grabianka's society in St. Petersburg. Chapter 8 explores the remarkable history of Thérèse Bouche, who was active in the Avignon Society in the 1790s. She went on to promote herself as a prophetess in Marseille in the early 1810s, where she maintained links to former members of the society. She later enjoyed the status of a secret court prophet for Russia's Emperor Alexander and two of his most senior servitors between 1819 and 1821.

The members of the Avignon Society may not have defined the contours of this era, but as we will demonstrate, they were periodically sucked into the maelstrom of events that engulfed France after 1789 and the entire European continent during the Napoleonic Wars. Indeed, it is not hyperbole to state that key members of the society actively sought to intercede in political matters at crucial moments in European history. In chapter 5, for example, we document how Grabianka walked a precarious tightrope in Avignon in the 1790s. Whilst he formed cordial relationships with the leading revolutionary figures in the city, he also acted as an agent on behalf of the exiled Bourbon dynasty. Chapter 8 discusses the remarkable influence of Bouche on Emperor Alexander, at a time when he was arguably the most powerful sovereign in Europe. By this time, the initiatic society established by Grabianka, Brumore, and Pernety in Berlin had long ceased to exist. Yet Bouche continued to employ, with great success for a number of years, two of the most distinctive features associated with the society: the Holy Word oracle and a fervent millenarian vision.

NOTES

1. J.-P.-L. de Luchet, *Essai sur la secte des Illuminés* (Paris: n.p., 1789).

2. On the Bavarian Order of Illuminati, see Monika Neugebauer-Wölk, "Illuminaten," in *Dictionary of Gnosis and Western Esotericism*, ed. Wouter J. Hanegraaff (Leiden: Brill, 2006), 590–7.

3. Luchet, *Essai*, vi.

4. On the influence of Swedenborgian doctrine on English illuminism, see Clarke Garrett, "Swedenborg and the Mystical Enlightenment in Late Eighteenth-Century England," *Journal of the History of Ideas* 45:1 (1984): 67–81. On the wider European influence of Swedenborg on illuminist thought in the late eighteenth century, see August Viatte, *Les Sources occultes du romantisme: Illuminisme–théosophie 1770–1820*, vol. 1 (Paris: Honoré Champion, 1965), 71–103; Jane Williams-Hogan, "The Place of Emanuel Swedenborg in Modern Western Esotericism," in *Western Esotericism and the Science of Religion*, ed. Antoine Faivre and Wouter J. Hanegraaff (Leuven: Peeters, 1998), 201–52. On Schrepfer, see Renko Geffarth, "The Masonic Necromancer: Shifting Identities in the Lives of Johann Georg Schrepfer," in *Polemical Encounters: Esoteric Discourse and Its Others*, ed. Olav Hammer and Kocku von Stuckrad (Leiden: Brill, 2007), 181–200.

5. H.-G. Riqueti de Mirabeau, *Lettre du Comte de Mirabeau à M. . . . sur M. M. de Cagliostro et Lavater* (Berlin: François de Lagarde, 1786), 47.

6. See Wouter J. Hanegraaff, *Western Esotericism: A Guide for the Perplexed* (London: Bloomsbury, 2013), 1–18.

7. Mirabeau, *Lettre*, 48.

8. Luchet, *Essai*, vii–x.

9. See Carlo Denina, *La Prusse littéraire sous Frédéric II ou Histoire abrégé de la plupart des auteurs*, vol. 2 (Berlin: H. A. Rottmann, 1790), 430–3; Dieudonné Thiebault, *Mes souvenirs de vingt ans de séjour à Berlin*, vol. 2 (Paris: F. Buisson, 1805), 201–2.

10. Luchet, *Essai*, vi.

11. L.-S. Mercier, *Tableau de* Paris, vol. 5 (Amsterdam: n.p., 1783), 235. Saint-Martin came to prominence after the publication of *Des erreurs et de la vérité* in 1775.

12. Augustin Barruel, *Memoirs Illustrating the History of Jacobinism*, trans. Robert Clifford, vol. 4 (London: T. Burton, 1798), 143–4.

13. Barruel, *Memoirs*, vol. 4, 143.

14. Barruel, *Memoirs*, vol. 4, 487.

15. Henri Grégoire, *Histoire des Sectes Religieuses*, vol. 2 (Paris: Potey, Egron, Foucault, 1814), 17–20.

16. Thalès Bernard, "L'Alchimie," *L'Europe Littéraire*, no. 12 (Jan. 10, 1863): 181–4; no. 14 (Jan. 28, 1863): 212–14; no. 17 (Feb. 14, 1863): 264–6; no. 19 (Feb. 28, 1863): 295–9. Also see Thalés Bernard, "Notes sur Samuel Best, serviteur de dieu," *L'Europe Littériare*, no. 14 (Jan. 28, 1863): 219–20.

17. Marc de Vissac, "Dom Pernety et les Illuminés d'Avignon," *Mémoires de l'Académie de Vaucluse* 6 (1906): 219–38.

18. MC, MS. 3090, "Cahiers de correspondence concernant la secte des illuminés d'Avignon."

19. Vissac, "Dom Pernety," 229–30. See C.-F.-H. Barjavel, *Dictionnaire Historique, Biographique et Bibliographique du Département de Vaucluse*, vol. 2 (Carpentras: P. L. Hamy, 1841), 248.

20. See Joanny Bricaud, *Les Illuminés d'Avignon: Étude sur Dom Pernety et son groupe* (Paris: Amici Librorum, 1927); M. Meillassoux-Le Cerf, "Dom Pernety," *Histoire, économie et société* 2 (1988): 285–9; Meillassoux-Le Cerf, *Dom Pernety et les Illuminés d'Avignon* (Milan: Archè, 1992). For an informative article on the living quarters of *illuminés* in Avignon, see Adrien Marcel, "Quatre Maisons des Illuminés d'Avignon," *Mémoires de l'Académie de Vaucluse* (1922): 85–101. For studies that focus on the society's use of the oracular Holy Word, see Alice Joly, "Le Sainte-Parole des Illuminés d'Avignon," *Cahiers de la tour Saint-Jacques* 2–4 (1960): 98–116; Serge Caillet, "Des Illuminés d'Avignon à la Fraternitié Polaire: Deux oracles numériques aux XVIIIe et XXe siècles," *Politica Hermetica* 21 (2007): 26–47.

21. RGIA, Fond 1163 (Komitet okhraneniia obshchei bezopasnosti, 1807), op. 1, d. 16a, 16b, 16v.

22. Mikhail Longinov, "Odin iz magikov XVIII veka," *Russkii vestnik* 28 (1860): 579–603.

23. A. Pypin, "Materialy dlia istorii masonskikh lozh," *Vestnik Evropy* 1 (1872): 203–14.

24. Iu. E. Kondakov, *Rozenkreitsery, martinisty i "vnutrennie khristiane" v Rossii kontsa XVIII-pervoi chetverti XIX veka* (St. Petersburg: RGPU im. A. I. Gertsena, 2012), 104–43.

25. A. J. Rolle, *Tadeusz Leszczyc Grabianka Starosta Liwski i Teresa z Stadnickich Jego Małżonka* (Lviv: We Lwowie Winiarz, 1875).

26. See Józef Ujejski, *Król Nowego Izraela* (Warsaw: Kasy im. J. Mianowskiego, 1924); M. L. Danilewicz, "'The King of the New Israel': Thaddeus Grabianka (1740–1807)," *Oxford Slavonic Papers*, n.s., 1 (1968): 49–73; J. Siewierski, *Upłaty anioł z Podola. Opowieść o Tadeuszu Grabiance* (Warsaw: Wydaw. CiS, 2003).

27. Clarke Garrett, *Respectable Folly: Millenarians and the French Revolution in France and England* (Baltimore: Johns Hopkins University Press, 1975), 97–120.

28. Renzo de Felice, *Note e ricerche sugli "Illuminati" e il misticismo rivoluzionario (1789–1800)* (Rome: Edizioni di storia e letteratura, 1960), 121–56.

29. Andreas Önnerfors, "'Envoyées des Glaces du Nord jusque dans ces climats': Swedish Encounters with *Les Illuminés d'Avignon* at the End of the Eighteenth Century," in *Diffusions et circulations des pratiques maçonniques XVIIIe–XXe siècle*, ed. P.-Y. Beaurepaire et al. (Paris: Classiques Garnier, 2012), 167–94.

30. See Viatte, *Les Sources Occultes*, vol. 1, 96, 99–102; Garrett, *Respectable Folly*, 113–17. For a short overview of the Avignon Society, see Jan Snoek, "Illuminés d'Avignon," *Dictionary of Gnosis and Western Esotericism*, 597–600.

31. On Saint-Germain, see Isabella Cooper-Oakley, *The Comte de Saint Germain, the Secret of Kings* (London: Whitfriars Press, 1912). On Casanova, see Ian Kelly, *Casanova: Actor, Lover, Priest, Spy* (London: Hodder & Stoughton, 2008).

32. On Cagliostro, see, for example, Heinrich Conrad, *Der Graf Cagliostro* (Stuttgart: Verlag Robert Lutz, 1921); Iain McCalman, *The Last Alchemist: Count Cagliostro, Master of Magic in the Age of Reason* (New York: HarperCollins, 2003).

33. See Henrik Bogdan, "An Introduction to the High Degrees of Freemasonry," *Heredom* 14 (2006): 1–37; Pierre Mollier, "Freemasonry and Templarism," in *Handbook of Freemasonry*, ed. Henrik Bogdan and J. A. M. Snoek (Leiden: Brill, 2014), 82–99. Also see René Le Forestier, *La Franc-Maçonnerie templière et occultiste aux XVIIIe et XIXe siècles* (Paris: Aubier-Montaigne, 1970).

34. On Cagliostro's Egyptian Rite, see Serge Caillet, *Arcanes et rituels de la Maçonnerie Égyptienne* (Paris: Guy Trédanie, 1994).

35. See, for example, Nicholas Goodrick-Clarke, *The Western Esoteric Traditions: A Historical Introduction* (Oxford: Oxford University Press, 2008), 131–90; Paul Kléber Monod, *Solomon's Secret Arts: The Occult in the Age of Enlightenment* (New Haven, CT: Yale University Press, 2013); Andreas Önnerfors, "Illuminism," in *The Occult World*, ed. Christopher Partridge (Abingdon: Routledge, 2015), 173–81. For a fascinating recent study on C. F. Tieman's involvement in illuminist currents between the 1770s and 1802, see Antoine Faivre, *De Londres à Saint-Pétersbourg: Carl Friedrich Tieman (1743–1802) aux carrefours des courants illuministes et maçonniques* (Milan: Arché, 2018).

36. Christine Bergé, "Illuminism," *Dictionary of Gnosis*, 600.

37. A variety of terms have been coined to try to encapsulate the meaning and prevalence of what we refer to as illuminism in the present work. In 1994, for example, Joscelyn Godwin referred to the "Theosophical Enlightenment." See Joscelyn Godwin, *The Theosophical Enlightenment* (Albany: State University of New York Press, 1994). The term "the dark side of the enlightenment" was used by John Fleming in 2013 to encompass the "wizards, alchemists and spiritual seekers" who flourished in an era of rationalist philosophy. The author admits that his use of this categorisation is playful. Still, it unnecessarily accentuates negative connotations with "the occult" that came to the fore in the twentieth century. See J. V. Fleming, *The Dark Side of the Enlightenment* (New York: W. W. Norton, 2013). In 1974, James Webb used the term "occult underground" when writing about influential illuminist figures in the late eighteenth century. See James Webb, *The Occult Underground* (La Salle, IL: Open Court, 1974).

38. Edelstein argues that the term "Super-Enlightenment" better encapsulates the sense of complementarity of the intellectual strands associated with the Enlightenment and illuminism. Although we do not disagree with his overall argument, we use the term "illuminism" in the present study. See "Introduction to the Super-Enlightenment," in *The Super-Enlightenment: Daring to Know Too Much*, ed. Dan Edelstein (Oxford: Voltaire Foundation, 2010), 6.

39. Antoine Faivre, *Theosophy, Imagination, Tradition: Studies in Western Esotericism*, trans. Christine Rhone (Albany: State University of New York Press, 2000), 20.

40. See Karlheinz Gerlach, *Die Freimaurer im Alten Preussen 1738–1806: Die Logen in Berlin* (Innsbruck: Studien Verlag, 2014), 539.

41. See J. A. M. Snoek, "Swedenborg, Freemasonry, and Swedenborgian Freemasonry: An Overview," in *New Religions in a Postmodern World*, ed. Mikael Rothstein and Reender Kranenborg (Aarhus, Denmark: Aarhus University Press, 2003), 28–32.

42. French would remain the lingua franca of the society throughout its existence, although several initiates, most notably Ottavio Cappelli (Italian) and William Bryan (English), could only converse in their respective mother-tongues.

43. For general works, see, for example, Garrett, *Respectable Folly*; W. H. Oliver, *Prophets and Millennialists: The Uses of Biblical Prophecy in England from the 1790s to the 1840s* (Auckland: Auckland University Press, 1978); J. F. C. Harrison, *The Second Coming: Popular Millenarianism, 1780–1850* (London: Routledge and Kegan Paul, 1979); Iain McCalman, *Radical Underworld: Prophets, Revolutionaries and Pornographers in London, 1795–1840* (Cambridge: Cambridge University Press, 1988); Nicole Edelman, "Magnétisme, somnambulisme et prophetesses-visionnaires autour de la Révolution française de 1789," *Politica Hermetica* 3 (1989): 17–31; Edelman, *Voyantes, guérisseuses et visionnaires en France, 1785–1914* (Paris: Albin Michel, 1995); Iain McCalman, "New Jerusalems: Prophecy, Dissent and Radical Culture in England, 1786–1830," in *Enlightenment and Religion: Rational Dissent in Eighteenth-Century Britain*, ed. Knud Haakonssen (Cambridge: Cambridge University Press, 1996), 312–35; K. C. Knox, "Lunatick Visions: Prophecy, Signs and Scientific Knowledge in 1790s London," *History of Science* 37:4 (1999): 427–58; Susan Juster, *Doomsayers: Anglo-American Prophecy in the Age of Revolution* (Philadelphia: University of Pennsylvania Press, 2003); Jon Mee, "Millenarian Visions and Utopian Speculations," in *The Enlightenment World*, ed. Martin Fitzpatrick et al. (Abingdon: Routledge, 2004), 536–50; Deborah Madden, "Prophecy in the Age of Revolution," in *Prophecy and Eschatology in the Transatlantic World, 1550–1800*, ed. A. Crome (Basingstoke: Palgrave Macmillan, 2016), 259–81; Francisco Javier Ramón Solans, "'Être-immortel à Paris': Violence et prophétie durant la Révolution," *Annales. Histoire, Sciences Sociales* 71:2 (2016): 347–76. For an Italian context, see Marina Caffiero, *La nuova era, mito e profezie dell'Italia in rivoluzione* (Genoa: Marietti, 1991). For a Spanish context, see Solans, "La hidra revolucionaria: Apocalipsis y antiliberalismo en la España del primer tercio del siglo XIX," *Hispania* 77:256 (2017): 471–96.

44. On Gott, see Nancy Jiwon Cho, "Dorothy Gott (c. 1748–1812) and 'God's Chosen People': A Disowned Prophet's Quest for Quaker Recognition in Late Georgian England," *Quaker Studies* 18:1 (2013): 50–75. On Buchan, see John Cameron, *History of the Buchanite Delusion: 1783–1846* (Dumfries: R. G. Mann, 1904). On Brothers, see Deborah Madden, *The Paddington Prophet: Richard Brothers's Journey to Jerusalem* (Manchester: Manchester University Press, 2010); J. P. Downing, "Prophets Reading Prophecy: The Interpretation of the Book of Revelation in the Writings of Richard Brothers, Joanna Southcott and William Blake" (PhD diss., University of Oxford, 2015). On Southcott, see James K. Hopkins, *A Woman to Deliver Her People: Joanna Southcott and English Millenarianism in an Era of Revolution* (Austin: University of Texas Press, 1982); Matthew Niblett, *Prophecy and the Politics of Salvation in Late Georgian England* (London: I. B. Tauris, 2015).

45. On Brohon, see August Viatte, "Une visionnaire au siècle de Jean-Jacques: Mademoiselle Brohon," *Revue des questions historiques*, 3rd ser., 2 (1923): 336–44. On Ruer, see Antoine Faivre, "Un Familier des Sociétés Ésotériques au dix-huitième siècle: Bourrée de Corberon," *Revue des Sciences Humaines* 126 (1967), 273–81. On Labrousse, see Paul Vulliaud, *Suzette Labrousse,*

prophétesse de la Révolution; suivi de Léon Bloy, prophète et martyr (Milan: Arché, 1988). On Théot, see Michel Eude, "Points de vue sur l'affaire Catherine Théot," *Annales historiques de la Révolution française* 198 (1969): 606–29; Clarke Garrett, "Popular Piety in the French Revolution: Catherine Théot," *Catholic Historical Review* 60:2 (1974): 215–32. Also see Francisco Javier Ramón Solans, "La Mesmérisme à la Rencontre de la Prophétie: Le Cercle de la Duchesse de Bourbon," *Annales historiques de la Révolution française* 1 (2018): 153–75.

1

In the Beginning Was the (Holy) Word

THE FOUNDATION OF THE INITIATIC SOCIETY AND ITS

EARLY YEARS IN BERLIN, RHEINSBERG, AND PODOLIA,

1779–1784

ON JANUARY 15, 1779, Antoine-Joseph Pernety, the librarian to Friedrich II of Prussia and a member of the Royal Academy of Sciences in Berlin, asked the following question to an oracle called the Holy Word (Sainte Parole): "Will my brief of secularisation soon have its effect?" He received a reassuring response, which promised that he alone had the power to finish the affair that he wished to one day see concluded. This was the first of 120 questions that Pernety alone would pose to the Holy Word up to October 30, 1782. This initial enquiry seems to touch upon Pernety's decision, in 1765, to abandon his calling as a Benedictine monk in the Congregation of Saint-Maur in Paris.[1] What effect was he hoping for?

Given that the majority of his subsequent questions concerned alchemy and, specifically, the means of perfecting the so-called *grand œuvre*, or philosophers' stone, it is likely that his first query concerned this endeavour. After all, Pernety published two parallel works in 1758—*Fables égyptiennes et grecques* and *Dictionnaire mytho-hermétique*—which, as Antoine Faivre notes, provided an alchemical reading of narratives of Greek and Egyptian mythology. Pernety posited that ancient fables provided "a coded description of the processes of transmutation."[2] A decade after these tomes had been published, when he had settled in Berlin, Pernety's passion for completing the alchemical magnum opus remained unabated. According to two fellow members of the Royal Academy in Berlin, Dieudonné Thiébault and Jean-Alexis Borrelly (1738–1810), Pernety met the mysterious Comte de Saint-Germain at the end of the 1760s in the Prussian capital. Thiébault

Initiating the Millennium. Robert Collis, and Natalie Bayer, Oxford University Press (2020) © Oxford University Press.
DOI: 10.1093/oso/9780190903374.001.0001

remarks that Pernety was "not slow in recognising" in Saint-Germain "the characteristics which go to make up an adept." However, when Pernety broached the subject of the philosophers' stone, the famed adventurer "curtly observed that most people who were in pursuit [of it] were astonishingly illogical inasmuch as they employed no agent but fire."[3]

Pernety's thirst for knowledge regarding the *grand œuvre* thus remained unquenched by his meeting with Saint-Germain. Another decade passed before he first consulted the Holy Word, which seems to have rekindled his active pursuit of the "great work." In February 1779 he asked a series of questions to the Holy Word relating to the *grand œuvre*. His principle preoccupation concerned whether two manuscripts in his possession, by Nicolas Flamel and by a certain Mardochée, "truly and sincerely contain the procedure of the *grand œuvre*."[4] He also asked practical questions relating to whether he was correctly following "to the letter" the necessary steps conveyed by the Holy Word: "Will I succeed in making the perfect powder of projection of the philosophers, which transmutes imperfect metals into gold and which is called the universal medicine?"[5]

During February and March 1779, Pernety pooled alchemical knowledge with three other Frenchmen in Berlin—Claude-Étienne Le Bauld de Nans (1735–1791), Charles-Pierre de Morinval (fl. 1772–1782), and Brumore—thereby establishing an informal circle of adepts. Of the three, Le Bauld's involvement seems to have been the most fleeting. Yet he did introduce the small circle to alchemical manuscripts attributed to Mardochée and to Elias Artista. Le Bauld was a respected comic actor, but his career was at a crossroads in early 1779 as he had lost his job as the director of the French Comedy House when it closed in 1778.[6] Consequently, the two questions he asked the Holy Word were more concerned with whether a new theatrical enterprise would be a success than with the search for the philosophers' stone. Morinval had no such employment worries; he was in his seventh year as a director of the Régie, the Prussian tax and excise department.[7] As we will see, he remained in this post until 1782, when he returned to France, and during that time he played a key role in the group's alchemical pursuits.

Besides sharing a nationality, Pernety, Morinval, and Le Bauld were also connected by a Masonic bond. All three belonged to the Loge Royale d'York de l'Amitié.[8] Notwithstanding this fraternal connection, it is unclear what role Masonic ties played in bringing them together within this small alchemical circle in early 1779. On the one hand, Le Bauld was a very influential figure in the lodge, being first the orator, in 1771, and assuming the position of Grand Master in 1787.[9] Pernety, on the other hand, despite being listed as a member in 1782, did not play an active role in the life of the lodge.

Moreover, the inclusion of Brumore, who does not appear to have been a Freemason, highlights that membership in the fraternity was not a prerequisite for involvement in the new alchemical circle. Indeed, Brumore was, in large measure, the linchpin of the group at this point. His importance lies not simply in his passion for alchemy, but in his role as the group's oracle, who, by utilising his mastery of arithmancy, acted as the medium between his fellow adepts and the supposedly divine Holy Word.

Like Pernety, Brumore was a lapsed clergyman, having been one of eight priestly canons at Langres Cathedral for a short time in early 1774.[10] In the same year he was enjoying a career as something of a court poet, publishing two panegyrics which lavished praise on Marie Antoinette, the new French queen, and Madame Louise, who became a Carmelite nun in 1770. The first work, *L'Inoculation par Aspiration*, paid homage to the new queen's promotion of the inoculation against smallpox, the disease that had killed Louis XV in May 1774. The second piece, entitled *Le Triomphe de la religion, ou Le Sacrifice de Madame Louise de France*, was a hagiographical poem, divided into four songs, which honoured the piety of Louis XVI's sister.[11] By 1778 Brumore had moved to Berlin, where his literary talents were sponsored by Prince Heinrich (1726–1802), the younger brother of the king. In this year, for example, he published two plays, "Les Calas" and "Les Salver, ou La Faute Réparée," in his capacity as an "attaché in the service of . . . Prince Henri."[12]

It is unclear why Brumore began to record his oracular communications in January 1779. The simplest explanation is that he became acquainted with Pernety around this time, who encouraged him to use his knowledge of arithmancy to obtain divine guidance for their alchemical pursuits. Whatever inspired Brumore to begin being an oracle, once he started, he evidently relished the role. Between January 1779 and May 1785 the Holy Word was consulted 362 times, by a variety of individuals, the majority of questions being asked before the summer of 1783.[13] Those who consulted the oracle during this time did so for myriad reasons, ranging from seeking advice on trivial issues to seeking guidance about life-changing decisions. Whatever the nature of the question, the Holy Word served a crucial purpose in what was to become a formal society: it provided divine validation for the actions and aspirations of those who consulted it. As we will see, the pronouncements made by the Holy Word could have a dramatic effect on the destinies of those who communicated with it.

A curious account of the crucial role played by the Holy Word, and of how it came to be employed by Brumore, can be found in a short pamphlet published in 1795 by Benedict Chastanier (1739–c. 1816), entitled *A Word of Advice to a Benighted World*. Chastanier had been an important London-based member of the Avignon Society up until 1789, when he severed ties with the group over their repudiation of Swedenborg (see chapter 3). Thereafter, Chastanier became an avowed Swedenborgian, and *A Word of Advice* crystallised his rejection of the religious doctrine espoused by the *illuminés* in Avignon. Nevertheless, despite its hostile tone, Chastanier did include a revealing section, "Soudkoski, or Grabianca's Account of the Formation of the Mago Cabbalistical Society," which sheds considerable light on the early importance of the Holy Word. As recited by Chastanier, an unnamed nephew (Brumore) inherited a "compendium of the Science called *Cabala*" from an uncle, which taught "in its purity how to make questions, and to receive answers from the written Word of God." Thereafter, Brumore and some other gentlemen made "various experiments, according to the rules therein . . . and always received . . . pertinent answers." Consequently, Brumore and these other early dabblers in the science of numbers soon consulted the Holy Word about decisions that often altered "the whole course of their life."[14]

In 1728 Ephraim Chambers included an entry on oracles in his celebrated *Cyclopædia*. His summation of contemporary opinion "among the more Learned," was that "*Oracles* were all mere Cheats and Impostures," who made their predictions for either their own avaricious ends or to serve "the political Views" of their paymasters. To validate this stance, Chambers cited as authorities Pierre Bayle, Anton van Dale, and Bernard de Fontenelle, who all concluded that oracles were "meer human Artifices."[15] Jaucourt's entry on oracles in the *Encyclopédie*, published in 1765, is more scathing still: "The desire so keen and so useless to know the future gave birth to them, imposture accredited them, and fanaticism put the seal on them."[16]

Yet despite this "enlightened" repudiation of oracles, Brumore published a letter in the December 1785 edition of *Journal encyclopédique* in which he sought to outline the principles of "the science of numbers, or of the true cabalistic art" to those who still questioned, distrusted and ridiculed the notion that there is "something supernatural and divine" in its practice.[17] This brief exposition of what Brumore refers to as the "science of numbers" or "cabalistic art" provides several fascinating insights: it helps us to understand the tradition on which he consciously drew and reveals something of his methodology when undertaking a calculation. Brumore is well aware of the lowly status of the oracular science of numbers, which he puts down to two contributory factors. First, he lambasts the simplistic division between white magic and black magic found in many books on the subject, which had only served to foment the "distrust and ridicule" of his cabalistic art. Second, he acknowledges the "culpable artifice" of charlatans, who by "false and frivolous operations" had brought about many erroneous predictions.[18]

Significantly, Brumore cites Swedenborg, a near contemporary, when establishing his genealogy of the science of numbers. Specifically, he references a passage in *Conjugal Love* (1768) in which the Swedish theologian commented on how the divine Word of Jehovah had been written down in *The Grand Triumphs of Jehovah and the Oracles of His Prophet*.[19] Brumore adds that Abraham had "put it in order," and crucially, it "still exists among us."[20] In other words, the "science of numbers," as understood by Brumore, was a quintessential form of "lost" knowledge, which, however, had been secretly transmitted down the ages. Having provided this Old Testament narrative, Brumore then asserts that Pythagoras, Al-Razi, Averroes, and Rabbi Akiva embraced this form of cabalistic art.[21]

After setting out the venerable lineage of the science of numbers, Brumore discloses its key principles. We learn that "the *cabale* proper is, then, only a given stem (a ninefold base) in a certain combination from which, by subsequent mechanical operations" based on the juxtaposition of the three names of Elohim, Adonai, and Jehovah, "are engendered in turn new numerical sequences." These numbers can then be transformed back into the letters of the alphabet "according to the idiom in which the request was formed." Even Brumore attests that it is "difficult to render sensible" the "sublime operations that succeed in appropriating the order of things." Indeed, he castigates the pride of those who scorn this divine science of numbers as something repugnant. In his opinion, those who are only able to think in rational terms find it "repugnant to admit that by the prestige of a simple calculation one could obtain a force above that of their reason."[22]

The public espousal of arithmancy Brumore issued in 1785 may have appalled many readers of the *Journal encyclopédique*, but it was symptomatic of a broader belief in the "science of numbers" in illuminist circles. In 1793, for example, an elderly Casanova wrote to Eve, the daughter of the Sabbatean Jacob Frank, and described his lengthy use of what he called his numerical *Kab-Eli*: "Through [this] I can arrive at an answer (expressed in Arabic numerals) to any question I had put in the same numerals. What I possess is a true oracle which, though often under a thick veil, always tells me the truth."[23] Casanova's use of his *Kab-Eli*, or pyramid, is frequently described in his memoirs from the 1750s onwards.[24]

Instructions for similar numerical oracles can be found among the papers of other leading figures of illuminism in the final quarter of the eighteenth century. Among the archive of L.-J. Prunelle de Lière, a leading member of the Martinist Order of *Elus Coëns* in the 1770s and 1780s, for example, can be found detailed instructions for a numerical oracle that he referred to as the "Regle de neuf."[25] Furthermore, in the collection of documents belonging to Charles Rainsford is a handwritten translation of a work by Ghillini entitled *La Vittoria*. Rainsford refers to this numerical oracle as the "Egyptian Cabbala," and it includes a base, pedestal, body, and crown in the shape of triangle. The instructions conclude with "an explanation of the oracle and how to have an answer from the pyramid."[26]

Hence Brumore was far from innovative in his espousal of "the science of numbers." However, we have no evidence to suggest that either Prunelle de Lière or Rainsford actively used their numerical oracles to foresee the fates of their peers. Even Casanova, who did utilise his numerical pyramid, did so in a seemingly haphazard manner and on a one-on-one basis. What distinguishes Brumore from his contemporary seers, therefore, is his deliberate employment of his oracular gift in a group setting. To be sure, for the first two months of 1779, this group seems to have been a relatively informal and small circle of adepts who largely limited their questions to alchemical matters.

The catalyst for the transformation of this small circle of adepts into a formal initiatic society was the arrival in Berlin of Tadeusz Grabianka, a Polish nobleman from Podolia, in around March 1779.[27] It is not known what brought Grabianka to the Prussian capital. We are, however, able to glean something about Grabianka's early involvement in what would later become the NIS from a report produced by the Russian authorities in 1807, based on their interrogation of the Polish gentleman after his arrest (see chapter 6).

This report states that Grabianka first became acquainted with Pernety in Berlin. At this meeting the Pole expressed no great interest in alchemy, but in "wisdom" (*mudrost'*). Pernety introduced Grabianka to Brumore, who did possess such wisdom, by having a "voice by means of Cabala or numbers." At this first encounter between Grabianka and Brumore, the latter is said to have exclaimed that he had come to Berlin two years previously to wait for a wandering pilgrim (*strannik*), "whom heaven wanted to make great."[28] In Brumore's eyes this *strannik* was none other than Grabianka.

Tellingly, the first question Grabianka posed to the Holy Word, on March 25, 1779, concerned whether he would "have the happiness to achieve the divine science of numbers via the person on whom I rely?" Grabianka did not receive a categorical response from the Holy Word, but was told to listen to his heart.[29] It is also significant that only three days later, Brumore consulted the Holy Word for the first time, seeking permission to consecrate Grabianka, as well himself and Pernety, at a ceremony that they had proposed conducting.[30] We know little about the deliberations that took place between Pernety, Brumore, and Grabianka regarding the nature of the rituals they would adopt for the consecration ceremonies. It seems, however, that a little power struggle took place on April 1, as both Brumore and Grabianka wished to be the *sacrificateur*. They subsequently consulted the Holy Word, who granted Grabianka the honour to be the first consecrate and *sacrificateur*.[31]

Grabianka's consecration began on April 12, 1779, and concluded on April 20, and Pernety, Brumore, and Brumore's consort, a certain Mlle Bruchié, began and finished two days later.[32] What is more, the fifth consecration ceremony, for Morinval, took place shortly afterwards (between April 18 and 26, 1779).[33] Although no detailed accounts of these early consecrations were written, the members of the new society did keep a record of their interactions with the Holy Word. In April 1779, several questions were concerned with the consecration rites that were either about to begin or were already underway. From these consultations we are able to glean several valuable insights. We learn, for example, that candidates were only permitted to begin and end their initiations with the approval of the Holy Word. At this point, the Holy Word did not prohibit any of the five initial candidates from completing their consecrations. However, this scenario did play out when the society relocated to Avignon in the late 1780s (see chapter 3). The early consecration of Bruchié (as the fourth initiate) also highlights the inclusion of women from the very foundation of the society.

It is also noticeable that the consecrations took place on a "mountain" over nine consecutive days and involved the tracing of a "circle of power."[34] The culmination of the nine-day rite involved the invocation of a guardian angel. In the case of Pernety, the angel was named Assadaï.[35] Yet the successful invocation of an angel was seemingly not guaranteed. A question posed by Grabianka on the last day of his consecration reveals that Brumore had led him to believe that he would be able to invoke his own guardian angel. To Grabianka's dismay, no such entity appeared to him, and subsequently he asked the Holy Word whether he was culpable for the failure of the theurgic operation.[36]

This entry hints that Brumore played a crucial role in devising these astonishing consecration rites. This is corroborated in a letter from January 1790, in which the author, Joseph Ferrier, who would go on to be one of seven leaders of the society in Avignon, describes the initial consecration ceremony practised in Berlin. Interestingly, Ferrier wrote that Brumore came into possession of a manuscript of the rite from an uncle in

France. This is redolent of Chastanier's account, although Ferrier asserted that Brumore in fact stole the manuscript and brought it to Berlin. Chastanier's brief history also noted that the "book . . . will shew you how to get acquainted with your guardian angel."[37] Ferrier's description also indicated that the mountain-top ceremony was meant to imitate Moses's encounter with God on Mount Sinai (Exod. 19).[38]

One other distinctive feature of the society's consecration rite was also employed from the very beginning—namely, the assignment of three numerals to each candidate on completion of the ceremony. The five first initiates, for example, received the following numbers: Grabianka (139), Pernety (135), Brumore (579 A), Bruchié (579 B), and Morinval (246 A).[39] According to Ferrier, the numbers were chosen by the candidates: the first digit represented their divine number; the second digit was their angelic number, and the third digit represented their personal number. Ferrier also explains that the numbers were imbued with mystical significance and provides two examples from recent initiates—Gustav Reuterholm and C. G. Silfverhielm—who chose the numbers 373 and 357 respectively. Reuterholm's numbers symbolised that the trinity was in between the seven planets, and Silfverhielm's digits represented the "perfect trinity carved with five wounds and the seven angelic choirs bring merriment."[40] No explanation is provided, however, for why letters sometimes follow the three digits. The simplest and most likely reason for this practice was to differentiate between initiates with the same three numbers. Thus Bruchié was recorded as 579 B because she was consecrated after Brumore, who was 579 A.[41] We will return to this remarkable consecration ceremony in chapter 3, when we will draw on first-hand descriptions of the rituals. It is worth stressing at this point, however, that the above-mentioned aspects of the society's initiation rite, which were already in place when it began its existence, remained an integral part of the consecration ceremony into the 1790s.

Interestingly, the flurry of consecrations that took place in Berlin in April 1779 marked a very rare (and fleeting) moment when Pernety, Brumore, and Grabianka participated together in the activities of the society. By the autumn of 1779, the three key founders of the society had dispersed: Pernety remained in Berlin; Grabianka returned to his home in Podolia; and Brumore took up residence at Rheinsberg Palace, some sixty-five miles north-west of the Prussian capital, at the court of Prince Heinrich. Grabianka was the first to leave Berlin, less than three weeks after Morinval had concluded his consecration. On May 3, 1779, Grabianka consulted the Holy Word about whether he should consecrate his wife, mother-in-law, and children in Poland or in Berlin. The next day, having interpreted the response from the Holy Word as a sign that he could consecrate his family in Poland, he asked whether he could also initiate his sister and brother-in-law and their children. His mind was already looking forward to sharing his sense of exaltation with his family. On his return to Podolia, Grabianka first consecrated Anna, his 6-year-old daughter, on June 22, 1779, and then, two days later, his mother-in-law, Martyna Stadnicka. Thereafter, he initiated his wife, Teresa, on July 14; followed by his brother-in-law, Jan Tarnowski, on August 4; and his sister, Tekla Tarnowska, on August 11. In the space of seven weeks Grabianka had doubled the size of the society. More importantly, he ushered in a new family dynamic in which young children and elderly in-laws could all participate. This dynamic would continue to be one of the most distinctive hallmarks of the society for more than a quarter of a century.

After quickly consecrating his family in the summer of 1779, Grabianka waited until September 1780 before approaching the Holy Word for permission to consecrate his aristocratic friend Michał Aleksander Ronikier and his wife, Teresa. Ronikier was a rich and powerful landowner, who had inherited properties in Podolia, Volhynia, and Galicia, and was also a general in the Polish army.[42] Grabianka's almost immediate desire to include his entire family in the society and then his closest landowning acquaintances shortly afterwards is revealing in terms of his culture of sociability at the time.[43] We see no split in his mind between the private, domestic realm and semi-public spaces, such as the Masonic lodge, from which women were mostly excluded and children were always barred.

Yet Grabianka's decision to include his family in the new society was soon sorely tested. On August 6, 1779, Grabianka prayed to the Holy Word and expressed the desire that his daughter would "preserve the innocence of her heart throughout her life." The reply he received was addressed to his daughter. It was to transform his life and would, to a large extent, lead to his estrangement from his wife and children for the remainder of his life: "Leave your father, leave your mother and your country; whoever is devoted to you must complete the sacrifice within seven years; you will be endowed with my science and by you all will be accomplished." Eight days after this answer was pronounced, Brumore asked the Holy Word whether Anna would be "gifted in the divine science of numbers?"

Interpreting the response in a positive way, Brumore and Bruchié subsequently probed the Holy Word as to whether it was the will of God that they assume the guardianship of the girl in order to oversee her instruction. Here we see the starkest example of the power of the deliberations of the Holy Word among initiates. Despite hesitating and stalling, Grabianka ultimately acquiesced to the command. In March 1780 he and his daughter travelled to Berlin, where she would undergo a ceremony atop the "mountain" and then be officially handed over to Brumore and Bruchié. It would be three years before Anna would see her family again. Even though Brumore decried the charlatans who were besmirching the divine science of numbers in 1785, it is hard not to interpret this episode as anything other than a manipulation of trust on his part. Irrespective of his intentions, the incident highlights the power Brumore held as oracle within the society.

By the time Brumore and Bruchié took in Anna as a ward, in March 1780, they had already taken up residence at Rheinsberg Palace. This is apparent from a question Brumore asked the Holy Word on November 22, 1779: "I beseech you to draw me out of my inquietude by telling me if it is under the good pleasure of God and by his holy will that we have come to stay in Rheinsberg?" According to Andrew Hamilton, Brumore became Prince Heinrich's resident "reader and poetaster."[44] Hamilton's scathing critique of Brumore's poetic talents may be true, but Prince Heinrich was a renowned patron of the arts. When the French Comedy Theatre was forced to close its doors in 1778, he established his own French theatre company at his private *Kavaliershaus* at Rheinsberg. The director of the company was Pierre-Jean de Blainville (1748–1781), and from 1780 the *Kappellmeister* was the composer and conductor J. A. P. Schulz.[45]

Thus Brumore was entering an intimate and thriving cultural milieu at Rheinsberg. In his panegyrical biography of Prince Heinrich, *La Vie d'un Prince Célèbre*, published in 1784, Brumore provides some fascinating insights into his involvement in the artistic culture promoted by his royal patron. Curiously, the position of prima donna in the theatre at Rheinsberg was taken by Madame Brumore. She had apparently been trained by Schulz in Berlin and is listed as being part of the French troupe in Rheinsberg in the 1770s.[46] According to Brumore, his wife (presumably Bruchié) "preferred the glory of serving Prince Heinrich" with the rarity of her singing voice in spectacles at the *Kavaliershaus* to accepting propositions from the Polish court and from Italy.[47] One such spectacle to be performed at Rheinsberg was entitled "Panomphée, ou Divertissement en Mélo-drame," which was staged in honour of Prince Heinrich's birthday. The *divertissement* was written by Brumore and "opens with a poet who seems absorbed in his subject." The role of the poet was sung by Madame Brumore and includes accompanying music composed by Schulz.[48]

The Brumores were resident at Rheinsburg until June 1783. During this time Blainville consulted the Holy Word on December 24, 1779.[49] However, there is no indication that he was in fact initiated into the society before his death (by suicide) at Rheinsberg in 1781.[50] This is not the case with Prince Heinrich, however, who received the numerals 999 and asked the Holy Word a series of questions in the winter of 1780–81. On January 5, 1781, for example, he enquired whether he would "pass the rest of his days in tranquillity."[51] It would seem Brumore had gained the prince's trust and felt confident enough to include a royal personage in what was still a small society.

It also seems likely that J.-A. Borrelly, who was consecrated on December 1, 1780, became involved with the initiatic society as a result of his close links to the court at Rheinsberg.[52] To be sure, Borrelly was acquainted with Pernety in Berlin, as both men were fellows of the Royal Academy of Sciences.[53] Yet in 1805 Borrelly reminisced about having been "constantly honoured with kindness, and, I dare say, the friendship" of Prince Heinrich. Indeed, he adds that he was in the prince's society and at "all the feasts" that were held in his palace in Berlin and in Rheinsberg.[54] Moreover, two of the eight questions posed by Borrelly relate to Rheinsberg and Prince Heinrich. In his first question to the Holy Word, on December 1, 1780, Borrelly asked if "the king will come soon to Rheinsberg," thereby indicating that he was already at the palace. Moreover, on March 7, 1781, he enquired about how he should comport himself with Prince Heinrich "in the route that God has traced for his glory."[55]

In Berlin at this time it would seem Pernety and Morinval were far more preoccupied with their alchemical labours than with actively seeking recruits for their society. In May and June 1779 both Morinval and Pernety seem to have been busy in their alchemical workshops, judging by the questions they posed to the Holy Word. The results, however, were not entirely successful. On June 3, 1779, for example, Morinval consulted the Holy

Word about what he should do as his crucible had overturned after he had poured into it twelve flacons of an undisclosed liquid.[56] What is more, Pernety soon felt the wrath of the Holy Word for an unstated misdemeanour connected, it would seem, with his *grand œuvre*. He was ordered to cease his alchemical labours, which evidently caused the society some frustration. On August 15, 1779, for example, Brumore asked the Holy Word when Pernety would finally be able to begin his alchemical work.[57]

In October Pernety was finally instructed what he had to do to resume his work on the *grand œuvre*: he needed to renew his incense atop the mountain. In other words, he needed to undergo a ritual of purification to cleanse his heart "in the waters of innocence." This ceremony was, in effect, a re-consecration, and Bruchié acted as the *sacrificateur* for the nine-day rite.[58] After finishing his purification rite, Pernety almost immediately asked the Holy Word if he and Morinval could share the advice they received from Heaven vis-à-vis their alchemical *œuvres*.[59]

Interestingly, Morinval seems to have been recognised as the pre-eminent alchemist within the society at this time. According to the Russian report of 1807, Grabianka referred to the initiation of an "Alchemist," in April 1779, besides Pernety, Brumore, and Bruchié. It can only have been Morinval, who had apparently had a revelation during his consecration about how to complete the *grand œuvre*.[60] Morinval's primacy in regard to the society's work on the *grand œuvre* is highlighted by the ceremony-cum-alchemical operation that he was instructed to perform in January 1780 atop the mountain "at the first hour of the day."[61] Pernety was evidently desperate to attend this rite in some capacity; he asked the Holy Word if he could accompany Morinval in order to pray with him before the commencement of his "mysterious operation." He would then retire before Morinval began.[62] Shortly after this ceremony Pernety also addressed the Holy Word and asked whether he had God's permission to consult an alchemical tract by Elias Artista that was in Morinval's possession.[63] This was likely the same tract Le Bauld had shown to the society the previous year. Evidently, Morinval was reluctant to share this knowledge of his own volition, and hence Pernety had to resort to the authority of the Holy Word.

Both Morinval and Pernety inundated the Holy Word with practical questions relating to alchemical endeavours for the remainder of 1780. Morinval's questions were related to the operation he had begun atop the mountain in January. On January 27, he consulted the Holy Word about when the would be able to open the flacon that he was working on. He asked eighteen times between February 20 and June 3 whether those particular days marked the moment when he could finally open his flacon.[64] Nearly six months then passed, before Morinval next communicated with the Holy Word. On December 2 he was miraculously cured of an extremely grave illness in three days, owing to having opened his "*flacon philosophique*." Morinval seems to have believed that his alchemical labours had been successful, and that he was now in possession of a panacea. This belief is confirmed by the Holy Word, which responded that Morinval now understood that he was at peace. Furthermore, the Holy Word pronounced: "I have given him wisdom and life as an inheritance."[65] Thereafter, Morinval continued to consult the Holy Word, but questions related to alchemy are noticeable by their absence. In short, his alchemical work was done.

Whereas Morinval had to wait patiently for his *œuvre* to be ready, Pernety restlessly consulted the Holy Word throughout the year regarding practical issues. On April 1, for example, he sought advice as to whether he had exposed his alchemical matter to too much fire and therefore corrupted his work. In August he enquired whether he needed to multiply his philosophical mercury more than once. In October he beseeched the Holy Word to advise him about whether he needed to defile and then re-defile his gold before purifying and re-purifying it in order to make it into a powder.[66]

After spending most of the year struggling with the intricacies of following alchemical recipes, by the end of the year Pernety finally seemed to be making some progress. On December 23, 1780, he declared to the Holy Word that he would soon "anoint you of the new chrism" and beseeches heaven to tell him how to prepare for the delivery of the unction.[67] Considering that this announcement heralded a major leap forward in his *œuvre*, it is puzzling that his subsequent consultations with the Holy Word hardly broach the topic. One explanation is that he had to wait patiently for his unction to mature. Yet unlike with Morinval, there is no indication that Pernety was eagerly awaiting the appointed time. One other explanation can be found in the official report produced by the Russian authorities in 1807. Herein, it states that the police banned Pernety from lighting strong fires in Berlin because they feared he would burn down the city![68] Such a decree would explain the abrupt cessation of alchemical enquires after December 1780. From his regular questions to the Holy Word it is also evident that Pernety must have lit a lot of fires in 1780. Moreover, his queries betray more than a little of the dilettante, who may not have been entirely competent in fire-management skills.

Thus Morinval and Pernety seem to have been by far the most engaged (and obsessed) alchemical adepts up until the end of 1780. However, by April 1782, a new triumvirate within the society—Brumore, Grabianka, and Ronikier—began to work towards the completion of their own alchemical endeavour.[69] Their goal was nothing less than to produce "the sublime essence of the Holy Chrism (*saint chrême*)." As we will demonstrate, it was highly significant that three initiates worked on this *œuvre*, which may well have been in imitation of the triune nature of the Holy Chrism.

Interestingly, such an interpretation had been propounded by the Paracelsian alchemist Pierre-Jean Fabre in *Alchymista christianus* (1632).[70] As Allen Debus notes, in this work Fabre was intent on indicating the compatibility of Roman Catholicism and alchemy. He "saw valid correspondences between the sacraments and chemical operations," and compared true alchemists to priests.[71] Of particular note for us is chapter 30, entitled "Chemical Oils Can Be the Symbol of Holy Chrism." Herein Fabre professes his admiration for the "threefold composition of the Holy Chrism, which has the nature of a common oil, Christ for form and the Holy Spirit as an indissoluble link." He concludes by stating that "it is not contrary to the Christian faith" to reproduce by natural means "the sacred mysteries of supreme wisdom."[72] In other words, it is permissible to try and create an alchemical *saint chrême* that is able to mimic the protective and healing qualities of the supernatural power of holy chrism "in relation to the body and this mortal life."[73] This is precisely what Brumore, Grabianka, and Ronikier tried to achieve over the course of nine months, between September 1782 and June 1783.

First, however, Ronikier had to be given some basic instruction in alchemy. He married Józefa Miaczyński (his third wife) in November 1781, and then the newlyweds travelled to Prussia.[74] Here, in early 1782, Józefa was consecrated into the society and Ronikier began to receive lessons on alchemy. On April 8, 1782, Pernety consulted the Holy Word on who should instruct Ronikier, and he was told that it should be Morinval. Three days later Ronikier asked the Holy Word when he would be able to return home and work on his *œuvre* from there. On April 22 Morinval consulted the Holy Word about how much he needed to teach Ronikier about the *œuvre*. Ronikier was still receiving instruction from Morinval on May 13.

By August or September 1782, Brumore, Grabianka, and Ronikier had begun to work individually on their own *œuvres*. The Holy Word has instructed them that their work was to last for nine months. It was to be like a child growing in the womb, or, in other words, the first matter of the philosophers' stone.[75] However, for the overall *œuvre* to be perfected and animated, the three adepts had to mix their liquids to make an unctuous matter that would create a sublime essence that they referred to as *saint chrême*.[76] Thus Brumore and Grabianka were instructed to bring their liquids in person to the home of Ronikier. Brumore duly departed Rheinsberg on June 9, 1783 (on the eve of Pentecost).[77] On July 24, Ronikier consulted the Holy Word and asked whether his own *œuvre* was ready to "suffer the operation for which our brother Brumore had been sent."[78]

This sequence of events tallies with the report made by the Russian authorities, which describes how Brumore and Grabianka, who was accompanied by his wife, converged on Ronikier's home to complete their alchemical work. It is not entirely clear what operations the three performed there. According to the Russian report, the alchemists merged their offerings and then burned the whole to ash, although the questions they posed to the Holy Word always refer to "the sublime essence of the *saint chrême*."[79] Irrespective of the composition of the final substance, the operation undertaken by Brumore, Grabianka, and Ronikier ended in failure.[80] Brumore's frustration at their lack of success is clear in his consultation with the Holy Word on September 15, 1783. He seems particularly exasperated by the fact that he had meticulously followed "all that was prescribed to me in the two operations for the complete perfection of the *œuvre*."[81]

According to the Russian report, the triumvirate of adepts did not immediately abandon their *grand œuvre*. Instead, they relocated to Warsaw, where they continued their alchemical endeavours in the autumn of 1783. Only one consultation with the Holy Word was made in this period, by Brumore on November 1, and it did not touch upon alchemy. However, the subject matter is intriguing and does suggest that Brumore was in Warsaw. The Holy Word is asked to advise Stanisław Kostka Bieliński about whether he should follow through on his plan to leave his homeland. Bieliński was evidently aggrieved at "the wrong that the king of Poland" had done to him by supposedly reneging on a promise to appoint him Marshal of the Court of the Crown in August 1783.[82]

Two months later, Bruchié consulted the Holy Word and confessed to being in despair, having witnessed the work (the *grand œuvre*) being destroyed. She is also "troubled by the new dispersion" that this has caused and "tormented by my mistrust." She even harboured doubts about whether Pernety still believed in the pronouncements of the Holy Word.[83] The "new dispersion" mentioned by Bruchié is not only a reference to Pernety's leaving Berlin in November 1783 for Valence in France, but also to Grabianka and Ronikier returning to their respective estates in Podolia.[84] At this juncture, it would seem Bruchié (and Brumore) felt somewhat cut adrift from the fraternal and alchemical bonds that had sustained them over the preceding five years in Berlin, Rheinsberg, and Poland.

This forlorn state of aimlessness did not last long. A rather prosaic entry in the manuscript record of the consultation with the Holy Word states that "Brumore and Mlle Bruchié left Poland and went to Hamburg, where Brumore saw 'Elie Artiste,' from whom he received two flacons of philosophical matter all prepared to receive the second mercury." Moreover, "he also received all the details necessary for the conduct of the œuvre." The next entry, on April 12, asks the Holy Word to confirm the veracity of the alchemical knowledge conveyed to Brumore and Bruchié by "Elie Artiste." After receiving an affirmative answer, the pair seem to have left Altona, after a stay of around three months.[85]

The reasoning behind their decision to seek out "Elie Artiste" in Altona is, in many ways, understandable. An alchemical tract by Elias Artista had circulated within the society since 1779, when Le Bauld first shared his copy. Morinval seems to have greatly valued his copy of this tract at the turn of 1780. In all likelihood, the manuscript possessed by Morinval and Le Bauld was a translation of *Elias Artista mit Dem Stein der Weisen* (1770).

Thus Brumore and Bruchié concluded in early 1784 that they needed to consult with the author of this tract in person to ascertain where they had gone wrong in their own alchemical operations. By means unknown, Brumore and Bruchié were able to glean that the author writing under the pseudonym of Elias Artista lived in Altona, near Hamburg. The German historian Reinhard Breymayer, in a series of articles written in the 1980s and 1990s, has argued convincingly that the musician and radical Pietist Johann Daniel Müller was the writer behind the tracts associated with Elias Artista at this time.[86]

Breymayer was greatly aided in his detective work by Brumore's typically extravagant praise of "this extraordinary man who called himself Elias Artista in several works, which appeared in the north of Germany." Brumore's lavish praise of Müller first appeared in 1784 in the former's translation of Swedenborg's *The Delights of Wisdom on the Subject of Conjugal Love*. In a lengthy footnote, Brumore proclaimed Müller to be "one of the prodigies of our age." According to Brumore, Müller was a phenomenal autodidact raised in a family of low status, who within two years of self-study was able to speak nearly every language. Significantly, Brumore also lauds Müller's treatise on alchemy, which he (and all those who believe in the *grand œuvre*) "regard as the key to the art."[87] Brumore's time in Altona, learning from someone he regarded so highly, re-energised his passion for alchemy. Moreover, he left northern Germany in possession of a prized commodity: two flacons of *prima materia*. By November 1784, Brumore had arrived in Avignon, where he was to stay for six months, eager to instigate a new attempt by the *illuminés* to complete the *grand œuvre*.[88] As we will see in chapter 3, Brumore did not live long enough to see this operation conclude (yet again in failure).

Brumore's above-mentioned translation of Swedenborg's *Conjugal Love* into French was published whilst he was travelling through Germany and France.[89] C. T. Odhner, the pre-eminent historian of the New Church, dismissed the work as "a fragmentary and faulty translation of selected passages" of Swedenborg's original Latin text.[90] Odhner's harsh critique took exception to Brumore's professed aim to "prune all the repetitions and theological proofs" in the original text in order that a wider readership would be able to "reach the truths" that Swedenborg endeavoured to establish.[91] Regardless of the literary merits of Brumore's translation, it does rank as the first French version of the treatise. Brumore's publication of this tract also highlights the sustained interest in Swedenborgian doctrine among the small circle of *illuminés* in Berlin, Rheinsberg, and Podolia.

The earliest reference to Swedenborg to be found among the records of the consultations with the Holy Word occurs in a question posed by Pernety on September 29, 1779. He approached the oracle to seek confirmation that he should "consider as true all that is contained in the tract entitled *Delitiæ sapeintiæ de amore conjugalis*." The Holy Word responded affirmatively: "He walked the road where Heaven has placed you, he had the wisdom of a sage; he has spoken truthfully."[92] Over the next eighteen months Pernety's interest in Swedenborg only deepened. On March 12, 1781, Pernety again consulted the Holy Word about the Swede and whether he should publish his translation of Swedenborg's *Heaven and Hell*.[93] Once again, the Holy Word responded enthusiastically, and Pernety obtained permission to continue. It may be coincidental, but Pernety's interest in, and translation of, Swedenborg's text occurred precisely at the time when he seems to have been forced to abandon his alchemical pursuits.

In October 1781, Pernety began to correspond with Carl Fredrik Nordenskjöld, who, along with his elder brother August, was one of the most prominent Swedenborgians in Sweden.[94] Part of Pernety's reason for writing to C. F. Nordenskjöld was to request biographical information and anecdotes about Swedenborg from August. He duly received a great deal of material, which he used extensively to write his "Observations ou Notes sur Swedenborg," which appeared before his translation when *Les Merveilles du Ciel et de l'Enfer* was published in 1782.[95] On January 15, 1782, prior to the publication of *Les Merveilles*, Pernety had once again consulted the Holy Word regarding whether to insert several responses he had received from the oracle in Berlin. He was particularly concerned with whether he should include those "relating to the appearance of my angel on the day of the renewal of my incense," which had taken place place in October 1779.[96]

The Holy Word ordered him not to include these descriptions, which were duly omitted from the printed version.

Yet even without these personal testaments to the invocation of Assadaï, Pernety's "Discours Preliminaire," which appears prior to his translation of *Les Merveilles*, emphasizes the influence of Swedenborg's doctrine. Swedenborg's angelology is especially pertinent in regard to the initiatic society that Pernety had helped to establish in 1779. Although Swedenborg's communication with angels was much more individual, he still looked to the prophets in the Old Testament and their communication with God to validate his own visionary experiences after 1744.[97] The way in which the *illuminés* in Berlin first began to practise theurgical rites atop a "mountain" in conscious imitation of Moses's encounter with God on Mount Sinai was aesthetically at odds with Swedenborg's own experiences. However, the mountaintop rite still functioned within the same spiritual framework Swedenborg had developed in the middle of the eighteenth century.

In *Heaven and Hell*, Swedenborg describes an everyday world in which angels are ever-present and, moreover, take on human form and can converse with those who are spiritually enlightened. As Swedenborg wrote: "That angels are human forms, or men, has been seen by me a thousand times. I have spoken with them as man with man . . . and I have seen in them nothing different in form from that of man . . . they have faces, eyes, ears, body, arms, hands and feet."[98] Such everyday encounters with angels feature very rarely in the manuscript that recorded the consultations with the Holy Word up to 1785. An exception can be found in a note written down on October 19, 1779, which describes Pernety seeing an apparition of two angels whilst he was burning incense atop the mountain during his rite of renewal.[99] The angels took human form and were apparently keen to talk to Pernety. However, angel encounters were documented much more frequently by *illuminés* in Avignon from 1787 (see chapter 3).

The group's growing interest in Swedenborgian doctrine went hand in hand with a pronounced turn to millenarianism. Yet, whereas conventional Swedenborgians in the 1780s preached that a New Jerusalem would soon descend to earth and usher in an "internal Millennium,"[100] Grabianka and Pernety embraced a far more literal premillennialism in which great tribulations would beset the world before the return of Christ. The principal stimulus for this millenarian turn seems to have been the visit of a Polish gentleman named Rohoziński to Grabianka's home in Podolia at some point in the first half of 1780.[101] By June 12, 1780, Pernety had received a message from Grabianka regarding the visit of Rohoziński and was instructed to ask the Holy Word the following question: "Pray tell us for our instruction, Holy Word, if the Polish gentleman named Rohoziński, who visited [Grabianka] with his sister and brother-in-law [Tekla Tarnowska and Jan Tarnowski], is a man inspired by the supreme being?" Pernety added that Rohoziński had already been announcing the imminent arrival of the "new reign of the Lord," since 1765. The response from the Holy Word was emphatic: "This is the time when you will believe in all those who will announce to the nations my new reign because my spirit is with them."[102] This endorsement of Rohoziński ensured that the prophetic utterances of this

obscure Polish gentleman would serve as the principal dynamo for the millenarian sentiments of Grabianka and Pernety for several years.

It is noteworthy that Podolia was at this time the epicentre of the eschatological Frankist
Movement, led by Jacob Frank. Frank drew on significant support for Sabbatianism
among Podolian Jews in the mid-eighteenth century. As Paweł Maciejko notes, "Podolia
was the only place in the world" at this time where "many Jews openly adhered" to the
seventeenth-century messianic teachings of Sabbatai Tsevi.[103] It is impossible to gauge the
influence of Frank on Rohoziński, given the paucity of information regarding the latter's prophetic career. Nevertheless, it is clear that the area provided fertile ground for
religious visionaries at this time.

The profound and lasting impact Rohoziński had on Pernety is vividly demonstrated
in a letter he sent to C. F. Nordenskjöld in Stockholm, dated October 20, 1781. Pernety
describes at length letters he has received from Grabianka in Podolia, whom he lauds as
"a man of great honour and veracity." Interestingly, Pernety provides some biographical
information about Rohoziński. We learn, for example, that he was a "gentleman who
has been for some time retired to the country, where he leads a very pious and exem-
plary life" and is "a *partisan* of Swedenborg." Moreover, in his retirement Rohoziński
conversed with whomever he saw fit "about the new reign of Jesus Christ on Earth, which
he depicts as being very near." Crucially, Pernety is prepared to proclaim to Nordenskjöld
that Rohoziński is "inspired by God" by including the entire response he had received
from the Holy Word some fifteen months earlier. This, Pernety declares, provides "the
most evident proofs of the truth of what is said about the new kingdom of God."[104]

As further proof the imminent onset of Christ's new reign, Pernety also recounts
Grabianka's description of two miraculous incidents that had recently occurred in
Podolia. He then narrates how two peasants who "were lately dead at a few months inter-
val, or at least dead in appearance," were "returned to life" when they were being carried
to their graves. They both "rose in perfect health, walking and praising God, and exhort-
ing all the attendants to conversion and immediate repentance." Pernety adds that "the
first of these extraordinary events passed in the country in the presence of the brother-
in-law of the gentleman who wrote the letter." In other words, Jan Tarnowski, who had
been consecrated by Grabianka in the summer of 1779, had conveyed this story to his
brother-in-law. The second incident, according to Pernety, occurred on the "estate of
the *Grand Échanson* of Lithuania, whose estate is in Podolia." This second miraculous
resurrection was therefore witnessed by Ronikier. A curious detail of Ronikier's report
was that the peasant he supposedly saw returned to life came back "with a cross and
spear very strangely worked upon his breast, which cannot be erased."[105] Further proof, if
Nordenskjöld needed it, that the resurrection of the dead (emblazoned, moreover, with
symbols associated with the crucifixion of Christ), as foreseen in the Nicene Creed, heralded the onset of the Second Coming in the near future.

In a further letter to Nordenskjöld, written on December 1, 1781, Pernety sought
to augment his previous "information concerning the definite announcement of the

approaching new reign of the Lord on Earth." He did so by referencing William Herschel's recent discovery of Uranus, which he considered "a sign given by God in announcement of His new reign."[106] He then cited the entire response he received from the Holy Word on November 21 in regard to this recent astronomical discovery. The answer from the oracle ended by beseeching Pernety to "be the messenger of the new reign."[107]

A fascinating aspect of Pernety's correspondence with Nordenskjöld is the way in which this auspicious news was communicated to like-minded millenarians across Europe. On May 27, 1782, for example, Thomas Hartley, the English Swedenborgian, wrote to thank Nordenskjöld for informing him about "the announcement of the remarkable and marvellous events that are told from Podolia."[108] The papers of Charles Rainsford also contain an English translation of Pernety's first letter to Nordenskjöld, which had been communicated to him by William Spence, another early English Swedenborgian.[109] The familiarity of English Swedenborgians with the prophetic utterances of Rohoziński in the first half of the 1780s helps us to understand how Grabianka vaunted his links to his fellow Pole when he first arrived in London at the close of 1785. An unknown prophet he may still be to us in the twenty-first century, but Rohoziński's prophetic utterances in the early 1780s fuelled millenarian sentiment far beyond Podolia and the small society of *illuminés* that had been established in Berlin in 1779.

NOTES

1. On Pernety's career as a Benedictine monk, see Linn Holmberg, *The Forgotten Encyclopedia: The Maurists' Dictionary of Arts, Crafts, and Sciences, the Unrealized Rival of the Encyclopédie of Diderot and d'Alembert* (Umeå, Sweden: Umeå University, 2014). Alongside Dom Brézillac, Pernety worked on the formation of universal dictionary of arts, crafts, and sciences between 1743 and 1755. For the manuscript material of this dictionary by Pernety, see BNdF, "Matériaux pour un Dictionnaire des arts et sciences, par dom Antoine-Joseph Pernety," MSS. 16979–16984.

2. Antoine Faivre, *Access to Western Esotericism* (Albany: State University of New York Press, 1994), 76. For a brief biography of Pernety, see J. A. M. Snoek, "Pernety, Dom Antoine-Joseph," *Dictionary of Gnosis*, 940–2. For a book-length biography of Pernety, see Meillassoux-Le Cerf, *Dom Pernety*.

3. Thiébault, *Mes souvenirs*, vol. 5, 97–9. Also see J.-A. Borrelly, *Caractere des personnages les plus marquans dans les differentes*, vol. 1 (Paris: Leopold Collin, 1808), 50–1.

4. Pernety wrote an essay in 1762 defending the alchemical *œuvre* of Flamel in response to the publication of Abbé Villain's *Histoire Critique de Nicolas Flamel* (Paris: G. Desprez, 1761). See A.-J. Pernety, "Lettre de Dom Pernety sur une Histoire de Nicolas Flamel," *L'Année Littéraire* (1762): 24–35.

5. Pernety to the Holy Word, Feb. 19, 1779, in Meillassoux-Le Cerf, *Dom Pernety*, 335.

6. Given Le Bauld's prominence within the small French theatrical milieu in Berlin, it is possible that he simply consulted the Holy Word as a result of his acquaintance with the dramatist Brumore.

7. See Walther Schultze, *Geschichte der preussischen regieverwaltung von 1766 bis 1786*, vol. 1 (Leipzig: Verlag von Duncker & Humblot, 1888), 59–60, 119, 131, 372. Morinval succeeded J.-M. Pernety, the younger brother of Antoine-Joseph.

8. Gerlach, *Die Freimaurer im Alten Preussen*, 522–3, 533, 539, 574, 853.

9. On Le Bauld's Masonic correspondence on behalf of the lodge, see François Labbé, *Correspondances Maçonniques 1777–1783: Franc-Maçonnerie, Illuminisme, Rose-Croix d'Or, Stricte Observance* (Paris: Honoré Champion, 2016), 23–33, 77–82, 87–8, 90, 254–5, 273–9, 281–2, 287, 292, 310–11, 327. He also composed many songs for the lodge. See, for example, *Chansons pour les Santés dans les Banquets* (Berlin, 1781).

10. ADHM, II G 75, 11–12.

11. See Abbé de Morveau, *L'Inoculation par Aspiration; épitre présentée a la Reine* (Paris: Chez Musier, Fils, 1774); Morveau, *Le Triomphe de la Religion, ou Le Sacrifice de Madame Louise de France* (London-Paris: Chez Musier, Fils, 1774). According to a biographer of his elder brother, the Abbé de Morveau spent several years at Versailles in "obscure employment," which included being a reader for Marie-Antoinette. See Georges Bouchard, *Guyton-Morveau, chimiste et conventionnel (1737–1816)* (Paris: Librairie Académique Perrin, 1938), 14–15.

12. Mr. de Brumore, *Drames Nouveaux* (Berlin: George Jacques Decker, 1778). Both were three-act plays, the first being in prose and the second in verse. It is noteworthy that "Les Calas" ranks as the first dramatic work in French to tackle the controversial subject of the execution, in 1762, of Jean Calas, a Protestant. The treatment of Calas in Toulouse was subsequently used as a case study of fanaticism by Voltaire.

13. See Meillassoux-Le Cerf, *Dom Pernety*, 335–448.

14. Benedict Chastanier, *A Word of Advice to a Benighted World* (London: n.p., 1795), 26.

15. Ephraim Chambers, *Cyclopædia, or, an universal dictionary of Arts and Sciences*, vol. 2 (London: n.p, 1728), 668. For an analysis of the attack on ancient oracles in the late seventeenth century, see J. I. Israel, "Fontenelle and the War of the Oracles," in *The Radical Enlightenment: Philosophy and the Making of Modernity 1650–1750* (Oxford: Oxford University Press, 2001), 359–74.

16. Louis Jaucourt, "Oracle," in *Encyclopédie, ou dictionnaire raisonné des sciences, des arts et des métiers etc.*, ed. Denis Diderot, vol. 11 (Neufchastel: Samuel Faulche, 1765), 531.

17. Abbé de Brumore, "Lettre à M. le marquis de Thomé," *Journal Encyclopédique* 60:8 (Dec. 1785): 286–97.

18. Brumore, "Lettre," 295.

19. Brumore published a French translation of this work in 1784. For the specific passage in his translation, see Emanuel Swedenborg, *Traité curieux des charmes de l'amour conjugal dans ce monde et dans l'autre*, trans. M. de Brumore (Berlin and Basel: George-Jacques & J. Henri Decker, 1784), 97–8.

20. Brumore, "Lettre," 294.

21. Brumore, "Lettre," 294.

22. Brumore, "Lettre," 294–5.

23. Giacomo Casanova to Eve Frank, Sept. 23, 1793. See Bernhard Marr, "La Kabbale de Jacques Casanova," in G. Casanova, *Memoires de J. Casanova de Seingalt*, vol. 3 (Paris: Éditions de la Sirène, 1926), ix.

24. See J. Casanova, *History of My Life*, trans. W. R. Trask, 12 vols. (New York: Harcourt, Brace and World, 1966–71), passim. Also see Aldo Ravà and Gustav Gugitz, eds., *Giac. Casanovas*

Briefwechsel (Munich: Georg Müller, 1913), 331–4; Ian Kelly, "Casanova and the Cabbala," in *Casanova: Actor, Lover, Priest, Spy* (London: Penguin, 2008), 210–20.

25. Prunelle de Lière, BNdG, "Regle de neuf" and "Procedé de la Regle de neuf," Notes, documents, desseins relatifs à l'étude de l'hébreu et de la cabale, T.4188, 12–13.

26. Charles Rainsford, "Translation from the Italian MS La Vittoria or Victory given me by Mr. Ghillini," KCUP, MS. Codex 1687, 118–27.

27. Little is known about Grabianka's early life. According to A. J. Rolle, Grabianka attended the Polish school in Luneville, France, until 1759, when he returned to Lviv to attend the funeral of his father. Grabianka married Teresa Stadnicka in 1771 and they had three children together (Anna, b. 1773; Antoni, b. 1775, and Erazm, b. 1777). See Rolle, *Tadeusz Leszczyc Grabianka*, 7–22. On October 8, 1777, Jan de Witte, a Polish engineer, architect, and the commander of the fortress at Kamianets-Podilskyi, mentioned Grabianka in a letter. Grabianka was preparing for the name-day of his wife, Teresa (on Oct. 15), and they attended a ball together. See Jan de Witte, *Listy Jana de Witte (1777–1779)* (Kraków: Czasu, 1868), 5.

28. RGIA, Fond 1163, op. 1, d. 16b, 206v.

29. Meillassoux-Le Cerf, *Dom Pernety*, 382.

30. Meillassoux-Le Cerf, *Dom Pernety*, 382, 428.

31. Meillassoux-Le Cerf, *Dom Pernety*, 383, 428.

32. Meillassoux-Le Cerf, *Dom Pernety*, 339–40, 383–4, 429.

33. Meillassoux-Le Cerf, *Dom Pernety*, 412–13.

34. Meillassoux-Le Cerf, *Dom Pernety*, 384–5, 412. Berlin and its surroundings are completely devoid of mountains. The highest hills are Tempelhofer Berg (66 metres) and Müggelberge (114 metres).

35. Meillassoux-Le Cerf, *Dom Pernety*, 340.

36. Meillassoux-Le Cerf, *Dom Pernety*, 384.

37. Chastanier, *Word of Advice*, 26.

38. "Breve dettaglio della Società, o Setta scoperta nell'arresto di Ottavio Cappelli, tratto dalle Carte allo stesso perquisite (1790)," BNCdR, Vitt.Em.245, 569r–569v. Ferrier added that the ritual practised by Moses on Mount Sinai had been transmitted to Abu Ma' Shar.

39. Meillassoux-Le Cerf, *Dom Pernety*, 382, 335, 428, 411.

40. "Breve," 572v–573r.

41. When L.-M.-F. de la Forest Divonne was consecrated in December 1789, he became known as 579 G, as he was most likely the seventh person to choose these three digits. See chapter 3 for more on Divonne's consecration.

42. On Ronikier, see Teodor Żychliński, *Złota Księga Szlachty Polskiéj*, vol. 4 (Poznan: Jarosław Leitgeber, 1882), 223–4. Teresa Ronikier died in 1781. The governess of Countess Ronikier, Catherine Baley, was also consecrated into the society, in April 1782. See Meillassoux-Le Cerf, *Dom Pernety*, 411. On Ronikier's estate Nowosiółki, in Volhynia, see Roman Aftanazy, *Dzieje rezydencji na dawnych kresach Rzeczypospolitej*, vol. 5 (Wrocław: Zakład Narodowy im. Ossolińskich, 1994), 319–23.

43. On Aug. 23, 1782, Grabianka also sought permission from the Holy Word to consecrate his valet, Franciszek Mikołaj Leyman, who was born in Gdansk and was around 18 years old at the time. See Meillassoux-Le Cerf, *Dom Pernety*, 396. Brief biographical details in relation to this marriage in Avignon, in 1797, can be found in ADdV, Pm An V, 51v.

44. Andrew Hamilton, *Rheinsberg: Memorials of Frederick the Great and Prince Henry of Prussia*, vol. 2 (London: John Murray, 1880), 109.

45. Richard Krauel, "Prinz Heinrich von Preußen in Rheinsberg," *Hohenzollern-Jahrbuch* (1902), 19.

46. See Brumore, *La Vie Privée d'un Prince Célèbre des Loisirs du Prince Henri de Prusse* (Veropolis [Berlin]: n.p., 1784), 36; Olivier, *Les comédiens français*, vol. 3, 13.

47. Brumore, *La Vie*, 36–7.

48. Brumore, "Panomphée, ou Divertissement en Mélo-drame," in *La Vie*, 70–81.

49. Meillassoux-Le Cerf, *Dom Pernety*, 440.

50. Blainville was buried at Rheinsberg. Prince Heinrich ensured that his gravestone was inscribed with a verse in praise of his acting talents. See Olivier, *Les comédiens français*, vol. 3, p. 15. Brumore wrote that Blainville did not have the strength to survive "the pain of being forgotten for a moment." See Brumore, *La Vie*, 31. It would seem Blainville fell out of favour with Prince Heinrich in 1781.

51. Meillassoux-Le Cerf, *Dom Pernety*, 437–8. It is likely that Alexandre Baligand de Ferrières (also referred to as Serrières), a librettist who was active in central Europe in the 1770s and 1780s and who consulted the Holy Word in September 1780, met Brumore through their artistic work. On Alexandre Baligand de Ferrières, see Robert Ignatius Letellier, *Opéra-Comique: A Sourcebook* (Newcastle-upon-Tyne: Cambridge Scholars, 2010), 331.

52. Madame Borrelly was also consecrated at some point between February 22 and March 10, 1781. See Meillassoux-Le Cerf, *Dom Pernety*, 409–10.

53. Borrelly became a member of the Royal Academy of Sciences in 1772. He went to Berlin on the recommendation of Jean d'Alembert, who proposed him for the position of professor at the Military Academy for Gentlemen. See J. L. von Hordt, *Mémoires historiques, politiques et militaires de M. Le Cte. de Hordt*, vol. 2, ed. J.-A. Borrelly (Paris: F. Buisson, 1805), 65–6.

54. See J.-A. Borrelly, "Preface," in Hordt, *Mémoires*, vol. 1, 3–4.

55. Meillassoux-Le Cerf, *Dom Pernety*, 407–11.

56. Meillassoux-Le Cerf, *Dom Pernety*, 414.

57. Meillassoux-Le Cerf, *Dom Pernety*, 343.

58. Meillassoux-Le Cerf, *Dom Pernety*, 346–7.

59. Meillassoux-Le Cerf, *Dom Pernety*, 417.

60. RGIA, Fond 1163, op. 1, d. 16b, 207r.

61. Meillassoux-Le Cerf, *Dom Pernety*, 418. A similar alchemical ceremony took place in Avignon in May 1787. See chapter 3.

62. Meillassoux-Le Cerf, *Dom Pernety*, 351.

63. Meillassoux-Le Cerf, *Dom Pernety*, 351.

64. Meillassoux-Le Cerf, *Dom Pernety*, 419–23.

65. Meillassoux-Le Cerf, *Dom Pernety*, 424.

66. Meillassoux-Le Cerf, *Dom Pernety*, 353–60.

67. Meillassoux-Le Cerf, *Dom Pernety*, 361.

68. RGIA, Fond 1163, op. 1, d. 16b, 207r.

69. Morinval returned to France on December 2, 1782, as commanded by the Holy Word. Had he complied with the instructions of the Holy Word, he would have travelled to Lyon. As early as July 19, 1779, Morinval had been told by the Holy Word that he was destined to marry a woman

named Montolivet in Lyon. See Meillassoux-Le Cerf, *Dom Pernety*, 416, 427. For a curious account of Morinval's search for Mlle Montolivet in Lyon, see Bernard, "L'Alchimie" (Feb. 28, 1863), 297.

70. P.-J. Fabre, *Alchymista Christianus* (Toulouse: Pierre Bosc, 1632).

71. A. G. Debus, *The French Paracelsians* (Cambridge: Cambridge University Press, 1992), 75. For a biographical study of Fabre, see Frank Greiner, "Introduction," in P.-J. Fabre, *L'alchimiste chrétien*, ed. Frank Greiner (Milan: Arché, 2001), vii–cxvii. For a broader analysis of analogies between alchemy and Catholic liturgical practices, see Michel Noize, "Le Grand Œuvre, liturgie de l'alchimie chrétienne," *Revue de l'histoire des religions* 186:2 (1974): 149–83.

72. Fabre, *L'alchimiste chrétien*, 214.

73. Fabre, *L'alchimiste chrétien*, 211.

74. Zofia Zielińska, "Michał Aleksander Ronikier H. Gryf," *Polski słownik biograficzny*, vol. 32 (Wrocław: Zakład Narodowy im. Ossolińskich, 1989), 23–5.

75. Meillassoux-Le Cerf, *Dom Pernety*, 398, 407, 434.

76. Meillassoux-Le Cerf, *Dom Pernety*, 398.

77. Meillassoux-Le Cerf, *Dom Pernety*, 434.

78. Meillassoux-Le Cerf, *Dom Pernety*, 406–7.

79. RGIA, Fond 1163, op. 1, d. 16b, 207r.

80. The Russian report notes that Teresa Grabianka viewed the alchemical labours of her husband, Brumore, and Ronikier as a sham and a costly pursuit that was draining her family's finances. Moreover, the report states that this was the last time she and her husband met. See RGIA, Fond 1163, op. 1, d. 16b, 207v.

81. Meillassoux-Le Cerf, *Dom Pernety*, 434.

82. Meillassoux-Le Cerf, *Dom Pernety*, 435. On Bieliński, who did become the last Marshal in 1793 (until 1795), see Adam Skałkowski, "Stanisław Kostka Bieliński," *Polski Słownik Biograficzny*, vol. 2 (Kraków: Skład główny w księg, Gebethnera i Wolffa, 1936), 56–7.

83. Meillassoux-Le Cerf, *Dom Pernety*, 435.

84. On Pernety's departure from Berlin and his time in Valence, see chapter 3.

85. Meillassoux-Le Cerf, *Dom Pernety*, 436.

86. As well as being an author of mystical and alchemical tracts, Müller was a violinist and music director. See Reinhard Breymayer, "'Elie Artiste': Johann Daniel Müller de Wissenbach/Nissau (1716 Jusqu'après 1785): Un Aventurier entre le Piétisme Radical et L'Illuminisme," in *Actes du Colloque International Lumieres et Illuminisme*, ed. Mario Matucci (Pisa: Pacini Editore, 1984), 65–84; Breymayer, "Müller (Johann) Daniel," in *Biographisch-Bibliographisches Kirchenlexikon*, vol. 6 (Nordhausen: Verlag Traugott Bautz, 1993), 255–67; Breymayer, "'Elias Artista': Johann Daniel Müller Aus Wissenbach/Nissau, ein Kritischer Freund Swedenborgs, und seine wirkung auf die Schwäbischen Pietisten F. C. Oetinger und P. M. Hahn," in *Literatur und Kultur im deutschen Südwesten zwischen Renaissance und Aufklärung*, ed. W. E. Schäfer (Amsterdam: Rodopi, 1995), 329–72. For a broader analysis of the myth of Elias Artista as the messiah of nature, see Herbert Breger, "Elias Artista: A Precursor of the Messiah in Natural Science," in *Nineteen Eighty-Four: Science between Utopia and Dystopia*, ed. E. Mendelsohn and H. Nowotny (Dordrecht: Springer, 1984), 49–72; Antoine Faivre, "Elie Artiste, ou le Messie des Philosophes de la Nature (première patie)," *Aries* 2:2 (2002): 119–52; Faivre, "Elie Artiste, ou le Messie des Philosophes de la Nature (seconde partie)," *Aries* 3:1 (2003): 25–54.

87. Brumore, "Avertissement du Traducteur," in *Traité curieux*, 14. Brumore repeated his praise of Elias Artista in December 1785 in his reply to the Marquis de Thomé. See Brumore, "Lettre," 289–90, 296.

88. Prior to arriving in Avignon, Brumore visited Strasbourg (where Bruchié had remained) and Basel. It seems highly likely that he was reunited with Prince Heinrich, who spent much of 1784 in France and Switzerland. Prince Heinrich's itinerary included a stay in Basel in July 1784, followed by Montbéliard, the home of the Duke and Duchess of Württemberg. In August, the prince visited Dijon and met Brumore's famous brother, L.-B. Guyton de Morveau, who entertained his guest with a demonstration of his recently invented hot-air balloon. Morveau had first piloted his balloon in April 1784. For confirmation that Brumore visited Strasbourg and Basel, see Meillassoux-Le Cerf, *Dom Pernety*, 436. On Prince Heinrich's visits to Basel, Montbéliard, and Dijon, see Richard Krauel, *Prinz Heinrich von Preußen in Paris während der Jahre 1784 und 1788 bis 1789* (Berlin: Ernst Siegfried Mittler und Sohn, 1901), 6–11. Also see Hamilton, *Rheinsberg*, vol. 2, p. 109. For a description of Morveau's balloon launch, see L.-B. Guyton de Morveau, *Description de l'aérostate* (Dijon: Causse, 1784).

89. The work was published in Berlin and Basel and was dedicated to Prince Heinrich.

90. C. T. Odhner, *Annals of the New Church* (Philadelphia: Academy of the New Church, 1898), 123–4.

91. Brumore, "Avertissement du Traducteur," 5–6.

92. Meillassoux-Le Cerf, *Dom Pernety*, 344.

93. Meillassoux-Le Cerf, *Dom Pernety*, 363.

94. For the Pernety-Nordenskjöld correspondence, which began on Oct. 21, 1781, and went through Feb. 12, 1782, see Viatte, *Les Sources Occultes*, vol. 2, 279–83. For the French originals and English translations of the letters, see ACSD, vol. 10, 1663.18, 1663.19, 1664.11, 1664.13, and 1664.16.

95. See A.-J. Pernety, "Observations ou Notes sur Swedenborg," in Emanuel Swedenborg, *Les Merveilles du Ciel et de l'Enfer*, vol. 1 (Berlin: G. J. Decker, 1782), 62–88. On Pernety as a translator and populariser of Swedenborg, see Williams-Hogan, "Place of Emanuel Swedenborg," 235–7.

96. Meillassoux-Le Cerf, *Dom Pernety*, 370.

97. Simon McCarthy-Jones and Charles Fernyhough, "Talking Back to the Spirits: The Voices and Visions of Emanuel Swedenborg," *History of the Human Sciences* 21:1 (2008): 10.

98. Emanuel Swedenborg, *Heaven and Its Wonders and Hell*, trans. J. C. Ager (New York: New-Church Board of Publication, 1892), 43, 45.

99. Meillassoux-Le Cerf, *Dom Pernety*, 348.

100. Jacob Duché to Mary Hopkinson, May 5, 1785, HSP, Mrs. Francis T. Redwood Collection, Am. 12905. Also see Clarke Garrett, "Swedenborg and the Mystical Enlightenment," *Journal of the History of Ideas* 45:1 (1984): 73.

101. A prominent branch of the Rohoziński family was based in the Lutsk area of Volhynia (in modern-day Ukraine). See Kasper Niesiecki, *Korona Polska przy Złotey Wolnosci Starożytnemi*, vol. 3 (Lviv: w Drukarni Collegium Lwowskigeo Societatis JESU, 1740), 873; Witold Filipczak, "Rozdwojone wołyńskie sejmiki poselskie w 1786 roku," *Res Historica* 36 (2013): 163–90.

102. Meillassoux-Le Cerf, *Dom Pernety*, 356.

103. Paweł Maciejko, *The Mixed Multitude: Jacob Frank and the Frankist Movement, 1755–1816* (Philadelphia: University of Pennsylvania Press, 2011), 10.

104. A.-J. Pernety to C. F. Nordenskjöld, Oct. 20, 1781, KB, Arkiv Klara Johanson, KB1/L 2. Also see Viatte, *Les Sources Occultes*, vol. 2, 279–80.

105. Pernety to Nordenskjöld, KB, KB1/L 2. Also see Viatte, *Les Sources Occultes*, vol. 2, 279.

106. A.-J. Pernety to C. F. Nordenskjöld, Dec. 1, 1781, ACSD, 1664.11, 3.

107. Meillassoux-Le Cerf, *Dom Pernety*, 369.

108. Thomas Hartley to C. F. Nordesnskjöld, May 27, 1782, UUB, G 180a, 254.

109. See Rainsford's English translation of the letter from Pernety to C. F. Nordenskjöld, Oct. 20, 1781, BL, Add MS. 23,669, 1.

2

In Search of Guidance

GRABIANKA, SWEDENBORGIANS, AND THE PROPHECIES
OF SAMUEL BEST IN LONDON, 1785–1786

⌒——

FOR A "PRETENDED" prophet, who held audiences with a remarkable array of personages in the mid-1780s, including King George III and L.-C. de Saint-Martin, Samuel Best
(1738–1825), who was commonly known as "Poor-Help," has received scant attention.[1]
A brief biographical note on Best by T. F. Henderson, published in 1885, characterises
him as having "a reputation for dishonesty," but concedes that "he was consulted by many
of the upper classes of London."[2] This Victorian-era appraisal principally drew on a contemporary account of Best by John Martin, a Baptist minister, who in 1787 published
a scathing exposé entitled *Imposture Detected: Or Thoughts on a Pretended Prophet*.[3] In
outlining his rationale for publishing a repudiation of Best's supposed prophetic gifts,
Martin acknowledged that Best had "excited the attention and gratified the curiosity
of many."[4] In concluding why such a clamour existed, Martin conceded that "between
insanity on the one hand, and a coarse kind of enthusiasm, strongly in favour of hypocrisy
and nonsense . . . there may be an influence that will bear inspection."[5]

It is surprising that, with the exception of Henderson, no other scholar has sought
to more fully examine Best's allure in metropolitan London in the decade prior to the
French Revolution. To be sure, since the 1970s several scholars have noted, in passing,
that Best was the most famous of the "fanatical adventurers" of his day and epitomized
the rise in the incidence of prophetism in London in the 1780s.[6] However, it is fair to say
that in recent years the full gaze of historians has largely concentrated on the tumultuous decade following the storming of the Bastille, in 1789.[7] The seismic events in France
formed a backdrop against which prophets in England, such as Joanna Southcott and
Richard Brothers, attracted the public's attention with their millenarian visions.

Initiating the Millennium. Robert Collis, and Natalie Bayer, Oxford University Press (2020) © Oxford University Press.
DOI: 10.1093/oso/9780190903374.001.0001

This chapter will take up Martin's remark that Best exerted an "influence that will bear inspection." It will do so by exploring a remarkable series of meetings—sixteen in total, of which twelve are recorded—between Grabianka and Best that took place over an eleven-month period between December 1785 and November 1786, when the Polish nobleman was resident in the British capital. Evidence of the extraordinary bond between Grabianka and Best that developed in London in the mid-1780s can be found in an in-depth journal produced by the former, in which he recorded the details of each of their meetings, along with a biographical sketch of Best and general comments. For more than 150 years, this rich source of material has been hidden in plain sight, contained, as it is, in the aforementioned article "L'Alchimie" by the French poet Thalès Bernard, which was serialised in the journal *L'Europe Littéraire* from January to February 1863.[8] Hitherto, a number of historians have stated that Grabianka met Best whilst in London, without providing either evidence or detail.[9]

A study of Grabianka's London journal substantially augments our knowledge of his activities during the period of his residence in London. It reveals a man deeply susceptible to messages conveyed by individual prophets in forming (or solidifying) his own mille-narian worldview and situating himself within this grand scheme. Moreover, the journal is revelatory in terms of enhancing our understanding of Best's status in the mid-1780s, as arguably one of the foremost prophets active in Europe, let alone London. Lastly, the journal broadens our understanding of the close links between Best and Swedenborgian members of the British Society for the Propagation of the Doctrines of the New Church (known as the Theosophical Society between 1783 and 1785). It also details how leading figures linked with this society, particularly Benedict Chastanier and William Bousie (b. *c.* 1731–after 1816), facilitated Grabianka's initial meeting with the London prophet. The links between Grabianka and the tight-knit Swedenborgian milieu in London have been discussed by a number of historians, without reference to their shared attraction to Best's prophecies.[10] Knowing of this mutual fascination with Best helps to embel-lish the picture of the common spiritual bonds between Grabianka and the London Swedenborgians that existed at the time.

Grabianka arrived in London on December 6, 1785, accompanied by two valets (Franciszek Leyman and a Monsieur Nicolas), after undertaking a lengthy peregrina-tion across Europe that had begun in Sutkowce, his estate in Podolia.[11] At the begin-ning of his journal, Grabianka declares that "the desire to know" Best, whom he calls an "extraordinary man, who was called the prophet of the Lord," was "the principal motive of my journey [to London]."[12] However, he adds that he had heard a great deal about Best only when in Holland and France. In other words, it would seem that Grabianka did not depart from his estate in Podolia with the goal of meeting Best in London. Whilst the itinerary of Grabianka's journey is largely unknown, it is possible to piece together some significant information from available sources that helps to trace his meandering journey to England. It is documented, for example, that

Grabianka went first to Warsaw, where he managed to secure travel funds from his sister, Tekla Tarnowska (d. 1805).[13]

Significantly, his initial destination was Altona, in northern Germany, where, as Grabianka later wrote, he assumed the name of Slonski.[14] We have no record of whom Grabianka visited, but a prime candidate is the alchemist and Swedenborgian J. D. Müller, otherwise known as Elias Artista. After all, as discussed in the previous chapter, Brumore had left Grabianka's estate in Podolia to visit Müller at the beginning of 1784. After this visit, Brumore described Müller as an "extraordinary man" and "one of the prodigies of our age."[15] Considering Brumore's high praise of Müller after their meeting, it would seem likely that Grabianka's curiosity was piqued. However, all that is known about Grabianka's time in Altona is that he was "made acquainted" by someone (probably Müller) with Chastanier's French translation of a manuscript by Swedenborg, entitled *Du Commerce établi entre l'ame et la corps* (1785).[16] A noteworthy feature of this work is that Chastanier, as editor and translator, includes a vignette about his recent encounters with none other than Samuel Best:

> There is now in London in the infirmary of the parish of Shoreditch, a very extraordinary man, who seems to me as well as to many others to have communications with spirits. His name is Best, but he calls himself Little Help, or *petit secours*. I have been to see him twice this year; when he saw me the first time, he said, looking at my right hand . . . that I had adopted the doctrine of Swedenborg, which I had well done, and told me by heart many texts of Sacred Scripture which had a real relation to my present situation . . . This man is of the utmost simplicity, occupies himself all day in making works of straw and wool, which he coarsely embroiders, and often declares astonishing things on account of Swedenborg; He does this, however, only with those who are acquainted with these theological writings, and who adopt them.[17]

It may well be that Grabianka's curiosity had already been piqued in Altona by Chastanier's sketch about meeting a "very extraordinary man." Chastanier himself stated, in 1795, that Grabianka "went on purpose to The Hague to get the rest of my translations."[18] In The Hague, Grabianka sought out Pieter Frederik Gosse, the Dutch publisher of Chastanier's translations of Swedenborg. Gosse himself was a Swedenborgian, and judging by a letter he later received from Grabianka, was on close terms with the Pole in 1785, writing, "While I was staying in The Hague, under the name of Janieski, I did not conceal from you that I have the good fortune of being one of the Members of a Society, in which we have revelations about the New Jerusalem." Moreover, Grabianka praises Gosse's "zeal" and "love for truth," which he states are "very familiar to me."[19] It is not known precisely when Grabianka arrived in The Hague, but it was most likely not long after Gosse had received a letter from Chastanier in London, dated August 23, 1785, in which he described a further meeting with Best. As Chastanier notes, he had accompanied the Marquis René de Thomé (1732–1805) on August 19:

> This Friday morning I was with the Marquis de Thomé to see this extraordinary man of Shoreditch . . . The Marquis, who went there with the purpose of asking whether it would be well to publish the *Apocalypsis Explicata* of Swedenborg. He replied deliberately and joyfully, that not only would it be very well to publish it; But that nothing should be lost or suppressed, or cut from all that he had left in Mss. and that it was to be translated without the slightest change or alteration whatsoever, nothing to subtract and nothing added to what he called the human elegance of morality (these are the terms used by Best) because the whole comes from God.[20]

Hence, when Chastanier later remarked that Grabianka was "pressed with a desire to see" him in person when he was in The Hague, it was not solely because of Chastanier's skills as a translator of Swedenborg's texts.[21] By the autumn of 1785, Grabianka was aware that Chastanier was closely associated with Best.

At the time, Chastanier lived at 62 Tottenham Court Road in London. The location was very well-situated for both his professional career, as a surgeon, and in his capacity as one of the leading proponents of Swedenborgian doctrine in the English capital and an early practitioner of animal magnetism. In 1783, he advertised an assembly for "all those who read the theological writings of Swedenborg" in his home, which formed the initial nucleus of the Theosophical Society.[22] In the autobiographical sections of *A Word of Advice to a Benighted World*, written in 1795, Chastanier, a Frenchman by birth, states that he settled in London in October 1763.[23] In 1768, shortly after he had experienced a vision in which a mysterious woman had declared that "it shall be given you to know of *all the Mysteries of the Lord*," Chastanier records that he first heard of "an extraordinary man, who was reported to be in constant converse with Angels and Spirits."[24] In the mid-1780s, Chastanier was not only one of the leading Swedenborgians in England, he was also a prominent Freemason who maintained close links with brethren in France.[25] Furthermore, at the end of 1785 Chastanier became a pupil of John Bonoit de Mainauduc, the most prominent and successful animal magnetizer in London at the time. Indeed, in June 1786 he advertised his services for those seeking "intellectual treatment of diseases by sensations."[26] In short, Chastanier was a pivotal illuminist figure in London in the 1780s.

According to Chastanier, his first direct contact with Grabianka took place on December 7, when the surgeon "went to meet him at the Hotel in the Adelphi." Evidently, the Polish nobleman was not short of funds when he arrived in the British capital. His lodgings, Osborn's Adelphi Hotel, located on the corner of John Street and Adam Street in part of the recently completed Adelphi Buildings, had quickly gained a reputation as one of the most prestigious places of its kind in London.[27] Two days after their first meeting, Grabianka records that Chastanier escorted the Pole to his first meeting with Samuel Best.

Significantly, William Bousie was also in attendance. Bousie was an Englishman by birth and a wine merchant by trade, who seems to have divided much of his time in the 1780s between Paris and London.[28] Very little has been written about Bousie, which is a surprising lacuna given the fascinating web of networks he spun in the last quarter of the eighteenth century. He grew up in England, but moved to Bordeaux in 1751, where he first became a clerk in the Boyd family wine merchants, before becoming a vintner in his own right. He moved to Paris in 1773, where his business thrived.[29] This may explain why the British authorities enlisted him as an agent in their espionage campaign against American colonists seeking independence.[30]

An early indication of both his interest in illuminist forms of Freemasonry and his considerable networking skills is his reception in 1763 into the Ancient and Honourable Order of Kilwinning, or Scotch Heredom in London.[31] On February 16, 1764, Bousie is recorded as being initiated into the *loge l'Amitié* in Bordeaux.[32] By the mid-1780s, Bousie was one of the most prominent illuminist Freemasons in France. It is noteworthy, for example, that he participated in the Convent of Paris between 1785 and 1787, organised by the Philalèthes.[33] Moreover, in June 1783, in preparation for this Masonic congress, he corresponded in detail with General Charles Rainsford in London to obtain answers to a series of queries regarding English and Scottish Freemasonry.[34]

Bousie's predilection for drawing close to the era's more colourful esoteric adventurers is testified by his enduring friendship with the notorious Cagliostro.[35] The bond between Bousie and Cagliostro is revealed in the journal of M.-D. Bourrée Corberon (1748–1810). Corberon, for example, described dining with Cagliostro and Bousie on June 30, 1781, whilst visiting Strasbourg.[36] After this initial meeting, Bousie and Corberon met on several occasions in July and August, the former seemingly keen to boast of his knowledge of Cagliostro's medical-alchemical recipes.[37] According to Corberon, Bousie had bragged about having tried all of Cagliostro's exotic recipes one by one when he had first met the Sicilian adventurer in London in 1776.[38] One such remedy was a green liquid that could apparently rejuvenate teeth and hair that were on the verge of falling out.[39]

In 1781, Bousie, Corberon, and Thomé also began to develop a shared interest in the writings of Swedenborg.[40] Indeed, Bousie's embrace of Swedenborgian doctrines was such that in 1784, C. F. Nordenskjöld recorded him as one of twenty-five devotees living in England, along with Chastanier.[41] Moreover, both Bousie and Chastanier were both elected as founding foreign members, alongside Pernety, of the Stockholm Exegetic and Philanthropic Society in 1786, a Swedenborgian group established by C. F. Nordenskjöld and C. B. Wadström.[42] This interest in Swedenborg was to last for the remainder of Bousie's life. And despite being rejected for inclusion in the newly formed New Church, after being nominated for entry in September 1787, Bousie continued to espouse Swedenborgian beliefs until at least 1816.[43]

Thus Grabianka's path to Samuel Best's door was facilitated by two of the most pivotal figures in Anglo-French illuminism in the 1780s. Both Chastanier and Bousie had many bows in their respective quivers, which included already being privy to the millenarian prophecies being proclaimed by Best. Their familiarity with Best is immediately revealed in Grabianka's description of his first meeting with the supposed prophet: "on December 9, I was led and escorted to Best by Bousie and Chastanier, who taught me what I should do when approaching the prophet." Thus having being instructed in advance, Grabianka presented his open right hand, with his thumb inclined as far as possible on the palm. Best then considered the folds in Grabianka's hand formed by his thumb, before he supposedly experienced the influence of heaven, which "inspires him with Scriptural passages relative to the state of the consultant."[44]

The form of palmistry practised by Best in mid-1780s London was far removed from the modern-day, end-of-the-pier variant offered for titillation. Crucially, Best combined the ancient divinatory art of chiromancy with a deep knowledge of scripture and pronounced his ability to converse with Archangel Gabriel to fashion himself as a millenarian prophet. Palmistry thus merely served as the preliminary step through which Best was able to channel his prophetic gift.

By the time Grabianka first met Best, the London prophet had already been performing the role of Poor-Help for at least three years. The earliest known description of Best dates from November 1782, when Thomas Langcake, a Behemist, wrote of meeting the "poor disorderly man" who quoted liberally from the "Book of Sensations."[45] At the time, Best was an inmate of Shoreditch Workhouse, where the following year he was visited by Dr. William Spence, an early English Swedenborgian. Spence later described that he had "heard strange reports" of Best's spiritual power of quoting scriptures and that when he visited him in his workhouse room, which was liberally adorned with straw works, he observed a man who "appeared to me visibly insane."[46] Given these negative portraits by mystically inclined nonconformists, it is hardly surprising that more derogatory descriptions soon followed in the press. One contributor to the *Gentleman's Magazine*, for example, derided Best's "wildness of enthusiastick inspiration."[47]

Yet despite the noted scorn and scepticism from many quarters, Best seemingly had enough (affluent) devotees by late 1785 to be able to extricate himself from the workhouse and set himself up in a private address at 90 Bunhill-Row.[48] Thus Grabianka's detailed account of his meetings with Best, which took place at the peak of the latter's renown, provides an invaluable counterpoint to the detractors' accusations, from the viewpoint of an ardent believer. For instance, Grabianka describes meeting a man who, as opposed to a wildly insane enthusiast, displayed "humility, reverence and respect" when he revealed "the word of god" and who afterwards exuded "a character of gentleness, simplicity and childish gestures." Moreover, in his general *Notes on Samuel Best, Servant of God*, Grabianka provides a sympathetic description of the prophet:

> Samuel Best, English, is (in 1788) a man of around fifty-two years, of medium size, and of a fairly loose corpulence. His face is elongated, thin, marked with smallpox, and his features announce a sweetness in character. His hat is rolled up only on two

sides in the fashion of the ministers of the holy gospel, who profess Lutheranism in the Prussian states.[49]

Interestingly, this written description is strikingly in accord with the only known portrait of Best, which was published in 1804 (see Figure 2.1).

After Best scrutinised his palm at their first meeting, Grabianka describes the extraordinary reaction he received: "Best, having regarded the folds formed by the thumb, appeared extremely surprised, and looked at me with astonishment; then, clasping his hands several times, he raised his eyes to heaven … and to express the joy he had in seeing me, he called me Mine, a name or quality which he gives only to those whom he sees with pleasure."[50] In this inspired state, Best then cited John 6:27, "Labour not for the meat

WONDERFUL MUSEUM.

Lewis, ad viv pinxt.   *Barts Sculpt.*

SAMUEL BEST,
alias
POOR-HELP.

Famous for interpreting certain parts of Scripture. His Prophecies, &c. &c.

Pub. Mar 1 1804 by Alex. Hogg, 16, Pater -noster Row.

FIGURE 2.1 Portrait of Samuel Best. William Granger, *The New Wonderful Museum, and Extraordinary Magazine*, vol. 2 (London: Alex. Hogg & Co., 1804), between pages 926 and 927.

which perisheth, but for that meat which endureth unto everlasting life, which the Son of man shall give unto you: for him hath God the Father sealed." Best then revealed the meaning of this citation, apparently correctly informing Grabianka that he had a mark under his right breast and that "this mark is a seal laid by the Lord." Best also pronounced to Bousie and Chastanier that it was Grabianka who would "overthrow the standard of Satan" and who would "raise the flag of Jesus Christ." These highly flattering remarks may have made Grabianka amenable to Best's prophetic utterances. It would seem, however, that the clinching factor for the visitor was Best's apparent knowledge of the answers Grabianka had received from the Holy Word since 1779.[51]

At the end of this first meeting, Grabianka describes Best making the startling announcement that six months earlier he had seen the spirit of Rohoziński, whom he refers to as a "servant of God," and that he had spoken of this vision with Jacob Duché.[52] At the time, Duché was the chaplain to the Asylum for Female Orphans in Lambeth, from where, every Sunday since 1785, he had led a discussion of Swedenborg's writings with members of the Theosophical Society.[53] How was it possible for Best and the Swedenborgian milieu in London to know about Rohoziński's relatively obscure prophecy prior to Grabianka's arrival in the city? Here one must look to the key role played by C. F. Nordenskjöld in transmitting knowledge about the Podolian prophet to England. After all, he lived in London between 1783 and 1786 and was a very active participant in the city's burgeoning circle of Swedenborgian followers. In October 1781 Pernety not only informed Nordenskjöld about the millenarian prophecy of Rohoziński, but also divulged that he had consulted the Holy Word on June 12, 1780, as to whether the Podolian gentleman was truly inspired from above.

Best returned to the subject of Rohoziński as a prophet of God six months later. On June 12, 1786, at a dinner at the home of Bousie, Best told Grabianka "much about the gentleman Rohoziński" and that "this servant of God would be much greater than Swedenborg." The Pole then "asked him if he said this on his own. To which he replied, "All that I say is through revelation because I am one of the prophets of God." A week later, at a meeting at Best's home, in the presence of Chastanier, the purported prophet once again discussed Rohoziński with Grabianka:

> And completing his quotations, he showed me a great deal of friendship; And telling me of Rohoziński, he assured me that he was a prophet of God, and that at present no one on Earth was more filled with the spirit and knowledge of the Lord than this Polish gentleman, who is, nevertheless, listened to by no one, and is deemed by all to be an enthusiast and a liar.[54]

The Shoreditch Prophet's admiration for his Polish counterpart was such that he beseeched Grabianka to send his countryman to England when he returned to his homeland. Best even offered to "give him his bed" if such a meeting of minds were to transpire.[55] Given the importance attached to Rohoziński as a prophet of God by the likes of

Grabianka, Pernety, and Best up to 1786, it is striking that this Polish gentleman seems to have disappeared off the millenarian landscape after 1787. One notable exception is a reference to Rohoziński as being one of two Poles (the other being Grabianka) who formed the core membership of "L'école Avignonnaise"—that is, the Illuminés d'Avignon—presumably in the late 1780s. However, this tantalising assertion is not borne out by any documentary evidence. We simply do not know whether Rohoziński passed away at some point in the late 1780s or merely cast off his prophet's garb or was somehow discredited. Whatever the case, Grabianka's journal of his meetings with Best testifies that the Polish prophet's influence continued to be tangible up until the end of 1786.

Grabianka's second visit to Best took place on December 28, 1785. On this occasion, he was accompanied by William and Mary Bousie and their daughter.[56] The session began with an admonishment of Grabianka, since when he had left Best at the end of the previous meeting, he had apparently not embraced him. One of the main topics of discussion on this second visit concerned Grabianka's relationship with the burgeoning Swedenborgian society in London. According to Grabianka, Best remarked that "the steps you take for the society of London are agreeable to your God." This endorsement, from someone Grabianka believed to be able to communicate with angels and to reveal the Word of God, would have had a powerful impact.

This seal of approval no doubt helped to ensure that the links that developed between Grabianka and the London-based Swedenborgians went far beyond mere acquaintance with Chastanier and Bousie. The extent to which Grabianka was embraced into the bosom of the Swedenborg society in London is discernible in the reminiscences of Robert Hindmarsh, an early English devotee of Swedenborg and one of the founders of the New Jerusalem Church. Hindmarsh's account makes for fascinating reading:

> The Count [Grabianka] attended all our meetings, joined in familiar conversation with each of us, and expressed the utmost satisfaction with all our proceedings. He appeared to be well acquainted with the leading doctrines of the New Church, and spoke in glowing terms of the personal character and the Writings of Swedenborg. At Mr. Duché's he was a frequent and welcome visitor: his conversation was always interesting and animated: and when he communicated the religious sentiments and feelings of his Society, he seemed to speak the very language of the New Church. All were delighted with his company: all were anxious to shew him tokens of their affection and esteem.[57]

As Hindmarsh's account vividly illustrates, Grabianka successfully wooed Swedenborgians in London with a combination of his theological prowess and personal charisma.[58] Moreover, it would seem that the group's warm feelings towards Grabianka did not dampen for some time after the Pole left London. This is reflected in Grabianka's being made an honorary member of the newly established New Jerusalem Church, on May 7, 1787.[59] It would seem the fondness was mutual. In a letter dated December 10, 1788, for example, Grabianka beseeched the unnamed recipient [William Bousie], who was evidently soon to visit London, to "embrace on arrival all the family of b[rother] Duché, the father, the mother, the son and the sisters, as well as the family of [William] Bryan, Best, [J. J.] Prichard, [George] Adams."[60]

Francis Dobbs, an Irish barrister, politician and writer, also offers a flattering portrait of Grabianka. In 1800 he recalled that in London, in 1786, he had been invited to attend a meeting at the home of William Bryan, a printer and bookseller, who between 1785 and 1786, sold several sermons by the Quaker Stephen Crisp, as well as numerous English translations of Swedenborg's works.[61] A striking feature of Dobbs's account is how it highlights the extent to which the Swedenborgian milieu in London at this time were gripped with millenarian fervour: "There I met nearly thirty persons, all of whom declared they had reasons out of the common order of things to think these times would produce mighty changes, that would end in the establishment of human happiness."[62] Dobbs describes that at the gathering, "three peculiarly claimed my attention": namely, Grabianka, Bryan, and Bousie, "a merchant of French extraction, then settled in London, but who afterwards removed to France." Significantly, both Bousie and Bryan later joined the Illuminés d'Avignon (as will be discussed in chapter 3). From Dobbs's description of their meeting in 1786, it is clear that they all shared a similar visionary expectation of the imminent millennium:

> I related to the Count [Grabianka] and the gentleman since removed to France [Bousie], that I had had a remarkable vision; namely, that the sun would soon miraculously withhold its light; that before that light returned, a star, far superior to any of the planets, would appear in the east, and that afterwards the sun should rise from the west. This had happened to me in Ireland. The Polish Count, who had never been in Ireland, declared he had had a similar vision; and so did the merchant I allude to. And, in fact, within these few days I find the same thing happened to the person at whose house we first met [Bryan]. That four persons should have been thus informed, without any communication or knowledge of each other, must be by supernatural means.[63]

The fervent belief in the imminent onset of the millennium, shared by the London Swedenborgians who welcomed Grabianka into their midst, helps to explain why some were also drawn to the chiliastic utterances of the Shoreditch Prophet.[64]

Judging by Grabianka's journal, Bousie and Chastanier were the two Swedenborgians in London who seem to have been most amenable to Best. In all, Bousie met Best five times with Grabianka. On two occasions, Bousie was accompanied by his wife and daughter (on December 28, 1785, as mentioned, and on October 11, 1786). Moreover, on November 1, 1786, Grabianka states that Augustin Bousie formed part of the company that visited Best.[65] Chastanier visited Best three times in Grabianka's company (December 9, 1785, June 19, 1786, and November 1, 1786). However, Grabianka's journal provides little insight into the conversations that took place between Best and both Bousie and Chastanier.

The third London-based Swedenborgian mentioned by Grabianka as being in his company when visiting Best (on three occasions: March 1, June 7, and June 12, 1786), was François-Hippolyte Barthélémon (1741–1808), the composer and violinist.[66] In 1784, Barthélémon became an early member of the Theosophical Society, shortly after being gifted a quarto volume of Swedenborg's writings by the Swedish ambassador, G. A. von Nolcken. Barthélémon's interest in Swedenborgian thought most likely stemmed from his friendship with Jacob Duché, from around 1780.[67] As with Bousie and Chastanier, Barthélémon was initiated into Freemasonry in the 1760s. In Barthélémon's case, he was a founding member of the French-speaking *L'Immortalitié de l'ordre* lodge in London, when it was established in 1766.[68] Thus, Grabianka's three principal companions when he visited Best had much in common: on the practical side, all were fluent French and English speakers; all were long-term Freemasons, and all were at the epicentre of London's Swedenborgian milieu. Moreover, all three figures went on to have close links with the Illuminés d'Avignon after Grabianka's departure from England (see chapter 3).

Bearing in mind the millennial zeal of the London Swedenborgians and Grabianka, as described by Dobbs, it is not surprising that the Shoreditch Prophet would arouse the curiosity of many among them. Yet, it is noteworthy that it was not until June 19, 1786, that Best began to pronounce the imminent onset of the kind of "mighty changes" discussed in the Swedenborgian assemblies. Grabianka states that he visited Best on this day, in the company of Chastanier. Significantly, at this meeting Best confided in Grabianka that he had been graced with "a visit from the angel Gabriel."[69] This is the first time, in his descriptions of each meeting, that Grabianka mentions Best being in communication with Gabriel. However, in his general character sketch of the prophet, the Pole indicates that this was a regular occurrence: "in speaking of the angel Gabriel, from whom he receives his influence, he calls him the messenger."[70] This tallies with other contemporary descriptions of Best's purported ability to relay messages from the archangel. According to John Martin, Best's principal detractor, "he would not gratify me with an account of his last visit from Gabriel . . . All I could learn from him was, that about a fortnight had elapsed since he had been honoured with so distinguishing a favour."[71]

Thus, Best fashioned himself as a privileged mediator. He was able to transmit the messages given to him by an archangel long associated in Christian thought with embodying the material incarnation of God's speech.[72] Hence, when Best conveyed to Grabianka that the archangel "spoke to me from the Lord, and this is what he dictated to me," the credulous Pole would have listened with bated breath. According to Grabianka's journal, Best's message on this occasion was brief and somewhat cryptic: "Best informed me that there would soon be earthquakes in Rome, and that in a short time I would receive good news. Both articles were verified shortly afterwards."[73] One can only guess about the nature of the good news received by Grabianka. However, records show that several seismic shocks did hit Rome shortly afterwards, on June 30, 1786, and again on July 30.[74]

No further meetings are recorded during that summer in the edited version of Grabianka's journal. The next encounter between Grabianka and Best, in the company of Bousie, occurred on September 27, 1786. On this occasion, Best went into great detail about tribulations about to be unleashed in Europe that would herald the Second Coming of Christ:

> Soon the earth will experience the greatest revolutions: the continent of England will be joined to that of another power, and Rome will experience great earthquakes. More sudden deaths will be seen than ever. A sore throat epidemic will lead a lot of people to the tomb in three days. Before four years [have passed] the righteous and the unjust shall be trembling; The former for the latter, and the latter for fear of punishment. I would gladly consent, says Best, to throw myself into the fire, to save one of those unfortunates whom their sins have condemned . . . It is in Ireland that Christ will be known first.[75]

Moreover, Best continued to expound upon the imminence of the long-awaited millennium in the remainder of his meetings with Grabianka, in the autumn of 1786. On October 11, for example, Best proclaimed that "terrible things will happen, which will carry terror in every heart." He warned that amid these great disasters there will be a tremendous blackness, "for in the middle of day shall be as the midst of the night." This darkness at noon will lead men to be "seized with fear and terror" and "misfortunes will be unheard of, and will carry terror in the hearts of the rich and the wicked of all conditions; for even today abominations of all kinds surpass those of Sodom and Gomorrah." Best predicted that thereafter, "a brilliant star will appear in the East; And this star will be to acknowledge the Lord."[76]

Best's remarkable outpouring of millenarian statements continued on November 1, during his meeting with Grabianka, Chastanier, and Augustin Bousie. Best told Chastanier that "the dead are already rising," and warned him to be hospitable to foreigners that came to his house, as some of them could be among the resurrected. At the end of the session, Best also predicted that "Holland was going to experience great troubles and great revolutions." He also said, more generally, that "within four years there would be disasters on Earth that would throw terror into the hearts of men."[77] In hindsight these predictions seem prescient. In September 1787, a Prussian invasion of Holland took place, an attempt to restore the Orange Stadtholders and to crush the Patriot movement. Moreover, revolutionary events in France began well within four years of Best's prediction.

A fascinating aspect of the millenarian themes broached at this November 1 meeting concerns Best's description to Grabianka of a recent audience with King George III. According to Grabianka, Best had told the king in person "of a revolution that is to arrive in London, during which there will be a tumult of carnage." Apparently, the king himself, mounted on a horse, would "walk in human blood up to the height of his [mount's] hooves." Best then emphasized that the king would witness these terrible events, before warning the monarch to "take care" on his departure from his royal audience.[78]

It would be easy to dismiss Best's account as the delusional ravings of a pretended prophet but for the remarkable fact that it tallies very closely with an account of the meeting provided by William Spence, the Swedenborgian physician. Spence describes how "it was reported on good authority" that "Best was sent for to Buckingham-house." On meeting the monarch, Best apparently looked into his right hand, as was his custom, and then cited the following excerpt from Jeremiah 13:18: "Say unto the King and to the Queen, humble yourselves, sit down; for the principalities shall come down, even the crown of your glory." Spence interprets Best's citation of this Old Testament passage as a humiliating reference to the king's madness, or as he puts it "the evil spirit [that] was hereby gaining to derange our gracious King."[79] The physician's reasoning is based on a different Hebrew translation of principalities as "head-tires," which is noted in the margins of the King James Bible. Spence's exegesis is understandable, written as it was after the king succumbed to a serious bout of mental illness. However, Best's description of his audience with the king, as well as the general outpouring of prophetic statements he made in the second half of 1786 regarding the imminent onset of the time of tribulations, strongly suggest that he understood principalities in the sense of the king's realm. In other words, the citation from Jeremiah is consistent with the description of Best's dire warnings of impending turmoil in England found in Grabianka's journal.

If Grabianka initially wondered what role he would personally play in anticipation of this time of immense upheaval, he did not have to wait long to receive guidance from the Shoreditch Prophet. At the end of September Best went to Grabianka's residence for the first time to convey a message that God had communicated to him vis-à-vis the Polish nobleman: "God has revealed to me that you must leave London, and that you must cross the sea and return to your destiny."[80] At their penultimate meeting, on November 1, 1786, Best elaborated on this theme: "After crossing the sea, says Best, you will go to the place where God calls you and when you arrive there you will find a prophet of the Lord." However, on Grabianka's previous visit, on October 11, Best had warned him that "there will also be prophets . . . who will make an effort to deceive the very elect. It is for this reason that we must not forget the Epistle of Jude."[81] The book of Jude does indeed warn against such false prophets "in the last time, who should walk after their own ungodly lusts."[82] It is impossible to gauge what role these predictions played concerning Grabianka's desire to seek out a "prophet of the Lord" yet also to be aware that he should simultaneously be on guard to ward off false messengers. Nevertheless, these warnings are worth noting, given the controversial role subsequently played by Ottavio Cappelli in the Union between 1787 and 1791 (see chapters 3 and 4).

The last meeting between Grabianka and Best took place on November 5, two days before the Pole's departure from London.[83] Best presented Grabianka with a farewell gift: a straw box three inches in diameter. The lid of this box was domed and raised in the form of an imperial crown, formed like a turban and surmounted by a stone or crystal carved in facets. Moreover, the surface of the box was apparently divided in an intricate fashion by bands of gold and silver stripes. Inside the box could be found silk-embroidered busts of Best and Grabianka, as well as stars that adorned the top and bottom and crosses sewn into the ribs. When presenting this elaborate box to Grabianka, Best had signified that it was of great importance. Although the present may well have been imbued with great significance, it seems Grabianka would have not been entirely surprised at receiving such a gift before his departure. Indeed, he may have reserved some space in his luggage in anticipation of one final offering, as in the preceding eleven months he had received no fewer than eleven other symbolic works of art.

Various contemporary accounts of Best refer to the abundance of straw works that adorned his apartment, which were "ornamentally disposed in regular order, and bearing types of Scripture events." Furthermore, Best's proclivity to bestow "straw rings, &c. as tokens of remembrance" was also noted by one commentator. Yet, though Best's singular talent for straw marquetry, as well as other forms of art, was discussed in passing by several commentators during his lifetime, only Grabianka's journal fleshes out the rich detail of the Shoreditch Prophet's craftsmanship.

In his biographical notes on Best, Grabianka reveals the significance of the Shoreditch Prophet's artistic creations. We learn, for example, that when Best was on his own, he would appear to be in communication with spirits, whilst often simultaneously embroidering hieroglyphic figures on canvas, wool, and works of straw marquetry. Grabianka notes that these creations—most commonly straw rings and pictures—were often given to those in whom Best detected heavenly signs and were always "relative to the destiny of the person." Significantly, Grabianka adds that these works of art, which were often adorned with crosses and stars, "are always emblems relating to the new Jerusalem, or to the wars that are to take place, or to events that relate to the new church."[84]

Hence, Grabianka's biographical notes on Best signpost, without providing details, how the gifts he received were imbued with personal significance vis-à-vis his role in the imminent advent of the millennium. Best was not slow to dispense presents to Grabianka; at their first meeting, on December 9, 1785, he gave the Pole two items: (a) an embroidered picture made from wool and framed in straw, which depicted a bouquet of seven large and five smaller flowers; the corners of the frame were decorated with stars, and a cross was also placed in the middle of the frame; and (b) a portrait of Grabianka, who is dressed in oriental attire (a rose-coloured camisole and a sky-blue coat).[85]

At the beginning of 1786 Grabianka received another picture, which on this occasion featured a man riding a white donkey. The man is clothed in purple, with red rays around his head and a stick or sceptre in his right hand. This representation seems to conflate Christ's entry on a donkey into Jerusalem on Palm Sunday with the attire mocking Roman soldiers forced him to wear immediately prior to the crucifixion.[86] The picture also included two women—one to the rear and one in front—holding red flowers in each hand. Best presented Grabianka with two very similar pictures later in 1786, which were essentially variations on a theme. Interestingly, one of the two variations was intended for Rohoziński and was embellished with two small trees that formed a cradle, under which were depicted Grabianka and a young girl.[87] Best also presented Grabianka with a portrait of himself and the Polish nobleman, who were depicted standing and looking at each other within a straw frame. They both had a single flower in each hand, with one wearing a green coat and black breeches and the other wearing a blue coat and black breeches. Behind both Best and Grabianka were tall flowers that bend over their heads. Besides these paintings, Grabianka also received two stone-shaped straw rings, each containing an image of a kitten. One of the rings was to be given to Rohoziński. Lastly, Grabianka was gifted a straw sword, the handle and scabbard of which were decorated with stars and crosses.[88]

All the gifts, which were intended for either Grabianka or Rohoziński, seem to have served purely symbolic functions. They reflected the important roles Best foresaw for the two Poles, as servants of God, in the impending millennial drama. However, on June 7, 1786, Grabianka records that Best also gave a straw ring to Monsieur Nicolas, one of Grabianka's two valets in London. This gift seems to have been intended to ease the sad plight of the valet, who was in the last stages of consumption. In conjunction with giving this ring to Nicolas, Best also dictated three remedies to be administered to the valet, which together would purportedly "serve to relieve a little . . . your servant."[89] That Best had pretensions as a healer was scornfully noted by John Martin, who referred to him as a "medical quack," who "pretends by licking the hands of his patient to discover his disease."[90]

Whether or not Best licked the hands of Nicolas is not disclosed, but by the summer of 1786 he was well aware of Nicolas's poor health, having met both of Grabianka's valets on several occasions. On December 28, 1785, Grabianka notes in his journal that Best quoted several passages from the Bible favourable to Leyman and Nicolas and looked upon them "with an air of satisfaction and tenderness."[91] Eleven days later, Best examined the palms of the valets and informed Grabianka that "they both cherish you."[92] However, Best added, Nicolas was sick. This was most likely obvious; Chastanier later noted that one of Grabianka's servants was already "in a deep consumption" on arrival in England.[93] Fascinatingly, Chastanier also describes how Grabianka "was so superstitious as to imagine he could cure him, by laying on him a *Pantecula*," in other words, a talismanic pentacle.[94] Was Chastanier here describing the straw ring given to Nicolas by Best?

Whatever the case, Nicolas's condition quickly deteriorated. On June 12, 1786, Best immediately scolded Grabianka at the beginning of their meeting for only giving Nicolas two of the three remedies he had prescribed. One week later, on asking Best whether he should leave London, Grabianka received the following reply, from 1 Samuel 9:27: "Bid the servant pass on before us (and he passed on), but stand thou still a while, that I may shew thee the word of God." Grabianka interpreted this as a signal that his valet would soon die and that he should stay longer in London: "this was promptly accomplished, for my valet Nicolas died shortly afterwards, and I remained until the 7th November."[95]

As mentioned, the last meeting between Grabianka and Best took place on November 5, when the latter presented the former with an intricately carved box. However, the next day the Shoreditch Prophet conveyed a farewell message to Grabianka—via Barthélémon—on the eve of the Pole's departure. Grabianka's journal records that Best went to Barthélémon's home during the day, evidently aware that the musician would later meet with the Pole at one of Jacob Duché's assemblies:

> Tonight you will see Sutkowski at the assembly; Do not forget to tell him that I came to announce to him that there would be great troubles in Poland; That I entreat him to listen to everything, to see everything, and to keep a great secret and profound silence over all things. Tell him also that Holland is sleeping at the moment and experiencing great troubles, and that I invite him, during the passage he will make, to stop there as little as possible.[96]

In his recollections, Hindmarsh confirms that Grabianka took "a most affectionate leave of the Society assembled at Mr. Duché's" at the end of 1786.[97]

By the time of his departure, Grabianka had developed an intimate relationship with Best over the course of eleven months, and had nurtured very cordial bonds with many of London's foremost Swedenborgians. The next chapter will discuss the legacy of Grabianka's time in London. It will demonstrate, for example, that it is possible to detect Best's continued influence on Grabianka after the Pole arrived in the papal enclave at the beginning of 1787. Moreover, it will show that the esteem in which Grabianka was held by many London Swedenborgians during his time in the English capital did not dissipate after he returned to Avignon. Indeed, the personal affection in which Grabianka was held by many of the Swedenborgian milieu in London ensured that a significant number—Bousie (and his family), Chastanier, Bryan, T. S. Duché, Barthélémon, and Rainsford—either joined or were attracted to the society that he began to openly promote after his arrival in Avignon.

What of Best in London after Grabianka's departure? At the beginning of 1787, Best still enjoyed visits from the leading proponents of European illuminism. In London, in January 1787, for example, Saint-Martin took the opportunity to seek out Best in Shoreditch. Fascinatingly, it seems that Grabianka played a role in bringing Best to the attention of the so-called *Philosophe inconnu*. On January 15, 1787, Saint-Martin wrote a letter from London to Jean-Baptiste Willermoz in Lyon. Saint-Martin thought it likely that Willermoz would have already met "a very interesting Pole who recently came from this country." Saint-Martin, who is undoubtedly writing about Grabianka, wonders whether "he will have spoken to you about a singular man"—that is, Best—"who he has seen here and whom I have just seen." Saint-Martin then proceeded to describe his recent meeting with Best: "he has a kind of inspiration which is manifested by passages from the Holy Scripture, which he quotes with such striking accuracy that one cannot help but be astonished." Saint-Martin reveals that he was also amazed by Best's knowledge of the "personal turns of my spiritual career and the different sorts of trials that I have had to endure."[98]

However, it seems likely that the flurry of negative press the Shoreditch Prophet received in 1787, most notably Martin's exposé, may have taken a toll on Best's éclat. Saint-Martin's favourable description of Best in early 1787 may represent the high watermark of his renown, as thereafter further positive testimonies are noticeable by their absence. Had Best's distinctive brand of prophecy simply exhausted its shelf life in London's metropolitan marketplace; its place usurped in the late 1780s and early 1790s by the likes of Dorothy Gott, Joanna Southcott, and Richard Brothers? This seems the most likely explanation.

In the relative furor that erupted after the publication of Brothers's *A Revealed Knowledge of the Prophecies and Times* in 1794, and his subsequent arrest for treason in 1795, a spate of prophetic broadsheets and pamphlets were published in England. One such publication was Best's *Poor Help's Warning to All*, printed by George Riebau in 1795. The pamphlet begins by announcing: "Take heed, watch and pray: as a thief in the night, so is doomsday. It comes suddenly; it will come shortly." A description follows of "some things [that] must precede the Judge's coming" over the course of fifteen days, such as "trees shall sweat blood" on the ninth day.[99] Significantly, Riebau was the principal publisher for Richard Brothers and styled himself the "Bookseller to the Prince of the Hebrews."[100] With this in mind, it would seem the initiative to publish Best's tract came from the printer, who may have been seeking to exploit the upsurge in demand for prophetic literature at the time. Confirmation that Best had not returned to the prophets' stage in London appears at the end of the tract, where it is written that the preceding warning been written "about five years ago." Yet the publication of this pamphlet shows that the Shoreditch Prophet was far from forgotten nearly a decade after his heyday as "Poor-Help."

NOTES

1. For Saint-Martin's description of his meeting with Best, which took place in 1787, see L.-C. de Saint-Martin, *Mon Portrait Historique: 1789–1803*, ed. by Robert Amadou (Paris: R. Juilliard, 1961), 70.

2. T. F. Henderson, "Best, Samuel (1738–1825)," *Dictionary of National Biography*, vol. 4 (London: Smith, Elder, & Co., 1885), 418.

3. John Martin, *Imposture Detected: Or Thoughts on a Pretended Prophet and on the Prevalence of His Impositions* (London: W. Smith, 1787).

4. Martin, *Imposture Detected*, 3.

5. Martin, *Imposture Detected*, 50.

6. See Garrett, *Respectable Folly*, 150–1; Harrison, *Second Coming*, 30–1; Juster, *Doomsayers*, 38–9.

7. A notable exception is the work of Nancy Jiwon Cho on Dorothy Gott, who began to attract attention as a prophetess in 1788 when she published *The Midnight Cry* (London, 1788). See Nancy Jiwon Cho, "Gott, Dorothy Newberry (1747/48–1812)," in *Handbook of Women Biblical*

Interpreters, ed. Marion Ann Taylor (Grand Rapids, MI: Baker Academic, 2012), 216–18; Cho, "Dorothy Gott (c. 1748–1812) and 'God's Chosen People': A Disowned Prophet's Quest for Quaker Recognition in Late-Georgian England," *Quaker Studies* 18:1 (2013): 50–75. On Gott's influence on William Blake, see Cho and David Worrall, "William Blake's Meeting with Dorothy Gott: The Female Origins of Blake's Prophetic Mode," *Romanticism* 16:1 (2010): 60–71. A number of other scholars have written on William Blake's links to millenarianism. See, for example, François Piquet, "Blake and Millenarian Ideology," *Yearbook of English Studies* 19 (1989): 28–35; Jonathan Mee, *Dangerous Enthusiasm: William Blake and the Culture of Radicalism in the 1790s* (Oxford: Clarendon Press, 1992); Tim Fulford, "Millenarianism and the Study of Romanticism," in *Romanticism and Millenarianism*, ed. Tim Fulford (Basingstoke: Palgrave, 2002), 1–22; Robert Rix, *William Blake and the Cultures of Radical Christianity* (Abingdon: Routledge, 2007).

8. The general (and misleading) title of Bernard's article may explain why historians have overlooked this valuable source of information on the millenarian worldview of Grabianka and the Illuminés d'Avignon. Bernard was evidently not fully aware of the significance of the material he published. See Bernard, "L'Alchimie," 12 (Jan. 10), 181–4; 14 (Jan. 24), 212–14, 219–20; 17 (Feb. 14), 264–6; 19 (Feb. 28), 295–9.

9. Longinov, "Odin iz magikov," 583. Longinov evidently consulted the Grabianka Archive in St. Petersburg, as he cites almost verbatim the account of the Polish nobleman's acquaintance with Best, found in "A Short Extract from the Dossier concerning Count Grabianka" (*Kratkaia vypiska po delu Grafa Grabienki*), RGIA, Fond 1163, op. 1, d. 16b, 207v–208r. The Polish scholar A. J. Rolle draws on Longinov's account; M. L. Danilewicz in turn draws on Rolle. See Rolle, *Tadeusz Leszczyc Grabianka*, 23; Danilewicz, "King of the New Israel," 63–4.

10. For discussion of Grabianka's links to Swedenborgians in London, see Danilewicz, "King of New Israel," 59–64; Garrett, "Swedenborg and the Mystical Enlightenment," 75–7; Peter J. Lineham, "The Origins of the New Jerusalem Church in the 1780s," *Bulletin of the John Rylands Library* 70:3 (1988): 113–14; Marsha Keith Schuchard, "The Secret Masonic History of Blake's Swedenborg Society," *Blake: An Illustrated Quarterly* 26:2 (1992): 42–4.

11. In London Grabianka took the name Sutkowski, a reference to his estate in Podolia. In France he often referred to himself as Count Ostap, a nod to his estate Ostapkowce ("Ostapkivtsi" in Ukrainian) in Podolia in Ukraine. See Grabianka's letter to P. F. Grosse, Feb. 24, 1787, in P. F. Gosse, *Portefeuille d'un ancient typographe, ou recueil de lettres* (The Hague, 1824), 84.

12. Bernard, "L'alchimie," Feb. 14, 1863, 264.

13. "A Short Extract," RGIA, Fond 1163, op. 1, d. 16b, 207v.

14. See Grabianka's letter to Gosse, Feb. 24, 1787, in Grosse, *Portefeuille*, 84. For corroboration of Grabianka's visit to Altona, see Chastanier, *Word of Advice*, 25.

15. Brumore, "Avertissement du Traducteur," in Swedenborg, *Traité curieux*, 13.

16. Chastanier, *Word of Advice*, 25.

17. Emanuel Swedenborg, *Du commerce établi entre l'ame et le corps*, trans. and ed. Benedict Chastanier (London and The Hague, 1785), 128.

18. Chastanier, *Word of Advice*, 25.

19. Grabianka to Gosse, Feb. 24, 1787. See Gosse, *Portefeuille*, 80. On May 7, 1787, Gosse was elected an honorary member of the newly formed New Jerusalem Church in London. See NCCL, *Minute Book of the Society for Promoting the Heavenly Doctrines of the New Jerusalem Church Eastcheap. London 7 May 1787 to 7 November 1791* (May 7, 1787).

20. Chastanier to Gosse, Aug. 23, 1785. See Gosse, *Portefeuille*, 5.

21. Chastanier, *Word of Advice*, 25.

22. R. L. Tafel, ed., *Documents concerning the Life and Character of Emanuel Swedenborg*, vol. 2, pt. 2 (London: Swedenborg Society, 1877), 1177.

23. Chastanier, *Word of Advice*, 15. For biographical information on Chastanier, see Tafel, *Documents*, vol. 2, pt. 2, 1176–80; James Hyde, "Benedict Chastanier and the Illuminati of Avignon," *New-Church Review* 14 (1907): 181–205.

24. Chastanier, *Word of Advice*, 21–22.

25. Chastanier was a member of *Loge Socrate de la parfaite union* in Paris. He was most likely initiated before he settled in London in October 1763. Whatever the case, he was elected Secretary for the Provinces of the Grand Lodge of France on December 27, 1765. For information regarding Chastanier's Masonic career in France in the 1760s, see FM Fichier Bossu (62) "Chastanier," BNdF; Daniel Kerjan, *Les débuts de la franc-maçonnerie française, de la Grande Loge au Grand Orient 1688–1793* (Paris: Éditions Dervy, 2014), 18. The records of the Convent of Paris, held between 1785 and 1787 and organised by the Philalèthes, a Masonic group saturated with elements of esotericism that emerged from the Amis Réunis Lodge in Paris in 1773, state that Chastanier sent a letter to the delegates attending the convent, which was discussed on March 29, 1787. See Charles Porset, *Les Philalèthes et les Convents de Paris* (Paris: Honoré Champion, 1996), 503.

26. The first advertisement promoting Chastanier's services as a practitioner of animal magnetism appeared in the *Morning Post* newspaper on June 14, 1786, and referred to the surgeon as a "pupil and assistant to Dr De Mainauduc." For a reprint of Chastanier's advertisement, see Daniel Lyson, ed., *Collectanea: or, A Collection of Advertisements and Paragraphs from the Newspapers Relating to Various Subjects*, vol. 2, pt. 2 (London: British Library, Pressmark, 1881), 156–7. On Chastanier and animal magnetism, see Patricia Fara, "An Attractive Therapy: Animal Magnetism in Eighteenth-Century England," *History of Science*, xxiii (1995), 140–2; Robert Rix, "William Blake: Trance, Therapy and Transcendence," *Litteraturkritik & Romantikstudier* 53 (2009): 8.

27. Eminent guests lodging at Osborn's Adelphi Hotel in the 1780s included John Quincy Adams (in 1783) and Edward Gibbon (in 1787). See John Quincy Adams and Charles Francis Adams, *The Life of John Adams*, vol. 2 (Philadelphia: Lippincott, 1871), 78; Leopold Wagner, *A New Book about London: A Quaint and Curious Volume of Forgotten Lore* (New York: E. P. Dutton, 1921), 106.

28. His home in Paris was on Rue de Petit Bourbon de St. Sulpice, and his London residence was in St. James' Place in Westminster. For mention of Bousie's Parisian home by M.-D. Bourrée de Corberon, see *Journal de Marie Daniel Bourrée Corberon*, July 4, 1781, MS. 3059, 146. Also see a letter from John Charretié to Benjamin Franklin, dated Dec. 28, 1783, in Ellen R. Cohn, ed., *The Papers of Benjamin Franklin*, vol. 41 (New Haven, CT: Yale University Press, 2014), 369. For a reference to Bousie's London home, see the list of subscribers in J. Hodson, *Jesus Christ the True God and Only Object of Supreme Adoration* (London, 1787), i.

29. Bousie's career in Bordeaux was aided immeasurably by his marrying Mary Johnston, the daughter of William Johnston, a leading wine merchant in Bordeaux, in 1762. On Bousie's early career and marriage, see L. M. Cullen, "The Boyds in Bordeaux and Dublin," in *Ireland, France, and the Atlantic in a Time of War: Reflections on the Bordeaux-Dublin Letters, 1757*, ed. Thomas M. Truxes (Abingdon: Routledge, 2017), 60, 62. Also see "Rapport de Poultier, représentant en mission," Avignon, 18 octobre 1793, AN, FN AF 11, 185. Published in F.-A. Aulard, *Recueil des Actes du Comité de Salut Public*, vol. 11 (Paris: Imprimerie Nationale, 1897), 498.

30. In July 1777 Bousie is recorded as serving as a cover to the British agent Isaac van Zandt (alias George Lupton) for receiving mail in Paris. See B. F. Stevens, *Facsimiles of Manuscripts in European Archives Relating to America, 1773–1783*, vol. 2 (London, 1889), no. 179, 6.

31. *Royal Order of Scotland Record Book*, 1750–1937, vol. 1, Museum and Library of the Grand Lodge of Scotland, Edinburgh. On this order, see Alain Bernheim, "Notes on the *Order of Kilwinning* or *Scotch Heredom*, the Present Royal Order of Scotland," *Heredom* 8 (2000): 93–130.

32. *Tableau des membres de la loge l'amitié* (1776), BNdF, FM2 170. On Feb. 28, 1767, Bousie became orator of the lodge. See FM Fichier Bossu (41), "Bousie."

33. See Porset, *Les Philalèthes*, 292, 497, 537.

34. See BL, Add. MS. 23675, 13, for the queries submitted to Bousie. For Bousie's letter to Rainsford, dated June 13, 1783, see BL, Add. MS. 23675, 15. For extracts from these documents, see Gordon P. G. Hills, "Notes on the Rainsford Papers in the British Museum," *Ars Quatuor Coronatorum* 26 (1913): 95–7.

35. In addition to Cagliostro, Bousie became acquainted with L.-C. de Saint-Martin, when the latter visited London in 1787. See L. Schauer and A. Chuquet, eds., *La Correspondence Inédite de L.-C. de Saint Martin dit le philosophe inconnu et Kirchberger, Baron de Liebistorf* (Paris: E. Dentu, 1862), 84.

36. *Journal de Corberon*, June 30, 1781, MC, MS. 3059, 127–8.

37. See *Journal de Corberon*, MC, MS. 3059, July 4 (146–7); July 8 (153–5); July 14 (174–7); July 25 (220); Aug. 2 (251).

38. *Journal de Corberon*, MC, MS. 3059, July 13, 1781, 175. It is noteworthy that Constantin Photiades refers to the fact that when Cagliostro resided in London for several months in the latter half of 1786, he "frequently visited" his "faithful friend Mr. Bousie" in "St. James's Place." As we know from Grabianka's journal, Bousie was resident in London for much of 1786, and he did live in St. James' Place at this time. However, Photiades provides no source for his information. See Constantin Photiades, *Count Cagliostro: An Authentic Story of a Mysterious Life* (Abingdon: Routledge, 2011), 219.

39. *Journal de Corberon*, MC, MS. 3059, July 13, 1781, 176.

40. *Journal de Corberon*, MC, MS. 3059, July 25, 1781, 220.

41. C. F. Nordenskjöld, "List of Those Devoted to Swedenborg's Doctrines," ACSD, vol. X, 1664.3101, 1.

42. "Membership List of the Exegetic and Philanthropic Society," ACSD, vol. X, 1665.18, 3.

43. For the vote (12–1) against Bousie's membership in the recently formed New Church, see NCCL, *Minute Book of the Society for Promoting the Heavenly Doctrines of the New Jerusalem Church Eastcheap. London 7 May 1787 to 7 November 1791* (Sept. 3, 1787). Robert Hindmarsh describes visiting Paris on September 5, 1802, where he attended a meeting of about twelve French Swedenborgians. Among the congregation was Bousie, who "read a few pages of one of Swedenborg's Works." See Robert Hindmarsh, *Rise and Progress of the New Jerusalem Church in England, America, and Other Parts* (London: Hodson & Son, 1861), 181–2. In the autumn of 1816, C. A. Tulk visited Paris, where he describes having "had the pleasure of being introduced" to Bousie, who was one of only "three receivers of the New Doctrines." See *The New Jerusalem Church Repository, for the years 1817 & 1818*, vol. 1 (Philadelphia: American Society for the Dissemination of the Doctrines of the New Jerusalem Church, 1818), 137.

44. Bernard, "L'Alchimie," Feb. 14, 1863, 264–5.

45. Thomas Langcake to Henry Brooke, Nov. 30, 1782. See DWL, Brooke Letterbook, Walton MS. 1.1.43, 37–8.

46. William Spence, *Essays in Divinity and Physic Proving the Divinity of the Person of Christ, and the Sense of Scripture* (London: R. Hindmarsh, 1792), 47–8.

47. Clio to Mr. Urban, *Gentleman's Magazine* 61 (1787), 309.

48. In 1787, John Martin wrote "that Mr. B. about two years ago, was removed from the paupers, in the parish of Shoreditch, to what was then thought a more convenient location in Bunhill-Row." He also cited a card circulating in 1787, informing people that "Poor Help" had "removed from No. 90 Bunhill-Row" to a new address in Kingsland Road. See Martin, *Imposture Detected*, 4.

49. Bernard, "L'Alchimise," Jan. 28, 1863, 219.

50. Bernard, "L'Alchimie," Feb. 14, 1863, 264.

51. Bernard, "L'Alchimie," Feb. 14, 1863, 265.

52. Bernard erroneously refers to Rohoziński as "Kohozinski" throughout the article.

53. On Jacob Duché, see Kevin J. Dellape, *America's First Chaplain: The Life and Times of the Reverend Jacob Duché* (Bethlehem, PA: Lehigh University Press, 2013); Clarke Garrett, "The Spiritual Odyssey of Jacob Duché," *Proceedings of the American Philosophical Society* 119:2 (1975): 143–55; Charles Higham, "Jacob Duché," *New-Church Magazine* 15 (1896): 389–96 and 459–66; Charles Higham, "The Reverend Jacob Duché, M.A.: His Later Life and Ministry in England," *New Church Review* 22 (1915): 404–20.

54. Bernard, "L'Alchimie," Feb. 14, 1863, 265.

55. Bernard, "L'Alchimie," Feb. 28, 1863, 296.

56. Mary Bousie (née Johnston; b. 1729) married William in 1761 in Bordeaux. She was the daughter of a Scottish wine merchant, William Johnston. The name of Bousie's daughter is not known. See "Rapport de Poultier," published in Aulard, *Recueil*, vol. 11, p. 498.

57. Hindmarsh, *Rise and Progress*, 41–2. Hindmarsh also describes how Grabianka distinguished twelve of the leading members of the London society by referring to each of them as one of the apostles. For example, Hindmarsh was John; his father, Rev. James Hindmarsh was Peter; and George Adams, the mathematical instrument makers, optician, and writer, was James.

58. Chastanier's brief account of Grabianka's stay in London dwells little on the Pole's links to Swedenborgians. However, he does emphasize that Grabianka gave an account of the "formation of their Society . . . particularly to young Mr. [Thomas Spence] Duché . . . at his father's, the Rev. Mr. Duché, of the Asylum," as well as to Bousie. See Chastanier, *Word of Advice*, 27. In an undated letter to Grabianka, written several years after 1786, Charles Rainsford fondly recalls their shared study of the "writings of the great Man Swedenborg" in London. See BL Add. MS. 23,669, 123. As chapter 3 will demonstrate, both T. S. Duché and Rainsford went on to establish links to the Illuminés d'Avignon in the late 1780s.

59. See NCCL, *Minute Book of the Society for Promoting the Heavenly Doctrines of the New Jerusalem Church Eastcheap. London 7 May 1787 to 7 November 1791* (May 7, 1787).

60. Letter from Grabianka to William Bousie, Dec. 10, 1788, HSD, Fond D4 No. 589/13. Joshua Jones Prichard was the secretary of the British Society for the Propagation of the Doctrines of the New Church in 1785. See Odhner, *Annals*, 125.

61. In 1785 Bryan was a bookseller for John Clowes's translation of Swedenborg's *A Summary View of the Heavenly Doctrines of the New Jerusalem Church* (London: R. Hindmarsh, 1785). In 1786, Bryan printed and sold the following series of sermons by Crisp: "Baptism and the Lord's

Supper Asserted," "Captive Sinners Set Free by Jesus Christ," and "The Sheep of Christ Hear His Voice." For information on Bryan's publication of sermons by Crisp, see Joseph Smith, *A Descriptive Catalogue of Friends' Books*, vol. 1 (London: Joseph Smith, 1867), 474. The works by Swedenborg that Bryan sold in 1786 were as follows: *The Doctrine of the New Jerusalem concerning the Lord*, originally translated by Peter Provo and revised by George Adams and printed by Hindmarsh; *The Doctrine of the New Jerusalem Concerning the Sacred Scripture*, which was translated by Provo and printed by Hindmarsh; and, *The Doctrine of the New Jerusalem*, which was translated by Clowes and printed by Hindmarsh. All these works were sold from Bryan's shop at No. 7 Mark Lane in east London.

62. Francis Dobbs, *A Concise View from History and Prophecy, of the Great Predictions in the Sacred Writings* (Dublin: John Jones, 1800), 259.

63. Dobbs, *Concise View*, 259.

64. Hindmarsh in his reminiscences alludes to meeting Best at the time of Grabianka's residence in London, although he provides a highly negative (and not entirely accurate) account of the supposed prophet's irreligiosity: "About the period when the Polish nobleman . . . visited our Society, I accidentally fell in company with a person residing in Kingsland Road, near Shoreditch, whose religious (or rather *irreligious*) frenzy had induced him to believe and to assert in the most positive terms, that there was *no God in the universe but man*." See Hindmarsh, *Rise and Progress*, 44. Significantly, at this time Best moved to 40 Kingsland Road. See Martin, *Imposture Detected*, 4.

65. Very little is known about Augustin Bousie. He was most likely William Bousie's brother.

66. On March 1, 1786, Barthélémon and Grabianka were accompanied by Brayer and Rey, whose identities we have been unable to ascertain. For biographical information on Barthélémon, who was born in Bordeaux and was of French-Irish descent, see Cecilia Maria Henslowe, "Memoir of the Late F. H. Barthélémon, Esq.," in *Selections from the Oratorio of Jefte in Masfa* (London: Clementi, Collard & Collard, 1827), 1–10; Charles Higham, "Francis Barthelemon," *New Church Magazine* 15 (1896): 1–13.

67. In 1784 Barthélémon became a guardian of the Asylum for Orphans Girls in Lambeth, where Duché was chaplain. In 1785, he wrote the music for a series of hymns and psalms for use in the asylum. For the musical score, see William Gawler, *The Hymns and Psalms Used at the Asylum or House of Refuge for Female Orphans* (London: W. Gawler, 1785).

68. See "The Annalist: Some Transactions of the French Lodge Formerly Held in London," *Freemasons' Quarterly Review*, 2nd ser., (March 1845): 33; W. Wonnacott, "De Vignoles and His Lodge 'L'Immortalité de l'ordre,'" *Ars Quatuor Coronatorum* 34 (1921): 139, 162, 165. In 1771, Barthélémon was orator of the lodge.

69. Bernard, "L'Alchimie," Feb. 14, 1863, 266.

70. Bernard, "L'Alchimie," Jan. 24, 1863, 219.

71. Martin, *Imposture Detected*, 17. A contributor to the *Gentleman's Magazine* also described, in March 1787, how Best told a visiting lady that "he would consult the angel Gabriel, at such an hour the three subsequent nights" and that he then "declared the result of his inquiry with the angel Gabriel." See Clio to Mr. Urban, *Gentleman's Magazine* 61 (1787), 309.

72. On Gabriel as a material incarnation of the Divine Word, see Meredith J. Gill, *Angels and the Order of Heaven in Medieval and Renaissance Italy* (Cambridge: Cambridge University Press, 2014), 103.

73. Bernard, "L'Alchimie," Feb. 14, 1863, 266.

74. Robert Mallet, "Third Report of the Facts of Earthquake Phænomena: Catalogue of Recorded Earthquakes from 1606 B.C. to A.D. 1850 (continued)," in *Report of the Twenty-Fourth Meeting of the British Association for the Advancement of Science* (London: John Murray, 1855), 13–14.

75. Bernard, "L'Alchimie," Feb.14, 1863, 266.

76. Bernard, "L'Alchimie," Feb. 28, 1863, 295.

77. Bernard, "L'Alchimie," Feb. 28, 1863, 295.

78. Bernard, "L'Alchimie," Feb. 28, 1863, 295.

79. Spence, *Essays on Divinity*, 51.

80. Bernard, "L'Alchimie," Feb. 14, 1863, 266. Bernard records this meeting as having taken place on Sept. 24, 1786. However, the number 248 attributed to the meeting follows on immediately from Grabianka's visit on Sept. 27, 1786. In other words, it seems more likely that the meeting took place on Sept. 28 or 29, and that 24 was a typographical error.

81. Bernard, "L'Alchimie," Feb. 28, 1863, 295.

82. Book of Jude 1:18 (King James Version).

83. Benedict Chastanier states that "on the 7th of November 1786, this good but deceived Count left us." See Chastanier, *Word of Advice*, 34.

84. Bernard, "L'Alchimie," Jan. 24, 1863, 219. Grabianka also describes Best's daily routine, whereby early in the morning he would begin to paint characters and hieroglyphics on his shoes and on the walls of his room, which supposedly were related to events that would occur to him during the course of the day.

85. Bernard, "L'Alchimie," Feb. 14, 1863, 264. Best gave Grabianka a similar portrait on Dec. 28, 1785, the only difference being that Grabianka is shown in a darker blue coat.

86. See John 12:14 for Christ's triumphant entry into Jerusalem on an ass. See Matthew 27:28–29 for a description of how Christ was dressed when he was being mocked by the Roman soldiers: "And they stripped him, and put on him a scarlet robe. And when they had platted a crown of thorns, they put *it* upon his head, and a reed in his right hand: and they bowed the knee before him, and mocked him, saying, Hail, King of the Jews!"

87. The young girl is possibly an allusion to his daughter, Anna, born in 1773.

88. Bernard, "L'Alchimie," Feb. 14, 1863, 264.

89. Bernard, "L'Alchimie," Feb. 14, 1863, 265.

90. Martin, *Imposture Detected*, 27.

91. Bernard, "L'Alchimie," Feb. 14, 1863, 265.

92. Bernard, "L'Alchimie," Feb. 28, 1863, 296. On Nov. 1, 1786, Best proclaimed that he saw "much spirituality" in Leyman's "hand and his eyes," before embracing him and saying "you must not leave your master until death; take a sabre and a belt, adorn thy loins and, if needs be, remember that thou must be ready to shed thy blood for him." See Bernard, "L'Alchimie," Feb. 28, 1863, 295.

93. Chastanier, *Word of Advice*, 34.

94. Chatanier, *Word of Advice*, 34. Chastanier refers to a relevant passage from H. C. Agrippa's *De Occulta Philosophia*, which describes how pentacles "may excell with wonderful vertues." See Heinrich Cornelius Agrippa, *Three Books of Occult Philosophy*, trans. John French, Book III (part 5) (London, 1651), 578.

95. Bernard, "L'Alchimie," Feb. 14, 1863, 266.

96. Bernard, "L'Alchimie," Feb. 28, 1863, 296.

97. Hindmarsh, *Rise and Progress*, 45. The timing of this farewell assembly at Duché's home, on the evening of Nov. 6, 1786, also accords with Chastanier's description that "on the 7th of November 1786, this good but deceived Count left us." See Chastanier, *Word of Advice*, 34.

98. Saint-Martin to J-B. Willermoz, Jan. 15, 1787. See Robert Amadou, ed., "Louis-Claude de Saint-Martin le Philosophe inconnu: Lettres a Jean-Baptiste Willermoz (1771–1789)," *Renaissance Traditionnelle* 53 (1983): 66.

99. Samuel Best, *Poor Help's Warning to All* (London: G. Riebau, 1795), 3, 5. The only known extant copy of this pamphlet is held at the International Institute of Social History in Amsterdam (shelf mark: Bro 1238–8).

100. See Richard Brothers, *A Letter of Richard Brothers, (Prince of the Hebrews) to Philip Stephens, Esq.* (London: G. Riebau, 1795), title page. On Riebau as a radical millenarian printer and bookseller in 1790s London, see Garrett, *Respectful Folly*, 205–6.

3

The Era of the Seven Brothers in Avignon, 1783–1790

COUNT GRABIANKA ARRIVED in Avignon in early 1787, after two years of peregrinations across Europe that had taken him from Podolia to Hamburg, The Hague, Paris, and London. This meandering route to the papal enclave had been "a thorny path" that had been "pointed out to him by Heaven."[1] During this time, A.-J. Pernety was enjoying a far less peripatetic life, having settled in Valence, in the Dauphiné (seventy-five miles north of Avignon), in late 1783. An entry under Pernety's name in the manuscript of the Holy Word on February 11, 1785, informs us that he came to the city "to be with his family."[2] Indeed, his younger brother, Jacques-Maurice, was Director of Tax Farms (*directeur des fermes*) in Valence, having assumed the post in 1776.[3] As mentioned in chapter 1, A.-J. Pernety had followed his younger brother to Berlin nearly a decade earlier, in 1766, when Jacques-Maurice was appointed a financial adviser (*conseiller intimé*) to Friedrich II of Prussia.[4] J.-M. Pernety left Berlin in 1772, when his initial contract of employment expired.[5] A decade passed before the elder Pernety consulted the Holy Word, on April 28, 1782, about whether he was destined to "find a new life" before the year had passed in the Midi. The answer Pernety received was to the point: November. This instruction was followed and, on November 10, 1783, Pernety departed from Berlin en route to Valence.

In the three years between Pernety's settling in Valence and Grabianka's arriving in Avignon, the former was able to lay the foundations for a transformation of the society that had been loosely established in Berlin in 1779. To be sure, it was modest in scope, but by the end of 1786, Pernety had successfully cultivated a loyal cabal of at least six new initiates—François-Louis Bourgeois de la Richardière (b. 1749), Antoine-Etienne Bouge (1743–after 1818), Claude-François Delhomme (1742–1807), Jean-Agricol Leblond (1745–1824), Joseph Ferrier (1736–after 1820) and Thomas-Nicolas-Jean de Rozières (b. 1751)—from the Dauphiné, the Comtat Venaissin, and Provence, who were more than

Initiating the Millennium. Robert Collis, and Natalie Bayer, Oxford University Press (2020) © Oxford University Press.
DOI: 10.1093/oso/9780190903374.001.0001

willing to be involved in the promotion of a highly distinctive millenarian and esoteric society.

Yet, without diminishing Pernety's role in cultivating a new group of devotees, it it can be said that the initial spark that rekindled the society was lit by the six-month presence of Brumore in Avignon.[6] He arrived in the papal enclave at the end of October 1784, after receiving a command from the Holy Word to go to Avignon at the beginning of the month. He came to the Midi beset by doubts but, vitally, in possession of two phials of (supposed) *prima materia* after his three-month alchemical sojourn with J. D. Müller in Altona at the beginning of the year.[7]

On November 9, 1784, shortly after his arrival in Avignon, Brumore beseeched the Holy Word to command him what to do with the *œuvre*—that is, his alchemical labours. His request is saturated with an air of utter despondency as he reflects on how his brothers and sisters, as "children of the new kingdom," had begun to despair about being dispersed across Europe and about the fulfilment of the promises made to them. The response he received was categorical: the Holy Word informed Brumore that the door had been closed on his alchemical pursuits and that he was to pass on his work on the *œuvre* to another labourer.[8]

The mantle was soon transferred to Richardière, whom Brumore perceived as the worker foreseen by the Holy Word. This may well explain why Richardière seems to have been the first individual to be consecrated in Avignon between March 12–20, 1785; evidently he could not begin his labours on the *grand œuvre* until he had been initiated.[9] The day after his consecration Richardière consulted the Holy Word and was told that he was the "worker of the testimony." Only six days later, Richardière began his labours on the *grand oeuvre* by beginning the process of calcination, whereby he placed the *prima materia* from Altona that had been brought by Brumore over a fire. The date he chose was highly symbolic, being Easter Saturday—that is, the deathly period before Christ's resurrection. The new adept then added the second philosophical mercury, which was typically used to break down metals into their constituent parts. Patience was needed by Richardière. He was instructed to wait 1200 days, that is until July 13, 1788, before being able to remove the matter from the fire.[10]

We know that besides Richardière, Bouge, Delhomme, and Rozières were all consecrated whilst Brumore was resident in Avignon. The Holy Word manuscript reveals that Bouge began his nine-day consecration on March 15, 1785, but does not indicate the extent to which he aided Richardière in the society's alchemical pursuits. The Médiathèque Ceccano in Avignon, however, holds a manuscript written by Bouge that contains a detailed recipe for the fabrication of potable gold.[11] Furthermore, a question posed to the Holy Word by Richardière, on May 14, 1785, cites the recent initiation of Delhomme: "Fr[ère] Perneti, whom the children of the new age call their patriarch, and whom it has pleased the Sabaoth to name his *sacrificateur*, having just consecrated Delhomme, my *frère*."[12] Furthermore, a report by Russian officials based on documents seized from Grabianka in St. Petersburg in 1807 (see chapter 6) explicitly states that

Delhomme and Rozières were also initiated by both Brumore and Pernety, along with their respective spouses.[13]

The consecration of Richardière, Bouge, Delhomme, and Rozières in 1785 may have been driven by Brumore's vision, but it was made possible by Pernety's networking ability. It is highly telling that all four *illuminés* were members of the Société Académique et Patriotique de Valence, which Pernety had helped to establish in 1784. In many ways, the Société Académique mirrored the wider intellectual culture in France for local forms of scholarly association. On the surface, in its learned deliberations and promotion of academic-prize contests, the society seemed to embody, as J. L. Caradonna notes, "the enlightenment in practice."[14]

Pernety played a very active role in the society, as both vice president and secretary.[15] The most public demonstration of Pernety's input was the pivotal role he played in overseeing an annual scientific competition, open to all, which the society first began to publicize widely in 1785. In July 1785, for example, the *Allegmeine Literatur-Zeitung*, published in Jena and Leipzig, carried an announcement about an essay contest based on the following two questions: (a) Has artificial electricity since its discovery thus far really contributed to the progress of physics? (b) Considered as a remedy, has it been more advantageous than harmful in its administration to the human race?[16] A substantial prize of 300 livres would be awarded the following year, and all responses were to be addressed to Pernety.[17]

At the same time, Pernety was also able to use his authority and connections within the society to identify members with like-minded interests in decidedly more esoteric and millenarian passions. Here we have a fine example of the liminality of the age, in which the boundaries between "respectable" learning and the embrace of illuminism were highly porous. Indeed, it is striking how Pernety was able to successively network by drawing on three intersecting strands of his life in Valence: academic sociability, Masonic fraternalism, and bonds of kinship.

Of the four *illuminés* consecrated by Pernety and Brumore, Rozières was the most active participant in the Société Academique between 1784 and 1791. Rozières, a captain in the Royal Engineering Corps, held the post of vice secretary within the society, although by 1787 he often deputised for the absent Pernety. In the 1780s, Rozières established himself as one of the foremost experts on the scientific study of the power and benefits of electricity. He was not only the chief instigator of the Valence society's interest in the benefits of electricity, in terms of physics in general and in healing, but also conducted a series of experiments that he circulated among learned circles throughout France. In December 1786 and April 1787, for example, Rozières wrote to the Comte de Buffon about his experiments involving magnetism and electricity.[18] In 1791, he published an essay in the influence of electricity on the germination and vegetation of plants.[19]

Significantly, Rozières was also the son-in-law of Jacques Pernety (who was also a member of the Société Academique), having married his daughter, Honorée-Louise, in 1781.[20] What is more, Rozières was a prominent Freemason in Valence, and was listed as Venerable Master of Loge la Sagesse in 1783.[21] Delhomme was also a member of la Sagesse and the Société Academique. His name features in the 1774 table of members of la Sagesse and he occupied a number of positions within the lodge (orator in 1776, senior warden in 1783, master of ceremonies in 1785, and treasurer in 1786 and 1787).[22] Moreover, Delhomme was the first person to be accepted as an associate member of the Société Academique, where he is listed as a doctor of medicine and law from Valence.[23] Thus Pernety was able to attract two of the most prominent Freemasons in Valence to join his illuministic society without himself being a member of any lodge in the city. He was able to do this because of both family ties and the vital role played by the Société Académique in the culture of sociability in Valence at this time.

Besides Delhomme, Richardiére, and Bouge were also doctors of medicine, though they both practised in Avignon. Bouge's membership in the Société Académique and as an early *illuminé* is noteworthy. He was, after 1774, one of the principal cultivators of a form of high-degree Freemasonry in Avignon that was infused with hermetic and alchemical philosophy.[24] Indeed, Bouge played a pivotal role within his lodge, St. Jean d'Écosse de la vertu persécutée, in the establishment of the Académie des vray maçons.[25] Between 1784 and 1788, Bouge was the sole member of the lodge to carry the title of Vray Maçon Sage Académicien, which effectively recognised his seniority in its esoteric academy.[26] Tellingly, Bouge's ascension to the rank of a Sage Academic of True Masonry occurred in the very year that he joined the Société Académique in Valence and came into close contact with Pernety.

Interestingly, one other member of La Vertu persécutée—Leblond—was one of the first *illuminés* to be consecrated prior to Grabianka's arrival. It is no coincidence that Leblond was second in seniority within the lodge's Académie des vray maçons. In 1788, it was Leblond who became the only other brother of the lodge to attain the rank of Vray Maçon Sage Académicien.[27] In other words, Bouge seems to have been highly selective in introducing his fellow brethren to the parallel spiritual and esoteric delights offered by Pernety's select group of *illuminés*. In many ways, Leblond was, for well over a quarter-century, only slightly less influential than Bouge in promoting a distinct form of high-degree Freemasonry in Avignon. Leblond's name appears first, for example, on a list of members of the Les Sectateurs de la Vertu lodge in a petition sent to the Grand Orient de France in Paris on October 26, 1774.[28] Thirty-two years later, the names of Bouge and Leblond appear first and second respectively on a list of signatories from La Vertu persécutée in a letter to the members of the Contrat Social lodge in Paris.[29] Very little is known about Leblond, despite his being one of the most influential Freemasons in Avignon at the time. Outside his involvement in the lodge, all we know with certainty about him is that he was a third-generation print seller and engraver.[30]

It has been erroneously claimed that Richardière was also a founding member of La Vertu persécutée in Avignon.[31] Besides his name not appearing on any lodge membership list, the extant manuscript of the consultations with the Holy Word records that the physician only arrived in Avignon on June 21, 1784. He then spent the autumn and winter of 1784–1785 in Valence, where he soon became an associate member of the Société Académique.[32] However, unlike with Rozières, Delhomme, Bouge, and Leblond, no evidence has come to light to show that Richardière was a Freemason.[33] We know very little about Richardière prior to his arrival in Avignon, apart from that he hailed from Paris and was a doctor of medicine.[34] We also know that he worked for several years in that capacity in Russia, as a surgeon in the household of Anna Nikitichna Naryshkina (née Trubetskaia).[35] In St. Petersburg, Richardière also became acquainted with Gilbert Romme, and the two men entered into correspondence in 1781, when Romme journeyed to Siberia. The letters written by Richardière reveal that he mixed with the foremost scientific figures in Russia of the era, including S. G. Domashnev, the director of the Academy of Sciences, who wanted to purchase Richardière's herbarium. Richardière also updated Romme about his efforts to establish a literary society and gazette in Petersburg.[36]

Lastly, Joseph Ferrier, a lawyer from Arles, was consecrated at some point before January 1787. Interestingly, Ferrier is the only known early *illuminé* in the Midi with no apparent links to either Freemasonry or the Société Académique in Valence. However, Ferrier and Bouge did share a common bond with the Jesuit Order in Provence. Ferrier had been a scholastic at the Jesuit college in Arles prior to the order's suppression in France in 1764.[37] Bouge, from nearby Aix-en-Provence, was also a Jesuit brother (*frère coadjuteur*), that is, a non-ordained man who has vowed to dedicate his life to the society's mission.[38]

Whereas the six-month stay of Brumore was important in reinvigorating the society in the Midi, it was the arrival of Grabianka, in early 1787, that ushered in a three-year golden era for the *illuminés* in Avignon. As much as members of the society believed their actions were dictated from above, it is striking how much the direction of the group was dependent upon dynamic and charismatic individuals. By early 1787, Brumore was dead and Pernety's advanced years may have stymied his active promotion of the society. It therefore seems that Grabianka became the leading light in the group after his arrival in Avignon. The leaders of the society (except Rozières, for some reason) quickly formed themselves into a council of seven who were not distinguished by rank. Nonetheless, Grabianka was regarded as the undeniable *primus inter pares* both inside and outside the group.

For over three years this Council of Seven Brothers—Grabianka, Pernety, Richardière, Bouge, Delhomme, Leblond, and Ferrier—remained unchanged and projected a unified front in all its transactions with correspondents and visitors alike. We have no record of how and why the *illuminés* in Avignon decided to form the Council of Seven, but it seems likely that they wished to imbue some degree of significance to this number. One explanation could be tied to a prophecy Grabianka received from the Holy Word, on April 14, 1779, in which he was assured that he would "do great things." However, he "must have seven arms to be strong . . . because you will become seven times as tall . . . the will of God will be fulfilled."[39]

The *illuminés* could also draw on a wealth of literature by Christian exegetes pointing to the importance of the number seven as the number of perfection (as epitomized by the Seven Pillars of Wisdom in Proverbs 9:1) and citing its symbolism throughout the Bible. Most notably, the number seven is abundantly used in the book of Revelation (7 churches, 7 seals, 7 trumpets, etc.). Moreover, early modern Christian cabalists, theosophists, and alchemists could draw on a wealth of ancient thinkers, including Pythagoras and Hermes Trismegistus, to point to the occult significance of the number. Alchemists needed to complete seven stages, for example, on the path of seeking material and spiritual gold.[40] By establishing the Council of Seven, the *illuminés* in Avignon may have wished to cast themselves as wise sages able to lead the elect beyond the contemporary time of tribulations and on to the New Jerusalem.

Whatever the case, by January 1787, with Grabianka in Avignon, the Seven Brothers were ready (and had evidently been instructed by the Holy Word) to come out of the shadows and promote their society to like-minded individuals and groups throughout Europe.[41] Over the following two months, with Grabianka acting as *primus inter pares* in all correspondence, they dispatched a series of letters to individuals and groups they deemed worthy of being informed about what to them was a momentous development. The recipients of these letters were either already "in the truth" or had demonstrated a "desire to know and embrace it."[42] In short, they were all, to varying degrees, influenced by Swedenborgian theosophy.

On February 12, 1787, for example, the Seven Brothers wrote a letter to "the Children of the New Kingdom in London," that is, the members and associates of the Theosophical Society in the English capital whom Grabianka had met the previous year. The letter begins with pleasantries about "the civil and distinguished" way Grabianka had been treated by the Swedenborgians in London, and thanks them for sending several works by Swedenborg to Avignon. This is followed by a cursory history of the establishment of their own society in 1779 and how they had "passed away" the subsequent eight years in "obscurity and silence." At last, the Seven Brothers declared, the "happy day" had arrived, "wherein we are to open our hearts to our brethren, and draw from theirs that reciprocation of fraternal friendship which we bear towards them in Jesus Christ."[43] Moreover, it was their duty to "dispose them to receive revealed truths, and prepare the way for his new people." Significantly, the letter promotes a distinct form of ecumenicism by proclaiming that "the Spirit of God . . . breathes in the Souls of all Men" and "elects indiscriminately from all Nations."[44] A fervent millenarian pronouncement ensues that draws strongly on the book of Revelation: "Very dear brethren, the angel that stands before the face of the Lamb is already sent to sound his trumpet on the mountains of Babylon, and give notice to the nations that the God of heaven will soon come to the gates of the earth, to change the face of the world."[45]

On February 24, 1787, Grabianka alone wrote a similar letter to the bookseller P. F. Gosse in The Hague, whom he had met in 1785. An interesting aspect of this letter, which is absent from the earlier missive, is what appears to be an attempt by Grabianka to assuage any confessional doubts Gosse may have harboured as a member of the Dutch Reformed Church. Grabianka highlights the society's non-hierarchical nature and sole reliance on the will of God: "In our society no one commands, but each is glorified and honoured to obey the will of God . . . We cannot admit anyone without the direct command of Heaven . . . No worldly distinction between us occurs." Grabianka seeks to distance the society from any outward similarity to the Catholic Church by emphasizing the absence of vestments, lavish ceremonials, and decorative hieroglyphs.[46]

Notwithstanding his pronouncing to Gosse that the society in Avignon was non-hierarchical, Grabianka was very much the dynamic force that drove the publicity campaign in early 1787. At this time, Grabianka also wrote similar letters on behalf of the society to C. F. Tieman,[47] Edouard Maubach,[48] J.-P. Parraud, and C.-P.-P. Savalette de Langes.[49] The latter was the founder of the high-degree lodge of Les Philalèthes in Paris and organised Masonic congresses in the French capital in 1784–1785 and 1787 to discuss contentious issues relating to the doctrine and history of the fraternity.[50] Tieman, Maubach, and Parraud attended this congress, and all rank as leading lights in the illuministic milieu in Western Europe in the 1780s.[51] At a session of the congress held on March 29, 1787, de Langes, Maubach, and Parraud communicated the content of letters they had received from Grabianka, which closely resembled that of those sent to the Swedenborgians in London and to Gosse in The Hague.[52]

Besides dispatching promotional letters to London, The Hague, and Paris, Grabianka also began to actively proselytise in person with prospective novitiates. One such candidate was Bourré de Corberon, who, since being initiated into the highest degree of the Melissino Rite in St. Petersburg, in 1777, had been an enthusiastic adherent to the major contemporary strands of European illuminism, namely, alchemy, Mesmerism, Swedenborgianism, Christian Cabala, and millenarianism.[53] In February 1787, Corberon wrote to C. A. von Brühl, an old friend and fellow illuminist, about having recently met Grabianka, whom he describes as "an extraordinary man." The pair enjoyed over three hours of conversation, and Grabianka spoke at length about the society in Avignon.[54] Brühl replied in April and confirmed that he was acquainted with Grabianka and pronounced that "if you embrace his system, I think I can compliment you."[55] By this time Corberon and Grabianka had already begun to correspond.[56] Corberon and his wife, Charlotte (née von Behmer), soon became *illuminés* and were actively involved in the society until at least April 1791.[57]

Much like the strategy of targeted marketing on modern-day social media platforms, the Grabianka-led advertisement campaign for the Avignon Society in 1787 was specifically aimed at a sympathetic audience. Although the *illuminés* in Avignon never explicitly claimed to be a Swedenborgian society, they were initially more than happy to portray themselves and to be perceived as exponents of the theosophical doctrines associated with Swedenborg. In letters the Seven Brothers sent to the Swedenborgians in London, much was made of how they had received the gift of Swedenborg's works "with Transports of the most lively Joy" and that they would "take that Care of them that they deserve . . . as the precious Mark of your friendship."[58] Moreover, Grabianka began his letter to Gosse by proclaiming that Christ "prepares everything by his Servants for his new

Kingdom, of which he has long since laid the foundations through the works of Emanuel Swedenborg."[59] On reading the letters sent to Savalette de Langes, Maubach, and Parraud, the delegates at the Philalèthes congress concluded, in March 1787, that they represented "an almost public manifestation of the new [Swedenborgian] doctrine."[60]

This reasoning is entirely understandable. After all, the promotional letters merely bolstered the Avignon Society's reputation as a haven of Swedenborgianism; they did not announce the sudden emergence of the group ex nihilo. The recipients of the letters would have been aware of the French translations of Swedenborg's works by Pernety and Brumore. Indeed, Pernety had only months earlier published a French edition of Swedenborg's *Angelic Wisdom, concerning the Divine Love and the Divine Wisdom*.[61] It is surely not coincidental that an anonymous work was published in Avignon in 1786 that attacked illuminist Freemasons for their dangerous espousal of the works of Saint-Martin, as well as their enthusiastic pursuit of the philosophers' stone and embrace of animal magnetism. Significantly, the author also warned *illuminés* of the dangers that awaited them if they continued to advance the false doctrines advanced by Swedenborg, who had "traced a new plan riddled with errors."[62]

It is noteworthy that Grabianka was so successful in ingratiating himself with the Swedenborgian community in London that his honorary membership in the Theosophical Society was formally recognised by the New Church when it was officially established, on May 7, 1787. It is therefore not surprising that many among the initial wave of new visitors to and initiates into the Avignon Society in 1787 were drawn from the illuminist wing of the burgeoning Swedenborgian milieu in Europe.

One of the earliest visitors to Avignon in 1787 appears to have been F. H. Barthélémon, who became well acquainted with Grabianka in London. Barthélémon was not only one of the most prominent Swedenborgians in the English capital in the 1780s, he also seems to have been one of the principal conduits between Samuel Best and the loose group of Swedenborgians that met at the home of Jacob Duché. In the summer of 1787 his role as a messenger for Best was to extend beyond the streets of London, as he was charged by the Shoreditch Prophet to convey several prophetic messages destined for Grabianka and to deliver a letter for all the brothers of the Avignon Society. Prior to these communications, on January 17, 1787, the Avignon brothers sought guidance from Archangel Gabriel as to whether they were to consider all the predictions and citations Best had given to Grabianka in London as being divinely inspired. The response they received was in Latin and affirmed that they could trust the prophecies laid out to Grabianka. This oracle can, in all likelihood, be regarded as an early mediation by Ottavio Cappelli, the purported prophet from Siena. First, the brothers beseeched Archangel Gabriel for divine advice, which, as we will see, was Cappelli's modus operandi in Avignon. Second, the reply was received in Latin, which also indicates his involvement.[63]

The messages are simply dated "March 23," but a numbering of all such notes between Best and Grabianka in chronological order indicates that the year was 1787.[64] Poland is a central theme in three of the five pronouncements, and Best predicts that Grabianka "would soon hear of troubles or war" in the country. The Shoreditch Prophet also informs Grabianka that it will be some time before he returns to Poland, but that when he does, he is to ask "the Polish gentleman Rohoziński" to visit Best in London. On a positive note, Best foresees that "many inspired servants of God will gather together" in Grabianka's society. Lastly, Best beseeched Grabianka to "pray" with his brother "for Barthélémon to be initiated."[65] The short letter from Best is dated June 17 and was addressed to Grabianka and his brothers. Crucially, the heading stipulates that Barthélémon deliver the letter in person.[66] The missive simply informs the Avignon brothers that Best had been "commanded by God, by His Holy Spirit in me" to send a batch of scriptural texts to them. Furthermore, he had been instructed to relay a message concerning how they would shortly "begin to receive and suffer persecution."[67]

By the autumn of 1787 the promotional seeds planted earlier in the year began to yield a rich harvest. In October Thomé, arguably the foremost French Swedenborgian of the era, visited Avignon to observe the society in person.[68] He left no record of his impressions. However, more than a year later Grabianka referred to him in a letter as "brother" and someone "whom I always love tenderly," which strongly suggests that Thomé was a member of the society.[69] When Thomé was in Avignon, Tieman also spent ten days in the city, ostensibly as part of a Grand Tour he was conducting as the governor of B. A. Golitsyn.[70] The city had much to offer in terms of sightseeing, but Tieman's itinerary was not based on an appreciation of its historical gems. Instead, he and Golitsyn went to Avignon in order to appreciate first-hand the spiritual milieu Grabianka had lauded in his letter from earlier in the year.

In a letter to Willermoz, written near the end of his stay in Avignon, Tieman reported that he had had the "opportunity to closely observe the society" over the course of eight days. The remainder of the letter is effusive in its praise of what he had seen. He confesses to Willermoz "in the sincerity of my heart" that he had never "seen anything greater, more striking [and] which bears more of the imprint of a higher vocation." He describes that they are "seven in number," before lauding them as being "wise men, enlightened and infinitely interesting by their manner of being, both in themselves and with their friends." His veneration is so great, he writes, that he "prostrates" himself "in dust" every time he leaves them. The overwhelming impression given by Tieman is that he has been allowed to enter a unique kind of monastic order, in which the brethren act with a great simplicity of heart. He elaborates by highlighting the worldly sacrifices made by three of the Seven Brothers, who he states abandoned their wives, children, and fortunes to follow their spiritual calling in Avignon.

A striking feature of Tieman's account is his focus on the Seven Brothers' spiritual purity and earthly asceticism, as opposed to their being steeped in occult philosophy. In other words, he perceives them as an elect union of "God's people" who are ready for the imminent tribulations that will descend on the nations of the earth. He emphasizes that "I have no doubt that it will be from among them that a very great Revolution will commence in the Church of Christ and that this Revolution is very near." Tieman seems inspired by the fervency of the society's millenarian vision and proclaims: "The world must be purified in all its parts and the new Church will appear." Lest Willermoz conclude that he had been overcome by enthusiasm, Tieman concluded his letter by stressing that "after the coldest reflection . . . I repeat: This is the finger of God: it announces a great revolution."[71] The form of millenarianism Tieman described reflects a distinctive aspect of the Avignon Society's doctrine which remained constant throughout its existence: a vision of an imminent literal millennium that would entail political upheavals among nations followed by a spiritual revolution ushered in by the elect. This did not align with the beliefs of many orthodox Swedenborgians, in England in particular, who held to Swedenborg's emphasis on the dawn of a new age prefigured on the individual achievement of an internal spiritual millennium.[72] Yet it did appeal to many on the eclectic fringes of the Swedenborgian milieu, as well as to illuminist Freemasons such as Tieman, as social and political tensions came to the fore in France in the late 1780s. Tieman remained closely associated with the Avignon Society until the end of 1789, as we will see, but his desire to join the group was apparently never sanctioned by Heaven.

The entire focus of Tieman's early description of the Avignon Society, in 1787, is on the millenarian ethos and spiritual purity of the group. Yet the *illuminés* in Avignon were at this time still very much preoccupied with the quest for the philosophers' stone, which had been doggedly pursued by the likes of Brumore, Ronikier, and Grabianka in Berlin, Rheinsberg, and Podolia, and continued by Richardière and Bouge in Avignon. We know of Grabianka's continued interest in alchemy from a red notebook seized by the Russian authorities in 1807. According to a summary of this notebook, Grabianka consulted the group's oracle three times between March and June 1787 on matters pertaining to the *grand œuvre*. On March 26, he sought advice about dissolving the philosophers' stone into a liquid. In other words, he was seeking counsel about how to prepare potable gold, or the elixir of life. The reply he received assured him that "trust overcomes labour in destroying the stone" and instructed him that the tincture should be sealed in bottles for twenty-six days. Lastly, he was commanded to pour the elixir into three parts: one part to keep and the other two parts to be given to his brothers. A curious anecdote also features in this entry. It tells of how a speck of dust fell into the elixir and how the wife of the alchemical toiler extracted it with an iron needle which subsequently turned a golden colour. The original scribe noted that "this miracle is known to every apothecarist, because iron not only takes on a golden colour in copper vitriol solution, but even turns into copper."[73] To be sure, many alchemists, including Paracelsus, noted that blue vitriol (copper sulphate) had the power to transmute iron into copper.[74]

The red notebook also contained an entry, dated May 27, 1787, which instructed the *illuminé* to conduct a remarkable alchemical procedure: Grabianka was ordered to go to the hill "de la roche," most likely a reference to the Rocher des Doms in Avignon, a rocky outcrop on the banks of the Rhône. The procedure was to take place during a full moon and at midnight to collect *"lumen Christi."* A belief in natural magic and, more specifically, the special virtues of the moon at this specific moment, which could be harnessed in the alchemical process, seem to be at play here. This *lumen Christi* was then to be put in vinegar; and the solution distilled and then corked in a bottle. This recalls *Faust*, and the instructions of Mephistopheles to prepare a remedy by distilling the ingredients "carefully in full-moon light."[75] The secret fluid used for the transmutation of metals was to be poured in a second bottle.[76] Six days later the *illuminés* received a third instruction related to their alchemical endeavours. They were told to keep the *lumen Christi*, the liquid for making gold, and the *Cabala* separate and out of sight.[77] The reference to cabala here suggests that the *illuminés* in Avignon were practicing a form of cabalistic alchemy. This had first been advocated in the early sixteenth century by G. A. Pantheo and was subsequently practised by the likes of Paracelsus, John Dee, and Heinrich Khunrath.[78]

Only one further entry related to alchemy from the notebook in Grabianka's possession was noted down by the Russian authorities. The date is highly significant, as it was July 8, 1788. In other words, the *illuminés* consulted the oracle only five days before the date given to them in 1785 in regard to when to remove the philosophers' stone from the sealed crucible. Alchemists often recommended a lengthy period of incubation as the final stage of the *grand œuvre*. Indeed, as John Read explains, "the central and crucial feature of the Great Work consisted in a prolonged and controlled heating of the proximate material, under the right conditions, in the sealed vessel of Hermes."[79] Having waited more than three years for the "egg" to incubate, it is understandable that in the days leading up to July 13, 1788, the *illuminés* were eager to receive instructions about how to proceed.

The oracle did not disappoint them. On July 8 it provided detailed directions for completing their own Great Work. They were ordered to return to the hill to carry out the procedure. There, they were instructed to mix seven pounds of iron powder, a pound of the spirit of wine, nine drops of *lumen Christi*, "and the same amount of the other liquid" into a crucible. This smelting pot was then to be closed and wrapped in paper before being buried in the ground so that the top surface remained exposed to the air. The *illuminés* were also told in no uncertain terms not to leave the buried crucible unattended "whilst the miracle is happening," as "Satan will hinder [the process], so [they must] drive him away." Once they had succeeded in banishing the devil, they were "to pick up what he left." According to the red notebook, Leyman was given the responsibility of guarding the crucible during the night but saw "neither the devil nor money nor a miracle."[80] In other words, they failed for a second time in their prolonged endeavour to produce the philosophers' stone. Significantly, the Russian authorities noted that this unsuccessful operation seems to have marked "the end of their work with the philosophers' stone," since the subject was not broached again in any subsequent questions to the oracle. The failure to produce the philosophers' stone in 1788 must have been bitterly disappointing for the *illuminés*. It is understandable that they subsequently lacked the collective will to embark on further lengthy and time-consuming alchemical quests to perfect the illusive divine quintessence.

The society's cessation of alchemical activities coincided with the direct involvement of Cappelli, a denizen of Rome, in the group's activities in Avignon. A scarcity of evidence relating to Cappelli's time in the papal enclave makes it hard to fully gauge his impact on the *illuminés* during his stay in Avignon, which occurred roughly between the autumn of 1787 and the end of 1788. However, enough evidence exists to suggest that Cappelli, in the guise of a prophet, sought to refashion the society, in some ways into a more conventional Catholic entity. Specifically, he championed Marian devotion, at the same time placing far less importance on esoteric pursuits, such as alchemy, and waging an outright attack on the popularity of Swedenborgian doctrine among the *illuminés*.

The earliest documented contact between Cappelli and the Avignon *illuminés* took place in 1786, when Ferrier met the Italian in Rome.[81] Cappelli confessed to the papal authorities in 1791 that he had come into contact with the society in 1786.[82] It is not known how this meeting transpired, but the most plausible explanation is that Cappelli met Brumore at some point after the latter's arrival in Rome, in June 1785. It is highly likely that by this time Cappelli had already begun to imagine himself to be a prophet, and thus would have piqued the curiosity of Brumore.

According to a report produced by the papal authorities in 1790, Brumore died in Rome on February 28, 1787.[83] The death of Brumore at this time, alongside Cappelli's growing influence, may well explain why Grabianka journeyed to Rome in March 1787, shortly after his arrival in Avignon. This visit is corroborated by Corberon, who wrote, on February 23, 1787, that he had met Grabianka before his departure for Italy. The Russian authorities also noted, in their summary of the documents seized from Grabianka, that he had posed a question to the oracle from Rome on March 26, 1787. This invaluable source also documents that Cappelli was in Turin on June 4, 1787, and was met there by Grabianka, Richardière, and Ferrier. This itinerary is confirmed by the trial papers of the *Giunta di Stato* in Rome, dating from 1799 (see chapter 4). In these, Cappelli testified that he travelled to Avignon via Turin because Ferrier had promised that he would be able to enlist him in military service. Cappelli's earthly concerns are also evident in the entry made by the Russian authorities relating to June 4, 1787, which states that "III [Cappelli] demanded 5,000 *livres* by command of Raphael." Here we have the first documented instance that Cappelli used his supposed prophetic ability to relay messages from the archangels Raphael and Gabriel to further his own agenda.

Six days later Cappelli, who was probably still in Turin, wrote to Pernety and unleashed an extraordinary attack on the latter's devotion to Swedenborgian doctrine. This assault on Swedenborgianism can be traced to January 1787, when the oracle issued two messages apropos the Swedish theologian. Presumably, Cappelli had by this point already taken on the role of prophet in the society and thus was acting as the sole mediator between members and Heaven. In the red notebook that documents oracles, for example, an entry for January 10, 1787, states that "not everything in Swedenborg is false: he converted six members."[84] The next entry in the notebook is much more strident in its denunciation of the Swede's doctrine: "It is forbidden to read the works of Swedenborg, so as to not corrupt your faith."[85]

This trenchant style is evident in Cappelli's letter to Pernety. According to the Russian summariser, Cappelli, who was yet to meet Pernety, began by stating that "our inspirations have finally affected your heart." Cappelli's condemnation of Pernety and Swedenborgianism rests on three core pillars of Roman Catholic doctrine: belief in the Holy Trinity according to the Athanasian Creed, veneration of Mary as the Mother of God, and the position of the pope as the sole, authoritative Vicar of Christ based on the decision made at the Council of Chalcedon in AD 451. From the outset, Cappelli did not mince his words. He immediately questioned whether Pernety was a true Roman Catholic and believed in the Holy Trinity. He then moved onto a discussion of the Swedenborgian's disavowal of the Athanasian Creed, whereby they rejected the notion of Christ and the Holy Spirit as consubstantial entities of the threefold essence of God. Moreover, Cappelli reminded Pernety that "they [Swedenborgians] do not believe that Mary is the Mother of God," and moreover, "everyone wants to live according to their own [beliefs] . . . What nonsense! Do not be among them." Lastly, Cappelli not only beseeches Pernety to return to the fold, but also indicates that he needs to ensure that his "sons live in the one God and will not cease to love Him, so that they recognise the same vicar as their forefathers recognised, so that they do not listen to this [Swedenborgian] teaching, otherwise they will be the victims of the horror of desperation in their terrible hour of death."[86] In other words, Cappelli was indicating to Pernety that he, as patriarch of the Avignon society, had a responsibility to preserve his flock within the Roman Catholic Church. This unambiguous censure occurred before Cappelli had even arrived in Avignon. Alongside a demand for money, the letter reveals that Cappelli was already aware of the power he was able to wield over the credulous *illuminés* in Avignon. Both Grabianka and Pernety had long been susceptible to the supposed gifts of prophets, and in 1787 Cappelli was no exception to this rule.

It took a little over a year after Cappelli's arrival in Avignon, in the autumn of 1787, for the society to publicly renounce Swedenborg and to pronounce something of a Marian cult. Perhaps aware of the implications this move would have for the society among non-Catholics, Grabianka waited until the end of 1788 before openly adopting the dramatic doctrinal shift. However, in a letter addressed to his fellow brethren in Paris, on December 10, 1788, Grabianka mentions that he and Richardière had already begun to communicate with them regarding "the Most Holy Virgin Mary and Emanuel Swedenborg."[87] This indicates that the seven brothers in Avignon had already taken Cappelli's doctrinal critique on board, but had not immediately disseminated that information to all members of the society. Instead, a selective approach had been adopted.

In his letter of December 10, Grabianka responds to a query from William Bousie, who was clearly privy to the new doctrinal stance, as to whether he was now permitted to communicate this important development to other members of the society. In response, Grabianka declares that "the time has finally come when we no longer [need to] keep the secret of the incomparable Mary, virgin and mother." It was Bousie's respon-sibility to convey this news "to our brothers and sisters in London." Moreover, Bousie was instructed to not simply relay this information, but to proclaim to "even the most stubborn in their false light"—that is, Swedenborgians—so that they "will finally recog-nise their error regarding the Most Holy Virgin Mary."[88] Grabianka explains this decision to Bousie by emphasizing that Swedenborg had been "unfortunate enough to give in [to] mistakes and serious illusions." He then repeats that "it is now permissible for us to openly declare that in his works the ideas of man have too often been mingled with those of rev-elation." What is more, Grabianka posits that Swedenborgians would realise the error of their ways if they were to scrutinise the works of Swedenborg "without enthusiasm," as they would then clearly see that he "advanced things quite contrary to Holy Scripture."[89]

In December 1789, a year after Grabianka had first indicated that the society could openly reveal its anti-Swedenborgian stance, a letter by William Bryan, an English mem-ber of the group, expressed sentiments that were very much in keeping with this com-mand. Replying to an acquaintance who had requested that Bryan elaborate on why in his new doctrine he believed Swedenborg was mistaken, Bryan asserted that Swedenborg "had erred in 6 points." Bryan added that this was "certainly true, since it was revealed to our society by an immediate communication with Heaven, & will in its proper time be fully explained & made public, till then we dare not declare it." Bryan, one of the Swedenborgians Grabianka had met in London in 1786, freely conceded in 1789 that he had once been "a lover of the truths I found in his writings & still I love them," before adding, "I could not help always seeing in them some manifest contradictions & also that they did in some places oppose the Holy Scriptures."[90]

The decision to openly and publicly repudiate Swedenborgian doctrine, alongside revealing a fervent espousal of Marian worship, explains Pernety's publication, in 1790, of *Les vertus, le Pouvoir, la Clémence et la Gloire de Marie mère de Dieu*. Here we have the most incontrovertible demonstration of Pernety's complete acquiescence to the demands first presented to him in June 1787. In the introduction to this text, Pernety extolled Mary as a "unique source of enlightenment (*lumières*), filled with grace."[91] Yet until Cappelli's arrest in Rome in September 1790 (see chapter 4), the tensions engendered within the Avignon Society by the embrace of Marian devotion in particular and Catholic doctrine in general did not fully erupt. To be sure, they were festering near the surface, but it was Cappelli's fall from grace that acted as the catalyst for schism within the society.

Indeed, though Cappelli's influence was sowing the seeds of discord as early as 1787, the society in fact thrived between this time and the beginning of 1790. We have been able to identify forty-seven individuals who joined the society between March 1787, when the Council of Seven announced themselves to their peers, and the end of 1789, as well as several who had extremely close ties to the group (see appendix 1). In all likelihood, many more people were initiated into the society during this time—spouses and family members, as well as like-minded Freemasons and illuminists—whose imprints have not been preserved. Among the family members who we do know joined during this period were Jacques Pernety; his wife, Françoise (née Gardelle); and their daughter, Honorée-Louise, who married Rozières.[92] Surprisingly, only one fellow Mason from the loge La Vertu Persécutée in Avignon seems to have joined Bouge and Leblond in the society of *illuminés* in the city. This was a certain Deravine, who undertook his consecration into the society of *illuminés* in November 1788. At this time, he is listed on the Tableau des frères of La Vertu as being a second degree (*compagnon*) Mason and an officer in a hussars' regiment.[93]

One explanation for this may be that the Council of Seven simply set their gaze beyond the city walls of Avignon after distributing the letters pronouncing their existence to their peers, in February and March 1787. In fact, the sights and ambitions of the society were now much greater. From this time until the end of 1789, the Seven Brothers in Avignon were undeniably very successful in attracting a diverse and far-flung stream of prospective consecrates from across the length and breadth of Europe. In this respect, the advertising campaign unleashed in early 1787 was something of a minor triumph. At the same time, it seems that the Seven Brothers did not simply sit back and wait for candidates to arrive in Avignon. Instead, they appear to have delegated a degree of authority to two individuals—Guillaume de Paul (1738–1793) and William Bousie—who were able to draw on their extensive networks of influence to attract potential novitiates. Both Paul and Bousie participated in the first Philalèthes convent in Paris in 1784–1785, and both were prominent figures in illuminist circles in France in the 1780s.[94]

Paul hailed from Marseille. By the 1780s he was one of the most prominent officials and cultural authorities in the city and remained so for nearly four decades. He had since 1758 presided over law and order in the city as Lieutenant-générale civil honoraire, and in 1763 he was elected to the Académie de Marseille. Writing in 1808, Casimir Rostan praised Paul as "the veritable Maecenas of his native land" because of his patronage of the arts and sciences in Marseille." The biographer then added: "is it any wonder that M. Paul has surrendered himself, for some time, with ardour, to the study of magnetism, hermetic philosophy, theosophy and has frequented societies of all kinds, which promise their adepts great revelations and great progress?"[95] It is entirely in keeping with this description that Paul ranks as one of the earliest proponents of Swedenborgianism in France. Indeed, as early as February 1782 Paul had written a reply to Pernety in Berlin apropos Swedenborg: "It is very true, Sir, that I ardently seek after the sovereign Good and sovereign Truth. After the Holy Scriptures, I have found no works more inspiring of good and more revealing of the truth than those of the late Mr. Emanuel Swedenborg."[96] One such society that Paul frequented was high-degree Freemasonry, the Loge de Saint-Jean d'Écosse in Marseille, whose membership lists recorded that he was *premier surveillant* in 1786 and Chancelier Garde des Sceaux the following year.[97]

At some point prior to July 1788, Paul was also consecrated as an *illuminé* of the Avignon Society. This is unsurprising, given his absorption in the main illuminist currents of his day and prior correspondence with Pernety, as well as the logistical ease of travelling between Avignon and Marseille. Proof of Paul's initiation into the Avignon

Society is found in an anonymous letter addressed to F.-M. de Chefdebien, a leading high-degree Freemason and member of Mesmer's Society of Harmony in Paris:

> Mr. de Paul, whom I saw yesterday ... charged me to write to you to inform you that you are admitted by the *Me[ssieu]rs* of Avignon. He has received some preliminary instructions, very wise and very interesting ... He promised to propose me too ... Mr. de Paul has a very happy hand since his four proposed [candidates] have been admitted, so I hope to get the same favour.[98]

This letter not only reveals Paul's membership of the Avignon Society, but also shines a more general light on the group's internal structure as it expanded in the late 1780s. Borrowing from the playbook of Freemasonry, the Council of Seven in Avignon seem to have taken on the guise of a "mother-lodge," which maintained strict control over admittance to affiliate branches. In this instance, Paul seems to have been at the head of an affiliate group in Marseille that had been sanctioned by the Council of Seven. Those wanting to join Paul's branch of the society in Marseille had to initially approach him and receive his approval. He then had to nominate his candidates to the Seven Brothers in Avignon, who would have consulted their oracle for guidance on whether to accept each individual. Evidently, by July 1788 Paul had successfully nominated four candidates besides Chefdebien. Furthermore, Paul had received some "very wise and very interesting" instructions. This suggests Paul was invested with the authority as a *sacrificateur* to consecrate initiates in Marseille. At the end of 1788 Grabianka asked that a copy of the important announcement about the society's renunciation of Swedenborg to be sent to "F[rère] Paul for all the f[rères] of Marseille," adding that the seven brothers in Avignon had "not written to them for a long time."[99]

The hypothesis that Paul was the appointed *sacrificateur* in Marseille is strengthened by bearing in mind that, in December 1789, Gustaf Adolf Reuterholm (1756–1813) was invested with the title "Sacrificateur du Nord" after completing his consecration in Avignon.[100] By bestowing this title on Reuterholm, the Seven Brothers had granted the Swede the power to initiate candidates when he returned to Sweden. Besides Chefdebien, we do not know the names of the other successful candidates nominated by Paul, except for Marcus Lemort de Métigny and his wife. In December 1788 Grabianka wrote that he was "sensitive to the memory of the good and dear f[rère] and s[oeur] de Métigny, these children of faith, trustful and docile." He wished to reassure them that a happy fate awaited them and that Richardière would confirm this again "with the grace and permission of Heaven."[101] It seems very likely that Paul proposed the Métignys; according to Rostan, Marcus Lemort was his "disciple and pupil," who generously furnished him with the means to complete a doctorate in medicine at the prestigious Ludovicée in Montpellier, in 1784.[102]

Whereas Paul wielded his influence in Marseille, Bousie's sphere of influence was in Paris, although he made frequent trips to London, principally on account of his work as a wine merchant. When Cagliostro, Grabianka, and Saint-Martin visited London between 1776 and 1787, they each turned to Bousie to facilitate their entry into the city's illuminist milieu (see chapter 2). In the 1770s and 1780s Bousie was arguably the foremost conduit of illuminist currents between Paris and London. By the late 1780s, Bousie's remarkable Anglo-French network of fellow illuminists of various hues included the Swedenborgian attendees of the gatherings at the home of Jacob Duché, in Lambeth, and the Philalèthes, in Paris. The Seven Brothers in Avignon would have been aware that by enlisting Bousie as a fellow *illuminé* of their ambitious society, they would be able to tap into an invaluable reservoir of potential support.

As with Paul, it is not known exactly when Bousie was initiated into the Avignon Society.[103] It is apparent that by December 1788 when Grabianka wrote to Bousie, he was already a well-established member of the society. Furthermore, the content of the letter reveals that he had been entrusted with overseeing the dissemination of important messages from the Seven Brothers to brothers and sisters in Paris, London, and elsewhere. The instructions Grabianka conveyed to Bousie, as well as the numerous requests to pass on greetings to brothers and sisters, provides a fascinating insight into the expansion of the society and Bousie's pivotal role in this.

Grabianka begins his important and lengthy letter by clearly establishing that it is intended for William Bousie, whom he calls "dear brother," and for "the brothers Bousie, your son, and Maglasan, your friend, as well as for all our brothers and sisters in J[esus] C[hrist] our Lord, who are in Paris and in London." Thus the letter is effectively divided into five parts, and only the first directly concerns the recipient. In this, the shortest section, Grabianka mildly rebukes Bousie for seeking to consult heaven about whether he should travel first to Bordeaux or to London. The second and third parts of the letter are devoted to Bousie's son, Robert, and the elder Bousie's friend and fellow wine merchant and business partner, Alexander Mackglashan, who were both already initiates of the society. As with Bousie senior, both sought advice from the society's oracle vis-à-vis their plans to return to Jamaica and Scotland, respectively.[104]

Interestingly, Robert Bousie enjoyed success in Jamaica between 1784 and 1786. In April 1784 he was awarded a patent for refining and making muscovado sugar from cane juice and was granted the sum of £1000 by the Assembly of Jamaica to implement his plan.[105] Yet in 1788 Grabianka provided him with the following guidance: "Can you still have the idea to return after what was said to you from Heaven: 'When the moment is near, is it the time to form projects and to follow blind fortune at random?'" He was telling Robert in no uncertain terms to stay with his parents because the advent of the New Jerusalem was near and he needed to forget about worldly schemes.[106]

Turning to Mackglashan, who wished to know whether he should return to Scotland to be with his parents, Grabianka relayed a positive answer from the oracle, albeit one laden with millenarian fervour: "Say and repeat: inform them of the arrival of the new reign of the Lord, which comes nowadays; teach them that the impious, the unbelieving will be exterminated by fire, by water, by civil and external wars, by famine, by plague, by earthquakes." It is not known whether Mackglashan heeded this advice, but he did continue to reside in Paris into the mid-1790s. Indeed, his name appears on Saint-Martin's list of the friends he mixed with after returning to the French capital in 1794.[107] Thus we learn from the first half of Grabianka's letter that Bousie had succeeded in attracting a family member and a fellow British wine merchant into the Avignon Society by 1788.[108]

After conveying lengthy oracular responses to the prior questions of R. Bousie and Mackglashan, Grabianka begins to address "all our brothers and sisters who are in Paris and London." In respect of London, Grabianka conveys his wish that F[rère] Chastanier be "in charge of communicating copies of the present [circular] to those who wish to read it."[109] On the one hand, it is relatively unsurprising to note the crucial role Chastanier played at this time as a brother of the Avignon Society in London. After all, he and Bousie had been pivotal in introducing Grabianka to Best and to the theosophical milieu in the capital. On the other hand, by 1795 Chastanier was branding the Avignon Society the "anti-type" of the New Church; and its members, "lying prophets."

The basis of Chastanier's dramatic disavowal of the Avignon Society lies in the content of the letter Grabianka asked him to distribute in December 1788. In this dispatch, the Seven Brothers in Avignon for the first time revealed their open hostility towards Swedenborgian doctrine and their espousal of Marianism. This appalled Chastanier and led him to sever all ties with the Avignon Society by the close of 1789. In a separate cover note to the letter, not meant to be read by Chastanier, Grabianka assures Bousie that the brothers "love" Chastanier and "will always love him, as he must be among the fortunate." However, this praise is tempered by the next line, which warns Bousie that he must "watch over" Chastanier's spirit "as it can infect the pure intentions of his right and good heart."[110] Here we detect a hint of tension between the seven in Avignon and Chastanier, their principal representative in London.

Writing in 1795, some five years after publicly professing to be "one of the strictest followers of these [New Church] doctrines of immortal truth," Chastanier reveals that his breech with the Avignon Society stemmed from their accusations against Swedenborg: "Grabianca . . . tried to persuade me, that this faithful Servant of the Living God [i.e. Swedenborg] was in reality no faithful servant at all, having intermixed his own apprehension of things, with what the spirit had revealed to him."[111] Chastanier notes that "at first . . . I could not . . . believe this grievous accusation," though he adds, "I did not positively deny the possibility of his having committed some errors." Thus after receiving Grabianka's letter of December 1788, informing him of the society's disavowal of Swedenborg, Chastanier replied, "wishing to know in what respect, and where those errors laid." According to Chastanier, he received only "vague and evasive" responses, and still worse, his "spirit was accused of versatility, and I was recommended to repent of faults that were not at all manifest to me." Still, even after being subjected to what he felt was harsh criticism, Chastanier did not break with the Avignon Society, owing to the "good opinion" he entertained of Grabianka. Indeed, he held Grabianka in such high esteem that he had made the Pole to "believe he might be right and Swedenborg might really not be, in all respects, the man intended to form the true establishment of the Lord's true Christian Church, and the Avignon society might still . . . be the very society appointed by the Lord for that purpose." The final straw for Chastanier was the society's "openly enjoining at last the Worship of the Virgin Mary as well as a subaltern Worship of the Angels Raphael, Gabriel, Michael and others."[112]

Who in England belonged to the Avignon Society and was therefore meant to receive a copy of this highly contentious letter, which had been conveyed via Bousie in Paris and then Chastanier in London? Grabianka does not list all members who should receive it, but he does ask Bousie "to embrace in writing . . . all the family of F[rère] Duché. The brother mentioned here is Thomas Spence Duché (1763–1790), the son of Jacob. In his denunciation of the Avignon Society, in 1795, Chastanier noted that Grabianka had given an account of the formation of the society "to several others in this Metropolis, particularly to young Mr. Duché." In other words, Duché had received a copy of the letter despatched to London by the Seven Brothers in early 1787. Duché spent the summer of 1788 in France, mainly to try to restore his failing health. On August 6, 1788, Duché's mother, Elizabeth, wrote to his maternal grandmother in the United States about the people her son had met in France: "In almost all the places our son has passed through, there are religious Societies." Among these societies, the "Avignon Society have been united to the London Society for this some time past."[113]

Besides Duché, Grabianka also mentions having written to "F[rère] Bryan." This unquestionably refers to William Bryan, but is somewhat puzzling because the date precedes the Englishman's stay in Avignon, alongside the Yorkshireman John Wright, a carpenter, between January and August 1789. Chastanier's polemic against the Avignon Society is illuminating in this regard; he describes having to translate and copy a letter the Seven Brothers sent to Bryan from Avignon on April 16, 1788.[114] His aim in highlighting this letter was to pour scorn upon the Seven Brothers' claims to be divinely inspired, as they had been collectively unable to read the English text of Bryan's query. The date of the letter in question is crucial, as it tallies with a query they had received from Bryan only two days earlier. In this question, Bryan "begs thou will tell him if the dislike he feels to join exteriorily with any, in their forms of worship, is from HEAVEN or not?"[115] Significantly, he uses his three-digit number (147), which confirms that he was *already* a member of the society. The most probable explanation for Bryan's being admitted to the society prior to his journey to Avignon is that Chastanier had been authorised to act as a *sacrificateur* in London.

The only other London-based brother who is explicitly named by Grabianka in the letter is Barthélémon.[116] Grabianka's mention of Barthélémon is intriguing because he states that the Seven Brothers had already written to him apropos a certain Grosjean. "No, no, we are not afraid of the evil spirits of Grosjean, and we must declare this truth: let her be seduced by hell, and we declare a warning to everyone who follows her principles and counsel." This warning was based on a message, supposedly received from heaven, that pronounced that "the Lord says to Grosjean that she has been seduced by the infernal."

Grabianka then explains that a Parisian member of the society, who is "a docile infant of faith and trust," will be able to explain the meaning of the advice they had received from Heaven.[117]

Who was this Grosjean who so alarmed Barthélémon and earned the ire of the Seven Brothers in Avignon? She does not appear to have been the subject of any scholarly attention, her mark no doubt blurred by the myriad visionaries plying their trade in Paris at the time. However, in his reminiscences, Saint-Martin recalls that he very nearly did not travel to Strasbourg in 1788 because a certain "Mlle Labourot made me hope for the knowledge of the famous Grosjean."[118] Moreover, Grosjean was also included among the regular guests of the Duchess de Bourbon (alongside Suzette Labrousse, Saint-Martin, Dom Gerle, and the Marquis de Thomé) at her home in Petit-Bourg, which had been a hub of illuminist activity.[119]

The dire warning pronounced against Grosjean in 1788 was, it seems, subsequently ignored by at least some members of the Avignon Society in Paris. On March 5, 1791, for example, L.-M. Gombault wrote to Corberon and recollected that "it is more than a year since Grosjean told me that Mr. de Juignié will not come back, and that the Bi[shop] of Babylon would be named in his place, half of the prophecy has already been verified."[120] This note was written shortly after Archbishop de Juignié left Paris and before the appointment by the French government of J.-B.-J Gobel later the same month. The content of this note aroused the interest of the revolutionary authorities in 1794, when Gombault was arrested and his correspondence seized. In response to being directly asked what he knew about this Grosjean, Gombault answered that she was a cook presently living in the home of Corberon.[121]

After addressing members in London, Grabianka turns his attention to brethren living in Strasbourg, Regensburg, and other, non-disclosed locations. First and foremost, Grabianka asks Bousie to transmit a copy of the letter to F[rère] Tieman in Strasbourg and to "tell him that we cherish him sincerely and cordially: for he must also be among the happy ones because he has the love of good and the veritable zeal of truth."[122] In February 1789 Tieman again journeyed to Avignon and spent six days in the company of the *illuminés*. During this visit, he acted as an interpreter for the Englishmen Bryan and Wright, and he was charged with conveying "some particulars" to the pair.[123] However, despite his closeness to the society and, indeed, sincere desire to be initiated, it seems that Tieman was never fully consecrated. In December 1789, L.-M.-F. de la Forest Divonne (1765–1838) arrived in Avignon to be consecrated. From Avignon, he wrote to C. D. von Meyer, a mutual friend of his and Tieman's, and provided an explanation of why their friend had had to wait so long to be initiated into the society:

My friend T[ieman] has long been called to be among the chosen ones to whom Heaven deigns to grant particular graces, that the F[rères] of A[vignon] are persuaded of it, that they ardently desire that the time when he is to be initiated will soon arrive, that they are afflicted of the delay that has been ordered on this in this respect, but they are not masters to accelerate it.[124]

This disclosure suggests that it was possible to be recognised as a fellow "brother" or "sister" in "Jesus Christ," who had been "called to be among the chosen ones," but that the Seven Brothers were powerless to grant full consecration without the permission of Heaven, conveyed in oracular form. As we will discuss, individuals with this lower status could still participate in some of the ceremonials and social events of the society, but they were excluded from the most significant rites.

Besides Tieman, Bousie is asked to pass on greetings to Baron Seiffert and M.-A. Bouët, Comte de Martange, who were both aide-de-camps to Prince Franz Xavier of Saxony.[125] A request to "embrace the dear F[rère] Parraud can also be found in the letter at this point. Parraud was one of the early recipients of a letter announcing the Avignon Society in 1787, as mentioned, but little else is known about his life apart from his work as a translator. Furthermore, a copy of the circular was to be sent to C.-M., Chevalier de Roqueville in Regensburg, who served as the Resident Minister to the Bishopric of Liège at the Imperial Diet.[126] We know nothing more about the role of these individuals in the Avignon Society, but their involvement in 1788 points to the extent to which the recruitment drive begun in 1787 was having some success in attracting interest from across Western Europe.

Lastly, Grabianka asks Bousie to embrace "all the F[rères] and S[oeurs] in Paris. Only a few Parisian members are marked out for special mention: Chevalier John Macgregor, a certain Bellery, and the aforementioned Thomé and Corberon and "the dear S[oeur], his wife."[127] Macgregor left his native Scotland after the Jacobite uprising of 1745 and entered French military service. The Scottish journalist James Anderson recalled meeting Macgregor and Mackglashan in Paris, in 1786.[128] Thus, Macgregor formed part of a small Anglo-Scottish clique (with Bousie) in Paris within the wider circle of Avignon *illuminés* in the city. Little is known about Bellery, but he may well have been a professor of mathematics and a hydraulic engineer at the time.[129] It is not surprising that Corberon and his wife were *illuminés* by 1788, given his rapturous account of meeting Grabianka in February 1787.

Corberon's membership of the Avignon Society predates May 1788, when he wrote a twenty-page letter to Grabianka from Paris. The letter begins reverentially, with Corberon greeting Grabianka as his "most dignified, most dear and most respectable brother." What ensues is a semi-confessional account of Corberon's association with J.-B. Ruer, who saw himself as the last descendant of David, who would rule as king in the imminent New Jerusalem. Ruer was not simply a supposed prophet, but also projected himself as an alchemical and hermetic adept. The society of adepts that gathered around Ruer from late 1784 included Corberon and his wife, as well as Bousie, Thomé, and Seiffert. One other key member of this society mentioned by Corberon was François Picot, a baker residing in Saint-Maur, who is said to have been cured of possession by Ruer.

Corberon provides little biographical information regarding "the honest Picot." However, a manuscript, housed at Harvard University, suggests that Picot and his wife, Marie-Elisabeth Colas, played an active and enthusiastic role in the Ruer circle in the mid-1780s. The document, entitled *Epitome des merveille de la nature et de la philosophe hermetique*, dates from 1784–1785, and contains four lengthy sections.[130] The second part of the manuscript, "Le livre des adeptes ou les adeptis . . . resident à St.-Maur de l'année 1785," indicates the importance of Picot and Colas within the alchemical-hermetic circles of Paris .[131]

By May 1788 Ruer's acolytes—Corberon, Bousie, Thomé, and Picot—had largely severed ties with their former leader. However, Corberon's lengthy history of their association with Ruer was penned in order to ask Grabianka's advice as to whether to cut all links. Bousie thought Corberon should never set foot in Ruer's house again, and Picot came to regret all the money he had squandered in support of the supposed prophet and adept. Only Thomé recommended that Corberon should maintain partial contact. In July 1788 Grabianka replied and instructed Corberon not to break from Ruer. Grabianka's apparent magnanimity was most likely based on a sense of self-assurance and confidence in the trajectory his society was on, in contrast to the waning fortunes of Ruer. By this time Bousie, Thomé, and Corberon cherished their membership in the Avignon Society. What is more, Picot and Colas were soon initiated into the same group, and by the end of 1789 were in Avignon.[132]

A fascinating insight into the key role Bousie played in effectively directing the Parisian branch of the Avignon Society is provided by the travel journal of Reuterholm.[133] The Swedish nobleman arrived in Paris in the autumn of 1789, accompanied by C. G. Silfverhielm (1759–1808), the nephew of Swedenborg.[134] Both Reuterholm and Silfverhielm were immersed in a variety of esoteric pursuits in Sweden—alchemy, animal magnetism, cabala—and were prominent high-degree Freemasons and members of the Exegetic and Philanthropic Society.[135] It is therefore unsurprising that they quickly fell into Bousie's company. Reuterholm describes his first visit to Bousie's home, which took place on October 9, 1789, in glowing terms, lauding Bousie as "an honest Englishman . . . who received us in the most-friendly manner." Moreover, Reuterholm noted, "his honest and sincere approach, as well as that of his good wife and modest children" ensured that the day he spent in their household was the most pleasurable he had experienced in Paris.[136] Significantly, it was the very next morning that Reuterholm wrote a letter to the Seven Brothers in Avignon in which he beseeched them to allow himself and Silfverhielm to be consecrated into the society and to be able to share in the "sublime knowledge" that the "Most Merciful Father" has allowed in "your sanctuary." It would seem Reuterholm and Silfverhielm were aware of the society's turn against Swedenborg, because they professed (rather misleadingly) to be neither adherents to their countryman's doctrine nor members of the Exegetic and Philanthropic Society.[137] After penning this petition Reuterholm, went to dine with "the good-natured Bousie," where the two consulted "several curious mystical collections."[138]

Reuterholm returned to dine at Bousie's home on October 18. On this occasion the Swede did not sample a scene of domestic bliss, but instead participated "in a gathering of all of this sect, members or at least admirers of the society in Avignon." Among those in attendance was a certain Mr. Davidson, who has "constant visions," and is someone "who fights with the devil." Reuterholm's interest was particularly piqued by a Madame de Borde, whom he describes as being "inspired" and who said "curious things" at the dinner table "after crossing herself and making a bunch of sigils." She predicted to Reuterholm that he would be "an Apostle and High Priest, among other things, for the enlightenment of my duke, my country and the world." According to Reuterholm, the voluble prophetess was "the oracle for the whole of this sect." It seems that Reuterholm was initially impressed by Madame de Borde; he and Bousie went to visit her the following day and "heard many peculiar things."[139]

The Swedish barons had to wait until November 8 to receive a reply from Grabianka, who informed them that the Seven Brothers had obtained permission from heaven to consecrate them into the society in Avignon. Grabianka then proclaimed that they were on the threshold of "great knowledge of the New Reign of the Lord, of his new Church and his New people." Indeed, they were "already daily in our prayers." The Polish nobleman added that "you have already been instructed about our society by our brothers who are in Paris."[140] In other words, Bousie, principally, had been readying them for full initiation. It is apparent from Reuterholm's journal that the Swedes had also been schooled by Gombault, "one of the Avignonnaise." On October 21, for example, Reuterholm noted that he and Bousie had dined at the home of Gombault, and that they had "only talked about mystical matters."[141] For the next four weeks, until their departure for Avignon, the Swedish noblemen met Bousie and Gombault on at least eight occasions.[142]

After spending a week on the road, Reuterholm and Silfverhielm arrived in Avignon, on November 24, 1789, where they would stay until December 20. Reuterholm's record of his twenty-six days in Avignon provides us with an insightful account of not only his own consecration, but also the everyday routines and rituals followed by key members of the society. Moreover, the Swede's journal records a particularly active period in the society's existence, when it was, arguably, at the pinnacle of its renown.

However, prior to examining this period we will focus our attention on a year earlier, when the Seven Brothers were graced with the presence of Friederike, the Duchess of Württemberg (1736–1798). She had been accompanied from her family home at Montbéliard by S. I. Pleshcheev (1752–1802), a Russian naval captain at the time and close confidante of Grand Duke Paul Petrovich, who was her son-in-law, and two of her sons.[143] This visit was of particular interest to the Russian authorities in 1807, when Grabianka was arrested in St. Petersburg (see chapter 6). They compiled an invaluable source of material relating to a crucial period in the society's history—namely, Cappelli's year-long residence in Avignon.

Pleshcheev's arrival in Avignon at the beginning of November 1788 marked the culmination of a meandering pilgrimage to meet the foremost figures of illuminism in

France and Switzerland. A Freemason since 1776, Pleshcheev, like many of the Russian nobility at the time, was profoundly drawn to Western esotericism and mystical forms of Christianity.[144] This explains the itinerary for his Grand Tour in 1788, which included a meeting in Lyon with Willermoz, who was the foremost exponent of high-degree Freemasonry in France. In Strasbourg he met with Saint-Martin and, significantly, with Tieman, who had settled in the city after completing his Grand Tour with B. A. Golitsyn. If Pleshcheev had previously been unaware of the Avignon Society, Tieman, an old acquaintance, could have aroused his interest in this singular group. However, before heading to the Midi, Pleshcheev visited Paris, where he, among others, met the Duke de Croÿ d'Havré, a leading Freemason. Pleshcheev then travelled to Zurich, where he paid homage to Lavater, the pre-eminent physiognomist of his era. Thereafter he made his way over the Alps to the Château de Montbéliard, the ducal residence of a branch of the House of Württemberg, arriving on September 4, 1788.[145] By this time the duchess was well-known for hosting notable illuminists, such as Saint-Martin and R. A. Koshelev.[146]

The duchess and Pleshcheev arrived in Avignon two months later. On November 4, 1788, the Seven Brothers enquired to the "S[aint] A[nge] G[abriel]" as to whether the Russian was to be "called to the holy union." The following day the Duchess of Württemberg consulted the Holy Angel Gabriel vis-à-vis how to behave towards one of her good friends who lacked piety. The Russian authorities also noted down four questions Pleshcheev posed to Gabriel between November 6 and 20. The first question concerned whether he should marry the widow of his cousin. The two next questions related directly to his close ties with Grand Duke Paul and Grand Duchess Mariia Fyodorovna (see chapter 6), and in his final enquiry he desired to know whether the visions of a certain Buneman "originate from a natural effect or if they are inspired by Heaven?"[147]

Pleshcheev's queries provide documentary evidence of a change in the manner of consulting the society's oracle, which points to Cappelli's influence. No longer were members addressing the Sainte Parole and receiving answers via what Brumore referred to as "sublime operations"—that is, via a complex form of arithmancy using a ninefold base.[148] Instead, Cappelli acted as a mediator between initiates and the archangels, and the answers they received came directly from the Italian's mouth. In reply to the Duchess of Württemberg, for example, Cappelli, in the guise of Gabriel, told her to "speak to her heart through friendship, speak to her eyes by your example." However, if her friend's behaviour remained unchanged, God would apparently "satisfy" his "justice by unveiling to all eyes the falseness of her conduct and the penchants of her misinformed heart."[149]

The answers received by Pleshcheev were similarly hopeful at times, but this was counterposed with strident denunciations against Russia and menacing threats if he failed to heed the advice. In reply to the question of whether he should marry the widow of his cousin, Pleshcheev was informed that "your nation . . . has scorned my paths . . . But the Lord, to cleanse his wound, will soon shed the blood of the proud, the deceitful, and the ungodly without exposing the blood of his chosen ones." The Russian was then commanded to cease being "an accomplice to their iniquity, abjure your conduct, unite your fate to that which you desire." The answer by Cappelli has the flimsiest connection to the original question; instead he launches a thinly veiled attack on Pleshcheev's homeland and his Orthodox faith. As with Cappelli's direct attack on Pernety in 1787, here we see how he exerted pressure on the heterogenous and ecumenical elements within the society. A similar message depicting how a vengeful God will lay waste to Pleshcheev's homeland is presented in reply to the question about the visions of Buneman: "Tell the one who consults me . . . soon I will strike down the house of the impious and I will shake it to its foundations. I will curse her sceptre and her empire."[150]

These terrifying prophecies, filled with millenarian foreboding, were not directed at the Russian Empire alone. In 1789, John Wright, who spent eight months in Avignon, noted down the prophecies that had been revealed to the society by Cappelli, which contained dire warnings against many realms and their rulers: "The earth will be overflowed with blood, you will hear of the deaths of several sovereigns. They give themselves up to luxury, they live in pleasures, but at last one of them will fall and make an unhappy end . . . The ways are preparing, the revolutions are coming on."[151] The ferocity of Cappelli's prophecies, whether or not he believed them himself, was aimed at a select audience who were expectantly awaiting the onset of the promised new reign of Christ on earth. By replying to questions that touched on mundane, earthly matters in such a dramatic way, Cappelli effectively sustained the tense eschatological dynamic within the society, which fascinated members and prospective initiates alike.

The opportunity to receive divine counsel via Gabriel (and Cappelli) was far from the only contact with angels initiates could expect. Indeed, angels permeated the world of the *illuminés* in Avignon in a variety of ways. At his consecration in 1785, for example, Richardière was given his own guardian angel, named Ajadoth, who was principally envisaged as a "faithful servant" in the new initiate's alchemical labours.[152] This emulated the role assigned to Pernety's guardian angel, Assadaï, in 1779, who was charged, in the main, with watching over and aiding his alchemical work.[153]

Yet, in Avignon guardian angels were far from confined to the crucible. In their ability to assist humans in the operation of divine grace, they fulfilled a role that was in accord with conventional Catholic belief (and even veneration). Guardian-angel devotion was particularly strong among Jesuits in the seventeenth and eighteenth centuries.[154] Moreover, a cult of guardian angels, especially Raphael and Michael, developed in the Italian peninsula in the early modern period.[155]

It would seem that the *illuminés* often saw guardian angels during their travels or at sacred sites. An entry for November 25, 1786, in a blue notebook confiscated from Grabianka by the Russian authorities in 1807, for example, recorded how a guardian angel instructed an *illuminé* about which path to take at night when they were on the road. An entry in the same notebook for September 14, 1788, records that an *illuminé*, presumably Richardière, recognised the angel Ajadoth in the guise of a hunter when they met.[156] Thalès Bernard also cites an anecdote involving Grabianka. The Pole had apparently just celebrated Mass when a shepherd in dark-coloured clothes entered the place of worship and walked up to the pulpit. From there, he addressed the congregation and spoke of "new trials reserved for the righteous." By the intense way the shepherd looked at Grabianka, the latter concluded that it was none other than his guardian angel.[157]

The *illuminés* in Avignon also seem to have on several occasions observed angels in human guise atop the "holy mount" where consecrations took place. An entry in the blue notebook for November 20, 1786, for example, records that Gabriel affirmed that a boy seen on the "holy mount" at the spot where initiations took place was indeed an angel. Four days later the oracle also confirmed that a hunter seen in the same place was an angel.[158] A more in-depth description, but of a similar ilk, was given by Wright on his return to England. During his time in Avignon, in 1789, he recalled a "particular circumstance" after "all the Brethren received an order from the HOLY WORD to go unto a small mountain a little distance from the city on a *religious duty*." When they were in sight of their destination, they saw "a *man as we thought* sitting under a tree . . . who was apparently eating bread." The brethren asked who he was, and he replied that he was "a traveller that had come out of ITALY to see his relations at *Avignon* who were all poor." Hence, the *illuminés* gave him some money and left him alone. This straightforward explanation was inadequate for one of the *illuminés*, who had "some thoughts that he was something more than MAN" and thus "enquired at the *word* of the LORD, and the answer *was*, that it was the ARCHANGEL RAPHAEL."[159]

One of the early leaders of the New Church in London also recalled being told by Bryan and Wright about their interactions with angels. As told by Hindmarsh, the initiates in Avignon would "at certain seasons" assemble "at the top of a mountain, where an angel met and conversed with them." On one occasion this angel even presented the assembled initiates "with a glass phial (cork and all) filled with a red liquid, which he told them was the dew of heaven, and which, if carried in their bosoms, would be a continual protection to them against enemies, and would moreover enable them at all times to perform miracles."[160] Neither Bryan nor Wright write about this event in their published accounts, but the details described by Hindmarsh are consistent with both the manner and place in which the *illuminés* supposedly most often came into contact with angels.

The everyday presence of angels in the lives of the *illuminés* in Avignon was such that they often sensed their presence at their daily communal dinner. According to Wright, "very often when we have been sitting together, the furniture in the room has been shook, a[s] though it was all coming to pieces." When Wright and Bryan enquired as to the cause of these disturbances, they were told that they "announced the presence of angels" rather than a malevolent poltergeist. Indeed, the *illuminés* were apparently more anxious when they did not hear the furniture-moving angels as they thought "something was amiss, and so enquired at the *word* of the LORD."[161]

Encounters with angels, whether they appeared as personal guides in a church or laboratory or as agents of the divine atop mountains, do not go against Roman Catholic dogma. Indeed, in October 2018 Pope Francis delivered a sermon on the day of the Memorial of the Guardian Angels in which he praised their role as "protectors God places by our side."[162] However, the relationship between the *illuminés* in Avignon and angelic entities went beyond humans being mere receivers of benevolent aid and advice. This is made clear in the description of Pleshcheev's consecration, which took place over nine days, between November 11 and 19, 1788. The nine-day ritual was in conscious imitation of the Christian tradition of the novena in which devotional prayers were repeated every day over the duration of this time. The final rite, on the ninth day of his consecration, involved his being left alone at the initiation site "in order to summon his Guardian Angel."[163] In other words, it was the culminating act of a lengthy theurgical ritual, whereby the candidate was not merely initiated, but (in this case) was also able to invoke his own angelic entity. To be sure, from the late twelfth century, when the *Ars Notoria* first appeared in northern Italy, Christian theurgy was advocated by some as a legitimate form of angel magic. Apologists could cite pseudo-Dionysius' approval of divine operations that sought to invoke angelic entities. On the other hand, Augustine proved to be extremely influential in denouncing theurgy as an illicit art, akin to sorcery, in which "both classes are the slaves of the deceitful rites of the demons they invoke under the names of angels." Augustine differentiated these from Old Testament miracles, by the likes of Moses, which are acts performed by "simple faith and godly confidence."[164]

In contrast, theurgical rites involved a variety of complex and time-consuming operations that needed to be performed in a meticulous and prescribed sequence. This is typified by *The Key of Solomon*, one of the most famous grimoires, which first appeared in Italy in the around the fourteenth or fifteenth century. Herein one finds instructions on a variety of necessary factors, including specific prayers and conjurations; the optimal time of the day to perform the ceremonials; the use of incense, perfumes, water, and fire; and the need to trace circles in which to perform the theurgical operations.[165] As we will see, all of these aspects of *The Key of Solomon* were employed in the consecration of Pleshcheev.

In 1807, the Russian authorities found two manuscripts copies of *The Key of Solomon* among Grabianka's papers, which they described as being written with great thoroughness. They also found two notebooks devoted to summoning spirits. Furthermore, the authorities noted a question posed to the oracle, on November 3, 1787, about "whether or not to burn *The Key of Solomon*?" The response was unambiguous: on the contrary, it was necessary to "cherish this gift" as it will lead "many to the path of salvation."[166] In addition to consulting early modern texts, the *illuminés* could draw on recent precedent, and it seems highly likely they were influenced by the three-day theurgical rite devised by Martinez de Pasqually in 1768 for the *Ordre des Élus Coëns*.[167]

The description provided by the Russian authorities of Pleshcheev's consecration in November 1788 concurs with the two other (less detailed) accounts at our disposal: Reuterholm's journal entries between December 1 and 9, 1789, and a brief summary of the initiation rite Ferrier provided to Cappelli in a letter from January 9, 1790.[168] In combination they provide invaluable details of what transpired at the consecration ceremonies at this time. The only documentary evidence regarding the consecration rituals practised in Avignon prior to these descriptions can be found in the manuscript of the Holy Word stored in the Médiathèque Ceccano in Avignon.[169] Herein can be found cursory references to an "altar of mysteries" and a "circle of stones" and that the nine-day ceremony began at 5 o'clock in the evening, but little else of note.[170]

The Pleshcheev account describes his leaving Avignon at 2:30 in the afternoon, accompanied by Pernety, Grabianka, and Delhomme.[171] The destination was a hill outside the city. Reuterholm provides more detail here, as he describes leaving through La Porte de Saint Michel and thereafter following the Rhône for a "good while, after which we turned to the left into the forest upon a hill."[172] It is therefore likely that their ceremonies atop the hill also began at 5 p.m. Two circles of power (*rondes de Puissance*) were described prior to the commencement of the ceremony.[173] According to Ferrier, these circles were described by turning from the east, with the number nine—a further reminder of the significance of the devotional novena—being written in the four parts of the outer sphere.[174] The number of the candidate—the last of the three-digit numbers assigned to every initiate; three in the case of Pleshcheev (973)—was then written on the inner circle.

The beginning of the ceremony involved Pleshcheev reciting a prayer of consecration and then Psalm 30, before kissing his number in the three places it had been inscribed around the inner circle.[175] Next, Pleshcheev had to walk around the outer circle nine times from right to left and nine times from left to right whilst reciting the so-called Achabes incantation.[176] An almost identical rite, including the recital of the Achabes incantation, is described by Ferrier, although the sequence of walking round the two circles is reversed. During the uttering of this very esoteric incantation, a fire in the inner circle was lit by an attendant, who read Psalm 51 at the same time. It was most likely Delhomme who did this, taking on the role of deacon in imitation of the Liturgy of Preparation (*Proskomidiia*). In Russian Orthodoxy, Psalm 51 is recited whilst the deacon censures the altar and the entire church surroundings at the conclusion of the preparation for the Eucharist.[177] The name of Jevovah was then mixed with Pleshcheev's name, and then the candidate was instructed to throw the incense (consisting of frankincense, myrrh, and aloe) into the fire in his circle of power, whilst the Patriarch (Pernety) recited the universal prayer (used in Catholicism to conclude the liturgy of the word). In the final part of the rite, Pleshcheev had to walk around his circle three times from right to left and three times from left to right, before writing his number, 973, nine times inside his sphere. Lastly, he stood in the middle of his circle and once again recited the Achabes incantation whilst throwing the ash that had gathered inside his space to the "four winds," thereby banishing hell from himself.

Pleshcheev then returned to the hill for seven consecutive days and had to repeat his prayer of initiation.[178] On the ninth day Pleshcheev had to walk around his outer circle nine times whilst reading the Achabes incantation. Psalm 30 was also recited, along with several other prayers. The candidate then went to his inner circle and walked around it three times, still reciting the Achabes incantation. During the final circuit, Pernety entered Pleshcheev's circle of power, poured some spring water and then sprinkled it on the candidate's heart, lower back, and head, and then left. It was at that point that Pleshcheev was able to summon his guardian angel. Thereafter, the *illuminés* descended from the hill and gathered in the chapel of Notre-Dame des Sept-Douleurs. At the time, one chapel with this name existed in Avignon, which formed part of an Observantins monastery.[179]

The account of Pleshcheev's consecration provides no insight into how the Russian nobleman felt during or after the ceremony. Reuterholm, however, did write down his thoughts about being consecrated in December 1789. After the first day of his initiation, he wrote that he had entered into "the most holy of all covenants with the Most High. May God grant me the grace to never forget my promises!!!" He added that it had been "one of the strangest days of my life" in which "the hand of providence led me all the way from the North to the border of the Alps and the foot of the Rhône, in order to make the last covenant with Him, and to find a part of the globe that had been prepared, sanctified and consecrated for me for time and eternity. On completion of his consecration on December 9, Reuterholm was ecstatic at what he had just experienced: "May the Supreme be praised eternally!!! . . . all this is deeply ingrained in my heart for time and eternity."[180]

Reuterholm's spiritual rapture was matched by Divonne's, who concluded his consecration on December 19, 1789. The pair, whose time in Avignon overlapped, became close friends, based partly on being able to share a similar sense of exultation at completing their consecrations at roughly the same time. In a letter to C. D. von Meyer, written shortly after completing his initiation, Divonne wrote: "Yes, I have found the truth and happiness, I have touched with my finger, the veil has been lifted from my eyes, and I have recognised that our mind alone is the cause of the darkness and doubts that surround us; I render grace to God for having taken pity on me and for calling me." Such was Divonne's spiritual joy that he confessed, as a Calvinist, to overcoming his doubts about the society's Marian worship: "It is now that I know the truth regarding the Blessed Virgin . . . I would like to convey to your heart all that I feel for her, I would like to penetrate you with her goodness, her power." Moreover, Divonne was not simply elated about his consecration, as he praised the "brothers of A[vignon]" as "men of God," who were at "this centre of wonders and marvels of the mercy of God."[181]

Reuterholm and Divonne forged a tender bond during their time together in Avignon, in December 1789. We know this because Reuterholm did not merely comment on his consecration, but also kept detailed notes of his daily life in the city. These journal entries, though far less ecstatic than those dedicated to his initiation, are very informative, as they provide us with by far the most comprehensive look into the everyday routines followed by the *illuminés*. What is more, the diary entries were recorded at a time of great activity in the society. The title bestowed upon Silfverhielm—"the North's Representative at this Large and True Convent"—indicates that the Swedish noblemen were part of a grand assembly, or reunion, of *illuminés* and candidates.[182] The renown of the society was arguably at its peak at this time. It is possible that the society benefitted somewhat from the social and political turbulence that began to be felt in Avignon in 1789. The papacy in the city was facing an unprecedented challenge to its authority, and a group of law-abiding religious enthusiasts was the least of its worries.[183] Thus the *illuminés* were able to come out into the open to a degree at the end of 1789. The authorities may have also turned a blind eye because in September 1789 Richardière became a deputy in a newly established militia of city grandees envisaged as a bulwark against the revolutionary forces.[184]

Prior to the Revolution, it seems that the *illuminés* in Avignon fell foul of the authorities on only one occasion. According to an entry in one of the society's notebooks, this occurred at midnight on the night of March 12, 1788, when forty armed grenadiers, eight mounted police, and officials from the municipal government broke down the doors and smashed windows during a search of the home of Richardière, Grabianka, and Françoise Pernety.[185] An entry made on March 18 states that the local officials were made to apologise on this day to Richardière for their conduct. This turn of events was described in the notebook as a miracle, which had come about because of some magical intervention, as well as Grabianka's noble status.[186]

This climbdown is surprising given the history of papal opposition to Freemasonry in Avignon. Lodges in the city were forced to close in 1751 in the wake of a papal bull against the fraternity. Masonic activity was renewed in Avignon in 1774, with Bouge and Leblond playing leading roles. However, the papal authorities soon sought to intimidate the resurgent Freemasons, paying an unannounced visit to Bouge, whose home was searched for three hours by an inquisitor and other officials.[187] Furthermore, in September 1776 the inquisitor-general of Avignon published an edict against Freemasonry. A decade later, in January 1786, the inquisition searched the lodge of Parfaite Union in Avignon, and nine months after that, the bishop of Carpentras issued an ordonnance for a new edition of the papal bull of 1751 against Freemasonry.[188]

We also glean a curious snippet of information regarding this raid: Grabianka, Richardière, and Françoise Pernety were living under the same roof. At the time Grabianka lived in Maison Neuve, on Rue de la Colombe in the Saint-Didier parish of Avignon.[189] Significantly, Richardière, in his deposition for a birth certificate, signed on September 21, 1786, attested that he, too, lived on Rue de la Colombe.[190] It seems Grabianka simply moved in with Richardière when he arrived in Avignon in early 1787. The reasons for the inclusion of Françoise Pernety, the wife of Jacques, among those present in the home are unknown. Whatever the case, this location, more than any other, served as the principal hub of activity for the *illuminés* in Avignon in the late 1780s.[191]

Before we examine Reuterholm's descriptions of his everyday experiences in Avignon, it is worth touching on two other fascinating aspects of the life of the society in 1789. First, the Saint-Didier parish baptismal registers show that the society marked the birth of two children to *illuminé* couples, on November 7 and 9, 1789. The first baptismal ceremony was in honour of the birth of Franciscus-Marinus-Malachias, the son of the above-mentioned Marcus Lemort de Metigny and his wife. The godparents are indicated as Delhomme and Anne-Marie-Olympe de Fumel, an *illuminé* whose name appears in various sources at this time.[192] Two days later Picot and Colas baptised their daughter. She was given the name Marie-Anne-Thadée; the last of these names was in honour of Grabianka. Grabianka and Anne-Claudia Le Maire d'Attigny (b. *c.* 1742) are also recorded as the godparents. Grabianka is listed as "gouverneur de la ville de Live en Pologne." He would have surely felt that Heaven itself wanted him to be godfather to this child—she is recorded as being the 139th birth of the year in the parish.[193]

D'Attigny had recently returned to France from St. Petersburg, where she had worked as a governess.[194] She evidently threw herself enthusiastically into the life of the society. Soon after her arrival in Avignon, she wrote two letters to John Paul Jones, the well-known naval officer, with whom she had become acquainted in St. Petersburg.[195] In his reply, written on February 8, 1790, Jones reveals that d'Attigny had invited him to become an *illuminé* in Avignon. He assured her that "as soon as circumstances permit, I shall feel eager to join the delightful society in which you are."[196] The pair continued to correspond in 1790, and Jones wrote the following on December 27: "Have you not sufficient confidence in my discretion to explain 'the enigma' of the happiness with which you say 'I will be loaded, and which will astonish me so soon as I know it.'"[197] Thus, d'Attigny became a keen proselytiser almost immediately after arriving in Avignon. Her name will feature prominently in the following pages: D'Attigny went on to become the so-called Great Mother of the society in the 1790s and resettled in the Russian capital in 1804, prior to Grabianka's arrival in the city (see chapters 5 and 6).

Second, it is also noteworthy that the departure of Cappelli in early 1789 led to a resumption of consultations with the Holy Word instead of beseeching Archangel Gabriel for advice. With Brumore dead and Cappelli in Rome, Bouge took on the role of "prophet" within the Avignon Society. Thus he was charged with the onerous task of mastering the science of arithmancy using the ninefold key to obtain divine responses. The earliest evidence of Bouge's new role spans the eight-month period (January to August 1789) in which Wright and Bryan were in Avignon. During this time, Wright copied all the questions they asked or that were related to them. Thus we know that Bouge (219) himself asked the Holy Word several questions about whether and when Bryan and Wright should be consecrated. He received something of a reprimand from the Holy Word on April 12 in reply to a query about whether "the three knocks which 1.4.7 [Bryan] heard in the night was ... supernatural." Bouge was told in no uncertain terms to "ask no more questions if thou has none to make of more importance."[198] Tellingly, no more questions in regard to the Englishmen were forthcoming from Bouge.

Wright posed three questions in total (two on April 16, 1789 and one on August 11, 1789). In April he asked whether "the Eternal has accepted of his incense" and "if the Lord approved of his leaving" a certain "society of CARR." His third question, in August, concerned whether he should return to his family.[199] Bryan's three questions concerned whether "his offering on the *mountain* was acceptable," and whether "it was the will of Heaven" that his wife should come to Avignon to be consecrated. Bryan also asked in August whether it was the will of Heaven that he should return to England.[200]

By the close of 1789 the task of being the society's oracle was proving troublesome to Bouge, who was charged with obtaining responses from the Holy Word to a growing volume of enquiries. In a letter to Reuterholm and Silfverhielm, penned on December 27, 1789, when they were en route to Rome, Grabianka sought to explain why they were yet to receive responses from the Holy Word: "The departure of some, the arrival of others ensures that 219 [Bouge] is very occupied. Added to this are various demands occasioned by a thousand circumstances among us." In short, Bouge was a victim of the society's own success, and he was simply not able to keep up with the volume of requests among *illuminés* in Avignon. Furthermore, Grabianka asks the Swedes to bear in mind the large number "of our brothers in different countries who address us for responses, as well as the many foreigners who must also be sure to know the Supreme Will." In case the Swedish noblemen did not grasp the point, Grabianka also informed them that Bouge presently has a stack of thirty urgent requests to answer.[201] Reuterholm and Silfverhielm would have to be patient.

The Swedes had to wait until March before receiving replies to some of their questions. In communicating the answers, Grabianka made sure to cite a general comment by the Holy Word: "Heaven did not want to answer the rest of your requests. The idea comes to me that, if you consider it appropriate, you can ask your other demands to St. Vieillard by way of 111 [Cappelli]."[202] If the Holy Word could not cope with the volume of questions posed by the Swedish noblemen (and others), it is hardly surprising that Bouge was also languishing under the weight of expectant enquiries!

Seven of the questions the Holy Word deigned to answer had been posed by Reuterholm; he responded to only one enquiry by Silfverhielm. Of Reuterholm's questions, three concern matters affecting his friends. He asks the Holy Word, for example, what he can do to reunite a married couple to whom he was deeply attached.[203] He also begged the Holy Word to reveal something that would provide happiness to a friend, as well as to provide some kind of consolation to Baron Carl Bonde.[204] The sixth question concerned whether he should return home to "the Prince" (most likely Duke Karl of Södermanland) "to receive the knowledge that he promised." Lastly, both he and Silfverhielm asked whether it was the will of God that they should remain celibate.[205]

As discussed, the remarkable consecration ceremony undertaken by Reuterholm had a profound effect on him. Yet, during his twenty-six-day stay in Avignon, he also immersed himself in the everyday routines and rituals of the society, which, though less dramatic, offer up a uniquely illuminating insight into the religious and associational culture of the group at the height of its influence. The Swedish travellers arrived in Avignon on Tuesday November 24, 1789. On reaching the city they headed directly to "Rue de la Colombe, Maison Neuve," where they enjoyed a "most heartfelt reception from Count Grabianka, Mr. De la Richardière and several other brothers, who were assembled there." Once again, the inference here is that Grabianka and Richardière both lived at this address.

The following day was impacted somewhat by Grabianka's feeling ill. Reuterholm, however, noted that he had dinner "at the home of brother Delhomme and Abbé Pernetty."

Again, the inference here is that Delhomme and Pernety were living in the same house. Moreover, a short biography of Pernety, written by J. B. Allier in 1838, attests that Pernety also rented a house in Rue de la Colombe after the Pole's arrival in Avignon.[206] Thus, it would seem that the leading lights of the society dwelled very close to each other in the late 1780s. Among the other guests at the home of Pernety and Delhomme were Madame d'Attigny ("a French woman arrived from St. Petersburg"), a certain Baroness Finnely and Deravine, the local Freemason who had been consecrated in November 1788, whom Reuterholm described as a "young polite man." Reuterholm may have been struck by Deravine's cultivated manners, but the overriding impression conveyed by his account is the opposite of a stifling assembly dictated by the rules of etiquette:

> This table was . . . the most remarkable at which I have ever been placed, garnished by people from all nations, brought together by Providence to form an entire family. This was both a new and touching experience for me. The friendship and bonhomie that reigned here cannot be described . . . You must see it yourself in order to believe it in such degenerate times as ours.[207]

In Paris Reuterholm had been particularly moved by the warmth he experienced as a guest in Bousie's home and among his host's family. In Avignon, however, Reuterholm sensed that he was experiencing his first taste of joining a new spiritual family, whose members had been brought together because of their piety. To finally be among such a family was an exhilarating moment for the eminent Swedish nobleman.

At 7 o'clock that evening Reuterholm went to pay his respects to Grabianka, but he did not stay, since only consecrated members of the society were allowed to attend the daily assembly. He records being admitted to this gathering for the first time on December 9, after he had completed his consecration, and that he only returned to his lodgings just before 10 o'clock that night.[208] The symbolism attached to this regular gathering is explained by Wright, who attended for five months after he was consecrated on April 1, 1789: "We met every evening at seven o'clock to commemorate the *death* of our LORD and SAVIOUR JESUS CHRIST, by eating bread and drinking wine."[209]

On November 26 Reuterholm visited Grabianka in the morning and again before the daily assembly at 7 p.m. This day marked the first time Reuterholm took lunch in "the hall."[210] With the exception of the final day of his consecration, when he intentionally remained in his quarters and fasted, Reuterholm thereafter took lunch in the hall every day. The Swede provides no details about the location or appearance of this dining hall. However, Wright describes being taken to a house across the street from where he was first received, where he was "shewn a large room where there was a table spread nearly the whole length." In other words, it is likely that this hall, which seems to have resembled a monastic refectory, was very near Maison Neuve in Rue de la Colombe. Tieman explained to Wright and Bryan that the "table was provided by the LORD, and when we wanted any thing to eat or drink we must come there, where we should find a servant ready to wait upon us."[211]

The first Friday Reuterholm spent in Avignon is the only day on which he did not participate in the society's busy schedule of social events, as he was suffering from a "severe migraine," which he thinks was brought on by the biting northerly wind.[212] The Swede was feeling better by Sunday and was able to attend his first mass at 8 o'clock that morning, which was led by Pernety, who was also assisted by Ferrier and Richardière, with "nearly the whole society" in attendance.[213] On this day Reuterholm merely noted the service was "in a church," but the following Sunday he added that the mass ministered by Pernety was "in *les Benedictins*."[214] Pernety, a former Benedictine monk, must have still been able to procure favours from his former monastic brethren. The location of the Saint Martial Benedictine Monastery-College in Avignon, with its southern edge running along Rue de la Colombe, could not have been more convenient.[215] Thus the Benedictine church used by the society for its weekly mass was only a stone's throw away from the living and dining quarters of its leaders. Reuterholm could therefore attend mass, visit Grabianka (who was still unwell), and take lunch in the hall with Pernety and other brothers, for example, on his first Sunday in Avignon without any inconvenience.[216] Besides the weekly Sunday service, Reuterholm also celebrated an 8 a.m. Mass with the society to mark the Feast of the Immaculate Conception on December 8; an unsurprising addition to their weekly itinerary given their veneration of Mary.[217]

On the morning of November 30, Reuterholm went for a stroll around the city with Grabianka, who was feeling better. After the usual lunch in the hall, he and Grabianka then went to visit "all the sisters," among whom were d'Attigny, de Fumel, Colas and Madame Nicolas.[218] Reuterholm's description of this visit suggests that the female members of the society were housed, or at least socialised, in separate quarters, which would tally with the monastic atmosphere that pervades his journal entries.

Madame Sophie Nicolas (née Rivoire) was the wife of Jean-François Nicolas (1738–1816), a physician from Grenoble and one of the foremost animal magnetisers in France.[219] He was also an *illuminé* and wrote of meeting Reuterholm and Silfverhielm in December 1789.[220] It would be natural that Nicolas and Silfverhielm were drawn to each other in Avignon: both were still enthusiastic proponents of animal magnetism at the time. Moreover, both Paul and Corberon were members of the Society of Harmony in Paris.[221] Yet, the only reference to the *illuminés* pursuing animal magnetism and somnambulism at the time appears in a letter to Chefdebien, written in July 1788. The unknown writer commented that "at least some of these m[essieur]s of Avignon are . . . occupied with Magnetism" and added that "on May 26 one of their somnambulists saw the Turks and Russians in a pitched battle."[222] Reuterholm makes no mention of animal magnetism in his journal. It seems that it did not preoccupy the society collectively in the same way it had previously, for example, in their search for the philosophers' stone up until 1788.

This is not to say that some of the *illuminés*, such as Nicolas, were not actively engaged in such pursuits. In April and June 1788, for example, the physician supposedly succeeded in curing a young woman and a peasant in villages close to Avignon by inducing "crises of Somnambulistic magnetism."[223] It is likely that Nicolas also encouraged Bouge and

Richardière, his medical colleagues and fellow *illuminés*, to indulge in the healing techniques employed by animal magnetists. In 1801 the prefect of Vaucluse reported that Richardière "established a *baquet* of Mesmer with the physician Bouge, his cousin in illumination."[224]

A bizarre and fascinating testament to the continued use of animal magnetist techniques by Nicolas and Bouge can be found in the idiosyncratic work *Les Farfadets* (1821) by A.-V.-C. Berbiguier. In French folklore, *farfadets* were devilish imps, but Berbiguier defined them in a more sinister fashion as "the élite secret agents of the infamous Beelzebub."[225] Berbiguier, after making the fateful decision to consult with Nicolas and Bouge in Avignon regarding his insomnia, came to believe that all doctors were evil. He regarded their Mesmerist cures as satanic, and labelled Nicolas as a "representative of Moloch" and Bouge as a "representative of Pluto!"[226]

Esoteric pursuits in general do not seem to have figured in the society's collective culture at the close of 1789. An important aspect of Reuterholm's stay in Avignon involved the daily instruction he received from Ferrier in his home. This instruction began on December 4, that is, three days after Reuterholm had begun his consecration ceremony, and concluded nine days later, on December 12.[227] It was surely no coincidence that this instruction lasted for nine days. Reuterholm does not, however, disclose what knowledge Ferrier was imparting, although spiritual matters seem most likely. Each session could last for several hours, and the instruction also seems to have formed a necessary part of becoming an *illuminé*. On December 7, for example, Divonne began his own course of instruction a day after arriving in Avignon, and four days before his consecration began.[228]

It is clear from Reuterholm's journal that he and Divonne enjoyed an instant connection. After they both attended Ferrier's instruction on December 7, for example, they then spent the rest of the day together. Thereafter they were practically inseparable. On December 14, for example, they went to their respective circles of power together. Three days later Reuterholm noted that he had gone on a long stroll around Avignon "with his good friend" and then spent the evening with him after the daily assembly. On the eve of his departure, Reuterholm describes how he and Divonne "took tender leave and promised each other eternal friendship. I then wiped away my tears and went home to mind to seek some rest for my distraught senses." Reuterholm met many fellow *illuminés* during his time in Avignon, but only Divonne elicited such warm sentiments from the Swede.[229]

The sense of shared ecstasy enjoyed by Reuterholm and Divonne in December 1789 is testament to the profound impact of the Avignon Society, in a relatively short space of time, on the landscape of European illuminism. The Seven Brothers began to promote their society in February 1787 and soon attracted candidates from across Europe. Those who sought entry into the Avignon Society were drawn to the tantalising mix of ardent millenarianism, strands of esotericism (Cabala and alchemy, in particular) and Swedenborgianism. Moreover, the ceremonial splendour of conventional Catholic liturgical practices was merged with theurgy to create an astonishing nine-day consecration ritual, the likes of which could not be experienced anywhere in Europe.

The rejection of Swedenborgian doctrine, proclaimed within the society in December 1788, led to a permanent break with orthodox adherents of the New Church in London, such as Chastanier. However, this neither led to a mass exodus from the society, nor stymied the tide of prospective candidates. What is more, the society's fervent embrace of Marianism by 1789 did not (immediately) curb the enthusiasm of non-Catholics. This is epitomised by the consecration of Reuterholm, Silfverhielm, and Divonne at the close of 1789. Notwithstanding their Lutheran and Calvinist backgrounds (as well as Silfverhielm being Swedenborg's nephew), they still journeyed to Avignon in order to obtain what they believed was higher illumination.

Judging by Reuterholm's journal and Divonne's correspondence, their time in Avignon fulfilled their hopes and expectations. Reuterholm depicts a confident society that was able to openly go about its business in the centre of Avignon. He also conveys the spirit of communality, akin to a monastic order, that governed the everyday life of the society at this time. We hear nothing of Leblond, but the other six leaders of the society seemingly lived, worshipped, and dined hand in glove. This aura of tranquillity proved fleeting. Indeed, it may well have only been possible to enjoy such open worship because of the gathering storm clouds. Within months Avignon was beset by revolutionary and patriotic upheaval. Moreover, the unity of the society was rent asunder by events in Rome in September 1790, as we discuss in the next chapter.

NOTES

1. "Copie d'une lettre écrite d'Avignon le 12 février 1787," BL, Add. MS. 23,675. Also see Elizabeth Brownbill, *A Short Account of the Personal Appearance of Jesus Christ to Eliz. Brownbill* (Liverpool: R. Ferguson, 1788), 28.

2. Meillassoux-Le Cerf, *Dom Pernety*, 376.

3. See the list of *directeurs des fermes* in *Almanach Royal* (Paris: Le Breton, 1776), 493. Pernety was *directeur des fermes* in Toulon between 1774 and 1775. See *Almanach Royal* (Paris: Le Breton, 1774), 417; *Almanach Royal* (Paris: Le Breton, 1775), 456.

4. In 1766 J.-M. Pernety became one of four general directors of the newly formed Administration Générale des accises et péages (known as the "Régie"), which was staffed by around 250 Frenchmen. Pernety's services were not retained after 1772, when his initial term of six years came to an end.

5. It seems highly unlikely that J.-M. Pernety returned to Berlin between 1779 and 1780 and was initiated into the society at this time. Three entries for "Perneti cadet" are listed in the manuscript of the questions posed to the Holy Word (Oct. 30, 1779; July 10, 1780, and Sept. 25, 1780). However, it seems much more probable that his elder brother asked these questions on his behalf. The manuscript also notes that J.-M. Pernety was consecrated between May 29 and June 16, 1787, which is more plausible. See Meillassoux-Le Cerf, *Dom Pernety*, 438–9.

6. It is not clear why Brumore departed from Avignon at the end of May 1785 and journeyed to Rome. One plausible theory is that he travelled to the Eternal City to meet with Ottavio Cappelli

and to establish the society there. However, no documentary evidence has come to light vis-à-vis any possible relationship between Brumore and Cappelli in Rome.

7. Meillassoux-Le Cerf, *Dom Pernety*, 436.

8. Meillassoux-Le Cerf, *Dom Pernety*, 436.

9. Meillassoux-Le Cerf, *Dom Pernety*, 444–5.

10. Meillassoux-Le Cerf, *Dom Pernety*, 445.

11. MC, MS. 3080. For a reproduction, see Bricaud, *Illuminés*, 105–7.

12. Meillassoux-Le Cerf, *Dom Pernety*, 446.

13. RGIA, Fond 1163, op. 1, d. 16b, 103v.

14. J. L. Caradonna, *The Enlightenment in Practice: Academic Prize Contests and Intellectual Culture in France, 1670–1794* (Ithaca, NY: Cornell University Press, 2012). For discussion of the Sociéte Académique et Patriotique de Valence, see 64, 167, 169, 238, 510.

15. On the society in general, as well as Pernety's role in it, see Henry de Colonjon, "Société académique et patriotique de Valence," *Bulletin de la Société départementale d'archéologie & de Statistique de la Drôme* 1 (1866): 90–9; Léon Amblard, "Jacques de Tardivon: Dernier Abbé de la Congrégation de Saint-Ruf et la Sociéte Académique et Patriotique de Valence," *Bulletin de la Société départementale d'archéologie & de Statistique de la Drôme* 27 (1893): 69–81.

16. On the fashion for medical electricity in the 1780s, see, for example, Geoffrey Sutton, "Electric Medicine and Mesmerism," *Isis* 72 (1981): 375–92.

17. *Allgemeines Literatur-Zeitung* (July, August, and September 1785), 80. Up until 1791 the society in Valence energetically promoted its contest and activities in learned journals in France and beyond. See, for example, *Journal politique: Ou Gazette des gazettes* (Oct. 1786): 64–5; *Journal des Sçavans* (Oct. 1786): 2093; *L'esprit des journaux François et étrangers* 4 (April 1787): 293; *Journal Politique de Bruxelles* (Oct. 1788): 40–1; *Journal Encyclopédique ou Universel* vol. 4, part 2 (1789): 325–30; *Journal Encyclopédique ou Universel* 8 (1791): 105–15.

18. For extracts of the letter sent on Dec.14, 1786, see Comte de Buffon, *Œuvres completes de Buffon*, vol. 11, ed. M. Flourens (Paris: Garnier Frères, 1855), 553–4.

19. See T.-N. de Rozières, "Essai sur cette question: Quelle est l'influence de l'Electricité sur la Germination et la Végétation des Plantes," *Observations sur la physique, sur l'histoire naturelle et sur les arts*, vol. 38 (1791): 351–65, 427–46.

20. L. De Magny, "De Rozières," in *Recueil de Généalogies de maisons nobles de France*, vol. 4 (Paris: Archives de la Noblesse, 1894), 3. Also see Meillassoux-Le Cerf, *Dom Pernety*, annexe 1, 284.

21. See "Tableaux des officiers composant la R. L. de St. Jean sous le titre distinctif de la Sagesse a L'O de Valence et Dauphine pour annee 5783 [1783]," BNdF, FM2 493.

22. See the table of members for Loge La Sagesse for 1774, 1785, 1787, and 1788, BNdF, FM2 493.

23. Colonjon, "Société Académique," 95. Delhomme graduated from the University of Avignon on April 8, 1763. See ADdV, D 99, certificates of study at the University of Avignon. He died in 1807 in Valence and was survived by two daughters. See the listing posted regarding the sale of Delhomme's household effects, *Le Journal de la Drôme* (July 8, 1807), 6.

24. On Freemasonry in Avignon in the second half of the eighteenth century, see Claude Mesliand, "Franc-maçonnerie et religion a Avignon au XVIIIe siècle," *Annales historiques de la revolution française* 41:197 (1969): 447–68; Mesliand, "Renaissance de la franc-maçonnerie avignonnaise a la fin de l'ancien regime (1774–1789), *Bulletin d'histoire économique et sociale de la*

revolution française (1970): 23–82. Also see J.-M. Mercier, *Les francs-maçons du pape: L'art royal à Avignon au XVIIIᵉ siècle* (Paris: Classiques Garnier, 2010).

25. See Thierry Zarcone, "Bouge, Antoine-Etienne-Augustin, docteur (1735–*après* 1818)," in *Le Monde Maçonnique des Lumières (Europe-Amériques & Colonies)*, vol. 1, ed. Charles Porset and Cécile Révauger (Paris: Honoré Champion, 2013), 493–8.

26. Bouge also fulfilled various other roles within the lodge, including being venerable master (1780) and senior warden (1785), and 1st Master of Ceremonies (1786). When Bouge became venerable master in 1780, he delivered a speech entitled "A Discourse on the Profundity of Our Mysteries, of which is particularly relevant the Sublimity of Écossisme." See AGA, "Registre de La Loge de la Fidélité," 162, 171–2. For his various other roles within the lodge, see BMdA, "Tableau des freres qui composent la T.R.G. Loge de St. Jean d'Ecosse de la Vertu Persécutée," (1783–1789), MS. 2951, nos. 46–52.

27. BMdA, "Tableau des freres" (1788), MS. 2951, no. 51.

28. BMdA, MS. 3072. Bouge is listed as being the secretary of the lodge.

29. BNdF, FM1 289. For a discussion of the correspondence between the lodges in Avignon and Paris in 1806, see Michel Chazottes, *La franc-maçonnerie avignonnaise et vauclusienne au XIXᵉ siècle* (Aix-en-Provence: Edisud, 1993), 23–4. In 1809 Bouge and Leblond are also listed as members of honour of the Loge ecossaise d'Isis in Lyon. See *Tableau des frères composant la R. L. ecossaise d'Isis* (Lyon: Pelzin and Drevon, 1809), 6.

30. For reproductions of a series of Christian engravings produced by Leblond's father, Claude, see Sylvain Gagnière, *Catalogue de l'imagerie populaire religieuse avignonnaise* (Avignon: Rullière, 1943), passim.

31. Bricaud, *Les illuminés*, 65; Colonjon, "Société Académique," 95.

32. Meillassoux-Le Cerf, *Dom Pernety*, 441.

33. Richardière's elder brother, Jean-Baptiste (b. 1744), is listed as being a Master Mason of the Saint-Alexandre d'Écosse lodge in Paris in 1783. See "Tableau des members qui composent loge Alexandre d'Écosse (1783), BNdF FM1 100bis.

34. On Sept. 21, 1786, Richardière obtained a "dèpôt de certificate de vie," which attests that he was born in Paris on Sept. 17, 1749, and was a doctor of medicine. See "Dèpôt de certificate de vie," AN, MC/ET/XXIV/952.

35. Richardière became embroiled in a financial dispute with A. I. Naryshkin in 1782, after the death of the latter's wife in Paris. Naryshkin's refusal to pay compensation to Richardière for debts owed by his wife resulted in the French ambassador in St. Petersburg, the Marquis de Vérac, taking up the matter with I. A. Osterman, the Russian vice-chancellor. Naryshkin's death in November 1782 no doubt complicated matters, and the affair seems to have dragged on into the spring of 1783. In April 1783, Martin de Lesseps, the French Consul General, reported that he had received a dispatch from a Russian ministry pointing out that Richardière had failed to properly register his claims against the heirs of A. I. Naryshkin. This protracted dispute suggests that Richardière would not have left the Russian capital without a resolution to the matter prior to the spring of 1783. It is not known when Richardière arrived in Russia, but it is recorded that his son, Antoine-Achille, who went on to become a renowned engraver of portraits, was born in Polna in the Pskov Governorate in March 1777. For information about A.-A. Richardière's birth, see AdP, AD-75, sous série V2E. On the diplomatic manoeuvres associated with Richardière's financial dispute with A. I. Naryshkin and his heirs, see AN, "Correspondance des Consuls de France à Saint-Pétersbourg (1713–1792)," AE/B/I/982–AE/B/I/989, 38r–39v, 56r–56v.

36. See Richardière to Gilbert Romme, June 27, 1781, SPF IRI, fond 8. Also see Gilbert Romme, *Correspondance 1779–1786*, vol. 2, tome 1, ed. Anne-Marie Bourdin et al. (Clermont Ferrand: Presses Universitaires Blaise-Pascal, 2014), 237–9.

37. Alfred Hamy, *Chronologie Biographique de la Compagnie de Jésus, 1re série Province de Lyon 1582–1762* (Paris: H. Champion, 1900), 90.

38. Hamy, *Chronologie*, 32.

39. Meillassoux-Le Cerf, *Dom Pernety*, 383.

40. On the meanings and symbolism associated with the number seven in Christian exegesis and in strands of thought associated with Western esotericism, see Annemarie Schimmel, *The Mystery of Numbers* (Oxford: Oxford University Press, 1993), 127–55.

41. On September 15, 1790, J. C. Lavater, the celebrated Swiss physiognomist, penned a brief description of his opinion of seven silhouettes of each of the Avignon brothers that had been sent to him the previous month by Tieman. He wrote: "I am disgusted by their entirely artificial and non-evangelical mannerism. It smells of something different than Paul, Peter and John." Lavater's evaluation may not have been positive, but it does testify to the renown/notoriety of the Seven Brothers by this time. See ZBZ, Fonds Johann Caspar Lavater, 584–71. Reproduced in Faivre, *De Londres*, 482–3.

42. Grabianka to Gosse, Feb. 24, 1787. See Gosse, *Portefeuille*, 80.

43. Brownbill, *A Short Account*, 29–30. This letter is also reproduced in Hindmarsh, *Rise and Progress*, 46–7.

44. Brownbill, *A Short Account*, 29.

45. Brownbill, *A Short Account*, 30.

46. Gosse, *Portefeuille*, 81–2. Grabianka also revealed that the society accepted both men and women.

47. Tieman wrote to the Lyonnais Freemason Jean-Baptiste Willermoz, on Mar. 19, 1787, and mentioned that he had "received a long letter" from Grabianka. See BMdL, MS. 5870 (21). For a reproduction of this letter, see Faivre, *De Londres*, 438.

48. Maubach was initiated into Les amis réunis Masonic lodge in 1781 and was close to Savalette de Langes. See Alain Le Bihan, *Francs-maçons parisiens du Grand Orient de France* (Paris: Bibliothèque national, 1966), 346. Maubach wrote to Charles Rainsford regarding the Philalèthes congress in June 1784. See BL Add MS. 23,669, 92. Maubach lived in London for several years in the 1780s and in 1785 published *A Natural Method of Teaching the French Language* (London: Hookham, 1785). In 1792 he published a work entitled "Essai sur l'éducation publique," and on May 6 addressed the Legislative Assembly in Paris regarding his thoughts on the importance of public instruction. See Alexandre Tuetey, *Répertoire general des sources manuscrites de l'histoire de Paris pendant la Révolution Française*, vol. 6 (Paris: Imprimerie nouvelle, 1902), 204.

49. Parraud translated several works by Swedenborg into French, the earliest being *Du Commerce de l'Ame et Du Corps* (Paris: Barrois l'aîné, libraire, 1785). In 1787 he also published the first French translation of the *Bhagavad-Gita*. For an informative obituary, see *Journal des Savans* (Sept. 1832), 566.

50. On the congresses, see Charles Porset, *Les Philalèthes et le Convents de Paris* (Paris: Honoré Champion, 1996). On Savalette de Langes, see J. E. S. Tuckett, "Savalette de Langes, Les Philaletes, and the Council of Wilhelmsbad, 1782," *Ars Quatuor Coronatorum* 30 (1917): 131–72; Robert Chabot, "Savalette de Langes, Charles-Pierre Paul," in *Le Monde Maçonnique*, vol. 3 (2013), 2488–97.

51. On their participation at the Philalèthes congresses, see Porset, *Les Philalèthes*, passim.

52. Porset, *Les Philalèthes*, 504–5.

53. On the influence of P. I. Melissino and the Melissino Rite on Corberon, who served as the French chargé d'affaires in the Russian capital between 1775 and 1780, see Robert Collis, "The Petersburg Crucible: Alchemy and the Russian Nobility in Catherine the Great's Russia," *Journal of Religion in Europe* 5:1 (2012): 56–99; Collis, "Illuminism in the Age of Minerva: Pyotr Ivanovich Melissino (1726–1797) and High-Degree Freemasonry in Catherine the Great's Russia," *COLLeGIUM: Studies across Disciplines in the Humanities and Social Sciences* 16 (2014): 128–68. On Corberon's saturation in the currents of illuminism in Russia and France from 1777, see Antoine Faivre, "Un Familier des Sociétés Ésotériques au Dix-Huitième Siècle: Bourrée de Corberon," *Revue des Sciences Humaines* (1967): 259–87. On Corberon's embrace of animal magnetism and participation in the Society of Harmony in Paris, see Robert Darnton, *Mesmer and the Age of the Enlightenment* (Cambridge, MA: Harvard University Press, 1968), 76–7, 116, 180–2.

54. Corberon to von Brühl, Feb. 23, 1787. MC, MS. 3060, 41r. For an analysis of this correspondence, see Faivre, "Corberon," 281, fn. 119.

55. Brühl to Corberon, April 10, 1787. MC, MS. 3060, 91r. At the time Brühl was the governor to the children of Friedrich Wilhelm II in Potsdam. Brühl was initiated into the highest degree of the Melissino Rite in St. Petersburg at the same lodge meeting as Corberon and played a key role in drawing the French diplomat into the illuminist milieu in the Russian capital. See L.-H. Labande, ed., *Un Diplomate Français a la cour de Catherine II 1775–1780: Journal Intime du Chevalier de Corberon*, vol. 2 (Paris: Librairie Plon, 1901), 2–3, 139, 175. Both Corberon and Brühl also participated in the Philalèthes congresses in Paris. See Porset, *Les Philalèthes*, 535–8.

56. Grabianka wrote to Corberon on Mar. 1, 1787, and the latter sent a reply on April 5. See MC, MS. 3060, 67v, 69r.

57. See chapter 8 for discussion of the Corberons attendance in Avignon in April 1791 at the baptism of a son of Thérése Bouche, alongside Grabianka and Bouge.

58. Brownbill, *A Short Account*, 27.

59. Gosse, *Portefeuille*, 80.

60. Porset, *Les Philalèthes*, 505.

61. A. J. P[ernety], *La Sagesse Angélique sur l'Amour Divin, et sur la Sagesse Divine*, vol. 1 (Paris and Lyon: Perisse, 1786).

62. *Observations sur La Franc-Maçonnerie, le Martinisme, les Visions de Swedenborg, le Magnétisme, &c* (Avignon, 1786), 259.

63. Bernard, "L'Alchimie," Feb. 14, 1863, 264.

64. The content of the messages also suggests that they were written after Grabianka's return to Avignon and the promotion of the society.

65. Bernard, "L'Alchimie," Feb. 28, 1863, 296.

66. Bernard, "L'Alchimie," Feb. 28, 1863, 296. In a letter to William Bousie, Robert Bousie, and Alexander Mackglashan, dated Dec. 10, 1788, Grabianka remarks that the brothers "had written to f[rère] Barthélémon. The prefix "f." is not used when Grabianka refers to other London acquaintances, such as Best, William Bryan, Joshua Jones Prichard, George Adams. See HSD, Fond D4 No. 589/13, 3v, 4r.

67. Bernard, "L'Alchimie," Feb. 28, 1863, 296. The note was signed "Poor Help (Best)." Among the manuscripts consulted by Thalès Bernard was one that matches Best's description. It is entitled "Recueil des citations de l'Écriture-Sainte par Best Anglois." Bernard, "L'Alchimie," Feb. 28, 1863, 298. On the Marquis de Thomé, see Porset, *Les Philalèthes*, 611–12.

68. BMdL, MS. 5870 (22). Also see Faivre, *De Londres*, 446.

69. Letter to W. Bousie, R. Bousie, and A. Mackglashan, HSD, Fond D4 No. 589/13, 4r.

70. On the Grand Tour undertaken by Tieman and Boris Andreevich Golitsyn, see Faivre, *De Londres*, 175–212. On Tieman's employment as a governor to the children of several other prominent Russian officials, see Faivre, *De Londres*, 12–35, 90–100.

71. Tieman to J.-B. Willermoz, Oct. 28, 1787. BMdL, MS. 5870 (22). Reproduced in Faivre, *De Londres*, 445–6.

72. Lineham, "Origins of the New Jerusalem, 110.

73. RGIA, Fond 1163, op. 1, d. 16b, 104r–104v.

74. See, for example, Paracelsus, *The Hermetic and Alchemical Writings of Aureolus Philippus Theophrastus Bombast of Hohenheim, called Paracelsus the* Great, vol. 1, ed. A. E. Waite (London: James Elliott & Co., 1894), 101–3. Also see "The Golden Tract," in *The Hermetic Museum, Restored and Enlarged*, vol. 1, ed. A. E. Waite (London: James Elliott & Co., 1893), 25; Fabre, *L'Alchimiste chrétien*, 212.

75. J. W. von Goethe, *Faust I & II*, vol. 2, ed. and trans. Stuart Atkins (Princeton, NJ: Princeton University Press, 1984), 162.

76. RGIA, Fond 1163, op. 1, d. 16b, 104r–104v.

77. RGIA, Fond 1163, op. 1, d. 16b, 104v–105r.

78. See Peter J. Forshaw, "*Cabala Chymica* or *Chemia Cabalistica*—Early Modern Alchemists and Cabala," *Ambix* 60:4 (2013): 361–89.

79. John Read, *From Alchemy to Chemistry* (Mineola, NY: Dover, 1995), 32.

80. RGIA, Fond 1163, op. 1, d. 16b, 105r–105v.

81. AdSdRm, Giunta di Stato, Fascicolo 7, busta 1, 12r.

82. *Noteficazione noi fr. Tommaso Vincenzo Pani da Rimino dell Ordine de Predicatori* (Rome: Camera Apostolica, 1791).

83. BNCdR, "Breve dettaglio della Società, o Setta scoperta nell'arresto di Ottavio Cappelli, tratto dalle Carte allo stesso perquisite (1790)," MS. Vittorio Emanuele, 245, 569r. Also see Renzo de Felice, *Note e ricerche sugli "Illuminati" e il Misticismo Rivoluzionario (1789–1800)* (Rome: Edizioni di storia e letteratura, 1960), 221.

84. RGIA, Fond 1163, op. 1, d. 16b, 106v. This would seemingly be a reference to the number of *illuminés* who had been "converted" to the Swedenborgian doctrine.

85. RGIA, Fond 1163, op. 1, d. 16b, 106v.

86. RGIA, Fond 1163, op. 1, d. 16b, 108r–108v. Swedenborg rejected the notion that the pope should be "acknowledged as the Lord's vicar." See Emanuel Swedenborg, *The Four Doctrines of the New Jerusalem* (Boston: Houghton, Mifflin, 1907), 186.

87. HSD, Fond D4 No. 589/13, 4v.

88. HSD, Fond D4 No. 589/13, 4v.

89. HSD, Fond D4 No. 589/13, 5r.

90. NA PRO, Privy Council, 1/18/19. On Bryan's anti-Swedenborgianism, see David Worrall, "William Bryan, Another Anti-Swedenborgian Visionary Engraver of 1789," *Blake: An Illustrated Quarterly* 34:1 (2000): 14–21.

91. A.-J. Pernety, *Les Vertus, le pouvoir, la clémence et la gloire de Marie, mère de Dieu* (Paris: Libraires Associés, 1790), 15.

92. For documentation regarding the consecration of Jacques Pernety, see Meillassoux-Le Cerf, *Dom Pernety*, 438–9. For confirmation that Françoise Pernety and H.-L Rozières were members of the society, see RGIA, Fond 1163, op. 1, d. 16b, 103v and 109v.

93. Deravine's name first appears on lodge records in 1785 as an apprentice. See MC, MS. 2951, nos. 43 and 46.

94. On their participation at the first Philalèthes convent, see Porset, *Les Philalèthes*, 537, 591, and passim.

95. Casimir Rostan, "Notice Biographique sur Monsieur Guillaume Paul," *Mémoires Publiés par L'Académie de Marseille*, vol. 7 (Marseille: Joseph-François Achard, 1811), 258. On Paul as a collector and patron of the arts and sciences, see Anne Jouve, *Guillaume de Paul: 1738–1793: Un collectionneur marseillais au siècle des Lumières* (Marseille: Musée des Beaux-Arts, 1994).

96. G. de Paul to A.-J. Pernety, Feb. 22, 1782. ACSD, vol. 10, 237–42.

97. Porset, *Les Philalèthes*, 591. On the Loge de Saint-Jean d'Écosse de Marseille, including mention of de Paul, see P.-Y. Beaurepaire, "Saint-Jean d'Écosse de Marseille: Une puissance Maçonnique méditerranéeanne aux ambitions Européennes," *Cahiers de la Méditerranée* 72 (2006): 61–95.

98. Anonymous letter to F.-M. de Chefdebien, July 5–7, 1788. Private collection of Philippe de Scorbiac. For a reproduction of the letter, see Faivre, *De Londres*, 459–61.

99. HSD, Fond D4 No. 589/13, 4r–4v.

100. "Rese Journal öfver min Utländska vandring," Dec. 12, 1789, RA, RA, Reuterholm-Ädelgrenska samlingen, vol. 22.

101. HSD, Fond D4 No. 589/13, 4v.

102. Rostan, "Notice Biographique," 256–7. Métigny's thesis is entitled "Tentamen Psycho – somato – iatrikon, seu Conspectus thesiformis de natura animi et corporis." It ranks as possibly the earliest learned treatise on psychosomatic medicine.

103. According to Benedict Chastanier, writing in 1795, Bousie was already a brother of the Avignon Society prior to April 16, 1788, when he was charged with translating a letter from English to French. See Chastanier, *A Word of Advice*, 38.

104. When visiting Paris in September 1786, the Scottish journalist James Anderson wrote the following: "I am well served with wines, by my obliging countryman Mr. Maclagan, who is in company with Monsieur Boussee, presently at London." See James Anderson, *The Bee, Or, Literary Weekly Intelligencer*, vol. 3 (Edinburgh: Mundell and Son, 1791), 194–5.

105. Bousie's method apparently "investigated the nature of the alkalis, the peculiar effects of various alkaline substances and the best mode of applying them in clarifying the juice." See Bryan Edwards, *The History, Civil and Commercial of the British Colonies in the West Indies*, vol. 2 (Dublin: Luke White, 1793), 222; George Richardson Porter, *The Nature and Properties of the Sugar Cane* (London: Smith, Elder and Co., 1830), 118. 184. On the private acts passed in 1785 and 1786 to secure the implementation of Bousie's invention, see *The Laws of Jamaica: Comprehending All the Acts in Force*, vol. 2 (St. Jago de la vega: Alexander Aikman, 1802), vii, ix.

106. To our knowledge there is no documentary evidence to suggest that R. W. Bousie did return to Jamaica.

107. Saint-Martin, *Mon Portrait*, 262. His name is listed as "Maglasson."

108. Bousie's wife, Mary, is not mentioned in this letter, but she became a member of the Avignon Society no later than August 1789. See Corberon to Grabianka, Aug. 30, 1789. MC, MS. 3060, 871. See the response of Nicolas Simonin, who was initiated into the Avignon Society in 1796 or 1797, when he was being interrogated by the Russian authorities in 1807: "I was acquainted with Mrs. Bousie, a very old lady; an English native; she also belonged to the society." See RGIA,

Fond 1163, op. 1, d. 16b, 28v. William and Mary Bousie lived in Avignon for several years from around 1790. See "Rapport de Poultier" published in Aulard, *Recueil*, vol. 11, 498.

109. Chastanier himself wrote in 1795 that all Grabianka's letters, "either to myself or to others of the friends [in England]" were "communicated to me." Chastanier, *A Word of Advice*, 36. On Chastanier and the Avignon Society, see James Hyde, "Benedict Chastanier and the Illuminati of Avignon," *New-Church Review* 14 (1907): 181–205.

110. HSD, Fond D4 No. 589/13, 4r.

111. For Chastanier's public avowal of New Church doctrine, see Benedict Chastanier, "To the Editors of the New-Jerusalem Magazine," *New-Jerusalem Magazine* (Mar. 1, 1790), 112–13.

112. Chastanier, *A Word of Advice*, 35–6.

113. Cited from Hyde, "Chastanier," 200. On T. S. Duhé, see A. F. Gegenheimer, "Artist in Exile: The Story of Thomas Spence Duché," *Pennsylvania Magazine* 79 (1955): 3–26.

114. Chastanier, *A Word of Advice*, 37–8.

115. Wright, *A Revealed Knowledge*, 60.

116. The Irish chemist Peter Woulfe (1727–1803) is not mentioned in Grabianka's letter, but was a member of the Avignon Society. He spent winters in London and summers in Paris. For a reference to Woulfe, who sent a letter to Cappelli on Mar. 8, 1790, see "Breve," 565v; Felice, *Note e Ricerche*, 219. Richard Brothers, the so-called Paddington Prophet, also wrote that Woulfe was "one of the Avignon Society" in 1794. See Richard Brothers, *A Revealed Knowledge of the Prophecies & Times* (London, n.p., 1794), 75. General Charles Rainsford (1728–1809), who was one of the foremost English illuminists in the 1780s, wrote to Grabianka in 1788. Furthermore, in a document that he wrote in 1794 listing the societies to which he belonged, Rainsford included one in Avignon. However, it is not entirely clear if this was the Avignon Society led by the Seven Brothers. See Rainsford to Monsieur le Comte [Grabianka], BL Add. MS. 23,669, 123–4; "Singular Avocations," BL Add. MS. 23,667. Lastly, Chastanier states that a certain Mrs. Olbeldeston visited the society in Avignon. See Chastanier, *A Word of Advice*, 36.

117. HSD, Fond D4 No. 589/13, 3v.

118. Saint-Martin, *Mon Portrait*, 90–1.

119. This information is based on the testimony of J. Gros, the secretary to the Duchess de Bourbon. See Eude, "Points de vue," 614, fn. 33.

120. L.-M. Gombault to Corberon, Mar. 5, 1791. AN, Police Générale, dossier Gombault, F/7/4728.

121. Report on the interrogation of L.-M. Gombault by the Committee of Public Security, 21 floréal, year II (May 10, 1794), AN, Police Générale, dossier Gombault, F/7/4728.

122. HSD, Fond D4 No. 589/13, 4r.

123. William Bryan, *A Testimony of the Spirit of Truth concerning Richard Brothers* (London: J. Wright, 1795), 27–8.

124. Christian Daniel von Meyer to Christian von Hessen-Darmstadt, Dec. 20, 1789. HSD, Fond D4, No. 591/1–1a. For a reproduction, see Faivre, *De Londres*, 467–8.

125. HSD, Fond D4 No. 589/13, 4r, 5v. On Seiffert (d. 1790; also known as Saiffert), see Germain Bapst, ed., "Lettres du Baron de Saiffert," *Revue de la Révolution* 7 (1886): 69–103. On Martange (1722–1806), see Charles Bréard, ed., *Correspondane inédite au general-major de Martange, aide de camp du prince Xavier de Saxe* (Paris: A. Picard et Fils, 1898). A certain "F[rère] Vineau" is also referred to at this point in the letter, but his identity is unknown.

126. On Roqueville, see "Chronique de la Société d'Art et d'Histoire du Diocèse de Liège," *Bulletin de la Société d'Art et d'Histoire du Diocèse de Liège*, vol. 11 (Liège: L. Grandmont-Donders, 1897), 26–7. On Feb. 3, 1782, the Marquis de Bombelles noted in his journal that Roqueville was the venerable master of a lodge, possibly diplomatic in composition, in Regensburg. See Marquis de Bombelles, *Journal*, vol. 1 (Geneva: Libraire Droz, 1977), 101.

127. HSD, Fond D4 No. 589/13, 4v.

128. Anderson, *The Bee*, 195–6. Macgregor was arrested in Avignon in October 1793 in the same company as A-J. Pernety and William and Mary Bousie, which suggests that he remained an active member of the Avignon Society for several years. According to a nephew, Gregor Macgregor, writing in the 1830s, he "was generally located in Avignon." On his arrest, see "Rapport de Poultier" published in Aulard, *Recueil*, vol. 11, 498. For the reminiscences of his nephew about Chevalier John Macgregor living in Avignon, see Gregor Macgregor, "Autobiographical Segment," NAS GD/50/112, 1. For a discussion of Gregor Macgregor, which mentions the chevalier, see Matthew Brown, "Gregor Macgregor: Clansman, Conquistador and Coloniser on the Fringes of the British Empire," in *Colonial Lives across the British Empire: Imperial Careering in the Long Nineteenth Century*, ed. David Lambert and Alan Lester (Cambridge: Cambridge University Press, 2006), 32–57.

129. See a text by Bellery entitled *Mémoire sur le jaugeage des navires* (Paris: Quai des Augustins, 1788). The author is listed as being a member of the Academy of Sciences of Amiens and the official hydraulic engineer for the Comte d'Artois.

130. HLHU, GEN MS. Fr 441.

131. Other sections are dedicated to hermetic philosophy (1st); infallible remedies that guarantee protection against rabid animals and other prayers (3rd) and alchemical recipes (4th). Picot writes in the manuscript that he is a native of Crépey in Lorraine. See HLHU, GEN, MS. 441, 124r.

132. In October 1801 a police report into the activities of "a society known to spread the spirit of royalty and fanaticism," noted that "one of the chiefs, La Richardière, is in Paris." Apparently, he liked to dine with Picot every Tuesday or Wednesday. The official from the Ministry of Police added that "Picot is one of the affiliates of this society." It would seem that Picot sided with Richardière when the Avignon Society splintered in 1791, and thereafter remained close to the leader of the splinter group. See "Echange de lettres entre le Ministère de la Police et le Préfet de Vaucluse," AN F. 7/7915. Reproduced in Meillassoux-Le Cerf, *Dom Pernety*, 323–6. On Picot and Colas in Avignon in 1789, see p. 91.

133. For an abridged version of this journal, see B. von Schinkel, *Minnen ur Sveriges Nyare Historia*, vol. 2 (Stockholm: P. A. Norstedt & Söner, 1852), 342–54. For commentaries on Reuterholm's travels, see O.-P. Sturzen-Becker, *Reuterholm efter hans egna memoirer* (Stockholm-Copenhagen: S. Trier, 1862), 117–28; Göran Anderberg, "Gustaf Adolf Reuterholms vallfart till revolutionens Frankrike och Italien," *Historisk Tidskrift för Finland* 3 (2005): 305–39.

134. See Andreas Önnerfors, "'Envoyées des Glaces du Nord Jusque Dans ces Climats': Swedish Encounters with *Les Illuminés d'Avignon* at the End of the Eighteenth Century," in *Diffusions et circulations des pratiques maçonniques XVIIIe–XXe siècle*, ed. P.-Y. Beaurepaire et al. (Paris: Classiques Garnier, 2012), 167–94.

135. Reuterholm is regarded as playing a pivotal role in the development of the high-degree Swedish Rite of Freemasonry, along with his patron Duke Karl of Södermanland. On Reuterholm's esoteric and Masonic passions, see Kjell Lekeby, *Gustaviansk Mystik* (Sala/

Södermalm: Vertigo Förlag, 2010); Lekeby, *Gustav Adolf Reuterholms hemliga arkiv från 1780-talet* (Stockholm: Pleiaderna, 2011); Lekeby, *Esoterica i Svenska Frimurarordens arkiv 1776–1803* (Stockholm: Pleiaderna, 2011). Silfverhielm ranks as the first animal magnetist in Sweden. See C. G. Silfverhielm, *Inledning til kunskapen om den animale magnetismen* (Stockholm: Kungl. tryckeriet, 1787). On the involvement of Silfverhielm (in particular), Reuterholm and Duke Carl in the Exegetic and Philanthropic Society in Stockholm, see Robert Sundelin, *Svedenborgianismens historia i Sverige under förra åhundradet* (Upsala: W. Schultz, 1886), 267–71; Al Gabay, "Swedenborg, Mesmer and the 'Covert' Enlightenment," *New Philosophy* (1997): 675–84. For the speech made by Duke Karl on becoming a member of the Exegetic and Philanthropic Society, on Aug. 29, 1787, see *New Jerusalem Magazine* (1790), 179.

136. Schinkel, *Minnen*, 344.

137. Reuterholm and Silfverhielm to Grabianka, Oct. 10, 1789, SFOA 121.141.5.

138. Schinkel, *Minnen*, 344.

139. Schinkel, *Minnen*, 344–5.

140. Grabianka to Reuterholm and Silfverhielm, Nov. 1, 1789. SFOA 121.141.4 (no. 1).

141. Schinkel, *Minnen*, 345.

142. Reuterholm was in the company of Bousie on Nov. 3, 6, 12, and 17; the company of Gombault on Nov. 7 and 16, and in the company of both men on Oct. 31 and Nov. 14. See RA, "Rese Journal."

143. We know that of the duchess's eight sons, Duke Ferdinand of Württemberg (1763–1834) accompanied her to Avignon and became an *illumine*. The identity of the second son who journeyed to Avignon is not known.

144. Pleshcheev was initiated in the Lodge of Oziris in St. Petersburg in 1776. See A. I. Serkov, *Russkoe masonstvo 1731–2000. Entsiklopedicheskii slovar'* (Moscow: ROSSPEN, 2001), 996.

145. Pleshcheev wrote down his itinerary and whom he met in a basic diary. See "Dnevnik Pleshcheeva," RNB, Fond 487 (Mikhailovskii), Q. 392, 1r–1v. For an analysis of Pleshcheev's grand tour, see S. A. Kozlov, *Russkii puteshestvennik epokhi Prosveshcheniia* (St. Petersburg: Istoricheskaia illiustratsiia, 2003), 149–52; Alexandre Stroev, "Franc-maçons aventuriers et voyageurs au XVIIIe siècle," in *La franc-maçonnerie et la culture russe*, ed. Jean Breuillard and Irina Ivanova (Toulouse: CRIMS, 2007), 73–90.

146. Saint-Martin, *Mon Portrait*, 117.

147. RGIA, Fond 1163, op. 1, d. 16a, 182v–184r. The Russian authorities in 1807 also noted down two questions to Gabriel posed by Richardière (on Oct. 14 and 16, 1788). RGIA, Fond 1163, op. 1, d. 16a, 183r–183v. Interestingly, the Russian scribe noted down the number for each question. Richardière's first question, on Oct. 14, 1788, was no. 397. The final query by Pleshcheev, posed on Nov. 20, 1788, is listed as no. 426. Thus, thirty questions were posed to the oracle over a period of thirty-seven days, of which only eight were recorded by the Russian authorities.

148. Brumore, "Lettre," 294–5.

149. RGIA, Fond 1163, op. 1, d. 16a, 183r.

150. RGIA, Fond 1163, op. 1, d. 16a, 183r–183v, 184r.

151. Wright, *A Revealed Knowledge*, 26.

152. Meillassoux-Le Cerf, *Dom Pernety*, 445.

153. See, for example, Meillassoux-Le Cerf, *Dom Pernety*, 340, 351, 353–6. Assadaï is also said to have watched over Pernety on his journey from Berlin to Valence (see p. 371).

154. See Trevor Johnson, "Guardian Angels and the Society of Jesus," in *Angels in the Early Modern World*, ed. Peter Marshall and Alexandra Walsham (Cambridge: Cambridge University Press, 2006), 191–213; Ingrid D. Rowland, "Athanasius Kircher's Guardian Angel," in *Conversations with Angels*, ed. Joad Raymond (Basingstoke: Palgrave Macmillan, 2011), 250–70.

155. See Konrad Eisenbichler, "Devotion to the Archangel Raphael in Renaissance Florence," in *Saints: Studies in Hagiography*, ed. Sandro Sticca (Binghamton, NY: Medieval and Renaissance Texts and Studies, 1995), 251–67; "Joseph Hammond, "The Cult and Representation of Archangel Raphael in Sixteenth-Century Venice," *St. Andrews Journal of Art History and Museum Studies* 15 (2011): 79–88.

156. RGIA, Fond 1163, op. 1, d. 16b, 106r–106v.

157. Bernard, "L'Alchimie," Jan. 24, 1863, 213.

158. RGIA, Fond 1163, op. 1, d. 16b, 106r–106v. The three entries found in the blue notebook between November 20–25, 1786 are also interesting as they were likely mediated by Cappelli in Italy. The timing of these questions makes it most likely that Ferrier was the querent.

159. Wright, *A Revealed Knowledge*, 19.

160. Hindmarsh, *Rise and Progress*, 48.

161. Wright, *A Revealed Knowledge*, 19.

162. Gabriella Ceraso, "Pope at Mass: Guardian Angels, Our Daily Gate to the Father," *Vatican News*. Oct. 2, 2018, https://www.vaticannews.va/en/pope-francis/mass-casa-santa-marta/2018-10/pope-francis-homily-daily-mass-guardian-angels-transcendence.html (accessed Jan. 7, 2019).

163. RGIA, Fond 1163, op. 1, d. 16b, 108r.

164. Augustine, *The Works of Aurelius Augustine*, vol. 1, *The City of God*, ed. Marcus Dods (Edinburgh: T.&T. Clark, 1913), 394. On Christian attitudes to theurgy up to the sixteenth century, see Claire Fanger, "Introduction: Theurgy, Magic and Mysticism," in *Invoking Angels: Theurgic Ideas and Practices, Thirteenth to Sixteenth Centuries*, ed. Claire Fanger (University Park: Pennsylvania State University Press, 2012), 1–33.

165. See *The Key of Solomon the King*, ed. and trans. S. Liddell MacGregor Mathers (London: George Redway, 1889).

166. RGIA Fond 1163, op. 1, d. 16b, 106r.

167. Le Forestier, *La Franc-Maçonnerie occultiste*, 290–313. For a succinct summary of the theurgic rite of the *Élus Coëns* in English, see Christopher McIntosh, *Eliphas Lévi and the French Occult Revival* (Albany: State University of New York Press, 2011), 21–5. On the contemporary theurgic rite practised as part of the *Arcana Arcanorum* in Cagliostro's Egyptian Rite of Freemasonry, see Massimo Introvigne, "Cagliostro," in *Dictionary of Gnosis and Western Esotericism*, ed. Wouter J. Hanegraaff (Leiden: Brill, 2006), 225–7.

168. "Rese Journal," Dec. 1–9, 1789; "Breve," 578v–579r.

169. See MC, MS 3090. Also see Meillassoux-Le Cerf, *Dom Pernety*, 333–448.

170. Meillassoux-Le Cerf, *Dom Pernety*, 444.

171. The Russian authorities wrote down "579 Morvo," assuming that the three-digit number referred to Brumore, most likely unaware that he was already dead. However, Reuterholm described being escorted at 2:30 p.m. by Pernety and Delhomme (Grabianka was ill). See "Rese Journal," Dec. 1, 1789. Moreover, a letter to Reuterholm and Silfverhielm from the Seven Brothers in Avignon, housed in the SFOA, is signed using the three-digit number of each illumine: 139 (Grabianka); 135 (Pernety); 219 (Bouge); 814, 579, 369 (Ferrier); 915 (Richardière). The fourth and fifth numbers belong to either Delhomme or Leblond. Given the strict observance of roles

within the society, it is highly likely that Delhomme acted as Pernety's assistant. See the letter from the Seven Brothers to Reuterholm and Silfverhielm, Feb. 20, 1790. See Seven Brothers to Reuterholm and Silfverhielm, Feb. 20, 1790. SFOA 121.141.4 (no. 11).

172. "Rese Journal," Dec. 1, 1789.

173. RGIA Fond 1163, op. 1, d. 16b, 107r.

174. "Breve," 579r.

175. RGIA Fond 1163, op. 1, d. 16b, 107r. Reuterholm, whose number was 373, would have also kissed his number three times.

176. RGIA Fond 1163, op. 1, d. 16b, 107r. The incantation was as follows: "Achabes, Vad, Venigrad, Psyche (*Psikhe*), Spirit (*Dukha*), Sinup, Ekha, Geokrub, Soobrad, Ekhero Arpa, Ekhero Alla, Hosanna, Hosanna, Hosanna, Sabaoth." Not all the names/words written down by the Russian authorities in Cyrillic are easy to recognise.

177. For a seventeenth-century example of the use of this psalm during *proskomidiia*, see Boris Uspenskii, *Krest i krug* (Moscow: Iazyki Slavianskikh Kul'tur, 2006), 138.

178. Deravine began his consecration on the second day of Pleshcheev's initiation. See RGIA Fond 1163, op. 1, d. 16b, 107v.

179. RGIA Fond 1163, op. 1, d. 16b, 107v. On this chapel, which was built in 1674, seized by a federalist during the Revolution and burned down in 1815, see Abbé Granget, *Histoire du Diocèse d'Avignon*, vol. 2 (Avignon: Seguin Aîné, 1862), 270–1.

180. "Rese Journal," RA, Dec. 1, 9, 1789. Also see Schinkel, *Minnen*, 347.

181. C. D. von Meyer to Christian of Hesse-Darmstadt, Jan. 19, 1790. CMCPF, Fonds Georg Kloss, "Maurerische Bücher-Sammlung," MS. X2V1-655. Also see, Faivre, *Londres*, 470–2.

182. Sturzen-Becker, *Reuterholm*, 123.

183. On the political situation in Avignon in 1789, see Eric F. Johnson, "The Sacred, Secular Regime: Catholic Ritual and Revolutionary Politics in Avignon, 1789–1791," *French Historical Studies* 30:1 (2007): 49–76; E. J. Kolla, "The French Revolution, the Union of Avignon, and the Challenges of National Self-Determination," *Law and History Review* 31:4 (2013): 717–47.

184. Charles Soullier, *Histoire de la revolution d'Avignon et du Comté-Venaissin, en 1789*, vol. 1 (Avignon: Th. Fischer, 1844), 14.

185. In 1801, the prefect of the Vaucluse region wrote a report on the *illuminés* in Avignon and stated that the Pope had issued a bull against the society in 1788. See "Echange de lettres," AN F. 7/7915; Meillassoux-Le Cerf, *Dom Pernety*, 324, 326.

186. RGIA Fond 1163, op. 1, d. 16b, 109v.

187. Bouge delivered a report about the raid by the Papal authorities to the lodge of *Saint-Jean d'Écosse*. See AGA, Fonds Alphandery, "Registre de la respectable loge Saint-Jean d'Écosse de la Fidélité," 59–63.

188. See Thierry Zarcone, "Franc-Maçons et illuminés face à l'inquisition dans l'Avignon pontificale (1737–1792)," *Politica Hermetica* 32 (2018): 83–111. Also see Mesliand, "Franc-maçonnerie et religion."

189. Letters to Grabianka were addressed to "Monsieur Heureuson, Maison Neuve, Rue de la Colombe." See, for example, Reuterholm and Silfverhielm to Grabianka, Oct. 10, 1789, SFOA 121.141.5. In 1857, Paul Achard wrote that Grabianka lived at No. 22 in this street. See Paul Achard, *Guide du Voyageur ou Dictionnaire Historique des Rues et des Places Publiques de la Ville d'Avignon* (Avignon: Seguin Aîné, 1857), 55.

190. AN, MC/ET/XXIV/952.

191. Numerous historians have claimed that A.-J. Pernety directed the activities of the *illuminés* from a château in the village of Bédarrides, near Avignon, owned by the Marquis de Vaucroze, which he renamed Mont Thabor. However, there does not appear to be any documentary evidence to support this claim. The earliest reference to Pernety overseeing assemblies of *illuminés* in Bédarrides seems to date to 1841. See C.-F.-H. Barjavel, *Dictionnaire Historique, Biographique et Bibliographique du Département de Vaucluse*, vol. 2 (Carpentras: P. L. Hamy, 1841), 248.

192. ADdV, GG 51 St. Didier Baptêmes 1776–1790, no. 136, Nov. 7, 1789, 274r. For mention of de Fumel's involvement in the society in 1789 and 1790, see Reuterhlom, "Rese Journal," Nov. 30, 1789; "Breve," 565v–566r.

193. ADdV, GG 51 St. Didier Baptêmes 1776–1790, no. 139, Nov. 9, 1789, 274v. It is also possible that her birth occurred on Grabianka's name-day (Oct. 28).

194. Richardière consulted the Archangel Gabriel on Oct. 14, 1788, about whether to contact d'Attigny in Russia about joining the society. See RGIA, Fond 1163, op. 1, d. 16a, 182r. For a brief biographical sketch of d'Attigny by Grabianka made during his interrogation in St. Petersburg in 1807, see RGIA, Fond 1163, op. 1, d. 16a, 298v–302r.

195. On Jones's residence in St. Petersburg in 1789, see J. H. Sherburne, *Life and Character of the Chevalier John Paul Jones* (Washington DC.: Wilder & Campbell, 1825), 313–21.

196. John Paul Jones, *Memoirs of Rear-Admiral Paul Jones*, vol. 2 (Edinburgh: Oliver & Boyd, 1830), 220–1.

197. Jones, *Memoirs*, vol. 2, 222.

198. Wright, *A Revealed Knowledge*, 60–1.

199. Wright, *A Revealed Knowledge*, 62–3.

200. Wright, *A Revealed Knowledge*, 60–3.

201. Grabianka to Reuterholm and Silfverhielm, Dec. 27, 1789. SFOA, 121.141.4 (no. 3).

202. Grabianka to Reuterholm and Silfverhielm, Mar. 5, 1790. SFOA, 121.141.4 (no. 12). On Reuterholm's interactions with Cappelli and the role of St. Vieillard (Raphael), see chapter 4.

203. Possibly an allusion to Baron and Baroness Staël. See chapter 4.

204. For a biography of Bonde, who was a diplomat and a wealthy landowner, see G. Carlquist, "Carl Bonde," in *Svenskt biografiskt lexicon*, vol. 5 (Stockholm: Bonnier), 381.

205. SFOA, 121.141.4 (no. 12).

206. J.-B. Allier, "Biographie de Dom Pernety," MPA, 3114-A-1. Also see Meillassoux-Le Cerf, *Dom Pernety*, 321.

207. "Rese Journal," RA, Nov. 25, 1789. Also see Schinkel, *Minnen*, 346.

208. "Rese Journal," RA, Nov. 25 and Dec. 9, 1789.

209. Wright, *A Revealed Knowledge*, 19.

210. "Rese Journal," Nov. 26, 1789.

211. Wright, *A Revealed Knowledge*, 18.

212. "Rese Journal," RA, Nov. 27, 1789.

213. "Rese Journal," RA, Nov. 29, 1789.

214. "Rese Journal," RA, Dec. 6, 1789.

215. Eusèbe Clément, *Le monastère-collège de Saint-Martial d'Avignon* (Avignon: Seguin Frères, 1893), 322.

216. "Rese Journal," RA, Nov. 29, 1789.

217. "Rese Journal," RA, Dec. 8, 1789.

218. "Rese Journal," RA, Nov. 30, 1789. Also see Schinkel, *Minnen*, 346.

219. For a biography of Nicolas, see Séverine Beaumier, *Jean-François Nicolas Médecin des Lumières* (Mollans-sur-Ouvèze: Le Garde-Notes Baronniard, 2003).

220. Faivre, *De Londres*, 486. Tieman added that "Mr. Nicolas of Grenoble . . . was initiated and . . . also seems convinced."

221. For a table of members of the Society of Harmony, which includes the names of Nicolas (no. 137), Paul (no. 279), and Corberon (no. 60), see "Institutions: Société de l'Harmonie," *Journal du Magnétisme* 11 (1852): 242, 570, 198 respectively.

222. Faivre, *De Londres*, 460.

223. J.-F. Nicolas, "Seconde Lettre de Grenoble le 28. février. 1789," in *Annales de la Société Harmonique des amis réunis de Strasbourg*, vol. 3 (Strasbourg: n.p., 1789), 264–7.

224. AN F.7/7915. Also see Meillassoux-Le Cerf, *Dom Pernety*, 324.

225. A.-V.-C. Berbiguier, *Les Farfadets*, vol. 1 (Paris: P. Gueffier, 1821), x.

226. Berbiguier, vol. 1, 4–5. Berbiguier writes about Nicolas and Bouge in all three tomes of his work. See vol. 1, 46–50, 53–5, 319–20; vol. 2, 115, 135–6, 162–73, 357; and vol. 3, 178, 220, 379–80. For an analysis of Berbiguier's work, see Massimo Introvigne, *Satanism: A Social History* (Leiden: Brill, 2016), 74–83.

227. "Rese Journal," RA, Dec. 4–9, 1789.

228. "Rese Journal," RA, Dec. 7, 1789.

229. In addition to those already mentioned, Reuterholm also hosted Abbé Barozzi, a Franciscan monk, on Dec. 11. Moreover, on Dec. 19 he met M.-D. and Charlotte Corberon and Macgregor, who had travelled from Paris to attend another consecration. See "Rese Journal," RA, Dec. 11 and 19, 1789.

4

A Wolf in Sheep's Clothing?

THE RISE AND FALL OF OTTAVIO CAPPELLI IN ROME, 1789–1800

ON JANUARY 29, 1800, Ottavio Cappelli met an ignominious and gruesome end: he was hanged in the Piazza Sant'Angelo in Rome.[1] He had been arrested by the Governing Committee (*Giunta di Stato*) on November 16, 1799, shortly after the fall of the Roman Republic. The offences for which he was hanged included being in possession of a "sabre, sword and bayonet" and illegally re-entering Rome.[2] However, a list of the possessions seized when the authorities searched Cappelli's home in Rome, which he shared with a certain Maria Dorsani, do not suggest that the accused posed an urgent insurrectionary threat to the re-establishment of papal authority. Besides plentiful pieces of women's clothing, the only items evidently in Cappelli's possession were two books: an unnamed comedy and a book of devotional prayers (*novenas*) to St. Archangel Raphael.[3] The latter tome indicates a veneration of Raphael, which, as we will show, was a distinctive feature of Cappelli's prophetic aura a decade earlier, at the height of his sway over the Union.

Why did the *Giunta di Stato* in Rome rush to mete out such a harsh punishment on Cappelli, given the paltry incriminating evidence against him? As Marina Caffiero notes, the haste and severity with which the authorities acted reflects the tumultuous political and military situation in Rome at the time.[4] This was an extremely turbulent period, when wild rumours swirled about Jacobin threats and about an imminent armistice between France and Austria, which would imperil the restoration of papal authority. In this fevered atmosphere, Cappelli, with his motley assortment of weapons, posed no real danger. Yet his presence in Rome *did* present a potential threat in terms of his proven ability at the turn of the 1790s to fan millenarian sentiment as a supposed prophet who had, for example, proclaimed a calamitous destiny in the near future for the pontiff and the papacy as a whole.

Initiating the Millennium. Robert Collis, and Natalie Bayer, Oxford University Press (2020) © Oxford University Press.
DOI: 10.1093/oso/9780190903374.001.0001

This chapter will primarily focus on this period of Cappelli's life. More specifically, it examines in detail a relatively short span of time between December 1789 and October 1790, when Cappelli enjoyed his greatest influence within the Union, as a prophet who was able to serve as an intermediary between the Archangel Raphael and members of the Union. We argue that Cappelli's authority peaked in around the spring of 1790, when he felt sufficiently emboldened to attempt to introduce significant revisions to the society's rituals, theological doctrine, and hierarchical structure. Yet the apogee of his influence within the Union was fleeting. By June 1790 some within the society were expressing doubts about the authenticity of his prophetic gift.

Moreover, calamity soon befell Cappelli, when, on September 27, 1790, he was arrested, along with his wife, son, and two clerical followers, by the Holy Office and charged with being the leader of a heretical sect.[5] As we will show, Cappelli's incarceration unleashed something of an eighteenth-century media storm, as newspapers across Europe disseminated scandalous tales and rumours about the nature and extent of his alleged crimes. Alongside the reactions of those unconnected to the Union, we will also examine how various members of the society responded to the dramatic developments in Rome. The imprisonment of Cappelli threw the Union into a state of internal turmoil, which soon tore the unity of the society asunder. In effect, members had to decide whether to remain faithful to Cappelli as a true prophet or whether to cast him off as a false messenger, a wolf in sheep's clothing who had deceived them.

In seeking to elucidate this critical period in the history of the Union, when Cappelli effectively sought to reconfigure the society according to his own theological vision, we draw heavily on two invaluable sources. The first is the extensive archival material related to Gustav Reuterholm's pilgrimage to meet Cappelli in Rome in early 1790. The journal kept by Reuterholm, alongside the considerable correspondence he conducted with members of the Union in Avignon and elsewhere at the time, affords us remarkable insights into how fellow members of the society viewed Cappelli. Most extraordinary of all, Reuterholm's personal archive also contains several documents—letters, short notes, and a series of prophetic statements—composed by Cappelli himself. These hitherto overlooked documents written by Cappelli provide us with an unprecedented glimpse into how the purported prophet interacted with and sought to guide fellow initiates of the Union.

In addition to sources related to Reuterholm's pilgrimage, we also examine the report entitled "Brief Details of the Society, or Sect Discovered on the Arrest of Ottavio Cappelli," drawn up by Holy Office shortly after he was taken into custody in 1790. As the unnamed author states, this document amounts to a summary of the fifty or so letters addressed to Cappelli by fellow members of the Union that the papal authorities discovered in his home at the time of his arrest. The seized correspondence ran from January 2 until October 1, 1790. Even in summary form, the subject matter offers penetrating insights into how members of the Union governed their religious, moral, political, health, and economic affairs according to what they believed were mediated oracles transmitted to them by Cappelli from Raphael. The report bemoans the fact that Cappelli apparently did not keep any of his correspondence from before 1790, depriving its author of the possibility to weave a more intricate tapestry of the society's machinations.

I

Over two centuries later it is still extremely difficult to ascertain much of note about Cappelli's activities prior to January 1790. We do know that after a little more than a year in Avignon, Cappelli returned to Rome, in early 1789. However, we know hardly anything about the precise timing and the motivations behind Cappelli's relocation to the Eternal City. It is notable, though, that the Italian peninsula, and Rome in particular, were the focus of dire prophetic warnings within the Avignon Society in early 1789. John Wright copied down many of these "Remarkable Prophecies" during his six-month stay in the papal enclave in 1789. His record of these prophecies, which, he explicitly outlines, were "relative to the present times, and approaching latter days," foresaw that "ROME will be the Theatre of great events . . . Troops will come down from the mountain . . . and the Capital of the world will experience great calamities."[6] Indeed, it is stated that "the PONTIFF will lose his power."[7]

It seems plausible that Cappelli's return to Rome was connected to the disasters predicted to befall the city in the near future. By June 1789 the society in Avignon was receiving regular letters "from the Union at ROME," which conveyed cryptic messages from Archangel Raphael. One such epistle narrated that the "ARCH-ANGEL RAPHAEL asked the brethren and sisters if the cold made them uneasy, and said, have a little patience, and the weather will be warm enough."[8] Is there a millenarian subtext to this coded message? Quite possibly, considering the sense of expectancy among the Union members in Avignon and Rome of imminent "terrible disasters" on the Italian peninsula. It is noteworthy that an extremely destructive earthquake did occur in central Italy on September 30, 1789.[9] This earthquake, which struck in Valtiberina in Tuscany, may well have been viewed by members of the Union as an affirmation of the dire predictions they had recently made about the fate of Rome.

Cappelli is not mentioned by name in the correspondence sent from the Union at Rome in the summer of 1789, but within the society only he enjoyed the status of a prophet who served as an intermediary between the archangels Gabriel and Raphael and the members. Interestingly, the surviving questions posed to the oracle by members of the society whilst Cappelli was resident in Avignon are addressed to the Archangel Gabriel. However, the correspondence sent by the Union in Rome to Avignon in June 1789 only mentions messages transmitted by Archangel Raphael. Thenceforth, for reasons unknown, Cappelli seems to have been solely in contact with the Archangel Raphael.

Despite the apparent regularity of communication between the Union in Rome and the society in Avignon in 1789, it seems that none of this correspondence is extant.

Consequently, not only do we know very little about precisely when and why Cappelli returned to Rome, but we are also faced with a dearth of material relating to his endeavours on behalf of and related to the Union until the close of 1789. In effect, this paucity of bona fide evidence is merely a continuation of a notable feature of Cappelli's earlier time in Avignon: the slenderest trace of an historical imprint.

II

On December 8, 1789, Reuterholm noted in his journal that Grabianka had received a "remarkable dispatch" from Rome. The Swedish nobleman does not elaborate on this message in his diary, but it is noteworthy that only one week later he pronounced that "I took the Lord's name, on my part, to travel to Italy." On December 20, 1789, only twelve days after Grabianka had received the extraordinary correspondence from Rome, Reuterholm and Silfverhielm left Avignon for the Eternal City. By 1789, Rome had for about two centuries been viewed as the destination par excellence for grand tourists seeking to satiate their thirst for classical knowledge.[10] Reuterholm's journal testifies that he and his compatriot did not neglect the traditional itinerary associated with Rome; it is replete with descriptions of the famous sites and artefacts that are common to travel accounts of the era.[11] Yet Reuterholm and Silfverhielm's sudden and unplanned departure for Rome was not primarily borne of a desire to observe the wonders of antiquity;[12] rather, it seems that the Swedes received some form of supposed command from Archangel Raphael via Cappelli, his intermediary.

It took nearly a month for the Swedish travellers to journey from Avignon to Rome, where they arrived on January 18, 1790. En route to Rome, Reuterholm received regular correspondence from various brethren of the society, who were eager for him to convey warm greetings to Cappelli and his family, as well as to the sisters and brothers of the society. A sense of anticipation is palpable in many of the letters sent to the Swedes at this time. On December 27, 1789, for example, Grabianka wrote to Reuterholm and asked him to embrace the brothers and sisters of the Union in Rome, including Cappelli (referred to using his three-digit number, 111). The following day, a fellow initiate of the society named Barozzi, a Franciscan monk of the Convent des Cordeliers in Moirans, near Grenoble, wrote to Reuterholm and Silfverhielm. In addition to providing the Swedes with numerous letters of introduction to Italian clergymen in Venice, Florence, and Rome, Barozzi also asked them to convey greetings to "those people who are dear to me"—namely Cappelli; his wife, Chiara (née Feltrini); and their son, Gerbonio (born circa 1781).[13]

The most enthusiastic messages Reuterholm received on his way to Rome came from the pen of Divonne, who had been initiated in Avignon shortly after the Swede. As discussed, Reuterholm and Divonne struck up something of an instant rapport in Avignon and their subsequent correspondence continues to reflect a close bond. On December

30, 1789, Divonne wrote to Reuterholm from Avignon, to say that he was waiting "with grand impatience" for news from his new friend. He also beseeches Reuterholm "not to forget me near our brother Octavio."[14] Divonne wrote to Reuterholm again on January 13, 1790, this time expressing his fondness for Cappelli and his family even more effusively: "I pray to dear brother Octavio and his whole family, according to the natural order and according to the spiritual order, to receive the assurance of the most tender attachment from a brother who knows them in God through the sentiments of his heart."[15] Divonne may have expressed the most gushing praise for Cappelli and his family at this time, but Grabianka was also not shy in lavishing compliments on Cappelli's children. In a letter to the Swedish travellers, dated January 16, 1790, for example, Grabianka refers to Cappelli's young daughter Margherita as "la petite sainte."[16]

As with Grabianka, Divonne also asked Reuterholm to pass on his greetings "to all our good sisters." Indeed, Divonne requests that Reuterholm ask the sisters to pray for him, "especially the Turkish sister."[17] We know precious little about the female members of the Union in Rome. However, it seems highly likely that this "Turkish sister" was the same woman who is mentioned by John Wright in a letter from Rome, which had arrived in Avignon on June 17, 1789: "The Union in Rome . . . informed us of a sister that is a daughter of a Turk, whom Brother Brimmore [Brumore] baptized at Silesia, between ten and fifteen years ago." This woman had returned to Alexandria in Egypt with her father, but on his death, "she was ordered by the Archangel Raphael . . . to fly into the Christian country."[18]

Barozzi and Divonne continued to shower tender greetings on Cappelli and his family throughout the twelve weeks that Reuterholm and Silfverhielm spent in Rome. In February 1790, for example, Barozzi wrote to the Swedes of his ardent desire to "be at your heels when you climb the stairs of my dear 111 [Cappelli], that I would gladly see the brave mother 9 [Chiara Cappelli] and the awakened Cherbo [Gerbonio]."[19] In March, Divonne asked Reuterholm and Silfverhielm to embrace Cappelli, whom he refers to as "the Job of our age," and his "dear and incomparable son," and to give the former an enclosed gift: a "little badinage" sent to him by "s[ister] 579," who, it is disclosed, is his 9-year-old daughter, who "has the same number (579) as me, inasmuch as she was received at the same time." This would appear to be something of a reciprocal gesture, as Divonne remarks that he has a portrait of "the amiable Cerbonio" above his bureau.[20]

Given the profuse expressions of affection for Cappelli's family conveyed by the likes of Grabianka, Barozzi, and Divonne, it is not entirely surprising that Reuterholm's description of his first meeting with the Italian, which took place on January 19, 1790 (a day after he and Silfverhielm had arrived in Rome), contains a fascinating vignette reflecting his domestic life. After settling into their accommodation, which had been arranged by Cappelli, Reuterholm describes how "the modest" Italian and his "little son Cherbonjo" effectively served as tour guides for the Swedes on a "long promenade" that took in St. Peter's Basilica, the outer halls of the Pope's Palace, the Raphael Rooms in the Vatican, the Pantheon, as well as many other places, including the most noteworthy columns and fountains.[21] The tour included a visit to Cappelli's home, situated on the Via della Croce.[22] Here Reuterholm and Silfverhielm met Cappelli's wife and "little daughter." A decidedly awkward scene then played out; Reuterholm describes how the guests "acted out a pitiful pantomime to them all, as they did not understand more French than we did Italian." The Swedish noblemen were then shown the principal sights Rome had to offer, and Reuterholm notes that it was very late before Cappelli and his son led them back to their lodgings.[23] Reuterholm's journal records visiting Cappelli at his home on ten further occasions before leaving Rome, on April 10. On that day, Reuterholm noted that Cappelli "followed me a good deal beyond the Porta del Populo," before they said their farewells.[24]

More insights into how Cappelli offered practical help to the Swedish travellers can be gleaned from a brief note that can be found among the Reuterholm papers housed at the archive of the Swedish Order of Freemasons. The billet seems to relate to the preparations made for a trip to Naples that was undertaken by Reuterholm and Silfverhielm between March 3 and 15. Cappelli writes that "the orders given to me from you . . . will be fulfilled tomorrow." This included making "a note of the provisions you will need if you don't want to perish on the road or be obliged to gather a great deal of provisions in the middle of the mountains." The note ends with Cappelli courteously hoping that they have "a pleasant trip and an equally pleasant return" and signing off with "I am faithfully yours III."[25]

III

As charming and helpful as Cappelli and his family may have been, Reuterholm and Silfverhielm's repeated visits to their home were not merely to observe scenes of domestic bliss or to receive practical aid. Of much greater consequence for the Swedes was the opportunity to experience direct contact with Raphael via Cappelli's supposed prophetic gift. In a letter to Duke Karl of Södermanland, written the day after his first meeting with Cappelli, Reuterholm describes his sense of exultation at being privy to such immediate correspondence with an angelic entity:

> Here [in Rome] I have found a person [Cappelli] supremely gifted by God . . . This man alone possesses more light than all the brethren in Avignon together, or more correctly: this is the source form which they receive all their light, and he is like a Deity. It is also through him [that they receive] the most remarkable information and instructions (of course, they come from heaven when I speak this way).[26]

According to Reuterholm, he "received a positive and quite clear command" to remain in Rome for holy week by "the one who has the right to rule over our fate."[27] Only at this time would he "receive the final seal of my initiation, my mission and the foundation of the sanctuary."[28]

At the time, Reuterholm and Silfverhielm's privileged access to "the one who has the right to rule over our fate" was commented upon with envy by Divonne, Ferrier, and Barozzi, who refer to him as "St. Vieillard" and "le venerable Vieillard" instead of using the name Raphael. A week after Reuterholm and Silfverhielm's departure from Avignon, for example, Divonne wrote to the former and exclaimed, "The Lord lets you see the St. Vieillard!" before expressing the hope that his friend "will be able to tell him two words" about him.[29] On January 2, 1790, when the Swedes were still en route to Rome, Ferrier also wrote to Reuterholm and expressed his pleasure that "you are permitted to see Saint Vieillard and that he gives you his blessing."[30] In February 1790, Divonne wrote to Reuterholm again and proclaimed, "I join with Cerbonio, dear brother Octavio and our worthy sisters to solicit Saint Vieillard in your favour, my good friend . . . Yes, he will grant you everything your heart desires." Around the same time, Barozzi also expressed a yearning "to be familiar with the venerable Vieillard."[31]

Members of the Union consistently use the name "St. Vieillard" when writing about Raphael at this time. On February 20, 1790, for example, the Council of Seven wrote to Reuterholm and Silfverhielm from Avignon to convey a sense of how fortunate the Swedes and the Union as a whole were: "You will surely meet our Saint Vieillard more than once, eh! May you acknowledge this, and be equally blessed for you, for us and for all those who are dear to our Union."[32]

Members of the Union not lucky enough to be able to travel to Rome to experience direct contact with St. Vieillard could evidently write to Cappelli to have the supposed prophet intercede on their behalf. The correspondence seized by the Holy Office in the autumn of 1790 is replete with letters from brothers and sisters in need of divine counsel. A particular feature of these petitions to Raphael is that the majority concern matters traditionally associated with the angel: health, marriage, and travel. It is noteworthy that Cappelli was born in Siena, where he may have been influenced by the cult of the Archangel Raphael that flourished in central Italy in the early modern period. In Florence, for example, where the cult seems to have been particularly strong, a youth confraternity, the Compagnia dell'Arcangelo Raffaello, existed until 1785. In other words, Cappelli's devotion to Raphael was redolent of the broader cult of the angel that was especially strong in Tuscany, where he grew up.[33]

A rich Christian tradition links Raphael with miraculous acts of healing. Not only did the angel cure the blindness of Tobit (book of Tobit 5:1–22), but he is also commonly associated with the angel who stirred the healing waters of the Pool of Bethesda (John 5:1–5).[34] With this in mind, it is understandable that the brothers and sisters of the Union sought to benefit from Raphael's healing powers via Cappelli, their very own conduit. In February 1790, for example, Barozzi wrote to Cappelli about "my friend and brother" Jean-François Nicolas, a physician, who was suffering from chronic leg pains. Barozzi beseeched St. Vieillard to indicate a remedy for Nicolas.[35] Interestingly, the physician

Delhomme also submitted a question to St. Vieillard regarding the best remedies for a chronic condition he was suffering from that was becoming more frequent.[36] Moreover, Divonne sent a note to Cappelli requesting advice and information on behalf of Sof'ia Stepanovna Razumovskaia, a Russian noblewoman, whose health was in a "most deplorable state."[37]

Members of the Union also wrote to Cappelli seeking marriage guidance from Raphael. The archangel's reputation as an astute matchmaker was, again, based on the book of Tobit, where he intercedes on behalf of God to ensure that Tobiah marries Sarah.[38] Richardière wrote to Cappelli, in May 1790, asking "Our Heavenly Benefactor Raphael" whether he can give any indication about the future destiny of his wife and children.[39] Ferdinand of Württemberg also wrote to Cappelli in 1790 so that the Italian could "present to our Holy Protector Raphael" a question regarding whether it is God's will that he must wait a long time before being able to fulfil the order to marry.[40]

In addition to his reputation as a healer and marriage maker, Raphael was (and is) venerated as a patron saint of travellers.[41] The widow Anne-Marie-Olympe de Fumel wrote to Cappelli to seek guidance about whether she should visit Etienne-Joseph Lespinasse, the governor of Pont-Saint-Esprit, some thirty miles to the north of Avignon, and, if so, who should accompany her on the journey.[42] The "Breve" also refers to a certain Sister Maire, who sought Raphael's approval for a journey to Grenoble, and to a question by unnamed brothers about whether they should pass through Avignon and other places on their return journey.[43] Thus distance did not deprive members of the Union from enjoying the privilege of questioning St. Vieillard. However, the correspondence of Divonne, Barozzi, and the Council of Seven in Avignon with Reuterholm and Silfverhielm strongly suggests that the Swedes had been granted special access to the angel, if not direct contact, through the intercession of Cappelli in Rome.

IV

Reuterholm's letter to Duke Karl, written the day after his initial meeting with Cappelli in Rome, conveys a distinct sense of euphoria. It is as if the Swede sensed that he was on the threshold of obtaining life-changing truths. Judging by this letter, it seems that Cappelli offered Reuterholm tantalising morsels of prophetic information that were relevant to his life. Most sensationally, Reuterholm wrote that he had been told that the reign of King Gustav III of Sweden would soon be coming to an end. This remarkable augury, bearing in mind Gustav's subsequent assassination in March 1792, offered a penetrating insight into a matter of utmost concern for Reuterholm. Cappelli clearly knew his audience at this first meeting, as less than a year had passed since Reuterholm was placed under house arrest by his sovereign for his opposition to the Union and Security Act (1789), which increased the king's powers at the expense of the aristocracy.[44] In other words, Reuterholm had a fraught relationship with Gustav III and at the time of his travels to Avignon and Rome, effectively a period of exile, he was acutely aware of how insecure his position at the Swedish court was. Thus, this initial snippet of information vis-à-vis his sovereign would have surely whetted the Swede's appetite for further perspicacious revelations. At the same time, Reuterholm's letter to his patron also contains a note of decided caution: "Do not fear my gracious lord, that I may be abused or deceived. The truth of it will soon be shown in the fullness of days."[45]

Given the sense of anticipation expressed by Divonne and Barozzi, as well as Reuterholm's own initial exhilaration after his first meeting with Cappelli, it is somewhat puzzling that the Swedish noblemen had to wait until March 20 before apparently experiencing a direct encounter with St. Vieillard. Reuterholm's brief and prosaic description of this event, which took place at Cappelli's home, is also perplexing: "Octavjo regaled us with an apparition of S[t.] V[ieillard]."[46] We cannot be sure how Reuterholm reacted to this meeting, but his underwhelming journal entry would seem to be telling.

Irrespective of Reuterholm's reaction to the apparition of St. Vieillard in March, we do know that the Swede's access to Cappelli enabled him to ask the celestial entity at least nineteen questions.[47] The series of enquiries written down by Reuterholm seemingly complies with a request by Cappelli himself, who wrote in an undated note: "All of the questions I have to ask S[anto] V[ecchio],[48] I will have listed and not told orally. Take comfort . . . that they will be great and of grand value. I have apprised them of this in Avignon."[49] It is notable that Reuterholm's questions touch on a wide variety of issues of pressing concern for the baron that go beyond the traditional categories of health, marriage, and travel strongly associated with Archangel Raphael among Roman Catholics. It may be that Reuterholm, as a Lutheran, was unfamiliar with the culture of Catholic veneration of the archangel. To be sure, Reuterholm did ask two questions about marriage, relating to his unconsummated (and evidently unhappy) marriage that had lasted for two years and whether he should seek another wife and, if so, how many children she would bear him. He also asked one question about travel, in connection with whether he should return to Avignon and Rome in the future.

In addition to these questions, Reuterholm sought advice about a wide array of other matters. Family affairs were broached in several enquiries, including whether he could receive direct communication with the spirits of relatives. He also posed two questions related to his brother—namely, whether his sibling should take a wife and whether he should remain in Finland, go to Stockholm, or travel. He also asked whether his brother should be consecrated into the society. Three other questions address the organisation of the society in Sweden, vis-à-vis the form of rituals to be adopted, the admission of women and whether Reuterholm could tell the other brothers about his experiences during his travels. Significantly, two questions focus on Gustav III: he asks if the monarch "will again intensify his persecution against me," and if he "should accept some other service as long as he [Gustav III] lives." Reuterholm also wishes to know more about his future career prospects in Sweden, in particular, whether he will be able to fulfil his wish to serve Duke Karl. Advice and "some comfort" are also sought on behalf of Duke Karl, and

Reuterholm also wishes to know more about Silfverhielm's precise role in spreading "the truth" in Sweden. Lastly, two questions highlight Reuterholm's continuing fascination with strands of esotericism. First, he wishes to ascertain from St. Vieillard whether Prince Charles of Hesse-Cassel did indeed have "a great knowledge of celestial truth" and if he should visit him in Holstein. Second, he asks permission from St. Vieillard to receive "the miraculous tincture and the Philosophers' Stone" from a man in Rome.

The nineteen questions posed by Reuterholm are fascinating, but in many respects, they are not surprising. They broadly reflect his principal preoccupations: an intimate bond with Duke Karl; the enthusiastic embrace of initiatic societies, particularly Freemasonry, and a passion for many aspects of Western esotericism, including alchemy; along with fairly typical worries concerning conjugal and family matters.[50] Notable by their absence are any enquiries regarding religion, which suggests that Reuterholm's mind was not overly vexed by theological concerns.

It would seem Reuterholm received no direct response to the nineteen questions, judging by the lack of any such document in his personal archive. However, there is a note (in Italian) among Reuterholm's papers that seems to be a response of sorts from St. Vieillard. It is a curious command and, to all intents and purposes, appears to be motivated by nothing other than vainglory on the part of Cappelli:

> The Elected Brother destined to spread truth and enlighten those who have lived blindly until this year is ordained by the Heavens to order Duke Karl in writing that without delay he is to immediately send notice in his name and bearing his personal wax seal to anyone who wishes to be present at the Baptisimal Font of the future Creature who is about to be born to the couple Ottavio and Chiara Cappelli, so that the visions in which they took part last year may be achieved.[51]

The wording of this note is identical to one confiscated from Cappelli by the Holy Office in 1790.[52] From the notes seized by the papal authorities, we also know that Ferdinand of Württemberg was named godfather of a daughter born to Ottavio and Chiara.[53] In other words, Cappelli sought to use his status as a prophet to bolster the standing of his children (and himself) through association with eminent personages.

Furthermore, a second note among Reuterholm's papers relates to his friend and countryman, Erik Magnus von Staël, the Swedish ambassador in Paris and a fellow Freemason.[54] It was commonplace for initiates of the Union to intercede on behalf of close acquaintances and family. In the case of Staël, Reuterholm evidently sought counsel from St. Vieillard in 1790 regarding his friend's troubled marriage with Germaine de Staël, the celebrated woman of letters:

> I am asking that our future Brother Stael approach the treacherous woman more calmly and succeed in distracting her amiably with a tour around Italy, which would

be the means to pull her away from the dreadful friendship that in such fashion she holds through diabolical means, thus in a short time he will be freed from every malady because I will take it upon myself to have her win the battle.[55]

The remarkable marriage guidance offered to Staël came at a time when his wife's affair with Louis, Comte de Narbonne, was public knowledge.[56] Moreover, it occurred at a time when Staël had also drawn close to several members of the Avignon Society, particularly Reuterholm, Bousie, and Gombault, and, it seems, intended to join the group himself. As with Reuterholm, Staël also frequently consulted with supposed prophetesses and prophets, and therefore it is not surprising that he sought to enlist his countryman's help in seeking Cappelli's intercession.[57]

However, though it is possible that Reuterholm did not receive a direct response to his nineteen questions, he did receive a twenty-nine-point document (in French), dated February 1, 1790, which brims with prophetic utterances, alongside an accompanying note (in Cappelli's hand in Italian).[58] In the note, Cappelli (in the guise of St. Vieillard) explains that "you should not let your heart decide what to do with these 29 points, but rather you need to follow and receive my orders in your hands."[59] Crucially, only when Reuterholm makes a "profession of faith" will men and women follow his precepts. Interestingly, the note also stipulates that the Swedish travellers should "return to your Patria, not before the tenth of April," although they are permitted to visit Turin and Paris en route to their homeland.[60] Reuterholm and Silfverhielm followed these instructions meticulously, leaving Rome, as mentioned, on April 10, 1790, and returning to Stockholm via Turin and Paris.

Yet Reuterholm would have certainly found it far more difficult to comply with many of the commands he supposedly received from St. Vieillard, which are contained in the twenty-nine-point document. Grabianka seems to refer to the French-language document in a letter to Reuterholm and Silfverhielm, written on March 5, 1790: "At the first mail you will receive, my dear friends, the translation of all that you have from the St. Vieillard for your instruction and your conduit, 369 [Ferrier] will do the translation without any delay."[61]

To be sure, not all twenty-nine instructions would have proved to be problematic for Reuterholm. The third instruction, for example, is infused with a millenarian fervour and proclaims that "in order to end the age a true society has been formed which has already begun to bring souls back." With this in mind, Reuterholm was commanded to "enter the premier route and commit yourself again under the banner of Jesus Christ, because it is now the time to be enlightened."[62] Yet, in sum, the instructions amount to little more than a diatribe against Protestantism and a call to embrace the Roman Catholic faith. This is most vociferously articulated in the sixth instruction, which exhorts Reuterholm and Silfverhielm "to recognise Jesus, the Church, and all the ecclesiastical hierarchy" in order "that they return without delay to their first state and that they completely abjure the sacrilegious dogmas of the scoundrel who made them."[63] This decidedly confrontational language would appear to refer to Luther and Lutheranism. Bearing in mind that Reuterholm had not broached the subject of religion in his nineteen questions, the tone of these instructions may well have come as an unpleasant and shocking surprise. The seventh instruction is slightly conciliatory in allowing the Swedes to forgo a public renunciation of their Lutheran faith, but the eighth instruction declares in no uncertain terms that "he will not be called our son if he does not abjure all the sacrilegious precepts, which, in the past, were promulgated and received" and "if he does not embrace the true religion again."[64] The tenth instruction invokes the example of the "heroine" Queen Christina, who abdicated from the Swedish throne in 1654 and converted to Roman Catholicism.[65] By citing this famous precedent and then proclaiming that "the time has arrived to save Sweden and restore the general peace," St. Vieillard is issuing a command for Reuterholm and Silfverhielm to follow Christina's example.

This strident call to Reuterholm and Silfverhilem to abjure Lutheranism and to accept solely the rites of the Roman Catholic Church was apparently not an isolated command. Indeed, the author of the "Brief Details of the Society" noted that though Cappelli undoubtedly abused and deceived the credulous members of the Union into believing he was a prophet able to communicate with and transmit messages from Raphael, he did so with the aim of obligating them to embrace the Roman Catholic faith.[66] Among the correspondence seized by the Holy Office on Cappelli's arrest were several letters from non-Catholic brothers directly related to this contentious instruction. Bousie, for example, an Anglican, wrote a letter to St. Vieillard regarding the abjuration of his religion and whether it applied to his whole family, and also whether it had to be a public or private renunciation.[67] Pleshcheev, who belonged to the Russian Orthodox Church, wrote to Cappelli to implore Raphael to advise him about whether he would have to marry according to Catholic practices and whether a fellow brother would have to receive the Roman Catholic communion.[68] The "Brief Details" comments on a letter from Ferdinand of Württemberg, who was apparently aghast that "the many brothers . . . who profess the religion of Luther, and Calvin, and others" will have to accept the Catholic doctrine of transubstantiation.[69]

Thus the time Reuterholm and Silfverhielm spent in Rome coincided with a period when Cappelli, using his considerable power as a supposed prophet, was seeking to introduce controversial doctrinal reform into the Union. The twenty-nine instructions transmitted to the Swedes on February 1, 1790, reflect Cappelli's attempt to effectively bring about the conversion of all non-Catholic initiates of the society via what he sought to portray as divine commands.

We know next to nothing about how Reuterholm and Silfverhielm reacted to the proselytising endeavours Cappelli enacted in the name of Raphael at this time. However, a curious letter exists among Reuterholm's papers, written by Cappelli on April 11, 1790— that is, the day after the departure of the Swedish noblemen. The letter, written to an unidentified ambassador who would appear to be a fellow initiate of the Union, begins with Cappelli explaining that "their departure caused a great deal of distress to everyone in the house." Cappelli also wishes the travellers "a most pleasant remainder of the trip . . . hoping that they will remember us as well." Yet these compliments are undercut by a scathing attack on Silfverhielm, who was apparently "not worthy" of the ambassador's protection because he had "trampled this city against God's will" and had cavorted with "many female subjects, about which I will remain silent." Cappelli also implies that he had not brought Silfverhielm before Santo Vecchio because of his scandalous behaviour. Another intriguing aspect of this letter is that Cappelli signs off by stating "I am the f[ratello] III Cardinal."[70] This letter provides the first evidence of Cappelli's title within the Union, which suggests a high level of seniority but one, it would seem, below that of Pernety (the pontiff) and Grabianka (the King).[71]

V

Eleven days after Reuterholm and Silfverhielm left Rome, on April 21, 1790, Cappelli beseeched "the holy Protector Raphael" to dictate a new form of consecration for the Union.[72] It would seem that Cappelli had harboured such a desire for several months. Tellingly, Cappelli had received a long letter from Ferrier, on January 9, 1790, in which the latter provided a lengthy description of the rituals and origin of the society's consecration, as it had been practised since 1779 in Berlin.[73] The twenty-nine instructions given to Reuterholm and Silfverhielm, along with the letters sent by the likes of Bousie, Pleshcheev, and Ferdinand of Württemberg, also demonstrate Cappelli's determination at the start of 1790 to enact unprecedented ceremonial and doctrinal reform within the Union.

On the same day Cappelli made his request, he wrote down the reply he supposedly received, entitled "Consecration dictated to brother III . . . from our H[oly] Protector R[aphael]."[74] The divine command purportedly communicated to Cappelli contained three pivotal revisions to the consecration ceremony, which, in effect, outlined a radically different vision for the eleven-year-old society. First, any new initiate wishing to be consecrated into the society would have to "abjure all maxims by iniquitous writers" that they had been taught. In other words, they would have to renounce all heretical Protestant creeds. They would then have to solemnly "swear and promise . . . to be a true follower of the Roman Apostolic Church."[75] As noted, this move had been in the offing for months, but now Cappelli was making a concrete effort to set this doctrinal alteration in stone.

In conjunction with this strict enforcement of Roman Catholicism, Raphael also purportedly instructed the society to transform the consecration rituals to reflect a much more pronounced avowal of Trinitarian principles and veneration of Mary. In other words, Cappelli—through his role as a perceived prophet—was seeking to make the Union a much more conventional Catholic society by casting out all the esoteric elements at odds with the doctrine of the Roman Church. Gone, for example, is the so-called Circle of Power and the emphasis on the symbolism of the number nine (the consecration lasts for nine days and candidates go around the Circle of Power nine times). Instead, the new consecration ceremony, written down by Cappelli, instructs the members of the society to form three circles, which should each contain the names of God and Mary three times. Moreover, the length of the consecration is cut from nine days to three days, to reflect the new pre-eminence of Trinitarian symbolism. On the third day, candidates even had to trace a triangle in the middle circle, and at the foot of this image, they had to light a fire and make an offering to the Holy Trinity of three ounces of incense.[76] The adoration of Mary included the ritual kissing of the Blessed Virgin's name. Candidates also had to beseech the Mother of God in the following manner: "pure Virgin, Immaculate Mary, I pray for your intercession, that you be a mediator for me."[77]

The third major reform stipulated in Raphael's communication of April 21 related to the introduction of a three-tiered hierarchy within the society. Hitherto no such division had existed, but now consecrated members were to be distinguished as (a) greater children (*figli magni*); (b) medium children (*figli medi*); and (c) lesser children (*figli minimi*). Only the *figli magni* were to receive the three personal numbers that had previously been given to all initiates; the *figli medi* were to be awarded two numbers; and the *figli minimi* were to receive a single digit.[78] The reasoning for implementing these hierarchical ranks is not entirely clear. It is possible that the rapid expansion of the society in 1789 led to a desire among some initiates for a recognition of their seniority. The tripartite system could have also been a reflection of the Trinitarian reconfiguration of the society's rites and symbolism.

The author of the "Breve" notes that the reforms commanded by Raphael and communicated by Cappelli came into effect in September 1790, at a special assembly of the society in Avignon.[79] However, we have no record of the discussions that took place in Avignon vis-à-vis the new instructions. Undoubtedly, the most incontrovertible proof of the positive embrace of Cappelli's reforms can be seen in *Les vertus*, the lengthy paean to Mary published by Pernety in 1790. In the introduction to this text, Pernety extolled Mary as a "unique source of enlightenment (*lumières*), filled with grace."[80] Pernety's reverence for Swedenborgian principles, which was so prevalent in the early years of the society, is nowhere to be seen in the pages of *Les vertus*. Instead, the tome is wholly in accord with Cappelli's vision of a faithful Marian and Trinitarian society of Roman Catholics. With complete justification, a commentator in the London-based *New Jerusalem Magazine* noted in 1790 that the society in Avignon "insist on the indispensable necessity of worshipping the Virgin Mary." What is more, they strictly adhere "to the Athanasian Creed with respect to the partition of the divinity into three distinct persons . . . so that on these and on many other considerations the Avignon Society may with great propriety be stiled [*sic*] the *Antipodes* of the New Church."[81]

VI

The Swedenborgians of the New Church were not alone in expressing disdain for the society's burgeoning cult of Mary. Most tellingly, Tieman, who had been raised as a Pietist, had hitherto sought to be initiated into the society in Avignon, and been an enthusiastic advocate of its pivotal role in the imminent grand millenarian drama, was, by the middle of 1790, aghast at the new Marian hue of the group. In a letter from this time to Friederike Sophia, Duchess of Württemberg, a Lutheran who had been initiated into the society in 1788, Tieman is not circumspect in expressing his disillusionment and scorn: "What have we done madame! Instead of searching for the Lord, who called us to worship God in spirit in truth, we would seek it in traditions, in councils, in apparitions & revelations of the Blessed Virgin & saints, in heaps of miracles without number."[82]

At the same time as Tieman was lambasting the society for its Marian cult, it is possible to discern the first aspersions beginning to be cast against Cappelli as a genuine prophet. On June 1, 1790, Divonne, a Calvinist, wrote a letter to Reuterholm, a Lutheran, in which there is no trace of the ardent sentiments of warmth and devotion to Cappelli that had been so prevalent up until April of that year. The letter, which is partly encrypted, conveys to Reuterholm how 379D, whose identity is not known, had recently stayed with Divonne at his home in Geneva and had told his host "that he was perfectly convinced . . . that 111 [Cappelli] was an imposter," and had irrefutable proof to back up this claim. Far from simply dismissing these accusations, Divonne informed Reuterholm that he would wait before irrevocably fixing his opinion on the matter.[83]

Four days later, Ferrier wrote a curious letter to Reuterholm, who was in Paris at the time, in which he vented his anger at Silfverhielm. According to Ferrier, "our dear brother" had "spoken too thoughtlessly about our society." Moreover, Ferrier was angry at Silfverhilem because he "gave birth to doubts where there certainly would not have been any." Although Ferrier's accusation is rather oblique, he does proceed to affirm that Reuterholm himself "did not have doubts about 111 [Cappelli]."[84] Ferrier does not disclose the nature of the doubts, but this letter reveals more evidence of the fraught relationship between Cappelli and Silfverhielm, which Cappelli first articulated in his vituperative attack on the Swede in April. We do not know the exact basis of Silfverhielm's disgruntlement with Cappelli, but a possible explanation is hinted at in a letter, dated September 11, 1790, from Staël to Reuterholm. Herein Staël relates that Bousie had said to him that "my friend was very hasty in his judgement of the man in Rome. He claims that my friend has not been robbed."[85] Could it be that Silfverhielm accused Cappelli, esteemed by the society as a prophet, of thievery and skulduggery? This would certainly explain the less-than-kind accusations flung at the Swede by Cappelli and Ferrier. Whatever the case, by September 1790 it is possible to detect a notable degree of disquiet among several non-Catholics closely associated with the group about Cappelli's role as a prophet within the society.

VII

Yet there is no indication that any member of the society foresaw the dire fate that was soon to befall Cappelli, on September 27, 1790, when he was arrested, along with his wife and two priests. The first report of Cappelli's incarceration by the Holy Office was written on October 2 and appeared a week later in *Gazzetta Universale*. This initial report referred to Cappelli as a "simple servant of the piazza and an innkeeper."[86] A follow-up report for the *Gazzetta Universale*, written on October 8, declared that there were "countless conversations taking place" about Cappelli's arrest. The newspaper reported that Cappelli was rumoured to be the head of a new sect called the Angelic Dance (*il Ballo Angelico*), which had recruited more than a thousand men and five hundred women. Exactly nine months after the detention of the infamous Count Cagliostro on similar grounds, the *Gazzetta Universale* declared that Cappelli's "disgrace" now appeared the more famous.[87] This would not seem to an exaggeration, as numerous eminent Romans were quick to comment on the cause célèbre. On October 9, for example, Luigi Gaetano Marini, the well-known natural philosopher, wrote that Cappelli was "said to be the leader of a society like the Illuminati and plotted great things." He also described Cappelli, whom he had met in April, as a "solemn rascal and imposter" and a magician who was able to predict the lottery and who conversed with the Madonna and with angels.[88] Count Girolamo Astorri was also of the opinion that Cappelli was a member of the Illuminati and a Freemason, as well as being an emissary of Russian Jesuits; and Reginaldo Tanzini, a Jansenist abbot from Florence, posited that Cappelli was an envoy of American Jesuits.[89] By November 1790, the level of notoriety surrounding Cappelli's arrest was such that numerous newspapers across Europe saw fit to inform their readers about the unfolding scandal in Rome.[90]

Cappelli's arrest sparked something of an eighteenth-century media frenzy, in which speculative rumour had free reign. Yet a curiously accurate feature of the reporting of the scandal, amid the swirl of hearsay, was the remarkable and bizarre fact that Cappelli was at the time in military service for both the Russian Empire and the House of Württemberg. Indeed, a letter to Pleshcheev from Gaspare Santini, the Russian consul in Rome and a prominent financier and art dealer, indicates that a total of six officers' patents were found during Cappelli's arrest: three were signed by no less than Grigorii Aleksandrovich Potemkin and three by Duke Ferdinand of Württemberg.[91] In addition to Ottavio Cappelli, the other patents related to Gerbonio (his son) and Ferrier respectively. Santini, who characterises Cappelli as a "good-for-nothing" commoner from Lucca, attests that it was precisely because Cappelli and the others started to adorn the military uniform of Württemberg and then Russia that the Roman authorities ordered them to be put under surveillance.[92] In truth, it may not have been too onerous a task to track Cappelli, judging by the remarks made by Tieman shortly after hearing of his arrest: "it was no doubt taken with umbrage to see him appear in a Russian uniform, which he put on with éclat and pomp. What good is this éclat, pomp and festivity?"[93]

According to the documents seized by the papal authorities, Cappelli received the military patents, in April 1790, by directly enlisting the help of Pleshcheev and Ferdinand of Württemberg. Other letters apparently indicated that Raphael had commanded such a course of action, in anticipation of imminent tumult in Rome. In 1790, Cappelli had been informed by members of the society in France of the prophecies of Suzette Labrousse, which predicted the fall of the temporal power of the pontiff.[94] Such predictions were very similar to the dire warnings expressed by Cappelli himself in 1789. If Rome was to soon be the stage for a grand upheaval, Cappelli evidently wanted to be waiting in the wings in a handsome uniform.

VIII

The incarceration of Cappelli in Rome brought the tensions within the society to a head. At least two of the Council of Seven—Ferrier and Richardière—remained loyal to Cappelli. They were the ones, after all, who had travelled to Turin in 1787 to meet the Italian and escort him back to Avignon. They had no doubt invested much in effectively bringing Cappelli into the fold of the Avignon Society. At the time, Corberon noted that Ferrier felt that Cappelli possessed more light alone than all the other brothers in Avignon.[95] This echoes Reuterholm's early eulogistic description of Cappelli, who, it should be remembered, received instruction from Ferrier in Avignon at the end of 1789. As mentioned, Ferrier, a former Jesuit, was godfather to one of Cappelli's children, and is known to have been one of the two other individuals who joined the Italian in donning military uniforms in Rome. His whereabouts at the time of Cappelli's detention are not known. Ferrier may well have been implicated in the Cappelli affair, hence it seems to have fallen upon Richardière to try to defend Cappelli and secure his release. In a letter to Pleshcheev, for example, Richardière attached a notebook for Potemkin, in which he outlined that Cappelli emanated from an ancient and eminent Venetian family. Furthermore, Richardière railed against the Russian consul in Rome, Santini, who was accused of intriguing against Cappelli.[96]

Richardière's intervention proved to be in vain, in no small measure because of Santini's seeming reluctance to defend the Russian military officer. Shortly after Cappelli's arrest, Tieman wrote to the Duchess of Württemberg and expressed his surprise that Santini, whom he knew well and knew to have "great credit with the Pope," was not able to bring about the release of someone who was in possession of an authentic Russian military patent. Tieman explains this reticence by adding that "there is an eel under the rocks"—that is, the authorities were aware of Cappelli's links to the Avignon Society. Significantly, Tieman expresses no concern whatsoever about Cappelli's fate, but is alarmed by the real possibility that Duke Ferdinand might be ensnared in the scandalous affair.[97] On November 15, some six weeks after his arrest, Cappelli's hopes for a short stay in prison were effectively quashed when Count Vittore Cassini, the Russian councillor of legation in Rome, informed the authorities that they had abandoned Cappelli "to the rigours of the law."[98] This was coupled with Cappelli's inability to produce a patent from Württemberg, which had apparently been lost at sea in a shipwreck![99]

Nearly fourteen months passed between Cappelli's arrest and the final verdict, which was reached on November 21, 1791, by Tommaso Vincenzo Pani, a Dominican inquisitor and the commissioner general of the Holy Office. From surviving correspondence, it seems that members of the Union were largely in the dark for several months about the reasons behind Cappelli's detention, as well as the likely outcome of the Holy Office's investigation. On February 11, 1791, for example, Divonne confessed to Reuterholm that "relative to Octavio, I am still in the same state of incertitude."[100] Less than a month later, Gombault wrote to Corberon and updated him on the latest (lack of) news about Cappelli: "369 B [Ferrier] did not give me much information on 111 [Cappelli]. It seems we do not know the reasons for his detention."[101]

The first definitive news about Cappelli's case would have surely shocked the members of the Union: on August 31, 1791, the Ante-Preparatory Commission of the Holy Office issued a death sentence against him. This decision was publicised by several newspapers across Europe, and some even speculated that Pope Pius VI would mitigate the sentence to life imprisonment.[102] This line of thinking may have gained momentum by the announcement, on October 1, 1791, that Chiara Cappelli had been released.[103]

Given the preliminary verdict, it is somewhat surprising that the final sentence, made public two days after being reached by Pani on November 21, 1791, confined Cappelli to seven years of imprisonment.[104] Pani outlined some of the distinctive features of the society (that it was millenarian, open to both sexes and all nations, made use of numerical identification, conducted cabalistic operations, and promoted fabulous apparitions and communications with angels) before condemning the sect for "holding secret and illicit assemblies," whereby "they clearly proved that their society had a perverse and criminal object." Cappelli is personally reprimanded for his "culpable temerity" and "impious superstition," as well as his "shameless imposture," which "should not remain unpunished." The leniency of the verdict against Cappelli was commented upon by Divonne, who posits that the testimony of those who knew him and swore that he was in good faith may have mitigated his sentence, "otherwise I do not understand how the judgement could be so moderate."[105]

Irrespective of the degree of clemency shown by the Holy Office, the damage done to Cappelli's reputation as a genuine prophet within the Union by his arrest and incarceration proved irreparable. As mentioned, only Ferrier and Richardière can be marked down as Cappelli loyalists. Grabianka said little about Cappelli in 1807 during his lengthy interrogations in St. Petersburg (see chapter 6), where, like Cappelli, he was accused by the Russian authorities, at a time when they were gravely threatened by external forces, of being a revolutionary and a member of the illuminati. However, Grabianka did, however, state that he had come to regard Cappelli as a "false prophet" when he realised he was being deceived and when the Italian began to scheme against his leadership.[106] It should be recalled that Grabianka had been warned about the dangers of false prophets by Samuel Best, on October 11, 1786 (see chapter 2). Yet contemporary testimony by the likes of Tieman and Reuterholm, who were once so enamoured of Cappelli, reveals the depths to which his repute and status had sunk among arguably the majority of members of the society. On November 29, 1791, that is, less than a week after Pani's judgement had been published, Tieman wrote a scathing indictment of Cappelli to the Duchess of Württemberg from Rome. He described having a conversation with Johann Friedrich Reiffenstein, the renowned cicerone, who told him that Cappelli "was an adventurer and a man of nothing," before adding that "it is almost impossible to believe that Heaven has chosen such an imbecilic man, so vain and so stupid to be his agent in the new Church."[107]

An equally trenchant repudiation of Cappelli was expressed by Reuterholm shortly after the Holy Office had published its verdict. On December 5, 1791, Reuterholm wrote to Duke Karl from Pisa, explaining that he, Divonne, and Ferdinand of Württemberg had undergone a complete volte-face in their estimation of Cappelli (and the society as a whole): "He will now receive his angelic visions during seven years of imprisonment. In this verdict, the society in Avignon is completely unmasked with all its principles, oracles, lies, rituals . . . And I realise that I have been the first to discover these spiritual deceivers."[108] Writing to Reuterholm on the subject in January 1792, Ferdinand confessed that he had been duped by a cunning trickster, but that "my amour-propre, profoundly humiliated, finds consolation in the idea that God, who alone scrutinises the heart of man, knows the purity of my intentions."[109]

IX

At the beginning of 1790 the Union in Avignon and Rome reached its apotheosis. A fresh wave of new initiates at the close of 1789, including Reuterholm and Divonne, demonstrated that the society was able to attract members from across Europe, from a wide variety of Christian denominations, and from the upper echelons of the continent's nobility. Up until this time the society in Avignon had promoted something of an inclusive, ecumenical millenarian vision, which found room for esotericists and Swedenborgians. In the guise of Cappelli, the society also seemed to possess its very own prophet, one who could offer to intercede with the archangels Gabriel and Raphael on behalf of newly consecrated members. Moreover, revolutionary events in France seemed to herald, for many, the advent of the new millennium. Yet by the end of 1790, the society was in crisis. It was initially convulsed by the provocative instructions conveyed by Cappelli, which effectively sought to make it much more of a conventional Catholic sect, and was then further rent by his arrest and subsequent conviction in Rome.

However, as we will see, though the society fractured irreparably, it was not dealt a fatal blow by Cappelli's incarceration. Indeed, it faired considerably better than the supposed prophet himself. In August 1795, Cappelli was pardoned by Pius VI, but was exiled from the papal territories and barred from returning to Rome. According to his own testimony in 1799, he then travelled to Livorno, Siena, and St. Petersburg, where in 1796 Catherine II awarded him the title of Major in Russian service. Several historians have taken this assertion at face value. It seems much more likely, however, that it was merely a false story concocted by Cappelli and his lawyer, Agostino Valle, in order to try and spare him the death penalty by lauding his renewed status as an officer in the Russian army.[110] No evidence whatsoever exists that Cappelli was accepted back into Russian service or even visited Russia. Indeed, Cassini confirmed as much in his letter of October 1799, in which he reaffirmed that Cappelli had been abandoned by Russia "to the rigours of the law" in 1790. Cappelli maintained that after travelling to St. Petersburg, he returned to Italy and settled in Florence. In all likelihood, Cappelli simply settled in Florence at some point after his release.[111] However, in November 1798 he did return to Rome, during the short-lived Roman Republic, ostensibly to settle matrimonial affairs with Chiara, his estranged wife.[112] Cappelli enjoyed his liberty for nearly a year in Rome, until the fall of the Republic, although next to nothing is known about his activities during this time. The extremely modest possessions seized by the authorities on his arrest in November 1799 indicate he no longer enjoyed any kind of reputation as a prophet. Instead, the authorities derogatorily referred to Cappelli as "the cleric bigamist" (*il chierico bigamo*) because of his cohabitation with Maria Dorsani and the clerical career that he had abandoned at the age of twenty-four.[113] Thus his execution in January 1800 had far less to do with eliminating an eminent threat to the new authorities in Rome than with sending an unequivocal signal to other would-be prophets who could potentially threaten the fragile regime.

NOTES

1. Alessandro Ademollo, *Le annotazioni di Mastro Titta, carnefice romano: Supplizi e suppliziati* (Citta di Castello: S. Lapi Tipografo Editore, 1886), 49.

2. "A a Eccma Giunta di Stato Romana per Ottavio Cappello Contro Il Fisco," no. 26, AdSdR, Giunta di Stato, fascicolo 7, busta 1.

3. "Nota delle robe, che Maria Dorsani tenura riposte in casa del Sig. Ottavio Capelli," AdSdR, Giunta di Stato, fascicolo 7, busta 1.

4. Marina Caffiero, "Cappelli, Ottavio," in *Dizionario biografico degli italiani*, vol. 18 (Rome: Istituto dell'Enciclopedia italiana, 1975), 727.

5. *Gazzetta Universale*, Oct. 9, 1790, 648. A report in this edition of the newspaper, written on Oct. 2, 1970, related that Cappelli had been arrested the previous Monday.

6. Wright, *A Revealed Knowledge*, 25.

7. Wright, *A Revealed Knowledge*, 27, 28.

8. Wright, *A Revealed Knowledge*, 43.

9. On contemporary reactions to the earthquake, see V. Castelli, "In Troubled Times, in a Divided Country: The 1789 Valtiberina Earthquake," in *Historical Seismology: Interdisciplinary Studies of Past and Recent Earthquakes,* ed. Julien Fréchet, Mustapha Meghraoui, and Massimiliano Stucchi (Dordrecht: Springer, 2010), 249–60.

10. See Jeremy Black, *Italy and the Grand Tour* (New Haven, CT: Yale University Press, 2003), 46–67.

11. For a discussion of the sites visited by Reuterholm in France and Italy, see Göran Anderberg, "Gustaf Adolf Reuterholms vallfart till revolutionens Frankrike och Italien," *Historisk Tidskrift för Finland* 3 (2005): 305–39.

12. Two days after arriving in Rome Reuterholm wrote to Duke Karl of Södermanland and complained of a lack of money and clothes, which he had left in Paris, clearly having not anticipated any trip to Italy. See Reuterholm to Duke Karl, Jan. 20, 1790, RA, Kungliga arkiv 371/10, 89.

13. Barozzi to Reuterholm and Silfverhielm, Dec. 28, 1789, SFOA, 121.141.8 (no. 3).

14. Divonne to Reuterholm, Dec. 30, 1789, SFOA, 121.141.4 (no. 4).

15. Divonne to Reuterholm, Jan. 13, 1790, SFOA, 121.141.4 (no. 6).

16. Grabianka to Reuterholm and Silfverhielm, Jan. 16, 1790, SFOA, 121.141.4 (no. 7).

17. Divonne to Reuterholm, Dec. 30, 1789, SFOA, 121.141.4. (no. 4).

18. Wright, *A Revealed Knowledge*, 43–4.

19. Barozzi to Reuterholm and Silfverhielm, Feb. 17, 1790, SFOA, 121.141.8 (no. 2).

20. Divonne to Reuterholm and Silfverhielm, Mar. 6, 1790, SFOA, 121.141.4 (no. 13).

21. "Rese Journal öfver min Utländska vandring," Jan. 19, 1790, RA, Reuterholm-Ädelgrenska samlingen, vol. 22.

22. Cappelli's home on the Via della Croce was in the "maison de Mr du Clos." This is most likely a reference to Charles Pinot Duclos, the well-known French author, who undertook a voyage to Italy in 1766. See Charles Pinot Duclos, *Voyage en Italie: Ou considerations sur l'Italie*, 2nd ed. (Paris: Buisson, 1791).

23. "Rese Journal," RA, Jan. 19, 1790.

24. "Rese Journal," RA, Apr. 10, 1790. The other visits to Cappelli's home took place on Jan. 23, 29; Feb. 15, 22, 26; Mar. 16, 18, 20, 29; and Apr. 9.

25. Undated note, SFOA, 121.141.7 (no. 6).

26. Reuterholm to Duke Karl of Södermanland, Jan. 20, 1790. RA, Kungliga arkiv 371/10, 88.

27. Easter Sunday in 1790 fell on April 4.

28. Reuterholm to Duke Karl, Jan. 20, 1790. RA, Kungliga arkiv 371/10, 89.

29. Divonne to Reuterholm, Dec. 30, 1789, SFOA, 121.141.4 (no. 4).

30. 369B [Ferrier] to Reuterholm, Jan. 2, 1790, SFOA, 121.141.6 (no. 7).

31. Barozzi to Reuterholm and Silfverhielm, Feb. 17, 1790, SFOA, 121.141.8 (no. 2).

32. The Council of Seven to Reuterholm and Silfverhielm, Feb. 20, 1790, SFOA, 121.141.4 (no. 11).

33. On the cult of the Archangel Raphael in early modern Florence, see Konrad Eisenbichler, "Devotion to the Archangel Raphael in Renaissance Florence," in *Saints: Studies in Hagiography*, ed. Sandro Sticca (Binghamton, NY: Medieval and Renaissance Texts and Studies, 1995), 251–67. On the Compagnia dell'Arcangelo Raffaele, see Konrad Eisenbichler, *The Boys of the Archangel Raphael: A Youth Confraternity in Florence, 1411–1785* (Toronto: University of Toronto Press, 1998). For a general account of the importance of Raphael in Renaissance Italy, see Meredith J. Gill, *Angels and the Order of Heaven in Medieval and Renaissance Italy* (Cambridge: Cambridge University Press, 2014), 151–202.

34. On the associations of Raphael (whose name means "God has healed" in Hebrew) as a healer in the Old and New Testaments, see Joseph Hammond, "The Cult and Representation

of the Archangel Raphael in Sixteenth-Century Venice," *St. Andrews Journal of Art History and Museum Studies* 15 (2011), 81; Eisenbichler, "Devotion to the Archangel Raphael," 251–2.

35. "Breve dettaglio della Società, o Setta scoperta nell'arresto di Ottavio Cappelli, tratto dale Carte allo stesso perquisite (1790)," BNCdR, 559v.

36. "Breve," 559v.

37. Note from Divonne to Cappelli, attached to a letter sent to Reuterholm, June 1, 1790, SFOA, 121.141.4 (no. 18). Razumovskaia did indeed suffer from very poor health related to a tapeworm. For a brief biography, see Nikolai Mikhailovich, *Russkie portrety XVIII i XIX stoletii*, vol. 3, no. 3 (St. Petersburg: Ekspeditsiia zagotovleniia gosudarstvennykh bumag, 1907), no. 110.

38. On Raphael's role in arranging the marriage between Tobiah and Sarah, see Geoffrey David Miller, *Marriage in the Book of Tobit* (Berlin: Walter de Gruyter, 2011), passim.

39. "Breve," 559v–560r.

40. "Breve," 560v.

41. Rosemary Ellen Guiley, *Encyclopedia of Angels*, 2nd ed. (New York: Facts on File, 2004), 310. Raphael's veneration as a patron saint of travellers is largely based on a passage in the book of Tobit, which describes how he served as a guide for Tobias on his journey to Media. See the book of Tobit, chapter 5.

42. "Breve," 560v.

43. "Breve," 560v. Sister Maire could be a reference to Madame Lemaire d'Attigny.

44. Kari Tarkiainen, "Gustaf Adolf Reuterholm," in *Svenskt Biografiskt Lexicon*, ed. Bertil Boëthius, vol. 30 (Stockholm: Norstedts, 2000), 43.

45. Reuterholm to Duke Karl, Jan. 20, 1790. RA, Kungliga arkiv 371/10, 88.

46. "Rese Journal," RA, Mar. 20, 1790.

47. See the undated document entitled "Mei domandi a Il S[t.] V[ieillard]," SFOA, 121.141.5. Published in Lekeby, *Gustaviansk mystik*, 178–81.

48. Santo Vecchio is the Italian form of St. Vieillard.

49. Undated note in Cappelli's hand, SFOA, 121.141.7 (no. 5).

50. For a concise summary of Reuterholm's vital role in the development of the Swedish Rite of Freemasonry, as well as of his passion for various aspects of Western esotericism, see Henrik Bogdan, "Freemasonry in Sweden," in *Western Esotericism in Scandinavia*, ed. Henrik Bogdan and Olav Hammer (Leiden: Brill, 2016), 168–81. For a comprehensive examination of Reuterholm's interest in esotericism, see Lekeby, *Gustaviansk mystik*.

51. Undated note, SFOA, 121.141.4 (no. 21).

52. "Breve," 565v–566r.

53. "Breve," 566r–566v. It is also stated that a certain Madama de Brivat di Bartier, Contessa di Rochefort was godmother (as well as being an initiate of the Union). A date of July 13 is stated but no year, although it is likely to have been 1789. The author of the "Breve" also notes that Joseph Ferrier and his sister, Ursule-Catherine Payan, were made godparents to a child of Ottavio and Chiara on Mar. 23 (probably 1790).

54. On Staël see, Charles Baille, *Notes sur le Baron de Staël* (Besançon: Paul Jacquin, 1895); P. L. M de Broglie Pange, *Monsieur Staël* (Paris: Les Éditions des portiques, 1931). Staël became a *Grand Profès*, the highest (and secret) degree in the Scottish Rectified Rite, led by J.-B. Willermoz, on June 3, 1783. See Alain Bernheim, "Notes a Propos du Rite Ecossais Rectifie," 13, https://archive.org/details/NotesAProposDuRiteEcossaisRectifie (accessed Jan. 19, 2019).

55. Undated note, SFOA, 121,141.4 (no. 21).

56. Francine du Plessix Gray, *Madame de Staël: The First Modern Woman* (New York: Atlas, 2008), 39.

57. Reuterholm's journal contains several entries in which he and Staël consult prophetesses in Paris in 1789 and 1790. Moreover, Staël enclosed a prophecy in a letter to Reuterholm from Sept. 11, 1790, regarding the latter's relationship with Duke Karl of Södermanland. See Staël to Reuterholm, Sept. 11, 1790, RA, 720741, vol. E5145, 3r.

58. Unsigned document, Feb. 1, 1790, SFOA, 121.141.5 (no. 7).

59. n.d., SFOA, 121.141.7 (no. 3, 2).

60. SFOA, 121.141.7 (no. 3, 1).

61. Grabianka to Reuterholm and Silfverhielm, Mar. 5, 1790, SFOA, 121.141.4 (no. 12)

62. SFOA, 121.141.5 (no. 7, 1).

63. SFOA, 121.141.5 (no. 7, 2).

64. SFOA, 121.141.5 (no. 7, 2–3).

65. SFOA, 121.141.5 (no. 7, 3). On Queen Christina's conversion to Roman Catholicism, see Oskar Garstein, *Rome and the Counter-Reformation in Scandinavia: The Age of Gustavus Adolphus and Queen Christina of Sweden 1622–1656* (Leiden: E. J. Brill, 1992), 525–764.

66. "Breve," 566v–567r.

67. "Breve," 562r.

68. "Breve," 561v.

69. "Breve," 562r–562v.

70. Cappelli to unknown recipient, April 11, 1790, SFOA, 121.141.7 (no. 2).

71. The "Brief Details" also refers to a letter by Cappelli, in which he signs off with "F[ratello] III Cardinal." See "Breve," 573v–574r.

72. "Breve," 576r–576v.

73. "Breve," 569r–571v.

74. "Breve," 576v.

75. "Breve," 577r–577v.

76. "Breve," 578r–578v.

77. "Breve," 577v–578r.

78. "Breve," 572v.

79. "Breve," 579v.

80. Pernety, *Les Vertus,* 15.

81. "Annals of the New Church," *New-Jerusalem Magazine* (1790), 175–6.

82. Tieman to the Duchess of Württemberg, undated, HSAS, G237 Bü 23, no. 6. Also see Faivre, *De Londres*, 491–2.

83. Divonne to Reuterholm, June 1, 1790. SFOA, 121.141.4 (no. 18).

84. 369B [Ferrier] to Reuterholm, June 5, 1790. SFOA, 121.141.4 (no. 20).

85. Staël to Reuterholm, Sept. 11, 1790. RA, Reuterholmska samlingen, 720741, vol. E5145.

86. *Gazzetta Universale*, Oct. 9, 1790, 648.

87. *Gazzetta Universale*, Oct. 16, 1790, 664. On Cagliostro's arrest, which took place on Dec. 27, 1789, see Constantin Photiadès, *Count Cagliostro: An Authentic Story of a Mysterious Life* (London: Routledge, 2011), 253–4.

88. Marini to Giovanni Fantuzzi, Oct. 9, 1790, in *Lettere Inedite di Gaetano Marini*, vol. 2: *Lettere a Giovanni Fantuzzi*, ed. Enrico Carusi (Vatican City: Biblioteca Apostolica Vaticana, 1938), 326–7.

89. For the letters by Astorri and Tanzini, see A. Ademollo, "Cagliostro e i Liberi Muratori," in *Nuova Antologia di Scienze, Lettere ed Arti*, 2nd ser., 26 (1881): 628–9.

90. Near verbatim translations of the report that appeared in *Gazzetta Universale* on Oct. 16, 1790, were published, for example, in Madrid, Hamburg, and London. See *Mercurio de España*, Nov., 1790, 553; *Historisch-politisches magazine, nebst litterarischen nachrichten*, vol. 8, 1790, 572–3; *Public Advertiser*, Nov. 24, 1790, 1–2.

91. RGIA, Fond 1163, op. 1, d. 16b, 110r. On Santini, see S. O. Androsov, "Gaspare Santini—diplomat i khudozhestvennyi agent v Rime," in *Vek Prosveshcheniia*, vol. 1, ed. S. Ia. Karp (Moscow: Nauka, 2006), 102–15.

92. RGIA, Fond 1163, op. 1, d. 16b, 110r.

93. Tieman to the Duchess of Württemberg, undated, HSAS, G237 Bü 23, no. 14.

94. "Breve," 586v–587v. For more on the prophecies of Labrousse and her influence in France at the turn of the 1790s, see Felice, *Note e ricerche*, 71–96; Garrett, *Respectable Folly*, 31–60.

95. RGIA, Fond 1163, op. 1, d. 16b, 110v.

96. RGIA, Fond 1163, op. 1, d. 16b, 109v–110r.

97. Tieman to the Duchess of Württemberg, undated, HSAS, G237 Bü 23, no. 14.

98. AdSdR, Giunta di Stato, fascicolo 7, busta 1. A letter in the *Giunta di Stato* archive, from Cassini to Giacomo Giustiniani, the head of the Governing Committee in Rome, dated Oct. 29, 1799, and written after Cappelli had been re-arrested, confirms that Russia abandoned him on Nov. 15, 1790.

99. AdSdR, Giunta di Stato, fascicolo 7, busta 1.

100. Divonne to Reuterholm, Feb. 11, 1791, RA, Reterholmska samlingen 720741, vol. E5125. NB: Divonne mistakenly wrote 1790 on the letter, but the content (he describes returning to Geneva from Italy) makes it clear that it was written in 1791.

101. Gombault to Corberon, Mar. 5, 1791, AN, F/7/4728, dossier Gombault, letter no. 2.

102. See, *Gazzetta Universale*, Sept. 10, 1791, 584; *Historisch-politisches magazine*, vol. 10, Sept., 1791, 361. For a report about the initial death sentence and the likelihood that the Pope would commute the sentence, see *E. Johnson's British Gazette and Sunday Monitor*, Oct. 16, 1791. Cappelli is described as being "the friend and accomplice of Cagliostro."

103. *Gazzetta Universale*, Oct. 8, 1791. The report dates from October 1.

104. *Notificazione noi Fr. Tommaso Vincenzo Pani*, Nov. 23, 1791. A French translation of the *Notificazione* was published in *Gazette Universelle, ou Papier-Nouvelles*, Dec. 19, 1791, 1409, 1413.

105. Divonne to Reuterholm, Feb. 13, 1792, RA.

106. RGIA, Fond 1163, op. 1, d. 16b, 110r–110v.

107. Tieman to the Duchess of Württemberg, Nov. 29, 1791, HSAS, G237 Bü 23. Also see Faivre, *De Londres*, 510–2.

108. Reuterholm to Duke Karl of Södermanland, Dec. 5, 1791, RA, Reuterholm-Ädelgrenska samlingen, 720742, vol. 35.

109. Ferdinand of Württemberg to Reuterholm, Jan. 23, 1792, RA, Reuterholmska samlingen, 720741, vol. E5122.

110. See, for example, Felice, *Note e ricerche*, 154; Chiara Pavone, *Esserci e desiderare: donne romane nei processi della giunta di stato (1799–1800)* (Rome: Biblink, 2014), 26; AdSdR, Giunta di Stato, fascicolo 7, busta 1.

111. In 1796 and 1797 Cappelli wrote at least three letters (Nov. 22 and 25, 1796, and Feb. 21, 1797) from Florence to Luigi Angiolini, the Tuscan minister in Rome. See Renato Mori, ed., *Le Scritture della Legazione e del Consolato del Granducato di Toscana in Roma dal 1737 al 1859*, vol. 8 (Rome: Tipografia Riservata del Ministero Affari Esteri, 1959), 53–4.

112. For a discussion of his matrimonial affairs with Chiara, see Pavone, *Esserci*, 25–30.

113. AdSdR, Giunta di Stato, fascicolo 7, busta 1. Also see Pavone, *Esserci*, 27.

5

Trials, Tribulations, and Transformation

THE ILLUMINÉS D'AVIGNON IN REVOLUTIONARY FRANCE, 1791–1802

ON JUNE 7, 1791, Gombault wrote to Reuterholm about the sorry plight of the Avignon Society. The Parisian bemoaned the unprecedented suspension of receptions in Avignon for the past seven or eight months, which, almost certainly, was a result of the fractious response to the news of Cappelli's arrest in Rome in September 1790. The letter also describes the sorry plight of Grabianka, who is "almost always sick." Indeed, Gombault confesses, "I do not know his destiny, but he has had very hard tests." What were these trials? Gombault makes no direct reference to the schism within the society, which pitted those loyal to Cappelli—led by Ferrier and Richardière—against those who disavowed the Italian as a false prophet, headed by Grabianka. Indeed, the only "test" Gombault brings up, apart from ill health, is the fact that Grabianka's trusted valet, Leyman, left the count's service to marry the widow Madame de Fumel. According to Gombault, the "marriage angered the count . . . and brought him much trouble."[1] Leyman later testified to the Russian authorities, in 1807, that Grabianka at around this time was kept in custody for twenty-four hours by the revolutionary authorities in Avignon on account of a letter he had received from Reuterholm in which the Swede mentioned Gustav III.[2] Even the slightest reference to a monarch was apparently sufficient grounds for arrest during this turbulent epoch. Moreover, in 1807 the Russian authorities recorded that Grabianka had accrued substantial debts as a result of feeding many families in the aftermath of a severe flood that affected Avignon. Official records show that the only such inundation of the River Rhône in the city at the time occurred in January 1791.[3]

Yet Gombault's allusion to the adversities Grabianka faced also points to the much-diminished status of the Avignon Society in the summer of 1791. Not only had Ferrier and

Initiating the Millennium. Robert Collis, and Natalie Bayer, Oxford University Press (2020) © Oxford University Press.
DOI: 10.1093/oso/9780190903374.001.0001

Richardière left the society, but Reuterholm, Divonne, and Ferdinand of Württemberg had become utterly disillusioned with the group's direction after Cappelli's incarceration. Two more members of the Avignon Council of Seven—Delhomme and Leblond—seem to have played no further part in the group's activities after 1790. Significantly, Pernety and Bouge did not abandon Grabianka during this period of internal schism, but the future of the society must have seemed gravely imperilled during the indefinite suspension of receptions.

It must be borne in mind that the discord within the society and the "hard tests" faced by Grabianka came at a time of seismic upheaval in the political landscape of Avignon and the surrounding Comtat Venaissin. By the summer of 1791, the papal enclave had already been experiencing severe convulsions for a year. The troubles erupted in Avignon on June 12, 1790, when a group of revolutionary French patriots succeeded in forcing the papal vice-legate, Philippe Casoni, to flee, and the pro-French municipal assembly declared that the people of Avignon desired to unite with France. However, Casoni merely retreated to Carpentras, located some sixteen miles north-east of Avignon, from where the papal official was able to harness support from many of the more conservative inhabitants of the Comtat. Thenceforth, civil strife beset the region for more than a year whilst the deputies of the National Assembly in Paris equivocated about how best to deal with the situation. The National Constituent Assembly finally decreed that Avignon and the Comtat were officially French territory on September 14, 1791, but the decision did nothing to douse the flames of animosity that had ravaged the region.[4] Indeed, in the short-term, hostilities were only fomented by this dramatic act, culminating in the murder of Nicolas Lescuyer, a leading Jacobin official in Avignon, by a Catholic mob. This event precipitated the notorious massacres, led by Mathieu Jourdan and Jean Duprat, of around forty papal sympathisers in the Tour de la Glacière of the Palais des Papes, on the night of October 16–17, 1791. A semblance of order was only (temporarily) restored when the National Assembly in Paris sent troops to oversee an uneasy peace.[5]

Despite their regular proclamations, in accord with their millenarian outlook, that France (and Europe as a whole) faced imminent tribulations, it seems that Grabianka, and the society as a whole were wholly unprepared for the cataclysmic reality of revolutionary upheaval in Avignon in 1790 and 1791. According to the Comte d'Avaray, who was one the closest companions of Louis Stanislas Xavier (the future Louis XVIII) in exile, Grabianka actually attempted to leave Avignon "at the moment the revolution broke out," but his escape was thwarted "by a very serious inconvenience" at the Alpine pass of Mont Cenis, on the Italian border, and he "was obliged to return" to the city.[6] We do not know the nature of this inconvenience, but it may well be related to the ill health Gombault commented on in the summer of 1791.

To be sure, Gombault was not prepared to predict Grabianka's destiny in the summer of 1791, the inference being that the Pole's abject circumstances, coupled with the anarchic political situation in Avignon, made it difficult to see a rosy future for the "king" of the society. With this in mind, this chapter focusses on how Grabianka endeavoured to navigate the stormy and disorienting waters of revolutionary Avignon in the 1790s. Any historian seeking to chart turbulent times is faced with the problem of having to rely on a dearth of archival documentation related to the topic under scrutiny. Our task here was no different, and we have had to piece together an impression of how Grabianka and the society fared from disparate fragments of source material, drawn primarily from hitherto overlooked archival sources in Russia and France.

What emerges from these sources is the remarkable role Grabianka played on the complex revolutionary stage that was Avignon in the 1790s. As we will demonstrate, the Polish gentleman with an avowedly millenarian outlook managed to foster cordial relationships with many leading revolutionary leaders, and at the same time played a vital role in harbouring fugitive royalists. Indeed, the links Grabianka cultivated with the revolutionary authorities in Avignon and Paris enabled him to play an unlikely role, primarily on behalf of the royalist cause, as a trusted go-between at the close of 1796 and early 1797.

In terms of the Avignon Society, this chapter will examine how Grabianka managed to prevent his rump of loyal supporters from completely abandoning his side in the early 1790s. We then examine how in the second half of the 1790s he succeeded in breathing new life into the group, presiding over the emergence of a new Council of Seven and the opening of a temple in which the society was able to perform newly formulated rituals. However, the favourable situation enjoyed by the society in Avignon did not last long; meetings in the temple were suspended on the eve of Napoleon's coup of 18 Brumaire in November 1799. Thereafter, we know very little about Grabianka's activities until 1802, when he successfully petitioned to obtain a Russian passport in Paris in order to return to his ancestral homeland in Podolia (which had been annexed by the Russian Empire as part of the Second Partition of Poland in 1793).

I

In spite of being questioned on one occasion by the revolutionary authorities during the fevered political atmosphere that engulfed Avignon in 1790 and 1791, it appears Grabianka suffered no serious persecution. An explanation for this apparent good fortune can be found in the testimony of Nicolas Simonin, who joined the Avignon Society in around 1796 or 1797. In 1807 Simonin was arrested in St. Petersburg by the Russian authorities (see chapter 6) and during the interrogation he was asked about Grabianka's connections with revolutionary leaders in Avignon. In response, Simonin described the cordial acquaintance the Pole enjoyed with Jean Duprat, a silk merchant and, until 1792, one of the leading revolutionaries in Avignon, who was implicated in the massacres at La Glacière.[7] According to Simonin, "Duprat wished to be acquainted with Count Grabianka [and] visited him often." What is more, Simonin even testified that during these tête-à-têtes, Grabianka "often conversed about divine laws" and succeeded in only a few conversations in leading Duprat away from being "a godless atheist and revolutionary" towards fully embracing Christian doctrine. Simonin also testified that Grabianka hosted the notorious Mathieu Jouve (nicknamed "Jourdan Coupe-Tête") on one occasion during the height of the civil turmoil in Avignon. According to Simonin, Grabianka "managed to soften him [Jourdan] with his conversation and courtesies and persuaded him not to carry out the murder of many people who were held in jail because they were committed to the previous form of rule."[8] Alongside Duprat, Jourdan was also implicated directly in the bloody La Glacière massacres, and both were soon to meet their end via the blade of the guillotine in 1793 and 1794 respectively.[9]

Leyman's testimony includes a fascinating justification of Grabianka's approach to dealing with the leading revolutionary personages in Avignon at this time:

As for the sentiments of these revolutionaries, he sincerely hated them, and consequently he could not form an intimate society of people of whom had such different attitudes than him. But he entertained them, he gave them dinners, suppers, he enlightened them about the times of the Terror, and so he made them as happy as possible, in order to have influence on them. But he told them that they were foolish, that they were cutting each other's throats unjustly, that they had to stop these iniquities and to remember that today they would kill and tomorrow others would come to kill them, and that therefore their wives and children would perish. He made the most of his influence on them to save himself and to save all those innocents that he could.[10]

Simonin painted a very similar portrait during his interrogation. When he was asked by the Russian authorities about Grabianka's conduct during the revolution, he stated that Grabianka "often rendered courtesies and pleasantries to them, entertaining them in the very best possible way." Simonin maintained that the raison d'être of this exercise in wining and dining was to save innocent lives.[11] In other words, Grabianka seemingly had the nerve and audacity to severely chastise some of the most notorious revolutionary figures in France. At the same time, he somehow managed to charm them over dinner at his home in order to spare the lives of a great many people.

It could be argued that Simonin and Leyman had ulterior motives for casting Grabianka as a trenchant, vocal critic of the revolutionary authorities and as the saviour of many who had been caught in the crosshairs of the revolutionaries. Yet, significantly, a very similar view was expressed by the Comte d'Avaray, in January 1797, when he described the "religious and even pious" Grabianka to Paul François de Quelen de la Vauguyon (a fellow member of Louis Xavier's four-man conseil d'état) by saying, "This extraordinary man ... did not refuse to receive in his house the factions of all parties; it seems that he reconciled their confidence and that he has used this to remove several honest persons from the greatest perils." What is more, d'Avaray continued, "he did not conceal from them at the time that he foresaw that all their plans would end up having a fatal outcome for themselves."[12] In other words, the descriptions offered by Simonin, Leyman, *and* d'Avaray provide a consistent account of how Grabianka went about trying to influence the revolutionaries in Avignon.

Further evidence of the extraordinary acquaintanceships that Grabianka was able to cultivate with revolutionary leaders in Avignon in the 1790s can be found in two letters the Pole wrote to Philippe-Charles-Aimé Goupilleau, on December 27, 1795, and January 21, 1796.[13] At the time, Goupilleau had recently become a deputy in the Council of Five Hundred, but between August 1794 and June 1795 he had served as a representative on mission in Vaucluse, whereby he fulfilled the role of an extraordinary envoy of the Convention sent to ensure the maintenance of law and order.[14] Goupilleau had his work cut out, as the Comtat Venaissin remained a place of anarchy and brigandage. The royalist "White Terror," led by the local Companions of Jehu and the Companions of the Sun in Provence, as elsewhere in the south-east, raged fiercely throughout much of 1795.[15] Indeed, on October 1, 1795, shortly after Goupilleau had returned to Paris, royalist forces under Alexandre Mottard Lestang briefly seized control of Avignon.[16]

Thus, Grabianka's letters to Goupilleau were written at a time of continued upheaval and violence in Avignon. However, no hint of civil strife can be found in the notes. In the first epistle, Grabianka is merely at pains to remind Goupilleau of the cherished friendship they apparently enjoyed in Avignon: "I rely on your friendship. I like to believe that you count on mine ... the attachment that you inspired in me is one of those feelings that time can never erase." Not content with these protestations of affection, Grabianka also proclaimed that "my heart ... loves you sincerely."[17]

The second letter, written at the beginning of 1796, provides a fascinating first-hand insight into how Grabianka was able to quickly ingratiate himself with the new representative on mission, who had arrived in the region at the end of October 1795. This was Louis-Stanislas Fréron, who was known in the region for the bloody reprisals he oversaw against royalist forces in the wake of the Siege of Toulon that ended in December 1793.[18] Despite his fearsome reputation as an enforcer of terror, Grabianka had nothing but praise for Fréron in his brief report to Goupilleau: "I had the pleasure dear and beloved friend to have the amiable Fréron to dine with me and to dine with him two days later ... He has so many happy qualities that one always ends up loving him when one knows him well." Alas, Grabianka was soon deprived of the opportunity to develop his acquaintance with Fréron, as the representative was recalled by the new Directory only five days after the Pole had written to Goupilleau.[19] Interestingly, as Greene notes, Fréron's second mission to the Midi stood "in stark contrast to his behaviour during his previous mission," in that he "managed to show great moderation."[20] It is impossible to gauge the extent to which Grabianka played a part in tempering the violent whims of Fréron. However, given the context, it would have surely been one of the principal underlying reasons behind the Pole's courting of the representative's friendship.

Despite the testimony of Leyman, Simonin, and d'Avaray, vis-à-vis Grabianka's efforts to protect royalists and the clergy from the Jacobin authorities, it seems only snippets of evidence are extant that are able to validate these assertions. In a summary of the Avignon

Society, which drew directly on documents seized from Grabianka in St. Petersburg in 1807, the Russian authorities noted that the Pole had helped to secure the release of A.-J. Pernety at a time when the clergy was being persecuted.[21] This almost certainly refers to Pernety's arrest in October 1793, along with Bousie and John Macgregor, which was documented by the then representative on mission, F.-M. Poultier.[22] All three were members of the Avignon Society, yet it is far from clear whether membership in this group was sufficient for them to fall under suspicion. If so, then why did Grabianka not suffer a similar fate? In his report to the Committee of Public Safety, written on October 18, 1793, Poultier explains that Bousie and Macgregor had been arrested as a result of a decree issued in the same month ("la loi sur les Anglais"), which stipulated that all British subjects had to be detained. However, no clear explanation is given for Pernety's incarceration. Indeed, Poultier ends his report by remarking on the "good conduct and innocence of the petitioners."[23] Given Grabianka's ability to befriend other representatives on mission, it is far from inconceivable that he also had the ear of Poultier and was able to bring about the speedy release of his brethren.[24]

A second reference to how Grabianka provided sanctuary for opponents of the revolution in Avignon appears in a recent biographical study by Serge Billard-Baltyde of Pierre Duclos, the Marquis de Bésignan. According to Billard-Baltyde, Grabianka offered refuge to Bésignan on the night of August 31, 1792 at his home in Avignon.[25] At the time the marquis was on the run, after his ancestral property, the Château de Bésignan, was besieged by revolutionary forces between August 25 and 29.[26] The seigneur's château was located some fifty miles north-east of Avignon, and therefore it is entirely plausible that he sought shelter with Grabianka two days after his home had been ransacked. Thereafter he made his way to Switzerland, where he quickly became an agent of Louis Joseph, the Prince of Condé. Moreover, on behalf of the royalist cause, Bésignan became one of the principal leaders of the armed gangs (*bandes*), who marauded throughout the Midi countryside in the mid-1790s.[27] Indeed, in 1796, the *Républicain du Nord* referred to Bésignan as the founder of the Companies of Jesus.[28]

The case for Grabianka having harboured Bésignan in 1792 is made vastly stronger by the astonishing content of the above-mentioned letter sent by d'Avaray to Vauguyon in January 1797. This note was composed by d'Avaray the day after he had met with Bésignan in Blankenburg, in Saxony-Anhalt, which was where Louis Xavier's court-in-exile was based at the time. D'Avaray informs Vauguyon that Bésignan had arrived at Blankenburg in order to convey an important message to Xavier, which had been entrusted to him by Grabianka. Hence, the description of Grabianka provided by d'Avaray in his letter to Vauguyon was essentially reliant upon the testimony of Bésignan. With this in mind, it is apparent that Bésignan held Grabianka in extremely high esteem. D'Avaray writes, for example, that Grabianka "has constantly offered all the elements of probity, virtue and even of piety."[29]

According to d'Avaray, the message intended for Xavier concerned an attempt by unnamed members of the Directory to facilitate the return to power of the Bourbon dynasty, on condition that they would be pardoned. D'Avaray elaborates by describing how they had recently come to perceive that "all their resources are exhausted" and that they had blindly fallen into an abyss of their own making. This realisation promoted them "to seek recourse to the legitimate authority neither by nor through the mediation of foreign powers, nor that of Frenchmen," but via Grabianka. In d'Avaray's words, they trusted the Pole to the extent that they "wish him to become their intermediary."[30] Such a scenario would sound preposterous, were it not for the evidence demonstrating that Grabianka did indeed enjoy cordial relationships with several leading revolutionaries of the day.

The plan conveyed by Bésignan, on behalf of Grabianka, to the court-in-exile, involved sending a trusted ambassador to the Pole in Avignon. This emissary was to travel to Lausanne, where he would find all the necessary passports and titles required for safe transit in France. Once the ambassador had reached Avignon, Grabianka would take care of all the necessary steps to bring about the negotiations between the members of the Directory and Xavier's envoy.[31] Ernest Daudet notes that this scheme was presented to the future king's council the day after it had been conveyed to d'Avaray. The plan was ultimately rejected by Xavier's council, but it did receive the support of Vauguyon, who even proposed the Abbé de Chaffoy as the most suitable person to undertake the mission.[32] Moreover, in his memoirs, the royalist Louis Fauche-Borel describes how Xavier was not entirely against the initiative, but that he demanded passports directly from the Directory, as he regarded them as the "touchstone of the truth of its relations with Count Grabianka."[33]

Irrespective of the opposition to this plan, the fact that it was seriously discussed by Xavier's council highlights Grabianka's rare gift: an ability to ingratiate himself with powerful and ardent republicans, whilst providing sanctuary and assistance to royalists. Hence, though this specific plan did not come to fruition, it still illustrates how Grabianka was able to successfully balance on the most precarious of tightropes in the tumultuous decade that followed the storming of the Bastille.

II

Grabianka's ability to chart a steady course through stormy waters may well have served him well in the early 1790s, in terms of trying to keep afloat the fractured hull of the Avignon Society. It would have been easy for the society to fully disintegrate in 1791. In terms of internal factors alone, the irreparable schism and sense of disillusion that stemmed from Cappelli's arrest led to an unprecedented suspension of receptions and the irrevocable departure of many members. What is more, these acute tensions were playing out against an anarchic and terrifying backdrop of civil strife in Avignon and the Comtat Venaissin.

Despite these grave pressures, a diminished version of the society, led by Grabianka, seems to have been active again in Avignon by 1792. Evidence to support this assertion can be found in the memoirs of Anne-Henri Cabot de Dampmartin, who was the commanding officer of two squadrons of troops sent to Avignon on the orders of the Legislative Assembly in Paris in November 1791 after the massacres at La Glacière.[34] Interestingly, his recollections for 1792 contain a detailed description of his encounters with Grabianka, Pernety, and other, unnamed, members of the society.

From the outset, Dampmartin's account of the society displays reverence and enthusiasm for the actions and conduct of the consecrates. Notwithstanding the dire situation he faced in Avignon at the time, Dampmartin professes that being billetted in the city gave him "the advantage of becoming acquainted with an astonishing society, whose members filled me with awe mixed with admiration." The officer recalls that Grabianka, referred to as "a Polish seigneur," was the leader, and that Pernety "exercised the functions of an apostle," Furthermore, "several known men showed themselves to be zealous disciples."[35] This brief hierarchical description is illuminating, because it not only demonstrates Grabianka's pre-eminence within the society, but also confirms that Pernety remained a member. Retaining the support of Pernety may well have played a crucial role in terms of legitimising the rump that remained loyal to Grabianka. After all, Pernety was the only other founding member of the society, besides Grabianka, still tied to the group.

Dampmartin's effusive reminiscences about the conduct of the society strongly suggest that it had recommenced many of its distinctive activities and features. He recalled, for example, that they placed full confidence "in the heavenly voice that regulated their actions."[36] In other words, Dampmartin indicates that many of their decisions were still determined after consultation with the Holy Word. Moreover, he reveals that "they predicted with astonishing clarity to me the events of which I have not ceased being the victim."[37] That is to say, he, too, was privy to the messages received from the Holy Word. In general, Dampmartin describes the manner in which the members of the society had welcomed him, "with an eagerness which penetrated me with gratitude," which initially made him desirous of being consecrated into the society. To him, their virtuous behaviour offered a "sublime contrast" to the "coalition of frenzied scoundrels" he had to contain in Avignon.[38]

Significantly, the impression Dampmartin conveys in his recollections is that he participated in some form of societal assembly, rather than simply being convinced of the merits of their primitive form of Christian piety via one-on-one discussions. Dampmartin ultimately decided not to be initiated into the society, based on the belief that he could not fully embrace all their views without deceiving them "by a hypocritical zeal."[39] However, the "sweet and precious" memories that Dampmartin recalled in 1799 are a valuable source, as they provide a unique insight into the Avignon Society's activities at a critical period following the crises that beset the group in 1791. Based on these recollections, it would seem that Grabianka was at the head of a society that had weathered the storm of the previous year and was re-emerging as a self-confident and dedicated group. In other words, Dampmartin's account demonstrates how Grabianka and his "disciples" had again begun to enact the pious expressions of millenarianism and to seek guidance about their worldly affairs from their other-worldly oracle.

III

French sources offer remarkably little information about the activities of the Avignon Society and Grabianka's continued influence on the group after 1792. In 1862, the Abbé Granget wrote, in his history of the diocese of Avignon, that Grabianka had departed from the city in 1792, leaving behind debts totalling 200,000 francs.[40] More recently, a number of French scholars have posited that the Avignon society dispersed in around 1793, and that Grabianka was already distancing himself from the group in 1791.[41] However, the Abbé Corenson correctly noted in the nineteenth century that Grabianka lived in Avignon at no. 22 Rue de la Colombe throughout the era of the Directory.[42] Adrien Marcel also highlighted Grabianka's continued presence in Avignon, by referring to a marriage certificate between the merchant Charles Bazin and Anne Berthout van Berchem, from March 31, 1797, that bears the Pole's signature as a witness.[43]

A far more accurate account of the Avignon Society's activities in the 1790s can be gleaned if one consults the relevant dossier of documents amassed by the Russian authorities in the wake of Grabianka's arrest in St. Petersburg in 1807.[44] Admittedly, these documents do not offer a comprehensive account of the period. They do, however, shine sufficient light for us to be able to discern the key features and personages of the society as it reacted to and sought to advance from the internal and external vicissitudes that beset it at the beginning of the decade.

Of crucial importance, as mentioned, is the fact that Pernety and Bouge did not desert Grabianka in the aftermath of Cappelli's incarceration. Indeed, Pernety remained the pontiff of the society up until his death in 1796, although he did become noticeably less involved in its activities. Bouge continued to be the Grand Prophet of the society up until the end of 1794 or the beginning of 1795.[45] In other words, he continued to be the principal mediator between consecrates of the society and the Holy Word, via his knowledge of how to operate the numerical oracle the society had utilized since 1779. The Grabianka dossier held in the Russian State Historical Archive (RGIA) includes information regarding three oracles dating from 1793 and 1794—that is, when Bouge was still the Grand Prophet. The first dates from January 23, 1793, and relates to the fate of Louis XVI. According to the summary produced by the Russian authorities, the oracle responded to a question set by Grabianka with the prophecy that the monarch would "leave prison in glory and triumph" as he would be protected by heaven. Alas, the king had been guillotined two days earlier. News of the monarch's execution reached Avignon on January 26. This reportedly led many initiates of the society to become disillusioned and "quietly leave," although we have no other evidence to suggest such a mass exodus occurred in 1793.[46]

The second response from the oracle documented in the Grabianka dossier dates from October 14, 1793, and almost certainly relates to the Pole's role as king in the society: "The king holds the place of Christ. Those who obey him will see his glorious reign."

Interestingly, during their interrogation of Grabianka in 1807, the Russian authorities directly asked him about the meaning of this oracle. Grabianka responded in the following way: "This oracle must be taken figuratively . . . Each father in a family, each master of a house, each chief in whatever order represents Christ."[47] It would seem that this response accorded with Grabianka's desire to be the indisputable leader of the society. In all likelihood, this oracle merely reinforced Grabianka's Christ-like authority within the society. After all, in his recollections of 1792, Dampmartin referred to the aged Pernety as a mere apostle of Grabianka and other members as his disciples. The third oracle, dating from February 17, 1794, also touches on hierarchical roles within the society: "The King is the principal stone of the grand edifice. The pontiff is also an essential stone. The Lord establishes his reign on the 1st; the second, the new church."[48] Thus, Grabianka's position as king of the New Israel is once again validated by the oracle, although a significant role is also afforded to the pontiff (Pernety).

The report drawn up by the Russian authorities in 1807 states that it was around 1793 or 1794 that Grabianka started to reconstitute the society according to his own ideas. Notably, he apparently jettisoned all esoteric pursuits (*tainstvennyia nauki*) previously practised by members of the society (alchemy, animal magnetism, and arithmancy), with the exception of correspondence with heaven.[49] At this juncture, Grabianka seems to have championed the prophetic gifts of a certain Allier, who was purportedly the son of a tavern keeper.[50] Indeed, it is stated that Grabianka deliberately promoted Allier as a prophet able to enter into communication with the voice of heaven via dreams. Apparently, Grabianka informed Allier that he needed to request to receive this prophetic voice from heaven, which was duly granted, and he was then officially consecrated as a prophet. When Bouge gave up his role as Grand Prophet in the society, Allier assumed the position. Thereafter, he was the primary conduit of the society's oracles, via prophetic dreams.[51] This is corroborated by Simonin, who testified that Allier was "a great friend and secretary of Count Grabianka" and that "for several years he himself pronounced oracles and dreams, to which he afterwards gave an explanation or interpretation."[52]

In the mid-1790s, against a backdrop of acute civil strife in Avignon, the oracle provided tidings of comfort and hope, supposedly via Allier's new-found prophetic gift. Hence, the voice of heaven proclaimed that it was necessary to remain loyal, be patient, and tolerate evil during this tumultuous period. Moreover, the king—that is, Grabianka—"would soon begin his glorious profession" and would be radiant like the sun. The exaltation of Grabianka continued: his wisdom was compared with that of Solomon; his strength with that of David.[53]

Significantly, the Russian report attests that the prophecies received by Allier in his dreams had no power without being confirmed by Grabianka.[54] It seems the king of the society had learnt his lesson from the Cappelli affair. Unwilling to be held hostage by the whims of fate, Grabianka asserted that within the society he had the singular gift to distinguish whether an oracle was true or false. We are afforded an intriguing insight into Grabianka's thinking on this vexing matter from his interrogation in St. Petersburg in

1807. In general, he believed that the End Times would bring forth a multitude of prophets, in accordance with the prophecy of Joel in the Old Testament, who proclaimed, "Your sons and your daughters shall prophesy, your old men shall dream dreams, your young men shall see visions."[55] Yet Grabianka also espoused a stark binary worldview, whereby "there is in the world the true and false, the good and the bad," adding that "we had among us [in the society] true and false prophets," the latter of whom he names as Richardière and Cappelli. How, though, did Grabianka judge whether a prophecy was true or false? In 1807, he explained that it was imperative to "absolutely know their basis and their foundation," as with all the sciences of the world. In essence, this necessitated heeding the advice of the Holy Scripture and "look[ing] upon the prophets as true if their prophecies are fulfilled and false if they are not."[56] However, this criterion seems at odds with his role as the sole arbiter of the true or false nature of Allier's oracles, in which it would seem he needed to make a relatively quick decision *before* events had necessarily played out.

Irrespective of Grabianka's opinion of Allier's dream oracles, the Russian author of the report branded the society's latest prophet as a crackpot madman, who came to believe in his own powers. To support this view, he cites how Allier described seeing Corberon transform into a beast, and recounts how the prophet also professed to having had conversations with clouds that metamorphosed into humans and several face-to-face encounters with the devil.[57] Despite this withering assessment from a Russian government official in 1807, Allier enjoyed increasing influence within the society in the second half of the 1790s. It was for this reason that when Pernety died in 1796, it was Allier who assumed the abbé's role as pontiff.[58]

The passing of Pernety not only signalled Allier's ascension in the society, but also seems to have led to renewed activity by the new Council of Seven, who were, however, subservient to Grabianka, their Christ-like sovereign. The new Council of Seven included Allier and three members who had been consecrated in the years prior to the 1791 schism. Deravine is listed in the Russian report as being the great prophet.[59] This suggests he would have played a pivotal role in pronouncing oracles. However, no mention is made in either the official report or in the interrogations of Grabianka, Leyman, and Simonin that anyone other than Allier fulfilled the role of chief conduit of the dream oracle. Deravine's elevated status within the society is, however, suggested by an undated oracle extract found in the material seized from Grabianka in 1807, which states that "Deravine shall sit beside you, he shall be at the king's right hand, like his sword."[60] Deravine was consecrated into the Avignon Society in November 1788, at the same time as Pleshcheev.[61] As mentioned, Deravine is listed as being a member of loge de St. Jean d'Écosse de la vertu persécutée between 1785 and 1789.[62] In other words, Deravine maintained the link between the Avignon lodge and the NIS into the late 1790s—that is, long after the likes of Leblond and Bouge. The new Council of Seven included a woman, Madame d'Attigny, who joined the society in 1789, and went on to assume the title of "Great Mother." In this role, she was envisaged as the embodiment of the Virgin Mother and was regarded as the equal of the pontiff (Allier). Lastly, the council also included Baron Louis-Dagobert Lefort, who hailed from a noble Alsatian family with Genevan roots.[63] Lefort was formerly an officer in the Royal-Nassau Hussars Regiment and in 1788 is listed as being a member of La Candeur Masonic lodge in Strasbourg.[64] Lefort seems to have joined the society in around 1789–1790.[65] By the mid-1790s he held the position of chancellor, which entailed overseeing the civil affairs of the society, as well as being the "grand judge of the people."[66]

Of the new members of the society, only Nicolas Simonin, the former military officer, was honoured with a title: the interpreter of dreams.[67] We are able to glean a little about this role from Simonin's interrogation in 1807, since his interlocutor posed several questions on the subject. According to Simonin, anyone in the society could present Grabianka with an account of one of their dreams. If he deemed the dream suitable, he gave it to Simonin to interpret. Yet Simonin testified that there was apparently no special art to his dream interpretation. He simply "told or wrote down what he deemed to be significant" in a dream "for the spiritual benefit of the person who saw the dream."[68] The other two members of the Council of Seven are named in the Russian report as Parmentier and Muratori, but no further information is supplied about these two consecrates.[69]

The emergence of this second Council of Seven (*conseil des intimes*) was not the only sign of the society's renewed vigour. Notable in this regard was the introduction of a new four-degree system. The highest degree was entitled "The Order of the Holy House of God," and was under the direction of d'Attigny and the protection of the Virgin Mary. Those holding this degree wore a green ribbon, which signified the hope for perfection. The third degree was presided over by Allier and was named "The Order of the Trinity," or "Adoption Sainte." The second degree was entitled "The Order of the Word Incarnate"; its holders wore a red ribbon. The first degree was named "The Order of the Holy Spirit," and initiates wore a sash of the colour of dawn on which was hung a dove (the Holy Spirit).[70]

In 1798 the society opened a dedicated chapel in Avignon, built in the manner of Solomon's Temple, benefitting from a slightly more stable political atmosphere in the city. The sanctuary of the temple, which only the most senior members of the society could enter, contained a throne on which could be found four crosses (three for the Holy Trinity and one for Mary) and seven candles. The temple also housed an altar, on which were placed sacrifices, bread, and wine. Regular morning services were held that were consistent with a Catholic mass. However, special rites were associated with so-called Royal Vespers (*Tsarskaia vecheria*), in imitation of the Last Supper. On these holy days, a midday prayer service would be held, during which the sins of those in attendance would be banished. The congregation would gather in the temple again in the evening, where they would sit at a table (reminiscent of the society's earlier evening assembly). Everyone wore a simple cowled robe with a girdle and bore a staff, with the exception of Allier, the pontiff, who was attired in a manner akin to the high priest Aaron.[71] Before sitting, the congregants walked around the table with burning incense to banish Satan, which had been lit according to Jewish rites. Grabianka then acted out the role of Christ and humbly served his "disciples" on his knees. The food offering consisted of a paschal lamb, the bones of which were burned afterwards.[72] In his interrogation, Simonin recalled taking part in such a ceremony on one occasion, when the participants "ate dried fruit, roast lamb . . . and after the feast prayers were recited that were contained in the Catholic Psalter." Moreover, in reply to questions about whether the rite involving the lamb served any magical purpose, Simonin stated that it was merely included in honour of the Last Supper.[73]

IV

The opening of a dedicated temple in Avignon in 1798 seemingly reflects the society's renewed sense of vigour and confidence at the time. This was no small achievement, considering the tumult and endemic disorder that continued to beset the region throughout the era of the Directory.[74] Yet in October 1799, meetings in the temple were suspended. According to the Russian official's account in 1807, Grabianka read out an oracle in this month that commanded the closing of the temple. Moreover, he considered it necessary to take careful measures and to conceal evidence that could compromise the society. Apparently, many members used this announcement as a plausible pretext to leave the society of their own volition. Those who remained were called to the temple on October 28, 1799, which, significantly, was the feast-day of Thaddaeus, after whom Grabianka was named. The assembled congregation were informed that because of their sins, they had to withdraw from the temple for a year. What brought about this reversal of fortune for the society at the close of 1799? Was it linked to the rise of Napoleon Bonaparte, as suggested by the Russian official?[75] In other words, was Grabianka guided by a prescient sense of foreboding? This may have been a factor—the suspension occurred only twelve days after Bonaparte had arrived in Paris and twelve days before the coup of 18 Brumaire. However, it is ultimately impossible to say with any certainty how Napoleon's machinations in Paris affected the Avignon Society. All we know, based on Grabianka's testimony at his interrogation in 1807, is that after a year had elapsed—that is, on October 28, 1800—not only did the temple not reopen, but all new consecrations were also suspended.[76] To all intents and purposes the Avignon Society was no more.

By 1800, Grabianka and many members of the society were destitute. Grabianka apparently lived a day-by-day existence in Avignon at the beginning of the nineteenth century, which involved hiding from his creditors and depending on others for sustenance. Lefort's plight was so desperate that he ended up in a debtor's prison for several months. The leaders of the society apparently consulted the oracle at this time to be guided about how best to pacify their creditors. The response they received was that Allier and

Leyman were to travel to Poland to try to secure funds. Allier was also entrusted with a secret undertaking to find ways to disseminate the teachings of the society during the journey. However, the creditors apparently would only agree to such a trip if they could send a trusted confidante with Allier and Leyman. Grabianka consulted the oracle again and received the following reply:

> Let Thaddaeus be joyous/: Count Grabianka:/ He was victorious . . . Every chosen one is obligated to him for his life . . . An Angel placed over Poland, he cast his gaze on Thaddeus and sees him writing letters and everything is set up in his favour. Poland needs a King: Thaddeus is appointed to be him by her [Poland's] Guardian Angel. Let Thaddeus be joyous! . . . Every chosen one is prepared to enjoy this happiness. This genius guarding Poland, prostrate before the chosen one, asking him Thaddeus to be the King.[77]

Thus the oracle indicated that Grabianka would receive a favourable reply if he entered into written correspondence with individuals in Poland. The oracle also foresaw, notwithstanding Grabianka's current abject plight, the count gloriously ascending to the throne of Poland, a realm that was in a similar pitiful state.[78]

In an attempt to placate his creditors, Grabianka was also "able to win over to his side the lawyer [Joseph-Marie] Verger," who was able to convince them to hold off from any further action until a response had been received from Poland. Indeed, Verger was apparently present when Grabianka penned the letter in question to Poland and even sealed it and personally sent it in the post.[79] Verger's involvement on behalf of Grabianka at this time is curious. Verger was not only a lawyer but also very well connected with Richardière and Ferrier, the former members of the Illuminés d'Avignon. Verger's links to the two former members of the original Council of Seven of the Avignon Society is revealed in his correspondence with J.-B. Willermoz, the leader of the Scottish Rectified Rite of Freemasonry in Lyon.[80] In a letter to Willermoz, dated October 24, 1801, for example, Verger informs him that he will be visited by "Mr. Ferrier, a friend of Mr. de la Richardiére and mine" and who is recommended as a "decent man."[81]

We know surprisingly little about the affairs of Richardiére and Ferrier in Avignon after 1791 considering their prominence within the Illuminés d'Avignon up until this point. However, two scraps of evidence, aside from Verger's correspondence with Willermoz, suggest that they maintained some form of illuministic society in Avignon after their split from the Grabianka-Pernety-led group. First, we know that on July 13, 1795, Esprit Calvet lent a consortium led by Richardière the considerable sum of 19,800 livres.[82] Furthermore, a report by the Ministry of Police, dating from October and November 1803, refers to Richardière as the head of a branch of illuminists who were still "propagating the spirit of royalism and fanaticism" in Avignon.[83]

Despite the glorious fate Grabianka was promised by the oracle, he evidently remained in Avignon until 1802, although we know little about his daily existence at this time.

Grabianka's pitiful circumstances only took a turn for the better at the beginning of 1802, when he managed to obtain a promissory note for 7900 livres to travel to Paris with Leyman. According to the Russian report, Grabianka resided in Paris for six months, whilst Parmentier sold a property in London to secure the funds Grabianka needed to return to his ancestral homeland.[84] Indeed, during his interrogation Leyman added that Parmentier also paid for their stay in the French capital, "so that we left as honest people . . . without not paying the inn or other people who gave us credit."[85] During Simonin's interrogation, he was asked why Grabianka sought to return to Podolia; he provided the following prosaic reply: "To put in order his affairs with his wife and to send money to his creditors."[86] In other words, financial necessity underpinned Grabianka's desire to return to Podolia for the first time since 1785, rather than any prophetic mission to claim the throne of Poland, let alone to lead the so-called People of God into the new millennium.

Grabianka received his Russian passport, which included Russian and French versions (see Figure 5.1), on October 27, 1802. Both copies were signed by Arkadii Ivanovich Morkov, the Russian ambassador in France and stipulated that Grabianka was to receive safe passage to Kamianets-Podilskyi in Podolia, which, as mentioned, had been part of the Russian Empire since the second partition of Poland in 1793. Grabianka thenceforth was officially recognised as a Russian subject. Presumably, Grabianka left Paris soon after receiving permission to travel, little knowing, perhaps, that he would never see France or Western Europe again.

Yet before we examine the five years that Grabianka spent in the Russian Empire, we should not overlook his half-year residence in Paris. This period was of interest to the Russian authorities, who during their interrogations of Simonin and Leyman in 1807, asked them several questions regarding Grabianka's activities in the French capital in 1802.[87] Although the line of questioning was not exhaustive, Simonin's and Leyman's replies shed considerable light on a phase of Grabianka's life that has hitherto remained in the shadows. When asked who had sought out Grabianka in Paris, for example, Simonin replied: "The people who came to see him were either members of his society or expressed a desire to be admitted to it." Simonin reveals few specifics, but he does indicate that in Paris Grabianka still enjoyed a degree of support from old members of the society, and was still able to attract prospective recruits. Simonin's interrogator does not push him to reveal names; instead, he probes the Frenchman about Grabianka's links to police and government officials in Paris. At this point, Simonin merely revealed that a certain Duprat, whom Grabianka knew in Avignon, visited the Pole on two occasions to thank him for persuading him to abandon his godlessness and to embrace Christian thought and a love of humanity.[88] This is most likely a reference to Jean-Étienne-Benoît Duprat, the younger brother of Jean Duprat, who rose to become a general in Napoleon's army and died at the Battle of Wagram in 1809.[89] Leyman was also asked whether he and Grabianka were ever taken to the police in Paris. He answered that they had only visited the police in order to present their passports from Avignon and to obtain the surety cards (*cartes de sûreté*) that foreign

FIGURE 5.1 Passport issued to Grabianka in Paris, October 27, 1802. RGIA, Fond 1163, op. 1, d. 16v, 93. *Image courtesy of the Russian State Historical Archive, St. Petersburg.*

residents in Paris were required to have at the time. Significantly, Leyman adds that a certain "Monsieur St. Charles" had accompanied them and helped to ensure that they encountered no problems with the police.[90] This is the only reference to Saint-Charles in what remains of the interrogatory notes relating to Leyman. We learn more about Grabianka's close relationship with Saint-Charles from Simonin's interrogation. When Simonin was directly pressed about his knowledge of Saint-Charles, he answered that Saint-Charles was formerly in the service of the French queen, that is, Marie Antoinette.[91] This morsel of information allows one to identify the individual in question as Ange-Charles Gabriel de Saint-Charles, who from 1770 was the intendant general of the queen's finances and master of the wardrobe.[92] Little biographical information about Saint-Charles exists, other than that he was the son of Ange-Jacques Gabriel, arguably the foremost French architect of the eighteenth century.[93]

Simonin attests that Grabianka wished to become acquainted with Saint-Charles, knowing of his great devotion to a certain prophetess in her seventies, who was known in Paris as *La Brébis* (the ewe), who had apparently said "very many kind things about the Count."[94] It has been remarked that "there were prophetesses everywhere" in France at the time, the most notable being Suzette Labrousse and Catherine Théot.[95] This surfeit of Pythian seers may explain why *La Brébis* has hitherto escaped the attention of historians. Whatever the reason for her historical anonymity, Grabianka was well aware of her reputation in 1802 and succeeded in making her acquaintance through Saint-Charles. According to Simonin, the pair would visit the prophetess together, and she, too, would visit Grabianka "at any hour of the night." At these meetings, *La Brébis* would be completely absorbed in herself and would speak in tongues and make lots of signs and crosses. Despite this penchant for glossolalia, Grabianka was apparently able to understand what she said enough to know that she foresaw "great prosperity (*blagopoluchie*) and a very advantageous arrangement in his affairs with his wife."[96] Such optimistic tidings would have heartened Grabianka enormously on the eve of his departure for Podolia, given his predilection for (sympathetic) prophets. Little did he know that the favourable outcome predicted by *La Brébis* would prove to be elusive.

NOTES

1. Gombault to Reuterholm, June 7, 1791, RA, Reuterholmska samlingen 720741, vol. E5127. The estrangement between Grabianka and Leyman is mentioned in the report of the society's activities produced by the Russian authorities in 1807, after the count's arrest in St. Petersburg. It is stated that "Grabianka did not permit Leyman to look him in the eye for three years, due to the fact that the latter married against his [Grabianka's] will." See RGIA, Fond 1163, op. 1, d. 16b, 84r. Leyman married again, on May 12, 1797, after the death of Fumel. His new wife was named Louise Frediere. The civil authorities in Avignon also noted that Leyman was resident on "Rue Colombe, section la fraternité." See ADdV, PM An V, 51v.

2. RGIA, Fond 1163, op. 1, d. 16b, 61v.

3. See Maurice Champion, *Les inondations en France depuis le VIe siècle jusqu'à nos jours*, vol. 4 (Paris: Dunod, 1862), 79–80. Damage in the municipality of Barbentane alone, near Avignon, was estimated at more than 100,000 livres.

4. See E. J. Kolla, "The French Revolution, the Union of Avignon, and the Challenges of National Self-Determination," *Law and History Review* 31:4 (Nov. 2013): 722–5.

5. On the massacre, see Charles Soullier, *Histoire de la Révolution et du Comté-Venaissin, en 1789 et années suivantes*, vol. 2 (Paris: Librairie Ecclésiastique de Seguin almé, 1844), 5–32; A. Segond, "Les foules révolutionnaires à Avignon," *Revue Provence Historique* 19 (1969): 307–28; Hubert C. Johnson, *The Midi in Revolution: A Study of Regional Political Diversity, 1789–1793* (Princeton, NJ: Princeton University Press, 1986), 134–5.

6. Comte d'Avaray to P. F. de Quelen de la Vauguyon, Jan. 9, 1797, AN, Fonds abbé André 444AP/1, no. 96, 1.

7. On Duprat, see Alphonse Rabbe, *Biographie universelle et portative des contemmporains, ou dictionnaire historique*, vol. 12 (Paris: F. G. Levrault, 1834), 1516–17.

8. RGIA, Fond 1163, op. 1, d. 16b, 26r–26v.

9. On Jourdan, see Adrien Faure, *Jourdan coupe-tête: l'histoire de Mathieu Jouve, enfact de Saint-Jeures de Bonas, general des braves brigands de Vaucluse, 5 octobre 1746–8 prairial an II* (Polignac: Roure, 2005).

10. RGIA, Fond 1163, op. 1, d. 16b, 61v.

11. RGIA, Fond 1163, op. 1, d. 16b, 26v.

12. D'Avaray to Vauguyon, AN, Fonds abbé André 444AP/1, no. 96, 1–2.

13. Comte Ostap [Grabianka] to Philippe-Charles-Aimé Goupilleau, Dec. 27, 1795, and Jan. 21, 1796, AN, AB/XIX/3491, dossier 2.

14. On Goupilleau's role as a representative on mission in Vaucluse, see Claude Gandrillon, "Philippe Charles Aimé de Montaigu, 1749–1823, représentant en mission dans le midi," *Recherches vendéennes* 17 (2010): 127–68; Michel Biard, *Missionnaires de la République: Les représentants du people en mission (1793–1795)* (Paris: Comité des travaux historiques et scientifiques, 2002), 518. Also see Michel Jouve and Marcel Giraud-Mangin, eds., *Correspondence intime du conventionnel Rovère avec Goupilleau (de Montaigu) après la Terreur (1794–1795)* (Nimes: Librairie Ancienne Debroas, 1908).

15. See Hugh Gough, *The Terror in the French Revolution*, 2nd ed. (Basingstoke: Palgrave Macmillan, 2010), 103.

16. See Pierre Charpenne, *Les Grands Épisodes de la Révolution dans Avignon et le Comtat*, vol. 4 (Avignon: Imprimerie Henri Guigou, 1901), 58–61, 120–7.

17. Ostap to Goupilleau, Dec. 27, 1795, AN, AB/XIX/3491, dossier 2.

18. On Fréron, see Karen L. Green, "The Rise and Fall of a Revolutionary: The Political Career of Louis-Marie-Stanislas Fréron, Representative on Mission and *Conventionnel*, 1754–1802" (PhD thesis, Florida State University, 2004), 77. For Fréron's own account of his role in subduing the royalist uprisings in the Midi, see L.-M.-S. Fréron, *Mémoire historique sur la reaction royale et sur les massacres du Midi* (Paris: Baudouin Frères, 1824).

19. Green, "Rise and Fall of a Revolutionary," 172.

20. Green, "Rise and Fall of a Revolutionary," 192.

21. RGIA, Fond 1163, op. 1. d. 16b, 213r.

22. AN, AF II, 185. Also see F.-A. Aulard, *Recueil des Actes du Comité de Salut Public*, vol. 7 (Paris: Imprimerie Nationale, 1894), 498–9.

23. Aulard, *Recueil*, vol. 7, 499.

24. It is noteworthy that Grabianka borrowed 9,900 livres in *assignats* from Esprit Calvet in September 1793, that is, immediately before the release of Pernety, Bousie, and Macgregor. It is not known whether any money was needed to secure their release, but Grabianka certainly had the funds if necessary. See BMdA, MS. 3623, 75, 77. Also see Laurence Brockliss, *Calvet's Web: Enlightenment and the Republic of Letters in Eighteenth-Century France* (Oxford: Oxford University Press, 2002), 52. For an undated letter from Grabianka to Calvet, see MC, MS. 3050, no. 547. The letter is courteous in tone, but does not indicate that Calvet was a member of the Avignon Society.

25. Serge Billard-Baltyde, "Histoire d'un Marquis pendant la Révolution Française: 1792," Billard-Balytde Generations (online), July 21, 2011, accessed February 15, 2019, http://billard-baltyde.fr/marquis-1792/.

26. See "Siège du Chateau de Bésignan en 1792," *Bulletin Historique et Archéologique de Vaucluse* 4 (1882): 11–22; P. Vaillandet, "Le premier complot du marquis de Bésignan," *Mémoires de l'Académie de Vaucluse*, 3rd ser., 1 (1936): 1–40.

27. See Ernest Daudet, *La Conjuration de Pichegru et Complots Royalistes du Midi et de L'est 1795–1797* (Paris: Librairie Plon, 1901), 136–44, 325–8.

28. *Républicain du Nord*, Feb. 8, 1796, 2.

29. AN, Fonds abbé André 444AP/1, no. 96, 1.

30. AN, Fonds abbé André 444AP/1, no. 96, 2.

31. AN, Fonds abbé André 444AP/1, no. 96, 2–5.

32. Ernest Daudet, *Histoire de l'émigration pendant la Révolution française*, vol. 2 (Paris: Librairie Hachette, 1905), 34.

33. Louis de Fauche-Borel, *Réponse de M. de Fauche-Borel* (Paris: Moutardier, Libraire-Éditeur, 1829), 31.

34. A. H. Dampmartin, *Événemens qui se sont passes sous mes yeux pendant la Révolution Française*, vol. 1 (Berlin, 1799), 253.

35. Dampmartin, *Événemens*, vol. 2, 4–5.

36. Dampmartin, *Événemens*, vol. 2, 5.

37. Dampmartin, *Événemens*, vol. 2, 6.

38. Dampmartin, *Événemens*, vol. 2, 5.

39. Dampmartin, *Événemens*, vol. 2, 6.

40. Granget, *Histoire du diocese d'Avignon*, vol. 2, 429, fn. 1.

41. Claude Mesliand, "Renaissance de la franc-maçonnerie avignonnaise à la fin de l'Ancien Régime, 1774–1789," in *Bulletin d'histoire économique et sociale de la Révolution française* (Paris: Bibliothèque Nationale, 1972), 79; Meillassoux-Le Cerf, *Dom Pernety*, 203, 223–4. Also see Snoek, "Illuminés d'Avignon," 599.

42. Abbé Corenson, "Infernale origine et cause de la grande Révolution française. Notes sur les Illuiminés d'Avignon," MC, MS. 2066, 15.

43. Marcel, "Les Quatre Maisons," 93. See ADdV, Mariages, E 464, an V, 92.

44. RGIA, Fond 1163, op. 1, d. 16b, 26–8, 212r–220v.

45. RGIA, Fond 1163, op. 1, d. 16b, 213v.

46. RGIA, Fond 1163, op. 1, d. 16b, 212v–213r.

47. RGIA, Fond 1163, op. 1, d. 16a, 235v–236r.

48. RGIA, Fond 1163, op. 1, d. 16a, 236r–236v.

49. RGIA, Fond 1163, op. 1, d. 16b, 213v.

50. RGIA, Fond 1163, op. 1, d. 16b, 213v. Interestingly, a Jean-Baptiste Allier, a doctor of ancient law and lawyer from Avignon, wrote a brief biography of Pernety in 1838. See MPA, 3114-A-1. For a published transcript, see Meillassoux-Le Cerf, *Dom Pernety*, 320–2. It is unclear whether this is the same Allier. The case for this being the Allier in question is strengthened by the birth of his son, Joseph Thadée Allier, on Nov. 20, 1792, in the St. Agricol parish of Avignon. J.-B. Allier is recorded as "citoyen et homme de loi." The middle name here is highly suggestive of a nod to Grabianka. See ADdV, GG37 St. Agricol N, M, D 1791–1792, 47.

51. RGIA, Fond 1163, op. 1, d. 16b, 213v.

52. RGIA, Fond 1163, op. 1, d. 16b, 40v.

53. RGIA, Fond 1163, op. 1, d. 16b, 214r.

54. RGIA, Fond 1163, op. 1, d. 16b, 214v.

55. Joel 2:28. For Grabianka's reference to Joel, see RGIA, Fond 1163, op. 1, d. 16a, 216r–216v.

56. RGIA, Fond 1163, op. 1, d. 16a, 215r–215v.

57. RGIA, Fond 1163, op. 1, d. 16b, 214r.

58. RGIA, Fond 1163, op. 1, d. 16b, 213v.

59. RGIA, Fond 1163, op. 1, d. 16b, 216v.

60. RGIA, Fond 1163, op. 1, d. 16a, 29v–30r.

61. RGIA, Fond 1163, op. 1, d. 16b, 107v.

62. See *Tableaux des Freres qui composent la T.R.G. Loge de St. Jean d'Écosse de la Vertu Persécutée* (1785–1789), MC, MS. 2951, nos. 48–52.

63. Louis de la Roque and Édouard de Barthélemy, *Catalogue des Gentilshommes d'Alsace* (Paris: E. Dentu, 1865), 18.

64. For the 1788 membership list of the La Candeur lodge, see HHStA, Kabinetsarchiv, Vertrauliche Akten 76-1-10, 112–15. Lefort's elder brother, Frédéric-Antoine-Henri, was a leading Freemason in Strasbourg in the 1780s, being venerable master of La Candeur lodge between 1784 and 1786. Lefort was a distant relative of François Lefort, his great-great-grandfather's brother, who made his name in the service of Peter the Great in Russia. For more on the Lefort family in Geneva, see Henri Le Fort, *Notice généalogique et historique sur la famille Le Fort de Genève* (Geneva: A. Kundig, 1920). For an ornate genealogical manuscript of the Lefort family, featuring Louis Lefort, and produced in 1769, see BNUdS, MS. 1049, f. 001.

65. In a letter written by Divonne to Reuterholm, dated June 1, 1790, Lefort is described as a "charming subject." Divonne suggests that he indoctrinated Lefort and that the young baron "wrote to me to express his joy at what he is going to receive." See Divonne to Reuterholm, SFOA, 121.141.4 (no. 18).

66. RGIA, Fond 1163, op. 1, d. 16b, 216r.

67. RGIA, Fond 1163, op. 1, d. 16b, 216v.

68. RGIA, Fond 1163, op. 1, d. 16b, 21v–22r.

69. RGIA, Fond 1163, op. 1, d. 16b, 216r.

70. RGIA, Fond 1163, op. 1, d. 16b, 216v.

71. In the Old Testament Aaron is described as wearing a "breastplate, and an ephod, and a robe, and a broidered coat, a mitre, and a girdle." See Exodus 28:4.

72. RGIA, Fond 1163, op. 1, d. 16b, 217r–217v.

73. RGIA, Fond 1163, op. 1, d. 16b, 27v.

74. On this disorder, see Jonathan Devlin, "The Army, Politics and Public Order in Directorial Provence, 1795–1800," *Historical Journal* 32:1 (1989): 87–106.

75. RGIA, Fond 1163, op. 1, d. 16b, 218v–219r.

76. RGIA, Fond 1163, op. 1, d. 16a, 205r.

77. RGIA, Fond 1163, op. 1, d. 16b, 219r–219v.

78. In his interrogation Simonin confirms this plan to appease Grabianka's creditors by sending Allier and Leyman to Poland to secure funds. See RGIA, Fond 1163, op. 1, d. 16b, 31r.

79. RGIA, Fond 1163, op. 1, d. 16b, 219v.

80. On Verger's links to Willermoz, see Alice Joly, *Un Mystique Lyonnais et les Secrets de la Franc-Maçonnerie Jean-Baptiste Willermoz* (Paris: Demeter, 1986), 311, 316. In 1808, Verger became a "Chévalier Grand Profès" and was awarded the honorary name "Eq. a tribus oleis stellatis." See Gustave Bord, "La Stricte Observance templière d'Allemagne," *La Franc-Maçonnerie Démasquée*, vol. 24 (1907), 64.

81. Verger to Willermoz, BMdL, MS. 5425, no. 32, 1.

82. BMdA MS. 5623, 77–8. See Brockliss, *Calvet's Web*, 52–3. It is not clear whether this consortium was an offshoot of the Illuminés d'Avignon. However, Calvet's will, of April 23, 1804, refers to the members of this consortium, who were still in his debt, as "*illuminés.*" See BMdA MS. 5628, 213.

83. "Document du Ministère de la Police générale de la République, Brumaire, An X." AN, F. 7/7915. Reproduced in Meillassoux-Le Cerf, *Dom Pernety*, 323–6. Interestingly, the report also mentions that Richardière was in Paris at the time, where he "regularly had a meal on Tuesday or Wednesday of each week at the home of Picot, the former *boulanger* to the Prince de Condé."

84. RGIA, Fond 1163, op. 1, d. 16b, 220r.

85. RGIA, Fond 1163, op. 1, d. 16b, 75r.

86. RGIA, Fond 1163, op. 1, d. 16b, 31v.

87. The full ninety-two questions that were posed to Simonin are extant; the record of Leyman's interrogation only includes questions 14–15, 33–9, and 62–5. See RGIA, Fond 1163, op. 1, d. 16b, 20r–36v, 51r–51v, 60r–62v, 75r–75v.

88. RGIA, Fond 1163, op. 1, d. 16b, 29v–30r.

89. See Georges Six, *Dictionnaire biographique des généraux et amiraux français de la Révolution et de l'Empire (1792–1814)*, vol. 2 (Paris: Librairie G. Saffroy, 1934), 406–7.

90. RGIA, Fond 1163, op. 1, d. 16b, 75r.

91. RGIA, Fond 1163, op. 1, d. 16b, 30v.

92. For brief biographical details, see Vicomte de Grouchy, "Artistes français des XVIIe et XVIIIe siècles," *Nouvelles Archives de L'Art Français*, 3rd ser., 7 (1891): 99–100. In the memoirs of Henriette Campan, a lady-in-waiting to Marie Antoinette, Saint-Charles is named as a lover of Cahouette de Villers, who sought to use the affair to gain access to the queen's apartments in Versailles. See Henriette Campan, *Mémoires sur la vie privée Marie-Antoinette, reine de France et de Navarre*, vol. 1 (Paris: Baudouin Fréres, 1823), 136.

93. A Saint-Charles is listed in the table of members of the Amis Réunis Masonic lodge in Paris for 1788 among those holding the seventh degree. See Gustave Bord, *La Franc-Maçonnerie en France*, vol. 1 (Paris: Librairie Nationale, 1909), 362.

94. RGIA, Fond 1163, op. 1, d. 16b, 30r–30v.

95. Winifred Stephens, *Women of the French Revolution* (New York: E. P. Dutton, 1922), 231.

96. RGIA, Fond 1163, op. 1, d. 16b, 30r–30v.

6

Light from the North

THE NEW ISRAEL SOCIETY REVIVED IN THE RUSSIAN EMPIRE, 1802–1807

THE COMMITTEE FOR the Preservation of General Security (CPGS) was established in St. Petersburg on January 13, 1807, at a time of national emergency. The War of the Fourth Coalition, which had broken out three months earlier, was proving to be a disaster for Russia. Napoleon's army took Berlin in October 1806, a victory that was followed shortly after by a Polish uprising and a Russian defeat, on December 23–24, 1806, in the Battle of Czarnowo. In the first two months of 1807, French and Polish forces had advanced deep into East Prussia and Poland, and were near the Russian frontier proper.[1] The CPGS was envisaged by its chief architect, N. N. Novosil'tsev, as a means to "avert and eradicate" the "evil intentions" of the "insidious French government" within the Russian Empire. The first article of the secret statutes that accompanied the official edict authorising the CPGS emphasizes the grave threat posed to Russia by "secret societies under the name of the Illuminati [and] Martinists." These groups were apparently being sponsored by the French with the aim, first and foremost, of "inserting harmful contacts inside the government" to sow discord and confusion at the highest level.[2] In a letter sent by Novosil'tsev to Emperor Alexander shortly after the establishment of the CPGS, the official justified the initiative by stressing that "our chancelleries are full of 'Martinists,' 'Israelites,' 'illumines,' and scoundrels of all shades."[3]

On February 6, 1807, less than a month after the establishment of the CPGS, Grabianka was arrested in St. Petersburg, where he had been residence since August 1805. The Polish nobleman's arrest occurred the day before the Battle of Eylau, just south of Königsberg, which proved to be inconclusive. However, defeat would have left the Russian capital seriously exposed to Napoleon's army. In early 1807, the rising sense of panic vis-à-vis the

Initiating the Millennium. Robert Collis, and Natalie Bayer, Oxford University Press (2020) © Oxford University Press. DOI: 10.1093/oso/9780190903374.001.0001

precarious military situation that was consuming Novosil'tsev and other tsarist officials in St. Petersburg was being exacerbated by influential conspiratorial theories promulgated by Augustin Barruel and John Robison at the close of the eighteenth century. Both men had argued that nefarious secret societies, including Freemasonry and "theosophical illuminés," were responsible for bringing down the Ancien Régime and unleashing the terror of the French Revolution.[4] The first Russian translations of principal works of Barruel and Robison were published in 1805 and 1806 respectively.[5] Hence, Novosil'tsev would have been able to contemplate the contemporary relevance of Barruel's virulent attack on the Illuminés of Avignon as "the most secret and monstrous of lodges," which formed "the most terrible tribunal for Kings."[6] The language Novosil'tsev used to justify the promulgation of the CPGS in January 1807 is strongly redolent of the virulent tone used by Barruel.

Moreover, Novosil'tsev's explanation of why it was necessary to establish the CPGS reflects the conspiratorial viewpoints of Barruel and Robison in terms of their conflation of two fundamentally different forms of illuminism. Thus the "scoundrels of all shades" Novosil'tsev claims are rife in Petersburg are seemingly perceived as the heirs to the radical atheistic and rational doctrine espoused by the Bavarian Order of Illuminaten, which was active between 1776 and 1785 and led by Adam Weishaupt. At the same time, these "scoundrels" were also devotees of a highly esoteric and millenarian form of theosophical illuminism, which authorities across Europe considered subversive because of its penchant for prophecies that foretold the cataclysmic downfall of the monarchical status quo. This rather amorphous combination of atheistic and theosophical strands of illuminism was first lumped together by Luchet, in 1789, in his *Essai sur la secte des Illuminés*.[7]

This conflation of the *illuminati* and the *illuminés* helps us to understand why Grabianka was arrested. It also helps us to understand the line of questioning and the accusations levelled against Grabianka, along with Simonin and Leyman, the only other two members of the NIS to be questioned by the Russian authorities. The surviving records of the interrogations of these three individuals provide us with fascinating insights into the fearful and uncertain attitude of the Russian authorities vis-à-vis the precise motives of the society in St. Petersburg.

The remainder of this chapter will demonstrate that Novosil'tsev was, to a great extent, justified in attesting that, at the beginning of 1807, government chancelleries were increasingly being infiltrated by Grabianka's followers, even if he was mistaken about any perfidious links to Napoleonic France or Polish rebels. Indeed, Grabianka's influence stretched beyond the walls of government ministries and into the homes of some of the most prominent noble families in the capital.

By December 1806, Grabianka had succeeded in initiating no fewer than sixty new members into the NIS, in the space of sixteen months since he had arrived in the capital. Grabianka's success in attracting so many members in Petersburg can be partly attributed to his personal charisma. But notwithstanding his charm, Grabianka was significantly aided in his efforts by being able to harness a network of Petersburg nobles who shared close links—either through family bonds or Masonic connections—to S. I. Pleshcheev, the first Russian to be initiated as an *illuminé* in Avignon, in 1788. Before we examine Grabianka's activities in St. Petersburg between August 1805 and his arrest in February 1807, we will discuss the significant legacy left by Pleshcheev, who died in 1802, which was, to a large extent, continued by his wife, Natal'ia Fedotovna Pleshcheeva (1768–1855), and closest friend and fellow mason, Aleksandr Alekseevich Lenivtsev (d. c. 1818). We also investigate the three-year period immediately prior to Grabianka's arrival in Petersburg, a time of networking that planted the seeds for the Pole's successful recruitment drive from August 1805. After undertaking an in-depth study of the impact of Grabianka's residence in St. Petersburg, we conclude by examining the reaction to his arrest among both his followers and detractors.

I

According to M. M. Muromtsov, who attended gatherings of the NIS in early 1807, "everyone was convinced (of course with the exception of his friends) that Count Grabianka was an agent or a spy of Napoleon," when word began to spread of his arrest.[8] This is unsurprising, given the explicit connection in the statutes of the CPGS, outlined by Novosil'tsev, between the French government and the *illuminés* resident in the Russian capital. Yet the surviving documents related to the interrogations of Grabianka, Leyman, and Simonin reveal that the CPGS had no solid evidence whatsoever that any member of the NIS was conducting any form of espionage or anti-Russian activity in St. Petersburg.

Despite this dearth of concrete evidence, the chief interrogator for the CPGS, a French legal referendary named Pierre Péchard-Deschamps, issued a damning indictment of Grabianka in his official summation of the grounds for his arrest. The charge sheet compiled by Péchard-Deschamps is wholly in line with Novosil'tsev's conspiratorial mindset, in that it conflates the worst imaginable extremes of the revolutionary illuminati and the millenarian *illuminés*. This was no easy task, but the French legal expert achieved his goal by painting Grabianka as a nefarious mastermind, unscrupulous in his ability to manipulate the society for his own ends. In his opinion, "the society had never existed without a political purpose, that all has been dictated in writing and ordered by Count Grabianka." According to Péchard-Deschamps, Grabianka saw himself as a Christ-like figure, who used the oracles to relay praise of him from heaven and to prescribe slavish worship of his leadership.

Péchard-Deschamps sought to portray Grabianka as a fanatical millenarian, who wished to hasten the advent of Christ's second coming by any means and was ready himself to rule over people. The tsarist official claimed that Grabianka had therefore ensured that the oracle approved of the Massacres of La Glacière in Avignon in 1791 and the slaughter of imprisoned priests by revolutionary sans-culottes in Paris in 1792. In chapter 5, we discussed Grabianka's acquaintance with Jean Duprat and Mathieu Jouve

Jourdain, who were both implicated in the massacres in Avignon. In his interrogation, Leyman was asked whether Grabianka formed a "*société intime* with Robespierreists, terrorists and cutthroats" from Avignon. Leyman did not deny that Grabianka had entertained such figures during the height of the Terror, but explained that "he made them as content as possible in order to have influence on them" and that he was prepared to scold them for cutting each other's throats.[9] Nonetheless, as we have seen, Grabianka was also on familiar terms with monarchists in Avignon in the 1790s. Several contemporaries testified to the Grabianka's heroic efforts to help, protect, and harbour monarchist figures, such as Bésignan. Leyman also defended Grabianka against the charge that he colluded with the revolutionaries, referring to an occasion in the early 1790s when the count was held in custody for twenty-hours after the revolutionary authorities had intercepted a letter from Reuterholm. Grabianka's old valet added that the revolutionaries "would have cut him into a thousand bits and pieces" if they had examined his papers.

A second principal accusation levelled against Grabianka by Péchard-Deschamps was that he was under the control of Russia's enemies, which, in the context of 1807, was a thinly veiled reference to France and Polish nationalists. Several questions following this line of enquiry were posed to Leyman and Simonin. During Leyman's interrogation, in June 1807, he was asked whether Grabianka had maintained a correspondence from Avignon with Polish agitators who sought to rebel against Russia. Leyman responded by categorically denying that his master had entered into any form of correspondence with Polish revolutionaries. Indeed, Leyman added, Grabianka was in possession of an oracle that foresaw the ruination of his kingdom.

Leyman's interrogator soon followed up with a second question regarding Grabianka's links to Polish rebels. On this occasion Leyman was asked a more specific question relating to whether Grabianka had received Polish rebels in Avignon who had fled to France after the failed Kościuszko Uprising in Poland, in 1794. Leyman provides an intriguing answer to this question: he initially insists that Grabianka "would be completely incapable of offering any revolutionary advice" and had "neither seen nor met at his house dissatisfied Poles who have retired to France." But the valet then reveals one exception: Major Klemens Liberadzki, a prominent officer in the uprising, had indeed stayed with Grabianka. Liberadzki hailed from Podolia and, according to Leyman, had saved Grabianka's sons, who were studying at a Jesuit college, during the uprising in Poland. Leyman adds that Grabianka tried to dampen Liberadzki's nationalist zeal and pronounced: "You are a fool to pursue the impossible dream of re-establishing Poland. I advise you to stay with me and to return one day with me to Poland where we will spend our lives in peace and in retirement." According to Leyman, Liberadzki promised to return directly to Poland after having already spent a considerable length of time in Avignon. However, instead of going to his homeland, Liberadzki enlisted in the Polish legion of Jan Henryk Dabrowski, which served as part of the French army in Italy, and was soon killed in action in Mantua, in April 1797.

A fascinating perspective on Liberadzki's relationship with Grabianka during his time in Avignon between 1795 and early 1797 is offered by Colonel Józef Drzewiecki, who served alongside Liberadzki during the Kościuszko Uprising and in the Polish Legion in Italy in 1797. In his memoirs, Drzewiecki describes how Liberadzki immersed himself in the millenarian milieu of the Avignon Society in the mid-1790s.[10] Drzewiecki asserts that Liberadzki especially trusted the society's prophet, who at this time would have been Allier. Apparently, Allier foresaw that Liberadzki would soon be killed in battle if he left Avignon and, consequently, Grabianka pleaded with his countryman not to leave.[11] Furthermore, even after Liberadzki had enlisted in the Polish Legion and travelled to Italy, in early 1797, he received a letter from the Avignon Society's prophet, who once again forewarned him about his imminent death if he continued his military exploits.[12]

Drzewiecki's description of the relationship between Grabianka and Liberadzki in Avignon highlights a bond that initially emanated from a shared Podolian noble heritage. Leyman's testimony also reveals the deep sense of gratitude Grabianka felt towards Liberadzki for saving his two boys. In fact, Liberadzki's time in Avignon appears to have been a period in which he was profoundly influenced by Grabianka's society, rather than one in which Liberadzki successfully promoted any form of revolutionary politics. In short, Péchard-Deschamps assertion that Grabianka sheltered Polish rebels in Avignon is decidedly misleading.

However, the interrogator could point to the reply Grabianka had received from the oracle in 1800, which proclaimed: "Poland needs a king: Thaddeus [i.e. Grabianka] is appointed to be him by her [Poland's] guardian angel." In the tense atmosphere pervading the Russian capital in 1807, this prophecy was indeed highly suspicious. Yet, when Simonin was asked directly whether Grabianka had come to St. Petersburg to restore the Polish monarchy, the former interpreter of dreams in the Avignon Society asserted the following: "I am confident that he never had a project or intention, through the help of his followers, to install a king in Poland." This tallies with Muromtsov's recollection that "adepts never once uttered a word about politics" at the gatherings of the NIS in St. Petersburg.[13] We discuss in more detail what did occur at the Petersburg assemblies later in the chapter; here, it is worth emphasizing that while he was resident in the Russian capital, Grabianka displayed no overt inclination, as far as surviving sources indicate, to bring about the fulfilment of the prophecy from 1800.

Péchard-Deschamps also placed a strong emphasis on the violent pronouncements contained within some of the prophecies received by members of the NIS that foretold the "destruction of the [Russian] empire and the assassination of the sovereign." Here the Russian authorities were in many ways no different to their British contemporaries. As John Barrell has demonstrated, in the wake of the French Revolution, in 1795, Richard Brothers was arrested by the Privy Council for the treasonable act of imagining the regicide of George III.[14] Thus Péchard-Deschamps could draw on recent precedent in arguing that by preserving these predictions for nineteen years, Grabianka was culpable in atrocious "grand crimes." Of critical importance here was Péchard-Deschamps's attempt to cast Grabianka as the sole author of all the prophetic replies received from heaven. In so doing, Grabianka alone bore the guilt of these thought crimes.

As evidence Péchard-Deschamps extracted a total of nine prophecies from the society's written records of each oracle, which the Russian authorities had confiscated from Grabianka's home. The two answers obtained by Richardière, as well as those already cited by Pleshcheev (see chapter 3), contain dire warnings that were directly related to the fate of Russia and her sovereign. The earliest prophecy cited by Péchard-Deschamps, dated October 14, 1788, was in answer to what seems like an innocuous question from Richardière: "S. A. Gabriel—Do you approve that I resume correspondence with Lemaire d'Attigny in Russia." As mentioned in chapter 3, Richardière spent several years in St. Petersburg as a chirurgeon to A. N. Naryshkina, until her death in 1782.[15] We also know that Lemaire d'Attigny was resident in Petersburg, where she was employed by several families as a governess, up until 1789, and it seems the pair were acquainted in the Russian capital.[16]

Although Richardière's question was seemingly mundane, the answer he received, purportedly from the Archangel Gabriel, was anything but. God's principal messenger commanded Richardière to transmit the following stark message to d'Attigny in St. Petersburg: "Leave these places that you inhabit if you do not want to perish. When I enter into combat, I will ravage the entire Empire; I will strike down the sovereign and my sword, shattering her days, will give her the justice that should have been delivered to her twenty years ago." The second dire prophecy stemmed from a cryptic question addressed to Gabriel by Richardière, on October 16, 1788, about what he should write "to Charlemagne in Russia to whom I am much obliged." Once again, Richardière is instructed to convey a dire prediction to his mysterious acquaintance in Russia:

Make your preparations to leave Russia because before two years have passed calamity upon calamity will ravage her. Here inhabitants will experience the fate of Sodom and Gomorrah. The Eternal has sworn that several of her towns, burned by rains of burning sulphur, will be consumed by flames; that others, buried in the abyss, will be covered afterwards by the highest rocks. That others again, swollen by the waters, will disappear in an instant, and that finally many, ravaged by iron, will be the prey of the enemies who will share the remains of the [Russian] Empire.

O Sodom! Impious leader! Bow your head and think of your crimes and moan your fate. He who menaces you is already on your doorstep . . . Rampant then will be those over who you reigned, who will immolate you to satisfy justice. The Veil of Death will come to cover the eyes and joy will clothe those who should be mourning you.[17]

These two ominous warnings received by Richardière cast Russia as a sinful realm ruled by an unrighteous sovereign that would soon witness cataclysmic events. It is therefore unsurprising that the Russian authorities honed in on them.

However, Grabianka rightly indicated in his testimony that these two prophecies had nothing whatsoever to do with him, as they were transmitted via Cappelli during the Italian's residence in Avignon. Moreover, he acknowledges the oracles as false. He under-cuts Péchard-Deschamps's argument by highlighting that he was not the society's chosen prophet in 1788 (or at any other point), *and* he categorically rejected the predictions as being truly divine messages from heaven.

II

The tsarist interrogator also honed in on a series of questions set by Pleshcheev shortly after his initiation into the Avignon Society in November 1788. Of particular interest to Péchard-Deschamps was Pleshcheev's enquiry on November 9, 1788, in which he asked the Archangel Gabriel whether "it is the will of God that he also teaches the Grand Duke [Paul] and the Grand Duchess [Mariia Fyodorovna]." In other words, Pleshcheev, fresh from being initiated himself, was seeking counsel about whether to reveal and teach the heir apparent to the Russian throne and his wife about the Avignon Society and its millenarian doctrine and esoteric practises. Pleshcheev was one of Grand Duke Paul's closest confidantes and had escorted the royal couple on their Grand Tour of Europe in 1781 and 1782. Moreover, Mariia Fyodorovna's mother and brother—Friederike Sophia Dorothea, Duchess of Württemberg, and Duke Ferdinand of Württemberg—were both initiated into the Avignon Society, in 1788 and 1789. Hence it may have seemed natural to Pleshcheev to share his new-found spiritual knowledge with his intimate friends in Russia.

The answer received by Pleshcheev, with Cappelli supposedly acting as a conduit, was far from discouraging. He was commanded to "guard your silence for six months and in six months you will speak to the one who guides you to speak to him [the Grand Duke] yourself a month later. Only after this time had elapsed was Pleshcheev to reveal to the Grand Duke "the terrible vengeance with which the Eternal comes to strike the ungrateful. Terror, pain, carnage already prepares the moment in which the uni-verse will be cleared of the guilty to deliver them to the most terrible torments." This terrifying prophecy is mitigated by the revelation that "the Eternal seeks his [Grand Duke Paul's] alliance" and that "he will revive in his heart his love, that he will pray to him, that he will love him and his power will magnify the sum of wonders." In other words, not only would Grand Duke Paul be saved by being privy to the secret religious knowledge known to initiates of the Avignon Society, but the Russian heir would play a significant and positive role in the impending millennium by helping to augment the number of prodigies.

Grabianka was asked directly about this prophecy during his interrogation in July 1807. He confirmed that he accepted the prediction in its entirety. But he went on to lament that "it was not accomplished." According to Grabianka, Pleshcheev had failed to "fulfil the conditions that were given to him," because "instead of waiting for six months, as was expressly instructed, Pleshcheev "spoke to the Grand Duke within the first days of his arrival" in Russia, apparently communicating "everything to him . . ., even giving him answers [and] enlightening him on these answers according to their true values."

Remarkably, a recorded conversation that took place between Emperor Paul and Stanisław August Poniatowski on September 4, 1797, seems to confirm that Pleshcheev did indeed reveal a great deal about the Avignon Society to the heir to the throne when he returned to Russia in early 1789. On this early autumn day, at the imperial residence of Gatchina, Paul initiated the conversation by asking the former Polish monarch, "Tell me, do you know of this society of Avignon, which knows many things?" Crucially, the emperor then adds, "I became aware of it about eight years ago." Specifically, he was informed about the group in 1789—that is, at exactly the time Pleshcheev returned to Russia, eager to reveal the prophetic warnings he had been permitted to tell the Russian sovereign. The knowledge of the society the emperor conveyed to Poniatowski in the remainder of their conversation is wholly accurate: "They were seven, they live very piously and they even continued their union in the midst of the troubles of France." Poniatowski then interjects to say that he was unaware of the existence of the group. Paul continues, adding, "I was told that in the year 1800, after terrible troubles in the world, there will come a great reparation and it will come from the North." Further, the emperor was not simply aware of this prediction but also gave credence to it in his conversation with Poniatowski: "Myself, I remain calm in my simplicity while awaiting the time of these great changes, which I confess I believe to be near . . . Are there not things in the holy books that permit this belief?" The eschatological theme of the conversation concludes with Paul I emphasizing his belief that the world was on the precipice of grand tribulations: "Anyway, remember what I tell you today that in three years you will see great and very astonishing things."[18]

Pleshcheev may have departed from Avignon at the end of 1788, but he remained in contact with Grabianka and Richardière in Avignon and Cappelli in Rome until September 1790.[19] In other words, Pleshcheev was an engaged member of the society for nearly two years after his initiation, albeit at a distance in Russia. This is significant; it was precisely in this period that Pleshcheev exerted his greatest influence in the mystical and moral instruction of Grand Duke Paul and his wife. In a letter he wrote to the grand duke on May 19, 1790, for example, Pleshcheev attached a collection of documents intended as spiritual guidance, which he entitled *The Letters and Moral Instructions of S. I. Pleshcheev*. We do not know the content of these moral and spiritual instructions, but Pleshcheev wrote that his "feeble efforts" were "for the advancement of his [the grand duke's] glory" and "peace of mind and salvation."[20]

Pleshcheev's enthusiastic embrace of the Avignon Society, alongside the likes of Reuterholm, Divonne, and Ferdinand of Württemberg, seems to have waned by the end of 1790. His disenchantment most likely stemmed from the fallout from Cappelli's arrest.

The revolutionary upheaval affecting Avignon at this time would have also made communication extremely problematic. Yet it is evident that, despite the rupture, Pleshcheev maintained a millenarian outlook, which was shared by Grand Duke Paul and Mariia Fyodorovna. This is demonstrated by an undated letter from the grand duchess to Pleshcheev, most likely written around 1794, in which she views contemporary events in Poland through a decidedly millenarian mindset: "The latest news about Poland is distressing. Present-day times recall, of course, what the Gospel preaches to us, and I confess that we are approaching the last days."[21] As mentioned, Emperor Paul expressed similar sentiments to Poniatowski's in 1797.

Pleshcheev's close relationship with Mariia Fyodorovna became the subject of court intrigue in 1794, and consequently he was banished to Moscow. However, his fall from grace was relatively short-lived, and he returned to court in Petersburg at the beginning of 1796. Shortly after returning to favour, he married N. F. Verigina, who had been a maid of honour (*fräulein*) to Mariia Fyodorovna since 1791.[22] By the time of his marriage, Pleshcheev was firmly ensconced in the Rosicrucian circle of the well-known publisher N. I. Novikov.[23] Novikov, during his interrogation, in the spring of 1792, by A. A. Prozorovskii, the governor of Moscow, revealed that Pleshcheev had been "appointed to be initiated into the theoretical degree" of the Order of Rosicrucians.[24] As Arthur Waite notes, this preliminary degree was "called a Rosicrucian School of Nature's Mysteries, for the education of members in love of God and their Brethren."[25]

Pleshcheev had been a Freemason since 1776, but it is highly likely that he was drawn to the Order of Rosicrucians by A. A. Lenivtsev, who served as the supervisor of the Theoretical Degree of the rite in St. Petersburg between 1788 and 1792.[26] Lenivtsev, whom I. V. Lopukhin referred to as "a person with rare gifts, mind and heart," had been at the forefront of illuminist Freemasonry in the Russian capital since at least 1785.[27] At this time Lenivtsev was the Masonic mentor to P. I. Titov. Lenivtsev's predilection for esoteric pursuits, including alchemy, is revealed by Titov, who describes how the two men met a certain Khariton Tsitseron at the end of 1786 at the home of an acquaintance in Petersburg. Here, Tsitseron boasted that he could make artificial marble and spoke in bad Russian about curious "secret sciences"; he also confided that he belonged to the Order of Rosicrucians. It seems that Lenivtsev and Titov were convinced by Tsitseron, because they hired him to be their tutor in the esoteric sciences. Titov notes that the three would meet every Sunday at midnight and stay together until dawn. Each meeting began with a prayer uttered by Tsitseron, with Lenivstev and Titov in a position of genuflection.[28] It did not take Lenivtsev and Titov long to realise that Tsitseron was a charlatan; nevertheless, this rather comic misadventure highlights their genuine desire to learn "secret sciences" from an adept who was supposedly a member of the Berlin-based Order of Rosicrucians. By 1788, Lenivstev had come into contact with authentic Rosicrucians in Moscow, and he returned to Petersburg with a "sincere wish to work for the Lord" by mentoring others in the Theoretical Degree of their rite.[29]

In May 1801, Pleshcheev and Lenivtsev, who were by this time fast friends as well as fraternal brothers, were entrusted by Russian Rosicrucians to go on a mission to Berlin to try to renew links with the order's leadership in Prussia.[30] However, by August they had already arrived in Frankfurt, having apparently achieved little in Berlin. It was the ill health of Pleshcheev, who was suffering from asthma, indigestion, and a fever, that had necessitated this journey to western Germany, not any Masonic business. In August, Pleshcheev began a two-month course of treatment at Bad Ems and nearby Wiesbaden.

During his treatment in Bad Ems, Pleshcheev began a correspondence with the renowned theosopher Karl von Eckartshausen.[31] Pleshcheev's urge to write to the German thinker, who lived in Munich, stemmed from his having recently read a Russian translation by A. F. Labzin of *Kosti's Journey from Morning to Noon* (1795).[32] In his first letter to Eckartshausen, Pleshcheev declares that he and Lenivtsev "love the march of righteousness" and that they wish to meet him in order to "learn the brilliant truths of which God has enriched your heart, your mind . . . in a manner so salutary for *hommes de désir*."[33] Pleshcheev's identification of himself and Lenivtsev as men of desire demonstrates the profound influence of L.-C. de Saint-Martin on the Russian noblemen.[34] His and Lenivtsev's eagerness to learn from Eckartshausen in person also highlights an important aspect of their characters and spiritual journey: an openness to seek "true" Christian enlightenment beyond the narrow parameters of Rosicrucianism alone.

Unfortunately, Pleshcheev's ill-health denied him the opportunity to travel to Munich. He spent the second half of the autumn of 1801 in Switzerland. He then offered to cover the costs for Eckartshausen to travel to stay with him at the Hotel du Corbeau in Zurich.[35] Although the German declined this offer, Pleshcheev's stay in Switzerland was not wholly devoid of stimulating company. Notably, Pleshcheev described meeting Divonne in Geneva to O. A. Pozdeev, a fellow Rosicrucian in Moscow, "He has great enlightenment from outside and also draws upon much light from within himself. Even though he does not follow our teachings [Rosicrucianism] he does not deny its value and lofty aims." Pleshcheev added that he "spent as much time" with Divonne as circumstances allowed.[36] The Russian nobleman had much in common with the Swiss aristocrat: both had been initiated into the Illuminés d'Avignon in the late 1780s, and both then distanced themselves from the society in the 1790s without abandoning their theosophical outlooks.

After departing from Geneva, Pleshcheev made his way to Montpellier, where he was the guest of General Charles de Frégeville, in the hope that the moderate winter climate would benefit his declining health. However, on February 4, 1802 Pleshcheev died and was buried within the grounds of Frégeville's property the Château du Domaine Grammont.[37] He and Lenivtsev had not succeeded in fulfilling their desire to meet Eckartshausen. However, only twenty-days later, N. F. Pleshcheeva wrote to Eckartshausen from Lausanne and expressed her own intention to visit the theosopher, in the company of Lenivtsev. In other words, Pleshcheeva had been travelling with her husband in Europe, although he had not mentioned her presence in his correspondence.

Despite her grief, the death of Pleshcheev allowed her to emerge from his shadow and to almost immediately seek to fulfil his goal of meeting Eckartshausen. On February 27, 1802, she informed Eckartshausen that it was her intention to pass through Munich in fifteen days and requested that Eckartshausen grace her and Lenivtsev with his company in order to relieve and console them by way of his "edifying conversation and advice."[38] Upon returning to St. Petersburg, Pleshcheeva penned another letter to Eckartshausen, in which it is clear that she and Lenivtsev did indeed visit the theosopher in Munich.[39] Significantly, it is almost certain that Divonne accompanied Pleshcheeva and Lenivtsev to their meeting with Eckartshausen. It is also likely that Divonne accompanied the Russian travellers on the return journey to St. Petersburg, where he resided for several months before departing for England.[40]

As we will demonstrate, Grabianka's success in attracting over sixty new members to the NIS in St. Petersburg between August 1805 and December 1806 was made possible in large measure by the enthusiastic networking skills of both Lenivtsev and Pleshcheeva. Although Grabianka undoubtedly possessed great charisma, it was the personal links to Petersburg society enjoyed by Lenivtsev and Pleshcheeva that enabled the society to flourish. More specifically, Lenivtsev succeeded in drawing in his old Masonic and Rosicrucian acquaintants in the capital, who were also very close to Pleshcheev before his death. In tandem with this Masonic dimension, Pleshcheeva proved highly adept at attracting relatives into the society from both her and her deceased husband's families. This mixture of fraternal and family connections was wholly in keeping with the way the society had operated since 1779.

III

Baron Louis Lefort, the chancellor of the NIS, arrived in St. Petersburg on August 21, 1802.[41] Despite his unfamiliarity with the northern climes of the Russian capital, he may well have felt a huge sense of relief at having escaped France, where he had suffered the ignominy of being incarcerated in a debtor's prison for three months as a result of being unable to support himself as a royalist officer in the revolutionary period.[42] According to Leyman, Grabianka managed to pay Lefort's bail. He was subsequently packed off to St. Petersburg by Ferdinand of Württemberg, who, according to Leyman, acted as a protector of the entire Lefort family.[43]

The timing of his arrival was fortuitous, as it coincided with the return of Pleshcheeva and Lenivtsev from western Europe and of Divonne, his old acquaintance and fellow initiate of the Illuminés d'Avignon. The baron's journey to the Russian capital took place when Grabianka was still in France. His entry into Petersburg society benefitted greatly from the letters of recommendation he had received from Duke Ferdinand, the brother of Empress Mariia Fyodorovna.[44] In a letter written to C. D. von Meyer in Strasbourg, a friend and fellow mason of La Candeur lodge in the city, Lefort wrote that he hoped to gain an audience with the empress the following week. Moreover, he described how he had quickly become reacquainted with Divonne, who was residing with Sof'ia Razumovskaia at the time.[45] Razumovskaia, who soon offered Lefort an apartment in her home, was a fascinating Russian noblewoman and seems to have enjoyed close links with many of the foremost theosophical minds of her era. She had been extremely close to Divonne since at least 1790, for example, and had first become acquainted with Saint-Martin in Paris in 1787.[46] According to Grabianka, Lefort also began to frequent Pleshcheeva's home in Petersburg shortly after his arrival and soon became the governor to Pleshcheeva's children.[47]

Was Lefort simply taking advantage of prior connections in order to eke out a living in a foreign country in 1802, or did he harbour the goal of promoting the NIS in Russia? A revealing passage in a letter, from June 10, 1804, to Bernard-Frédéric Turckheim, also a fellow member of La Candeur in Strasbourg, which states that he had not yet fulfilled his goal in travelling to Russia, suggests that Lefort was interested in more than the education of Pleshcheeva's children.[48]

If Lefort's goal remained unfulfilled in June 1804, his ensconcement in the illuminist milieu of the Petersburg nobility was nonetheless beginning to bear fruit. In a letter to Grabianka, dated April 16, 1804, for example, he described Pleshcheeva as a "really interesting and good little woman" and mentioned that Lenivtsev also lived in her home, adding that "the people who frequent this house are usually people of merit."[49] In other words, he was in a perfect position to exert influence on the formative salon-like gatherings that were taking place at Pleshcheeva's home. Further, he announced that he had just been commissioned by Pleshcheeva to offer Madame d'Attigny the post of governess to her children. This outcome would seem to have been achieved after considerable consultation with Grabianka; Lefort confides that "we have long debated the issue," and indicates that previous initiatives to secure such an outcome had been attempted.[50] In short, Lefort seems to have extensively vetted Pleshcheeva to ensure she was of a similar mindset and had a genuine desire to hire d'Attigny. A generous financial package was offered to d'Attigny, whereby she would receive a salary of a thousand roubles and full compensation for her travel expenses from Paris. Lefort ends his letter by expressing "how much I desire to see her here, while waiting for you [Grabianka] to come here yourself, dear friend."[51] In a second letter to Grabianka, written on June 5, 1804, Lefort reiterates, "it would be necessary, dear friend, that you should be ready to come to Petersburg during the summer season. If Providence would call you soon, I would be happier than I can tell you."[52] Lefort would have to wait another year before being reunited with Grabianka in Petersburg. However, by the end of the summer of 1804 d'Attigny had arrived in Petersburg and had entered the Pleshcheeva household and taken up employment as a governess. Thus, Lefort had been joined by d'Attigny, the Great Mother of the society, who, it seems, was equally adept at ingratiating herself into Pleshcheeva's illuminist circle. Although the pair made no attempt to formally establish a branch of the NIS in

Petersburg prior to the arrival of Grabianka, in August 1805, they did succeed in thoroughly preparing the ground for their leader's arrival in the city.

As mentioned in chapter 5, Grabianka successfully obtained a passport from the Russian ambassador in Paris on October 14, 1802—that is, a little over two months after Lefort's arrival in St. Petersburg. Grabianka may have wished to depart for Podolia earlier than the autumn of 1802, but he was hamstrung by the demands of his creditors. They were most probably placated by the sale of Liw Castle, some fifty miles east of Warsaw. The sale was most likely arranged by his estranged wife, Teresa, after she had been instructed in writing to sell the property by her husband.[53] By this time Grabianka may well have also had to sell other inherited assets, which included a castle at Rajkowce, fifteen villages, and thousands of serfs.[54]

We do not know the exact date of Grabianka's departure, but his passport states that he should be allowed to travel without hindrance to Kamianets-Podilskyi, the capital of Podolia Governorate. In other words, his destination was his ancestral home in Sutkivtsi (in modern-day Ukraine), located some forty-five miles north-east of the provincial capital. Grabianka seems to have spent very little time in Sutkivtsi before departing for St. Petersburg. Instead, he was based in the Galician city of Lviv from some point in 1803 until the summer of 1804, along with his valet Leyman and Simonin, whom he now employed as a secretary.[55] Whilst resident in Lviv, Grabianka began to reacquaint himself with prominent members of the old Polish *szlachta* from Podolia and Volhynia. In a letter he wrote to unnamed brethren in Avignon, he gives an account of his methods in drawing near to noble families from these regions and, crucially, his success in initiating them into the NIS. In this regard it is highly significant that Grabianka seems to have deliberately courted extremely wealthy individuals who were unambiguously aligned with pro-Russian elements among the old Polish nobility.

According to Simonin, Grabianka first succeeded in gaining the trust of Count Józef August Iliński (1766–1844), whom he initiated into the society in Lviv and who soon became one of his most ardent supporters. Indeed, Simonin states that Grabianka and Iliński resided together in Lviv.[56] This is entirely plausible; we know that Iliński was in the area for a period of time in 1803, undertaking a cure at the nearby balneological resort of Velikii Liubin.[57] Iliński was the marshal of the gentry of Volhynia and entered Russian service after the final partition of Poland, becoming a senator as early as 1797. He enjoyed the favour of Emperor Paul, partly as a result of paying off the sovereign's debts, and as a result was able to accumulate extraordinary wealth.[58]

During his residence in Lviv, Grabianka also socialised and proselytised with prominent members of the nobility in the surrounding area. Most notably, Simonin stated that Princess Elżbieta Izabela Lubomirska (neé Czartoryska, 1736–1816) was initiated by Grabianka, most likely at her country estate of Łańcut, located between Lviv and Lublin.[59] Grabianka enjoyed a long-standing friendship with Lubomirska, whose family hailed from Podolia. He had visited her in Paris in November 1786, on his way to Avignon from London, when she had given him a thousand francs, as well as various expensive items he could sell in order to fund the continuation of his journey.[60] Lubomirska dazzled Parisian high society in the years up to 1789, where she convened one of the most well-known salons, and was known for her political and cultural activities in Poland and beyond.[61]

Grabianka's wooing of the rich and influential Czartoryski family was evidently not restricted to Lubomirska. In the letter he wrote to his eldest son, in July 1804, he confessed that he had had to extend his stay in Galicia "because General [Adam Kazimierz] Czartoryski," Lubomirska's brother, "and everyone in [Velikii] Liubin obligated me to stay with them another month; I did not refuse them for many reasons."[62] This small and little-known balneological resort seems to have provided an environment that was conducive to Grabianka's efforts to attract the leading pro-Russian nobility of the region into his initiatic society. From this letter to his son, we also know that his residence in Galicia was coming to an end; the elder Grabianka informed the younger that he only planned to return to Lviv for a few days before departing eastward to visit his sister, Tekla Tarnowska. His sibling lived on the estate of her deceased husband (Jan Tarnowski, d. 1799) in the village of Berezce, near Kremenets in Volhynia. In all likelihood, this brief visit was occasioned by the declining health of his sister, who was to die the following year. Simonin and Leyman accompanied Grabianka to Berezce, but neither joined their master on his further travels. Simonin's stay was necessitated by ill health. Leyman may well have been charged with taking care of Grabianka's sister.[63] Whatever the reason, Leyman was still living at the Tarnowski residence in April 1807, when the Russian authorities requested that he be transported to St. Petersburg for questioning.[64]

Interestingly, Simonin testified in 1807 that Grabianka had also initiated Count Michał Mniszech (1742–1806) into the society in Volhynia.[65] Mniszech, once again, was firmly in the pro-Russian camp, having been made a privy councillor by Emperor Paul in 1797.[66] Moreover, his opulent residence Vishnivets'kii Palace was located only fifteen miles south of Berezce. Even during a trip primarily undertaken to visit his sister, Grabianka did not let slip an opportunity to initiate yet another rich and influential member of the old Polish aristocracy into his society.

By the autumn of 1804 Grabianka was the guest of Count Stanisław Szczęsny Potocki (1751–1805), one of the key figures behind the formation of the pro-Russian Targowica Confederation, at his grand palace in Tul'chin in eastern Podolia. Simonin also testified that Grabianka travelled to Kyiv to meet with Potocki and that the still-powerful magnate promised to render him great help after being initiated into the NIS.[67] Rolle corroborates Simonin's account by noting that the count's influence on Potocki was so great that the latter even promised to pay off Grabianka's debts and to redeem his estate (most likely Liw) from his creditors. However, Potocki died in March 1805, shortly after promising to resolve Grabianka's financial woes.[68]

This unexpected turn of events led Grabianka to swiftly depart for Iliński's sumptuous Romanov estate in Volhynia.[69] Iliński had apparently long-desired that Grabianka visit his famed palace, which was home to private theatre, ballet, and opera companies and two orchestras. Grabianka's arrival at Romanov also coincided with the opening of the first Institute for the Deaf and Mute in the Russian Empire.[70] The palace, which contained 155 rooms, was lavishly decorated and furnished throughout and was also home to works by Rubens, David, Poussin, and Vernet.[71] Grabianka even commented on Iliński's lifestyle in a letter to fellow brethren in Avignon, noting that he lived "rather like a king than a senator." A hint of scorn is palpable in this comment, but any sense of disapproval he may have felt did not preclude Grabianka from accepting the generous patronage of his enthusiastic new initiate. He added that "while waiting for Heaven to arrange otherwise for me, Count Iliński has offered me 300 Dutch ducats as long as I am near him." Each ducat contained 3.515 grams of gold, which would mean that at today's market price, 300 ducats would be worth approximately $40,000. To be sure, not a fortune, but certainly enough for a relatively short spell at Romanov. Grabianka also confided that Iliński "had prophesied to me that I will be in possession of my lands before May 18 of the following year."[72] This is almost certainly an allusion to the ancestral estates that Grabianka had been forced to relinquish rather than any wider reference to the partition of Poland and any desire on his part to be king of his homeland.

We know that Grabianka departed for the Russian capital in early June 1805, because he wrote a tender letter to his "beloved son" Antoni at the end of May, in which he informed his elder son that he would be leaving Romanov in eight to ten days.[73] He also expresses a desire to say farewell to both his "beloved children" before leaving Podolia, and confesses that "Aunt's death touched me, but let us not give up because there are medicines for this pain, so patience!"[74] The tone of the letter suggests that Grabianka had met with his two sons whilst in Podolia. His daughter Anna, who had been initiated into the society in June 1779 and who was raised by Brumore and Bruchié for a time, had died in 1796.[75] The last contact between Grabianka and Anna was most likely in 1795, when she wrote to her father in Avignon to ask for his blessings to marry.[76]

Grabianka was not, however, reconciled with his wife Teresa, who resided at her ancestral home in Ostapkivtsi. According to Simonin, Teresa never forgave her husband for abandoning her for nearly two decades, and the pair did not meet. She also feared that her sons would lose their inheritance if she agreed to fully pay her husband's debts in France. Simonin also asserted that Teresa began divorce proceedings against her husband as soon as he arrived in Russian-controlled Poland.[77]

Thus, Grabianka experienced mixed success during his time in his homeland. In the domestic realm, by the time he embarked on the journey to St. Petersburg in June 1805, he had irrevocably split from his wife, but the rupture was mitigated by his being able to maintain contact with his sons. In the social sphere, he had enjoyed great success in his proselytising among many of the richest and most influential members of the nobility in the region. What is more, these Polish aristocrats all enjoyed considerable favour at the imperial court in Petersburg. In other words, far from fraternising with Polish revolutionaries who were seeking to continue the cause of the Kościuszko Uprising, Grabianka astutely networked with pro-Russian individuals. As Lefort and d'Attigny were busy preparing the ground in Petersburg, Grabianka was establishing important connections in Galicia, Volhynia, and Podolia. The combination of all these things ensured that his initial reception in the capital among many of the Russian nobility would be highly favourable.

IV

On August 10, 1805. Grabianka wrote to Antoni from St. Petersburg. As a father, he seems keener to hear news about his son than relay news about his own recent arrival in the Russian capital. However, he does write that he is in good health and mentions that, though it is still summer, "many people are complaining about the climate here."[78] Grabianka's letter displays tenderness to his son, but it provides no indication that he is on the threshold of a new era, marked by resurgence, in the history of the NIS. To be sure, his arrest in February 1807 brought this period to a sudden halt. Yet it must be stressed that he was incarcerated because of his remarkable success in attracting a significant swathe of the Petersburg nobility into the society since his arrival in the Russian capital in August 1805.

We are able to glean vital insights into the composition of the society in St. Petersburg from a surviving list of new initiates.[79] This invaluable record documents that a total of sixty individuals—thirty males and thirty females—were accepted into the Union at twenty-four gatherings that were held between September 14, 1805, and December 30, 1806. What is immediately striking about this list is that a sizeable majority of the novitiates had close links to S. I. Pleshcheev in two ways: either through Masonic bonds stretching back in many cases to the 1770s, or via family connections to either Pleshcheev or his wife. By the time Grabianka arrived in St. Petersburg both these associational networks had been cultivated by Lefort and d'Attigny in anticipation of their leader's arrival. This twofold recruitment drive, which relied on both Masonic and family networks, had been a distinctive feature of the society since its inception in 1779 in Berlin. It was once again to prove highly effective in St. Petersburg.

Tellingly, the first Russian initiate into the NIS in nearly seventeen years, after Pleshcheev, was A. A. Lenivtsev. Admitting him, on September 14, 1805, was an astute move by Grabianka, who was no doubt guided by d'Attigny and Lefort. Lenivstev was not simply Pleshcheev's closest Masonic friend; he had enjoyed a preeminent position among Petersburg brothers since the mid-1780s. At the time, he was living in the home of Pleshcheeva and was therefore in day-to-day contact with d'Attigny and Lefort, who were both still in the noblewoman's service. Seventeen days later, Lenivtsev's brother, Mikhail Alekseevich (1763–1837), was initiated, though it seems he was not a mason. On July 7, 1806, Lenivtsev's youngest brother, Pavel, also joined the society. A. A. Lenivstev had no wife or children, and the initiation of his two brothers meant that he had persuaded his nearest family to join him among the so-called People of God.

The first indication that Lenivtsev's initiation encouraged his old Masonic brethren to follow suit can be seen on October 20, 1805, when three were initiated at the same gathering. Both Pyotr Iakovlevich Il'in (fl. 1758–1809) and Pyotr Ivanovich Timofeev (1756–1823) had been Freemasons since the 1770s and had obtained the Theoretical Degree of the Rosicrucian Order under the supervision of Lenivtsev.[80] Timofeev was also a founding member and the orator of the Dying Sphinx lodge in St. Petersburg, which had been established in 1800 under the leadership of Aleksandr Fyodorovich Labzin (1766–1825) with the goal of revitalising the Rosicrucian Order in the Russian capital.[81] Ivan Andreevich Petrov (1755–1824) was a second member of the Dying Sphinx lodge initiated at this time, who had been a Freemason since 1775.[82]

There was a second wave of Masonic recruits in the summer of 1806. The well-known artist V. L. Borovikovskii (1757–1825), for example, who joined the Dying Sphinx lodge in 1802, was initiated into the NIS on June 4, 1806.[83] On July 31, 1806, G. M. Pokhodiashin (d. 1820) also joined Grabianka's sect. By this time, Pokhodiashin had been one of Petersburg's most prominent Freemasons for around three decades. He was a member of various lodges in Russia, and worked under S. I. Gamaleia to receive the Theoretical Degree of the Rosicrucians. He had also been a key financial sponsor for N. I. Novikov in the 1780s.[84] In other words, by the summer of 1806, Lenivtsev's example had already persuaded many of Petersburg's most respected Freemasons to join Grabianka's society. This was acknowledged by Labzin, who in March 1807 reflected that "all local brothers joined there following behind A. A. Lenivtsev before me."[85] Labzin explained that though several brothers from the Dying Sphinx lodge had attempted to persuade him of the worthiness of the NIS, he had initially remained aloof. However, when he sensed that "the ones remaining loyal to me were hesitating," he convinced himself to visit one of Grabianka's gatherings. Meeting Grabianka allayed Labzin's fears, as he was assured that he would not have to abandon his Masonic connections and would not be asked to swear any oaths.[86] His doubts assuaged, Labzin was initiated into the NIS on December 9, 1806. Four other prominent members of the Dying Sphinx lodge were also initiated on this day: A. G. Cherevin (d. 1818), I. A. Turchilo (1778–?), D. G. Levitskii (1735–1822), and P. I. Rusanovskii (d. 1839).[87] In little over a year Lenivtsev had helped to ensure that Grabianka's NIS had been enthusiastically embraced by the leading figures of Freemasonry in the Russian capital.[88]

In accordance with one of the founding principles of the society, these Freemasons were encouraged to bring family members to gatherings in order to be initiated, irrespective of age or gender. Most noteworthy, perhaps, in this regard, were Labzin's family members. His wife, Anna (1758–1828), for example, was initiated at the same gathering as her husband and the four other members of the Dying Sphinx lodge. Thanks to the survival of fragments of her memoirs and diaries, we know that Labzina was an educated noblewoman who shared her (second) husband's religious mindset.[89] Far from merely acquiescing to her husband's commands, Labzina embraced his millenarian outlook and espoused a form of mystical Pietism that promoted inner faith. Labzina was an active participant in salons and literary life throughout her adult life, and played a pivotal role, along with her husband, in the short-lived *Sionskii vestnik* journal, which appeared in the first half of 1806, and which promoted contemporary expositions of chiliasm, including translated tracts by Jung-Stilling and Eckhartshausen.[90] Labzina went on to play a unique role in Russian Freemasonry as the only female permitted to participate in some of the rituals and educational pursuits of the Dying Sphinx Lodge. In 1809, for example, she was one of only seven individuals, including her husband, to be granted permission to study the Theoretical Degree of the Rosicrucian Order. A decade later, she was also made an honorary member of the lodge for her commitment to their Masonic endeavours.[91] We know far less about the life and spiritual outlook of A. F. Labzin's sister, N. F. Mikulina, but she, too, was initiated into Grabianka's society on December 30, 1806. Moreover, in her reminiscences, the maternal niece and adopted daughter of the Labzins, S. A. Laikevich (1797–1871), describes how she had her own number, which confirms that she must have been initiated in early 1807, before Grabianka's arrest.[92]

Anna Labzina was exceptional in that she was the only spouse of a Freemason to be initiated at the same gathering as her husband. Furthermore, she represents the only wife of a member of Dying Sphinx Lodge about whom we have a relatively extensive biography. But her initiation was by no means the first of the spousal and family consecrations. That distinction belongs to the wife of P. I. Timofeev, Tat'iana Timofeeva, who joined the society on February 14, 1806, a little less than four months after her husband. For reasons unknown, the remainder of the Timofeev family were only initiated on May 28, 1806 (four daughters and one son). The wives of Riabinin and Levitskii also followed their husbands into the society. P. Ia. Il'in was also soon able to enjoy the company of his two daughters and a nephew at gatherings, and Ivanov was joined by two female relatives. The first female initiate of the NIS in St. Petersburg, however, was N. F. Pleshcheeva, the widow of S. I. Pleshcheev and a close acquaintance of A. A. Lenivtsev. Her initiation on November 19, 1805, constitutes a milestone in Russian associational culture. Eighty-seven years had passed since Peter the Great had decreed that noblewomen could participate in assemblies. Yet, despite the relative popularity of so-called adoption lodges on continental Europe, no equivalent mixed-sex associations were established in the Russian Empire.[93] To be sure, a number of Russian noblewomen had attended adoption lodges in France in the 1770s and 1780s, including Sof'ia Razumovskaia.[94] Nonetheless, Pleshcheeva's initiation in 1805 marks the earliest known entry of a woman into an initiatic society on Russian soil.

In some ways it is surprising that Pleshcheeva was only the eighth initiate into the society in St. Petersburg, given the pivotal role she played in harbouring Lefort and d'Attigny, and providing a home for Lenivtsev. On his arrival in St. Petersburg, Grabianka wrote a letter to his brethren in Avignon in which he singles out "the widow Pleshcheeva [who] is very caring with me."[95] Moreover, Pleshcheeva's importance as a fulcrum for the society's expansion is highlighted by M. M. Muromtsev, who provides one of the few eyewitness accounts of the society's activities in St. Petersburg. He notes that "all the people" at the gatherings he attended "were either friends or relatives of N. F. Pleshcheeva."[96] On August 6, 1806, for example, Pleshcheeva's sister, M. F. Donaurova (1774–1848), and brother-in-law, M. I. Donaurov (1757–1817), were initiated into the NIS. Like her sister, Donaurova was a graduate of the Smol'nyi Institute for Noble Maidens. At the time her husband was a prominent nobleman, having been an aide-de-camp to Emperor Paul, who made him a Knight of the Order of Alexander Nevskii in 1797 and a senator and privy councillor in 1799. Donaurov was also a Freemason, but this seems to have played no role in his initiation into the NIS.[97] Rather, his familial connection to Pleshcheeva seems to have been crucial in facilitating Donaurov's entry into the millenarian circle orbiting around Grabianka.

A curious familial link also connects Pleshcheev with the five members of the Volkov family who were initiated into the society at three separate gatherings. On April 11, 1806, the matriarch of the family, E. D. Volkova (1746–1816), was initiated, along with two of her daughters (Praskov'ia and Elizaveta).[98] A third daughter, Mariia, was initiated on August 5, 1806, along with her husband, P. I. Ozerov (1778–1843), who was a steward (*gofmeister*) of the household of Grand Prince Konstantin Pavlovich.[99] Volkova's youngest son, Aleksandr (1779–1833), was initiated on May 8, 1806. That Volkov's initiation only took place four weeks after that of his mother and two of his sisters might be explained by the fact that he had been badly wounded at the Battle of Austerlitz in December 1805. Because of his injuries he could not walk for a considerable time and had to retire from military service. Soon after his initiation into the NIS in Petersburg, Volkov was appointed police chief of Moscow.[100]

Pleshcheeva would have been acquainted with Praskov'ia and Mariia Volkova, as they were all maids of honour to Empress Mariia Fyodorovna.[101] However, the real reason for the initiation of so many members of the extended Volkov family may well have been the alleged affair between Pleshcheev and E. D. Volkova in the 1770s and 1780s. Volkova's great-grandson, Apollon Kruglikov, wrote about what he called "la chronique scandale-use" in his reminiscences. According to Kruglikov, Pleshcheev had been "at the feet" of Volkova. He cited a rumour that all her children, apart from her three eldest (Apollon, Anna, and Varvara), were the offspring of this illicit affair.[102] It is interesting that none of the three older children joined their mother in the NIS.

Illegitimate offspring among the Russian nobility were far from uncommon at the time.[103] This scenario also casts a revealing light on why Pleshcheev devoted so much attention to the upbringing of Aleksandr Volkov. As Volkov's biographer writes: "Pleshcheev loved Volkov dearly from his very [earliest] childhood and was engaged in his education."[104] That Pleshcheev was romantically involved with Volkova and was the father of some of her children may help us understand two of the more cryptic questions he had asked the oracle in Avignon. On November 6, 1788, for example, Pleshcheev asked "if Heaven orders him to marry the widow of his cousin." The reply he received urged him to "abjure your conduct" and to "unite your fate to that which you desire," thereby repairing his "crime."[105] Significantly, the question was posed less than six months after the death of Volkova's husband. Moreover, the supposedly celestial advice suggests that Pleshcheev had been conducting an unlawful relationship. Six months after asking the oracle for matrimonial advice, in 1789, Pleshcheev submitted a new question regarding whether "it is the will of Heaven that he should send his children here or nearby to bring them closer to you." The response he received did not directly answer his query, but it did beseech Pleshcheev "to guide their childhood."[106] This question makes no sense unless Pleshcheev was asking about his illegitimate children, as he only married Natal'ia Fedotovna Verigina in 1796, who subsequently bore three girls.

We do not know whether Pleshcheev guided the education of any of Volkova's daughters. However, Aleksandr Volkov's profound sense of gratitude to and love of Pleshcheev was such that he undertook a seven-hundred-mile pilgrimage to Montpellier in 1819, from the spa resort of Františkovy Lázně in Bohemia, to erect a tombstone at Pleshcheev's burial place. The tombstone was duly placed on the grounds of the chateau and included an inscription written by A. Ia. Bulgakov on behalf of Volkov and N. F. Pleshcheeva.[107] The wording includes many tender protestations of love and respect for Pleshcheev, who is described as Volkov's "uncle and benefactor." And Volkov is described as "his nephew . . . who undertook the journey [to Montpellier] in order to pay his last respects to the remains of his beloved uncle."[108]

In numerical terms, eleven of the sixty initiates up to December 30, 1806 had family links to Pleshcheev (either legitimate or illegitimate). On top of this, a sizeable thirty-two members were connected with Pleshcheev via Masonic association (either as Freemasons themselves or as members of masons' families). Thus it can be ascertained that an impressive forty-three of the sixty initiates in St. Petersburg had links to the Pleshcheevs.

Several noteworthy individuals can be found among the seventeen initiates having no apparent links to either the Pleshcheev family or the Masonic milieu in St. Petersburg.[109] Arguably, the most eye-catching name is that of V. F. Malinovskii (1765–1814), who was initiated on October 20, 1805, along with four long-standing Freemasons.[110] Malinovskii is best remembered for his "Essay on War and Peace" (1803) and as the first director of the Tsarskoe Selo Lyceum when it was established in 1811.[111] Malinovskii does not appear to have been a Freemason, but there is evidence to suggest that he had already developed a religious outlook wholly in line with the millenarian doctrine of the NIS by 1805. In 1804, for example, Malinovskii translated fragments of Jung-Stilling's *Theobold, oder die Schwarmer* (1785).[112] Moreover, his grandson, E. A. Rozen, commented, "my grandfather . . . was a Martinist and a friend of Novikov."[113] In 1915, D. F. Kobeko directly posed the question of whether Malinovskii was a Martinist and, what is more, whether this had helped him secure the post of director of the lyceum. In addressing this subject, Kobeko included several letters by Malinovskii, written in 1811, in which the author indicates a continued close bond to M. I. Donaurov, M. F. Donaurova, and M. A. Lenivstev, who were all members of the NIS, as well as R. A. Koshelev.[114] Kobeko was unaware of Malinovskii's initiation into the NIS in 1805, which may well have brought him into contact with like-minded (and highly influential) members of the Russian nobility in

St. Petersburg. Alternatively, Malinovskii may well have already been on close terms with the likes of M. A. Lenivstev, which would explain why Malinovskii was one of the earliest initiates into the society.

A curious inclusion among the first initiates into the NIS was John Grieve (1753–1805), the Scottish personal physician to Emperor Alexander. His participation in the society ranks as the shortest, as he died of a stroke only sixteen days after his initiation in December 1805. Nevertheless, his brief dalliance with Grabianka's group is striking, as he was a relatively early initiate (recorded ninth on the membership list), one of only four non-Russians to join the society in St. Petersburg, and the only foreign member about whom we have been able to glean any biographical information.[115] Grieve enjoyed a successful medical career, having first served as military doctor in the Voronezh Division between 1778 and 1783 after graduating from the University of Glasgow. After practicing medicine in Edinburgh and London for fifteen years, during which time he was made a Fellow of the Royal Society (1794), Grieve returned to Russia in 1798.[116] A small insight into the religious worldview of Grieve can be gleaned from his connections to the Edinburgh Missionary Society, which established a Presbyterian colony in the village of Karass, near Piatigorsk in the North Caucasus. The early missionaries sailed to St. Petersburg from Leith, where they were assisted by Grieve. The physician also helped the Scottish missionaries in their negotiations with the Russian government up until his death.[117] Indeed, after he died, the society published a brief obituary in which they described his death as "a great loss to the Missionaries at Karass, to whom he was a warm and able friend."[118]

v

On May 2, 1807, Grabianka was summoned to appear before a tribunal in St. Petersburg. The interrogators probed the Pole about the requirements for becoming a member of what he referred to as "l'union de la Route de la vérité."[119] Grabianka's response provides a fascinating insight into the three-stage process of initiation prospective members were required to perform in St. Petersburg. As will be seen, Grabianka jettisoned the elaborate and esoteric preparatory rites practised in Berlin and Avignon. To be sure, the countryside outside Petersburg was devoid of the hills needed to replicate those rituals. Yet even had the Russian capital been situated in the middle of a mountain range, it is doubtful Grabianka would have continued with that rather laborious ceremonial. Instead, his strategy appears to have been to keep vestiges of the old rite, forgoing the theurgical aspects of the consecration as it was practised up until at least 1790 in Avignon. This approach had the advantage of making the initiation rite much more accessible to the Petersburg nobility, who simply had to gather within the salubrious residences of their peers.

In his testimony, Grabianka outlines three phases of the initiatory process practised in St. Petersburg: (a) preliminary preparation; (b) the nine-day *Novenne*; and (c) the reception of the proposed initiate. According to Grabianka, the initial stage involved the individual who wished to follow *la route de la vérité* being invited to speak frankly with him about his religious principles and attitudes towards the government. If it transpired that the candidate was not versed in the religious precepts of her/his religion, they would be encouraged to "return to the bosom" of their church. These preliminary discussions sought to ascertain whether a candidate was "imbued with the principles of modern philosophy [and] revolutionary principles." If so, Grabianka sought to persuade the candidate that "all authority comes from God" and that "the sovereign . . . holds for the social order the place of God here."[120]

A brief description of this preliminary stage can be found in the reminiscences of F. P. Lubianovskii, who attended a gathering of the NIS in late 1806 or early 1807. Lubianovskii recounts how Grabianka took his hand and led him to a window to engage him in a one-on-one conversation. Grabianka apparently spoke "a lot and quickly" about how he had been sent to Petersburg by Heaven to establish and organise "the new Kingdom of Jerusalem." After outlining his divine mission, Grabianka "volunteered to prepare and receive [Lubianovskii] into the society." Subsequently, the pair met for four preparatory conversations, after which Grabianka declared that he could not "take one step forward" while Lubianovskii "did not swear to keep further secrets." Lubianovskii was also shown a plan of the future temple in New Jerusalem, as well as the society's oath, before adjourning for a week of reflection as to whether he was ready to progress to the second stage of the path towards initiation. However, Lubianovskii was not persuaded by Grabianka's proselytising and he "went away . . . with the firm intention never to return. Faith in him went to the point of strangeness."[121]

If Lubianovskii was not won over by these spiritual and political conversations with Grabianka, at least sixty other individuals were evidently more enthusiastic and willing to begin the second preparatory stage. The nine-day novena practised in St. Petersburg was, in effect, a watered-down version of the elaborate rituals performed atop the hills outside Avignon and Berlin by the older members of the society. In short, it appears to have been a much more conventional form of novena, as practised by Catholics and Orthodox believers alike, which involved devotional praying for nine successive days. Grabianka described the form of novena used in his society in the following way:

> The individual who wants to enter the *route de la vérité* is obliged to prepare for nine days . . . through fervent prayers according to his religion; to attend church . . . to examine his conscience, to reconcile with his enemies, to pardon all offenses, to confess according to the dogmas of his religion, and to pray to God, that he will be good enough to make him worthy in the route.[122]

On completion of this novena, the candidate was ready to undergo the reception ceremony. Grabianka explains that because there was no dedicated temple in Petersburg, the candidate and attendees had to assemble in the home of a brother or sister of the union. The ceremony had to be witnessed by an unspecified number of initiates, who were allowed to assemble in ordinary clothing. Moreover, no specific formal ceremonies were enacted to mark the convocation.[123]

Next, Grabianka described the initiation ceremony itself, which began with the most senior member of the society present (normally himself) reading out the so-called act of aggregation.[124] This was most likely the twelve-point proclamation composed for the society in Petersburg and conveyed to new initiates. Of the twelve articles, the most significant include the second one, which states: "The purpose [of the society] is to announce, according to the command of God, the second and imminent coming of the Lord Jesus Christ and his glorious kingdom on earth." The sixth article reveals that initiates are able to correspond with heaven and "ask questions and receive answers even about the most seemingly insignificant matters."[125]

At the conclusion of the reading the assembled gathering prayed to God according to their own Christian denomination. Thereafter, the candidate was asked to examine her or his conscience and to beg God to forgive their sins and to declare that they were unworthy to enter the road of truth. Grabianka then proceeds to describe how the candidate beseeched God to render his grace in allowing her or him to join "his people" and thanked the Lord for communicating that the second coming was imminent and that he had allowed them to form his "new people on the earth" in anticipation of this long-awaited event. The candidate then donated an offering in recognition of his or her gratitude. To conclude the rite, Grabianka would kiss the initiate on the forehead as a received brother or sister. A collective prayer ensued, and then the new initiate selected an "election name consisting of three numerical digits."[126] As the list of members testifies, each new initiate did indeed receive a three-digit number, as had been the case since the very first initiation in Berlin in 1779.

However, Grabianka also emphasizes that the northern church established in St. Petersburg, envisaged as one of seven, was in its infancy and had only begun to develop after his arrival in the city. It still lacked a temple in which to perform the more lavish consecration rites that had occurred in Avignon prior to the abandonment of activities on October 28, 1800.[127] A plan to establish such a "northern temple" had been drawn up by M. A. Lenivtsev in September 1806, but it came to nothing after Grabianka's arrest.[128] Grabianka also reveals that the northern church in Petersburg lacked the requisite personages a temple needed to function, such as a pontiff, prophet, and king.

VI

The denizens of St. Petersburg had indulged in many forms of associational culture since the city's was founded in 1703, including bacchanalian clubs, prescribed assemblies, diplomatic receptions, court masquerades, literary and philosophical societies, and Freemasonry.[129] Arguably, the gatherings of the NIS offered something very distinctive by blurring many of the conventions that had governed elite associational culture in Russia in the eighteenth century. Unlike in pre-revolutionary France, educated Russian noble-women had not participated in Masonic adoption lodges and had not hosted salons.[130] The participation of women in the gatherings of the NIS was in itself a pioneering step, let alone that they seem to have been present in equal numbers as the opposite sex and were not excluded from any part of the proceedings. However, it should be borne in mind, as Gary Marker has noted about Anna Labzina, that the women in the NIS identi-fied not with the "Age of Reason or politesse, but with a sociability of piety"[131] and, what is more, a shared millenarian outlook. Initiation into the society thus not only ensured that women had access to meetings in the homes of the fellow members of the nobility, but also seemingly served the greater purpose of signalling their worthiness to dwell in the much-anticipated New Jerusalem. This higher purpose also underpins the inclusion and presence of young children at the gatherings; again, a hallmark of the society since 1779. At the same time, the solemn and righteous ceremonials of the society in Petersburg were accompanied by the embrace of earthly gastronomical delights.

Grabianka's testimonial in 1807 is illuminating in documenting how he adapted the rites of the NIS to his new surroundings in St. Petersburg. Nevertheless, he reveals little about what transpired at the many gatherings he presided over in the Russian capital. Fortunately, we can glean a great deal more about the associational culture of the society's meetings from three first-hand descriptions: by M. M. Muromtsov, the grandson of E. D. Volkova; S. A. Laikevich, the adopted daughter of the Labzins; and the aforementioned Lubianovskii, an acquaintance of Donaurov. All three accounts emphasize that the gath-erings were part religious assembly and part sumptuous feast, and portrayed Grabianka as a charismatic leader who seemingly revelled in performing a variety of interrelated roles.

Muromtsov provides the lengthiest account, which describes his attendance at several gatherings of the NIS over the course of a month after arriving in St. Petersburg at the turn of 1807. The fifteen-year-old youth had travelled to the capital to begin a military career and was temporarily lodging with his maternal grandmother, E. D. Volkova. According to Kruglikov's testimony, Muromtsov would have been Pleshcheev's grandson, as he was the son of Ekaterina Alekseevna (b. 1766). Whatever the case, Muromtsov met.

Grabianka for the first time at his grandmother's home. Volkova wasted no time in recommending her grandson as being worthy of receiving Grabianka's teaching. In other words, Muromtsov had been nominated to begin the preliminary preparations for initia-tion into the society.

Thenceforth, Muromtsov attended several meetings at the homes of M. I. Lenivstev and the Ozerovs. Grabianka alone seems to have had the authority to call a gathering of the society. The Podolian nobleman evidently relished the attention that was lavished upon him as a guest of honour at each assembly. Muromtsov explains that a carriage was sent to transport him to each meeting.[132] Lubianovskii describes Grabianka as he entered one such gathering, as a "grey, but still cheerful *starik* (old man) of medium height, with a red face, with bright fire in his eyes."[133] (See figure 6.1.)

FIGURE 6.1 Portraits of Tadeusz Grabianka. Image courtesy of Scientific Library of the Polish Academy of Learning and the Polish Academy of Sciences, Kraków.

At dinner at these assemblies Grabianka was always served his favourite dish. In her reminiscences, Laikevich describes that "an enormous and fine-looking bream was always served in his honour."[134] This choice of food is curiously revealing, as it is a playful pun on the Grabianka family's adoption of the Leszczyc coat of arms and name, which in Polish and in Russian sounds very similar to "bream" (Pl. *leszcz*; Ru. *leshch*). Food is mentioned in all three accounts: Muromtsov indicates that the dinners of M. A. Lenivtsev were especially "noteworthy for their sumptuousness," and Lubianovskii comments on the "dainty appetisers" that were served at the home of Donaurov.[135] The emphasis on food and dining at the gatherings fulfilled a social and functional role, as all banquets do, but did it also serve as a preparatory ritual in anticipation of a mystical experience? The choice of bream may well be significant in this regard, as it suggests a conscious nod to the cabalistic significance of names. Here it is worth citing Joel Hecker, who argues that food played "a significant role in preparing oneself for mystical encounters and for . . . mystical exegesis" for medieval zoharic kabbalists.[136] Moreover, as C. W. Bynum argues, the festive meal was "the central Christian ritual, the most direct way of encountering God."[137]

At the close of each dinner those in attendance would gather together and listen attentively to Grabianka. According to Muromtsov, Grabianka typically opened meetings by removing a notebook from his portfolio, which he used to preach and interpret religious texts, and to recount anecdotes about his own holy life. Both Muromtsov and Lubianovskii note that Grabianka continually muttered the Polish adage *iak sie zowie*

(what is it called) when speaking in French.[138] This slippage into Polish seems an affecta-
tion on Grabianka's part, to endear him to his Slavic audience, since his French was surely
flawless after spending two decades in Avignon. Irrespective of the artificiality of this
recourse to Polish, Grabianka's audience was apparently enraptured by his oratory. As
Muromtsov attests, "ladies especially worshipped him . . . whilst the men gave him special
presents."[139]

An example of Grabianka's penchant for anecdotes is provided by Muromtsov, who
recalls a gathering held in the Ozerov household at which it was announced that his aunt,
Mariia Alekseevna, was ill and would not be able to participate. The Pole apparently
began to soothe her husband and then told the following anecdote:

> In Paris during the time of the Terror . . . I was imprisoned. [In the prison] I sud-
> denly saw in front of me John the Baptist. I fell at his feet, and asked him to save me.
> John answered that knowing my innocence, he had descended into this dark cell.
> On these words, the doors of the prison opened and he guided me onto the street,
> where he gave me three seeds for remembrance and added: "If you want to heal
> someone, place these seeds in a glass of water and give it to the ill person to drink."[140]

On hearing this miraculous story, P. I. Ozerov beseeched Grabianka to perform this act
of healing on his sickly wife. Muromtsov attests that he saw the seeds, and that his aunt
was indeed cured. The onlooking adepts took this to be a genuine miracle, despite, as
Muromtsov adds, being "educated people."[141] Lubianovskii commented on the lofty status
of the members of the society attending a gathering at the home of Donaurov. He noted
that the attendees were "well-known for their minds and talents, for going grey owing to
the labours of their service, for their ranks, crosses and stars," that is, for their glittering
collection of medals.[142] Grabianka made a similar description in December 1806 when he
noted that "five or six with orders, generals, bishops, prelates, princes, senators and others" visited him every morning.[143]

Muromtsov's description of the veneration in which Grabianka was held by members
of the society in Petersburg is echoed by Laikevich and Lubianovskii. In her reminiscences, for example, Laikevich recalls how "some kind of *starik* began to visit us," that
is, in the Labzin household, and that everyone called him "Papa." Laikevich would have
only been 9 years old at the time, but she remembers that "many people gathered" at her
home "in the evenings and read."[144] She adds that she was also given her own number,
indicating that she must have been initiated at some point between December 30, 1806,
and Grabianka's arrest. Lubianovskii does not provide such a tender and patriarchal portrait of Grabianka, but does describe him as "a cheerful *starik*, of medium height, with a
red face, with bright fire in his eyes." As to the esteem in which he was held, he remarks
that "the most long-await blessed messenger would not be received with more hospitality
and respect."[145]

Despite being lavished with gifts and sumptuous food at the regular gathering of the NIS in St. Petersburg, Grabianka struggled with many aspects of his life in the Russian capital. This is all too apparent in a letter he wrote to Leyman in December 1806, in which he seems to feel at liberty to unburden his concerns to his old valet. He writes, for example, that he spent the summer in various dachas of his acquaintances and friends, which he found constraining and laborious. Matters only deteriorated on his return to Petersburg in the autumn. He twice fell so severely ill that he feared for his life and had only just returned to health. He complains about how the severe northern climate is negatively affecting his health. We learn that he "strongly desired" to leave with Iliński for Podolia, but had been unable to depart for reasons not disclosed. To his former long-term valet, Grabianka also moans that his new manservant is not very good at shaving and powdering him! Lastly, we learn that Grabianka was residing with P. Ia. Il'in at this time.[146] In short, the note conveys a sense of frustration at having to live off the charity of his rich Petersburg benefactors at a time when his health seems to have been deteriorating. However, Grabianka concluded his letter to Leyman on a positive note, insisting that "the year 1807, which will soon begin, will be favourable for all of us."[147] This optimistic prediction was to be proven disastrously inaccurate within a matter of weeks.

VII

It seems that neither Grabianka nor any of his followers in St. Petersburg foresaw the danger he was in. Indeed, the adoration in which Grabianka was held by his devotees is reflected in their shock at his arrest, on February 7, 1807. Muromtsov provides a vivid description of the sense of disbelief felt by his family members on hearing of the dramatic events. Indeed, Muromtsov was one of the first to learn first-hand the news that Grabianka had been placed under house arrest:

> My aunt Ozerova instructed me to take a note to the count in which she invited him to hers. I got up early in the morning and went to his. To my surprise I was stopped at the gates by a police officer, who asked why I was going to the count's. In my naivety I said to him that I was carrying a note for him. They allowed me in to him and ordered me to read the note to him aloud . . . The count asked me to send greetings to many people and to assure them that God knew of his innocence, and that he had been taken into custody, probably, according to some kind of misunderstanding. I rushed to pass on this catastrophic news to Uncle Ozerov. His initial surprise was so great that he did not believe me and attributed my story to some kind of gossip monger. But soon several adepts came to him and testified to the truth of the unexpected event. Many [adepts] discussed [the issue] among themselves and lodged a petition to release Count Grabianka with the authorities.

Prince Aleksandr Nikolaevich Golitsyn and other friends of his personally interceded on his behalf with the sovereign.[148]

Despite being written over half a century after the event, this account still makes palpable the sense of astonishment experienced by Ozerov. Interestingly, Muromtsov also cites A. N. Golitsyn's efforts to secure Grabianka's release. Golitsyn is not listed as being a member of the society prior to December 30, 1806. However, given his subsequent millenarian mindset and familiarity with other initiates (see chapter 7), it would not be surprising if he was acquainted with Grabianka at the very least.

The continued reverence felt towards Grabianka after his arrest is apparent in A. F. Labzin's correspondence with D. P. Runich, his friend and Masonic brother, in Moscow. A month after Grabianka had been placed under house arrest, Labzin forcefully defended his continued loyalty to the Pole: "And so, my dear friend, I never renounced, and will never renounce Freemasonry, [I] honor it and love it, and cannot not love it because it aided me in my greatest good: I honor the one who directed me in this; I pray for my first benefactors daily and will pray. I equally love Count Grabianka for the same [reasons]."[149] The sense of frustration felt by Labzin towards his Masonic brethren in Moscow in regards to their hostile treatment of Grabianka is not far below the surface here. On September 22, 1807, Labzin wrote to Runich again and continued to defend his loyalty to Grabianka. By this point, a tone of exasperation pervades his letter to his old friend, who, he argues, is all too ready to pass judgement on Grabianka without having met him: "I will tell you more: I will neither renounce a good nor a fictitious relationship, even if here were a Tartar, let alone a Christian. But even if I find good in a Tartar, I am not going to become a Tartar myself. And so today I am with Grabianka."[150] Two weeks later Grabianka was dead. He had been imprisoned since April in the notorious Peter and Paul Fortress, where his fragile health further deteriorated. There were rumours that he had poisoned himself, but it seems much more likely that he died from apoplexy, the cause of death listed in the church records of the Catholic Church of St. Catherine in St. Petersburg, where his funeral service took place.[151]

On hearing of Grabianka's death, O. A. Pozdeev, the leading Moscow Rosicrucian, did not hide his gloating sense of satisfaction at the shattering effect he thought this would have on his followers in Petersburg:

To know truth is power; how (can you) judge a weak person for the power he does not have; and so one should not judge Grabianka . . . . The *messieurs* from St. Petersburg who rushed headlong towards him, are now saying, as I hear: that he himself was obviously deceived; but before they were talking about him as if he (like Jesus) has all the Godly gifts. They had so much enthusiasm, because apparently he was supposed to live a long life, apparently Heaven announced this to him, and he convinced them of this. It is a dangerous business to assure yourself without God that one will live a long life.[152]

Pozdeev's evident satisfaction on receiving news of Grabianka's death reflects a sense of relief. He fundamentally disagreed with Labzin's pluralistic philosophy that embraced the millenarianism espoused by the charismatic Grabianka alongside a continued devotion to Freemasonry. For Pozdeev, Grabianka was at the head of a deviational group, which was leading his brethren in Petersburg away from the moral and spiritual truths that were exclusively revealed within the Rosicrucian Order. Indeed, two of the foremost scholars of Russian Freemasonry, A. I. Serkov and Iu. E. Kondakov, concur that Pozdeev was likely to have been directly involved in Grabianka's arrest and subsequent interrogation.[153] Tellingly, they point to the fact that A. I. Arsen'ev, who was in charge of Grabianka's interrogation and who authored a summary of the proceedings for Emperor Alexander, was a close acquaintance of Pozdeev and a fellow Rosicrucian.[154] Grabianka may have been silenced, but Pozdeev's gleeful belief that his disciples in Petersburg would simply abandon the millenarian doctrine associated with so-called *grabianizm* would prove to be woefully premature.

NOTES

1. See Dominic Lieven, *Russia Against Napoleon* (New York: Viking, 2010), 37–40.

2. "Uchrezhdenie Komiteta obshchei bezopasnosti, 13-go ianvaria 1807 goda," in N. K. Shil'der, *Imperator Aleksandr Pervyi: ego zhizn' i tsarstvovanie*, vol. 2 (St. Petersburg: A. S. Suvorin, 1897), 365.

3. Letter of N. N. Novosil'tsev to Emperor Alexander I, Mar. 5, 1807, cited in N. M. Romanov, *Imperator Aleksandr I* (Moscow: Bogorodskii pechatnik, 1999), 280.

4. See Augustin Barruel, *Mémoires pour servir à l'histoire du Jacobinisme*, 5 vols. (London: P. Le Boussonier, 1797–1798); John Robison, *Proofs of a Conspiracy against all the Religions and Governments of Europe* (Edinburgh: W. Creech, 1798).

5. Augustin Barruel, *Volteriantsy, ili Istoriia o iakobintsakh*, 12 vols. (Moscow: Selivanovskii, 1805); John Robison, "Dokazatel'stva zagovora protiv vsekh religii i pravitel'stv," *Moskovskie uchenye vedomosti*, nos. 18, 22–4, 26–7 (1806).

6. Augustin Barruel, *Memoirs Illustrating the History of Jacobinism*, vol. 4, pt. 4, trans. Robert Clifford (London: T. Burton, 1798), 497.

7. For a discussion of the misconceptions and conflations surrounding the understanding of illuminism in the late eighteenth and early nineteenth centuries, see Önnerfors, "Illuminism," 173–81.

8. M. M. Muromtsov, "Razkaz ochevidtsa o grafe Grabianke," *Sovremennaia letopis' russkago vestnika*, vol. 13 (1860), 21.

9. Simonin offered similar testimony during his interrogation in 1807. See RGIA, Fond 1163, op. 1, d. 16b, 26r.

10. Józef Drzewiecki, *Pamiętniki Józefa Drzewieckiego spisane przez niego samego (1772–1802)* (Vilnius: Nakładem i Drukiem Józefa Zawadzkiego, 1858), 79–80. Szymon Askenazy scornfully described how Liberadzki embraced the "unhealthy, superstitious eccentrics of the Illuminati" in Avignon. See S. Askenazy, *Napoleon a Polska*, vol. 2 (Warsaw: Towarzystwo Wydawnicze w Warszawie, 1918), 122.

11. Askenazy cites a letter from Liberadzki to Dabrowski, written in Genoa and dated March 28, 1797, in which the former wrote: "I left Avignon immediately, where I was among friends and a compatriot [Grabianka]." See Askenazy, *Napoleon*, vol. 2, 309.

12. Drzewiecki, *Pamiętniki*, 80–1.

13. Muromtsov, "Razkaz," 21.

14. John Barrell, *Imagining the King's Death: Figurative Treason, Fantasies of Regicide, 1793–1796* (Oxford: Oxford University Press, 2000), 504–47.

15. See AN, "Correspondance des Consuls de France à Saint-Pétersbourg (1713–1792)," AE/B/I/982-AE/B/I/989, 38r–39v, 56r–56v.

16. During his interrogation Grabianka confirmed that d'Attigny had been a governess in several families. See RGIA, Fond 1163, op. 1, d. 16a, 289r.

17. RGIA, Fond 1163, op. 1, d. 16A, 182r–182v.

18. Serge Goriaïnow, "Paul Iᵉʳ et Stanislas Auguste; Leurs entretiens en 1797 à Peterhof, Gatchina et St.-Pétersbourg," *Revue contemporaine* 33 (1911): 167–71.

19. See Felice, *Note e Ricerche*, 227.

20. E. S. Shumigorskii, *Imperatritsa Mariia Fyodorovna (1759–1828)*, vol. 1 (St. Petersburg: Tipografiia I. N. Skorokhodov, 1892), 362, fn. 44.

21. Shumigorskii, *Imperatritsa*, 427–8, fn. 57.

22. Pleshcheeva graduated from the Smol'nyi Institute for Noble Maidens in 1791. For a brief biography of N. F. Pleshcheeva, see N. M. Romanov, *Russkie portrety XVIII i XIX stoletii*, vol. 1 (St. Petersburg: State Papers, 1905), no. 145.

23. On Novikov and the Rosicrucian Order in Russia, see Rafaella Faggionato, *A Rosicrucian Utopia in Eighteenth-Century Russia: The Masonic Circle of N. I. Novikov* (Dordrecht, the Netherlands: Springer, 2005).

24. A. N. Popov, "Novye dokumenty po delu Novikova," *Sbornik russkago istoricheskago obshchestva* 2 (1868): 150.

25. A. E. Waite, *The Brotherhood of the Rosy Cross: A History of the Rosicrucians* (New York: Barnes & Noble Books, 1993), 536–7.

26. On Lenivtsev's role as supervisor of the Theoretical Degree in Petersburg, see Iu. E. Kondakov, *Orden zolotogo i rozovogo kresta v Rossii. Teoreticheskii gradus solomonvykh nauk* (St. Petersburg: Asterion, 2012), 241, 251, 258, 265, 307, 317.

27. I. V. Lopukhin, *Zapiski Senatora I. V. Lopukhina: 1859, London* (Moscow: Nauka, 1990), 84.

28. P. Ia. Titov, "Vtoraia redaktsiia ispovedi P. Ia. Titova," RGB, Fond 147. No. 90/M. 1967, 19r–19v. Also see V. I. Shcherbakov, "Neizvestnyi istochnik 'Voiny i mira' ('Moi zapiski' masona P. Ia. Titova)," *Novoe literaturnoe obozrenie* 21 (1996): 146.

29. Shcherbakov, "Neizvestnyi istochnik," 146.

30. See the letter from N. I. Novikov to Pleshcheev, May 13, 1801, in which the former discusses the Rosicrucian basis of the mission to Berlin. See N. I. Novikov, *Pis'ma N. I. Novikova* (St. Petersburg: Izdatel'stvo imeni N. I. Novikova, 1994), 59–61.

31. For a full reproduction of this correspondence, along with a commentary, see Antoine Faivre, *Eckartshausen et la théosophie chrétienne*, 2nd ed. (Hyères: La Pierre Philosophale, 2016), annexe, 1–32.

32. K. von Eckartshausen, *Puteshestvie mladogo Kostisa ot vostoka k poludniu*, trans. A. F. Labzin (St. Petersburg: Imperatorskoe tipografiia, 1801). Labzin was a friend of Pleshcheev and both were Rosicrucians.

33. Pleshcheev to Eckartshausen, Aug. 25, 1801, RGB, Fond 147.89.71.

34. See L.-C. de Saint-Martin, *L'Homme de désir* (Lyon: J. Sulpice Grabit, 1790). As Aren Roukema notes, "The man of desire is he who is so possessed of a soul that aspires for God that he is able to discover the spark of divinity that still remains within the self from its prelapsarian state of full unity with the divine. See Aren Roukema, *Esotericism and Narrative: The Occult Fiction of Charles Williams* (Leiden: Brill, 2018), 40, fn. 138.

35. See Pleshcheev to Eckartshausen, Nov. 14, 1801, RGB, Fond 147.89.71.

36. S. I. Pleshcheev to O. A. Pozdeev, Jan. 7, 1802, RGB, Fond 128, Sbornik rukoi O. A. Pozdeeva, 20r–21r.

37. Thanks to Pierre-Yves Kirschleger for relaying this information in a personal communication. Also see P.-Y. Kirschleger, "Cimetières de Montpellier," *Histoire des cimetières*, https://cimetieresdemontpellier.wordpress.com/histoire/ (accessed Nov. 5, 2018).

38. N. F. Pleshcheeva to Eckartshausen, Feb. 27, 1802, RGB, Fond 147.89.71.

39. Pleshcheeva to Eckartshausen, Dec. 16, 1802, RGB, Fond 147.89.71.

40. Divonne noted in a letter to Franz von Baader that he had met Eckartshausen in 1802. Moreover, in her letter to Eckartshausen dated Dec. 16, 1802, Pleshcheeva wrote: "My two travel companions wish you to recall their memory. One has left for England and the other is Lenivtsev." See Divonne to von Baader, Feb. 1, 1810, in Franz von Baader, *Lettres inédites de Franz von Baader*, ed. Eugène Susini, vol. 4 (Paris: P. U. F, 1967), 68–9; Pleshcheeva to Eckartshausen, RGB, Fond 147.89.71. A letter written by Louis Lefort in St. Petersburg on Aug. 27, 1802, refers to Divonne's intention to leave on a boat for England in the near future, which is consistent with Pleshcheeva's description in her letter to Eckartshausen. See Lefort to Christian Daniel von Meyer, Aug. 27, 1802, CMCPF, Fonds Georg Kloss, MS X2V1-655, 53r.

41. See the letter from Louis Lefort to C. D. von Meyer, Aug. 27, 1802, CMCPF, Fonds Georg Kloss, MS X2V1-655, 53r.

42. RGIA, Fond 1163, op. 1, d. 16b, 220r.

43. RGIA, Fond 1163, op. 1, d. 16b, 60r.

44. RGIA, Fond 1163, op. 1, d. 16b, 220v.

45. Lefort to Meyer, Aug. 27, 1802, CMCPF, Fonds Georg Kloss, MS X2V1-655, 53r.

46. See Saint-Martin, *Mon Portrait*, 129.

47. RGIA, Fond 1163, op. 1, d. 16a, 289r.

48. Lefort to B. F. de Turckheim, June 10, 1804, BNUdS, MS. Turckheim 141, F. 1-527.

49. Lefort to Grabianka, April 16, 1804, RGIA, Fond 1163, op. 1, d. 16v, 751r.

50. Lefort to Grabianka, April 16, 1804, 751r.

51. RGIA, Fond 1163, op. 1, d. 16v, 751v.

52. RGIA, Fond 1163, op. 1, d. 16v, 754r.

53. Simonin testified that Grabianka initially charged Allier and Leyman to travel to Podolia to discuss financial matters with his wife. However, they did not undertake this mission, and Grabianka soon received permission from his creditors to go Paris to obtain a passport. See RGIA, Fond 1163, op. 1, d. 16b, l. 39. On the sale of Liw Castle by Teresa Grabianka, see Rolle, *Tadeusz Leszczyc Grabianka*, 95.

54. For a description of Grabianka's inherited wealth, see Rolle, *Tadeusz Leszczyc Grabianka*, 11. In a 1764 census, 258 Jews in the village of Fulsztyn in Podolia were recorded as belonging to Grabianka's mother. See Stampfer, "1764 Census of Polish Jewry," 134.

55. Lefort wrote in February 1803 that "he had not heard of any news of the arrival of the Count [Grabianka] in Poland." See Lefort to C. D. von Meyer, Feb. 12, 1803, CMCPF, MS. X2V1-655, 65r. In 1807, Simonin testified that in 1802 Grabianka had invited him to travel to Podolia and to serve as his secretary. See RGIA, Fond 1163, op. 1, d. 16b, 39v.

56. RGIA, Fond 1163, op. 1, d. 16b, 32r.

57. Roman Aftanazy, *Dzieje rezydencji na dawnych kresach Rzeczypospolitej*, vol. 5 (Wrocław: Zakład Narodowy im. Ossolińskich, 1994), 402.

58. Aftanazy, *Dzieie*, vol. 5, 396.

59. RGIA, Fond 1163, op. 1, d. 16b, 40r.

60. RGIA Fond 1163, op. 1, d. 16 b, 101r. In a letter to his son Antoni, dated July 12, 1804, Grabianka wrote that he had returned to Lviv from Łańcut.

61. Lubomirska was also initiated into a masonic Adoption lodge. See S. Małachowski-Łempicki, *Wykaz Polskich Lóż wolnomularskich oraz ich członkow w latach 1738–1821* (Krakow: Nakladem Polskiej Akademji Umiejetności, 1929), 77.

62. Rolle, *Tadeusz Leszczyc Grabianka*, 105.

63. RGIA, Fond 1163, op. 1, d. 16b, 32r.

64. RGIA, Fond 1163, op. 1, d. 16a, 20r.

65. RGIA, Fond 1163, op. 1, d. 16b, 32r.

66. *Senatskii arkiv*, vol. 1 (St. Petersburg: Tipografiia pravitel'stuiushchago senata, 1888), 286.

67. RGIA, Fond 1163, op. 1, d. 16b, 32r.

68. Rolle, *Tadeusz Leszczyc Grabianka*, 105.

69. Rolle, *Grabianka*, 105.

70. On Iliński's Deaf and Mute Institute at Romanov, see Andrzej Kierzek, "Institut dla głuchoniemych w Romanowie," *Otorynolaryngologia* 11:4 (2012): 146–54.

71. On Iliński and cultural life at Romanov, see Roman Aftanazy, *Dzieje rezydencji na dawnych kresach Rzeczypospolitej*, vol. 5 (Wrocław: Zakład Narodowy im. Ossolińskich, 1994), 394–409; O. Kondratiuk, "Romaniv ta Rodina Ilins'kikh," *Volin'-Zhitomirshchina. Istoriko-Filologichnii zbirnik z regional'nikh problem* 7 (2001): 91–114; Kamil Kopnia, "The Paraliturgical Theatre of Count Józef August Iliński," *Teatr Lalek* 1–2 (2006): 15–22.

72. RGIA, Fond 1163, op. 1, d. 16a, 48r–48v.

73. Rolle, *Tadeusz Leszczyc Grabianka*, 106. Simonin initially stayed at Romanov in order to be the governor of Iliński's children, before later journeying to St. Petersburg on an unspecified date. See RGIA, Fond 1163, op, 1, d. 16. b, 530r.

74. Rolle, *Tadeusz Leszczyc Grabianka*, 106.

75. For a biography of Grabianka's daughter, see A. J. Rolle, *Niewiasty Kresowe* (Warsaw: Nakład Gebethnera i Wolffa. 1883), 189–243.

76. Rolle, *Tadeusz Leszczyc Grabianka*, 98.

77. RGIA, Fond 1163, op, 1, d. 16. b, 529r, 536v.

78. Rolle, *Tadeusz Leszczyc Grabianka,* 107.

79. RGIA, Fond 1163, op. 1, d. 16v, 406r–406v.

80. See Kondakov, *Orden*, 310–11, 340, 397. Il'in also features prominently in the diary of his brother, A. Ia. Il'in, who was also a Freemason. See A. Ia. Il'in, "Iz dnevnika masona (1775–1776 gg.)," *Chteniia v imperatorskom obshchestve istorii i drevnostei rossiiskikh*, bk. 4 (1908): 1–15.

81. On the Dying Sphinx Lodge, see Aleksandr Etkind, "Umiraiushchii Sfinks": krug Golitsyna-Labzina i peterburgskii period russkoi misticheskoi traditsii," *Studia Slavica Finlandensia* 13 (1996): 17–46; A. I. Serkov, *Istoriia russkogo masonstva XIX veka* (St. Petersburg: N. I. Novikov, 2000), 48–50.

82. Petrov is also frequently mentioned in Il'in's diary. A certain Anton Ivanov was also initiated on Oct. 20, 1805. We have not been able to ascertain the precise identity of this individual, but it is possible he is the same Ivanov who is listed as being a founding member of the Dying Sphinx lodge. See Serkov, *Russkoe masonstvo*, 1107.

83. On Borovikovskii's artistic career, see T. V. Alekseeva, *Vladimir Lukich Borovikovskii i russkaia kul'tura na rubezhe XVIII–XIX vekov* (Moscow: Iskusstvo, 1975).

84. On Pokhodiashin's links to Novikov and so-called Martinism, see E. M. Garshin, "Martinist i filantrop proshlago veka," *Istoricheskii vestnik* 9 (1887): 629–39.

85. Labzin to Runich, Mar. 8, 1807, RNB, Fond 656, d. 23, 19r.

86. A. F. Labzin to D. P. Runich, Mar. 8, 1807, RNB, Fond 656, d. 23, 20r.

87. On Cherevin, who was initiated into the Dying Sphinx lodge in 1801, see Serkov, *Russkoe masonstvo*, 871, 1106. On Turchilo (a member of Dying Sphinx since 1806), see Serkov, *Russkoe masonstvo*, 817, 1108. On Rusanovskii, who was the secretary of the Dying Sphinx when it was founded in 1800, as well as a member of lodges in Moscow in the 1780s, see Serkov, *Russkoe masonstvo*, 718, 955, 1106–7. On Levitskii, see B. L. Modzalevskii, "Zapiska D. G. Levitskogo k A. F. Labzinu," *Khudozhestvennye sokrovishcha Rossii*, no. 4 (1907): 90–3; N. Kiselev, "D. G. Levitskii i masonstvo," *Sredi kollektsionerov* 5 (1923): 26–8.

88. Other known Freemasons initiated into the NIS in St. Petersburg include A. E. Miasoedov (a member of the Neptune lodge on the island of Kronstadt since 1780); E. M. Riabinin (who is known to have visited various lodges in Petersburg in the 1810s); P. I. Ozerov (listed as a member of the Polar Star lodge in 1810); M. I. Donaurov (a Second-Degree mason in 1799); A. I. Kovalevskii (a Third-Degree mason in 1802), and G. E. H. von Hoyningen-Huene (a member of various lodges in Moscow, Riga, and in the military, who worked the Theoretical Degree of the Rosicrucian Order under the direction of N. I. Repnin). See Serkov, *Russkoe masonstvo*, 239, 312, 401, 949, 955, 957, 986, 989, 1051, 1061, 1089, 1107.

89. See A. E. Labzina, *Days of a Russian Noblewoman: The Memories of Anna Labzina 1758–1821*, trans. and ed. Gary Marker and Rachel May (DeKalb: Northern Illinois University Press, 2001.

90. Gary Marker, "The Enlightenment of Anna Labzina: Gender, Faith, and Public Life in Catherinian and Alexandrian Russia," *Slavic Review* 59:2 (Summer 2000): 372, 374.

91. Tira Sokolovskaia, "Podnesenie masonskikh perchatok A. E. Labzinoi. Epizod iz istorii russkogo masonstva (1819)," *Russkii arkhiv* 12 (1905): 532–5. For an English translation of Sokolovskaia's description, see Labzina, *Days*, appendix 2, 145–9.

92. S. A. Laikevich, *Vospominaniia Sof'i Alekseevny Laikevich* (St. Petersburg: Tip. M. P. S., 1905), 15.

93. On women and adoption lodges, see Jan Snoek, *Initiating Women in Freemasonry* (Leiden: Brill, 2012). Several adoption lodges were established in neighbouring areas of the Russian Empire, including in Mitau in the Duchy of Courland, Warsaw, Vilnius, and Zhitomir. See Serkov, *Russkoe masonstvo*, 944, 948, 950.

94. See Alexandre Stroev, "'Les Femmes Russes et la Franc-Maçonnerie Européenne à la fin du XVIIIe et au début du XIXe siécles," in *Les Rôles Transfrontaliers Joués par les Femmes dans*

la construction de l'Europe, ed. Suzan Van Dijk and Guyonne Ledu (Paris: L'Harmattan, 2012), 189–204.

95. RGIA, Fond 1163, op. 1, d. 16a, 1851.

96. Muromtsov, "Razkaz," 20.

97. On Donaurov, see Nikolai Kul'baka, *Istoriia dvorianskogo roda Donaurovykh* (Moscow: Staraia Basmannaia, 2013), 17–32.

98. E. D. Volkova's husband, Aleksandr Andreevich Volkov, a playwright and court herald master, died in 1788. See "A. A. Volkov, zabytyi pisatel' XVIII veka," *Khronika Leningradskogo obshchestva bibliofilov* (1931): 32–37.

99. *Mesiatsoslov s rospis'iu chinovnykh osob* (St. Petersburg: Imperial Academy of Sciences, 1805), 18. Ozerov was also an officer in the Mounted Life-Guard Regiment and had fought at the Battle of Austerlitz on December 2, 1805.

100. A. B., *Biografiia Aleksandra Aleksandrovicha Volkova* (Moscow: Tipografiia Avgusta Cemena, 1833), 5–6.

101. Mariia and Parsko'via Volkova were appointed maids of honour to Empress Mariia Feodorovna in 1797. See A. B., *Biografiia*, 4.

102. A. P. Kruglikov, *Moi vospominaniia* (Iaroslavl': Avers Plius, 2006), 25.

103. See Olga E. Glagoleva, "The Illegitimate Children of the Russian Nobility in Law and Practice, 1700–1860," *Kritika: Explorations in Russian and Eurasian History* 6:3 (Summer 2005): 461–99.

104. A. B., *Biografiia*, 15.

105. RGIA, Fond 1163, op. 1, d. 16a, 1831–183v.

106. RGIA, Fond 1163, op. 1, d. 16a, 1841–184v.

107. Bulgakov wrote that Volkov had asked him to write the inscription on Pleshcheev's tombstone in a letter to his brother. See A. Ia. Bulgakov to K. Ia. Bulgakov, Aug. 14, 1819, in "Iz pisem Aleksandra Iakovlevich Bulgakova k ego bratu, 1819–i god," *Russkii arkhiv* 10 (1900): 218.

108. The full wording of the inscription on Pleshcheev's grave was kindly relayed by P.-Y. Kirschleger.

109. The inclusion of Archpriest Vasilii Feodorovich Nalimov (1767–1820) is significant, as he ranks as the only known ecclesiastical figure to have been initiated in Russia. He served as a deacon and archpriest in the Semenovskii Lifeguard Regiment, before taking up a post as a teacher of French at the St. Petersburg Spiritual Academy, on Sept. 13, 1806 (four days after being initiated into the NIS). See I. Chistovich, *Istoriia S. Peterburgskoi dukhovnoi akademii* (St. Petersburg: Tipografiia Iakova Treia, 1857), 140. Nalimov is also credited as the translator of a French version of Bishop Feofilakt Gorskii's *Dogmas of the Orthodox Christian Faith*, published in St. Petersburg in 1792. See Feofilakt, *Dogmaty khristianskiia pravoslavnyia very* (St. Petersburg, 1792). The initiation of a certain André Kovalevskiy on Sept. 12, 1806, would seem to be a reference to Andrei Ivanovich Kovalevskii, who hailed from the village of Ivanovka near Kharkiv and who was a friend and protégé of the philosopher Hryhorii Skovoroda, who died on Kovalevskii's estate in 1794. Kovalevskii was also a member of the Kharkiv branch of the Russian Bible Society and corresponded with Labzin. See A. F. Labzin to Z. Ia. Karneev, July 24, 1816, "A. F. Labzin i ego ssylka (1822)," *Russkii arkhiv* 12 (1892): 356. According to Serkov, Kovalevskii was a Third-Degree mason in 1802. See G. P. Danilevskii, *Ukrainskaia starina* (Kharkiv: Izdanie Zalenskago i Liubarskago, 1866), 71; Serkov, *Russkoe masonstvo*, 401.

110. Malinovskii's wife, Sof'ia Andreevna, was also initiated on May 8, 1806; the couple's 13-year-old daughter, Elizaveta Vasil'evna, was initiated on Dec. 30, 1806.

111. For a biographical study of Malinovskii, see Paolo Ferretti, *A Russian Advocate of Peace: Vasilii Malinovskii (1765–1814)* (Dordrecht: Springer, 1998).

112. M. Shippan, "V. F. Malinovskii—perevodchik fragmenta romana 'Teobal'd, ili mechtateli' I. G. Iunga-Shtillinga," *XVIII vek*, vol. 22 (2002), 314.

113. See M. D. Filin, *O Pushkine i okrest poeta, Iz arkhivnykh razyskanii* (Moscow: Terra, 1997), 134.

114. D. F. Kobeko, "Pervyi direktor Tsarskosel'skogo litseia," *Zhurnal ministerstva narodnago prosveshcheniia* 1 (1915): 28–42.

115. The other initiates whose names suggest that they were not Russians were Hélène Laurent (?), Josephine Cuënod, Christine Wenigge, and Christine Krollé. RGIA, Fond 1163, op. 1, d. 16v, 406r–406v.

116. On Grieve, see John H. Appleby, "John Grieve's Correspondence with Joseph Black and Some Contemporaneous Russo-Scottish Medical Intercommunication," *Medical History* 29 (1985): 401–13; A. G. Cross, *By the Banks of the Neva: Chapters from the Lives and Careers of the British in Eighteenth-Century Russia* (Cambridge: Cambridge University Press, 1997), 153–5.

117. Thomas O'Flynn, *The Western Christian Presence in the Russias and Qājār Persia, c. 1760–c. 1870* (Leiden: Brill, 2017), 267, 278, 283.

118. *The Evangelical Magazine, 1806* (London: Williams and Smith, 1806), 230.

119. RGIA, Fond 1163, op. 1, d. 16a, 192v.

120. RGIA, Fond 1163, op. 1, d. 16a, 193v.

121. F. P. Lubianovskii, *Vospominaniia Feodora Petrovicha Lubianovskago, 1777–1834* (Moscow: Tipografiia Gracheva, 1872), 215–17.

122. RGIA, Fond 1163, op. 1, d. 16a, 193r.

123. RGIA, Fond 1163, op. 1, d. 16a, 195v–196r.

124. RGIA, Fond 1163, op. 1, d. 16a, 196r.

125. For the full twelve articles of the proclamation, see Longinov, "Odin iz magikov," 599–601.

126. RGIA, Fond 1163, op. 1, d. 16a, 196v–197.

127. RGIA, Fond 1163, op. 1, d. 16a, 204v–205r.

128. RGIA, Fond 1163, op. 1, d. 16a, part II, 186r. Lubianovskii describes being at a gathering where Grabianka showed him the blueprints of the temple. See Lubianovskii, *Vospominaniia*, 217.

129. See Ernest A. Zitser, *The Transfigured Kingdom: Sacred Parody and Charismatic Authority at the Court of Peter the Great* (Ithaca, NY: Cornell University Press, 2004); Paul Keenan, *St. Petersburg and the Russian Court, 1703–1761* (Basingstoke: Palgrave Macmillan, 2013), esp. chs. 3 and 4. Also see S. F. Platonov, "Iz bytovoi istorii Petrovskoi epokhi. I. Bengo-Kollegiia ili Velikobritanskii monastyr' v S.-Peterburge pri Petre Velikom," *Izvestiia Akademii Nauk SSSR* 7–8 (1926): 527–46; A. G. Cross, "The Bung College or British Monastery in Petrine Russia," *Newsletter of the Study Group on Eighteenth-Century Russia* 12 (1984): 14–24.

130. The earliest known *salonnière* in Russia was V. A. Iushkova, who in the decade before her death, in 1797, hosted literary evenings in Tula. However, noblewomen only began to act as hostesses of literary salons in St. Petersburg from the 1810s. See Lina Bernstein, "Women on the Verge of a New Language: Russian Salon Hostesses in the First Half of the Nineteenth Century," in *Russia Women Culture*, ed. Helena Goscilo and Beth Holmgren (Bloomington: Indiana University Press, 1996), 209–24.

131. Marker, "Enlightenment of Anna Labzina," 390.

132. Muromtsov, "Razkaz," 19–20.

133. Lubianovskii, *Vospominaniia*, 215.

134. Laikevich, *Vospominaniia*, 16.

135. Muromstov, "Razkaz," 20; Lubianovskii, *Vospominaniia*, 215–6.

136. Joel Hecker, *Mystical Bodies, Mystical Meals: Eating and Embodiment in Medieval Kabbalah* (Detroit, MI: Wayne State University Press, 2005), 5.

137. C. W. Bynum, "Fast, Feast and Flesh: The Religious Significance of Food to Medieval Women," *Representations* 11 (1985): 2.

138. Muromtsov, "Razkaz," 19; Lubianovskii, *Vospominaniia*, 216.

139. Muromtsov, "Razkaz," 19.

140. Muromtsov, 20.

141. Muromtsov, 19.

142. Lubianovskii, *Vospominaniia*, 215.

143. Grabianka to Leyman, Dec. 10, 1806, RGIA, Fond 1163, op. 1, d. 16b, 87v.

144. Laikevich, *Vospominaniia*, 15–16. The only other person named by Laikevich is Madame d'Attigny: "At this time a French woman, Madame d'Attigny, visited us; she lived with M[aria] A[ntonovna] Naryshkina and looked after her little daughter from H[is Royal Highness] A[lexander] P[avlovich]." Grabianka's testimony during his interrogation by the Russian authorities in 1807 tallies with Laikevich's description. He noted that Madame d'Attigny was presently living in the home of M. A. Naryshkina and had been entrusted with caring for one of her daughters. D'Attigny's role as the childrearer of Emperor Alexander's illegitimate daughter within the household of Naryshkina, his lover, may well explain why she escaped the same fate as Grabianka. For Grabianka's testimony, see, RGIA, Fond 1163, op. 1, d. 16a, 300r.

145. Lubianovskii, *Vospominaniia*, 215–16.

146. Grabianka to Leyman, Dec. 10, 1806, RGIA, Fond 1163, op. 1, d. 16b, 84r–90v. Il'in lived at "No. 229, near the Kharlamov Bridge."

147. RGIA, Fond 1163, op. 1, d. 16b, 89r.

148. Muromtsov, "Razkaz," 19–20.

149. Labzin to Runich, Mar. 8, 1807, RNB, Fond 656, d. 23, 19r–19v.

150. Labzin to Runich, Sept. 22, 1807, RNB, Fond 656, d. 23, 57v.

151. Franciszek Mackiewicz, who in 1815 became the bishop of Kamianets-Podilskyi, officiated at Grabianka's funeral. Grabianka was buried on Vasil'evskii Island in St. Petersburg. See Rolle, *Tadeusz Leszczyc Grabianka*, 121–2. For the records of death held by the Catholic Church of St. Catherine in St. Petersburg, see TsGIA SPB, Fond 347, op. 1, metricheskie svidetel'stva o rozhdenii, brake, smerti (1802–1823).

152. Pozdeev to L. K. Razumovskii, Oct. 25, 1807, RGB, Fond 14, ed. Kh. 631, 4r.

153. Serkov, *Istoriia*, 62; Kondakov, *Rozenkreitsery*, 137–8.

154. Arsen'ev was also an old masonic acquaintance of A. A. Lenivtsev from at least as early as 1785 in St. Petersburg. See Titov, "Vtoraia redaktsiia ispovedi," 145–6.

7

The Legacy of the New Israel Society

THE PLESHCHEEVA CIRCLE, 1807–1830S

IN JANUARY 1813, only weeks after Napoleon's Grand Army had left Russian soil,
O. A. Pozdeev, the leading figure of the revived Rosicrucian Order in Moscow, had other
matters on his mind. In a letter to a fellow brother, Pozdeev scornfully recalled how "A.
A. Lenivts[ev] and his followers went over to Grabianka, that most dangerous preacher
of the Illuminés d'Avignon (*Avin'ontsev*)." A more pressing concern for Pozdeev was that
Lenivtsev and his circle had "so deeply embedded . . . their roots that even now they are
succeeding in the intention of attracting many followers."[1] A year later he was still seething
at Lenivtsev for "violating his [Rosicrucian] oath" and leaving the order, and noted that
he was "heading towards sin."[2] In January 1817, nearly a decade after Grabianka's arrest,
Pozdeev wrote to L. K. Razumovskii and not so subtly instructed his friend to "read
more diligently" as only then "will God return you to your senses and will make clear to
you the false teachings of the *Avin'ontsev* or those who were deceived by the teachings
of Grabianka." Pozdeev's chastisement of Razumovskii is evidently borne out of a fear
that "this doctrine" has "once again begun to operate and the oracle helps."[3] Pozdeev, the
conservative Rosicrucian, had consistently decried what he perceived as Grabianka's pernicious influence in St. Petersburg during the Polish nobleman's residence in the capital
between 1805 and 1807. At the time he warned fellow brethren against being tempted by
the "promise of visions . . . the promise of correspondence with heaven, and even with the
Lord himself."[4]

Pozdeev's concerns about what he saw as the baleful impact of Grabianka among fellow
Rosicrucians in Petersburg up to 1807 were largely justified. The previous chapter demonstrated the extent to which the brothers of the Dying Sphinx Lodge, initially encouraged by A. A. Lenivtsev and backed up by A. F. Labzin, joined the NIS. Yet what are we

Initiating the Millennium. Robert Collis, and Natalie Bayer, Oxford University Press (2020) © Oxford University Press.
DOI: 10.1093/oso/9780190903374.001.0001

to make of his continued assertions in the 1810s that Grabianka's followers—particularly Lenivtsev—were, with some success, continuing to proselytise their leader's millenarian doctrine in Russia long after his death? We have not uncovered any evidence to suggest that formal meetings of the society and consultations with any kind of oracle continued after Grabianka's arrest.

However, a tight-knit circle of Grabianka's followers, led by N. F. Pleshcheeva and A. A. Lenivtsev, did continue to espouse the millenarian doctrine upheld in the society up to 1807. Indeed, Pleshcheeva and Lenivstev were by no means banished to the wilderness for their association with Grabianka. The opposite is in fact true: they succeeded in drawing into their circle two of Emperor Alexander's closest advisers—R. A. Koshelev (1749–1827) and A. N. Golitsyn (1773–1844)—in the years immediately prior to Napoleon's invasion of Russia. As numerous historians have noted, Koshelev and Golitsyn were, in turn, able to exert a profound influence on the religious mindset of the emperor at a critical moment in Russia's history, not least by playing a pivotal role in introducing him to two prophetesses—Barbara von Krüdener and Thèrése Bouche—who both enjoyed considerable favour with the monarch until 1822. Moreover, although Lenivstev died in around 1818, Pleshcheeva continued to be at the forefront of a like-minded millenarian circle in Petersburg until well into the 1830s. In other words, despite Grabianka's pitiful plight in a Petersburg prison cell for much of 1807 and the collapse of his society, his legacy, in Russia at least, was considerable.

I

On June 10, 1807, a report appeared in a Swiss periodical about an educational institute opened in 1805 in Yverdon by J. H. Pestalozzi. The pedagogical project of the Swiss educator, which was greatly influenced by Pietist forms of Christianity, soon attracted inquisitive visitors from across Europe and beyond.[5] Worthy of mention on this particular day is a small group of Russians that included Pleshcheeva, A. A. Lenivtsev, and Koshelev.[6] The Russian party was accompanied by Baron Lefort and a "Herr Allier."[7] In other words, prominent members of the NIS in Russia and in Avignon seem to have regrouped in Switzerland, at a time when the leader of the group was imprisoned in Petersburg and its impressive expansion in Russia had been curtailed.

The presence of Pleshcheeva in Switzerland was borne out of tragic necessity. Her sole surviving child, Mariia (b. 1798), was, as Grabianka had noted in 1806, "of extremely weak health," and her doctor ordered a change of climate. Hence, Pleshcheeva departed for Lausanne in August 1806, accompanied by Lefort and, almost certainly, Lenivtsev.[8] However, the pleasant climate in Lausanne did not act as the hoped-for salve for Maria, who passed away on March 30, 1807.[9] The devastating loss suffered by Pleshcheeva in Lausanne occurred two months prior to her visit to Pestalozzi's institute. Notwithstanding the emotional strain such a visit must have been for Pleshcheeva, the presence of so many trusted friends and like-minded individuals reveals that she was far from alone in her suffering. The religious atmosphere in the Vaud region of Switzerland, which was in the early throes of the Réveil movement, may well have provided comfort to Pleshcheeva.[10] However, though we know that key members of the NIS (Lefort, Allier, Pleshcheeva, and Lenivtsev) reassembled in the Vaud region in 1807, alongside Koshelev, Pleshcheev's brother-in-law, we know nothing about their discussions apropos religion in general or the fate of their group in particular.

II

In 1837, I. N. Bartenev, the noted memoirist, took breakfast at the home of his mentor, A. N. Golitsyn, who was in his mid-sixties at the time. On entering the dining room, Bartenev was immediately struck by the gallery of portraits adorning the walls that honoured those the prince held in the highest esteem. Alongside images of siblings and likely love interests, the prince also saw fit to pay homage to a selection of renowned Christian mystics: John Pordage, Saint-Martin, Krüdener, and Alexander Hohenlohe-Waldenburg.[11] The inclusion of Christian theosophers, supposed miracle workers, and a prophetess is unsurprising for a man who was profoundly attracted to a wide range of Christian mystical thought. Indeed, Golitsyn ranks as the most powerful and influential proponent of an ecumenical form of Christian mysticism in Russia, which was endowed with a rich vein of millenarianism, for a critical period in the country's history between 1810 and 1824. Golitsyn is credited with being the critical figure behind Emperor Alexander's turn to Christian mysticism in 1812. This subsequently led to Krüdener being able to provide spiritual guidance to the tsar, which culminated, in 1815, with the formation of the Holy Alliance at the Russian monarch's behest.[12]

By this time, Golitsyn was already the chief procurator of the Holy Synod and the overseer of all foreign confessions in Russia. His authority increased in 1816 when he was appointed to the post Minister of Religious Affairs and of the People's Enlightenment. Besides these official government duties, Golitsyn was also president of the Russian Bible Society (RBS) from its establishment in 1813 until it was banned by Emperor Nicholas I in 1826. Bearing in mind the pivotal role Golitsyn played in promoting a millenarian form of Christian mysticism at the Alexandrine court, it is highly significant that alongside the portraits of well-known Christian mystics were images of Pleshcheeva and Lenivtsev. Golitsyn's veneration in the late 1830s of the two main Russian proselytisers of the NIS in Petersburg between 1805 and 1807 is testament to the lasting impact of the group's millenarian vision.

We do not know exactly when Pleshcheeva, Lenivtsev, and Koshelev returned to Petersburg from their extended stay in Switzerland, but they were all resident in the capital by 1809. Around this time the triumvirate of Pleshcheeva, Lenivtsev, and Koshelev seem to have implemented a coordinated attempt to draw Golitsyn into their circle and to "awaken" him to their vision of Christian mysticism. This process may not have involved a formal initiation ceremony, but it did necessitate Golitsyn undertaking a spiritual rite of passage.

Golitsyn describes this process in detail in his reminiscences. The preliminary stage of the prince's "awakening" began when Koshelev approached him and invited him to his home. The chief procurator accepted and soon began to visit Koshelev regularly. Golitsyn recalls how *starik* Koshelev made a strong impression on him during their conversations, although he concedes that he only understood half of what his elder was saying. For Golitsyn at this time, Koshelev seemed to be the embodiment of a wise sage, one who had travelled throughout Europe and had personal connections to those who displayed the greatest "piety and Christian wisdom," such as Saint-Martin, Lavater, and Eckartshausen.[13] Thus Koshelev effectively undertook a successful process of drawing the younger Golitsyn into his spiritual milieu. The prince's reminiscences reveal that the next stage involved Koshelev introducing him to Lenivtsev at the former's home. Golitsyn's description of this meeting highlights Lenivtsev's charisma and powers of persuasion:

> Once Rodion Aleksandrovich [Koshelev] invited me to his and notified me that he had also invited Aleksandr Alekseevich Lenivtsev ... This Lenivtsev was known in Petersburg as a person of outstanding intellect and piety ... Lenivtsev had the rare gift of speaking sweetly and enticingly, and I probably guessed that Koshelev invited him [in order to] melt in me, so to speak, my permanent caution and incredulity. And, in actual fact, I discerned in Lenivstev a powerful and convincing eloquence; he combined this with an unusual kind of soft, clear exposition.[14]

The trio thereafter enjoyed regular sumptuous feasts, during which they would conduct "important and serious" discussions.[15]

These luncheons did not last for too long before Koshelev suggested that Golitsyn was ready to enter Pleshcheeva's inner circle. According to Golitsyn, Pleshcheeva, who was shy by temperament, initially considered him to be a sharp-tongued court wag. However, Koshelev managed to persuade Pleshcheeva that this was no longer the case and consequently she invited Golitsyn into her home.[16] The invitation signalled that the prince had been granted more than a private audience in Pleshcheeva's domestic realm. He had in effect gained admission to a select salon, regularly convened after her return to Russia, by a woman who may have been shy, but who was also highly educated.[17] Moreover, Pleshcheeva was both passionate and dedicated in her promotion of a religious circle in which she was able to consciously fashion a space in which the millenarian culture of the NIS could be continued, if not the formal rituals. The homes of a number of aristocratic women had been used as meeting places for assemblies of the NIS. Yet the women who hosted these gatherings cannot be regarded as *salonnières*, in the sense that they could not oversee admittance to the group or the promotion of any form of intellectual conversation.

Pleshcheeva, however, on her return from Switzerland, succeeded in fashioning herself as a genuine *salonnière*. According to Steven Kale, "a salon was a deliberately composed gathering of individuals selected by the *salonnière*." Moreover, the power of *salonnières* to issue invitations gave them "the freedom to create select groups ... and to arrange, making each salon an act of self-expression with its own character, and each *salonnière* the author of its particular qualities."[18] Kale's generalised definition describes Pleshcheeva's role as a *salonnière* who promoted a gathering of like-minded individuals who shared her vision of mystical Christianity. In the case of Golitsyn, it would seem that it took some time for her to be convinced of his genuine desire and worthiness to participate in her salon.

Golitsyn provides an excellent account of the first time he entered Pleshcheeva's salon. The initial part of the meeting was devoted to the "lofty, spiritual, in a word ... a Pietistic discussion." The second part of the meeting was dedicated to the reading of a spiritual text, on this occasion, one selected by Koshelev. Golitsyn notes that this seemed like a regular activity for the group. Koshelev's choice was entitled *Manuel des victimes de Jésus* by Jacqueline-Aimée Brohon, an eighteenth-century prophetess from Paris.[19] The rare tome was published posthumously in France in 1799. Golitsyn briefly notes that Brohon was at the head of the secret Society of Victims in France and that her *Manuel* contained "profound treasures of mysticism," along with descriptions of the visions of the prophetess.

Given the millenarian vision and mixed-gender dynamic at the core of the associational culture of the NIS, it is highly significant that the select members of the Pleshcheeva salon chose this tome. Brohon's *Manuel* was the last of a trilogy of posthumous works, published in the 1790s in the wake of the events of the French Revolution.[20] At the crux of Brohon's religious outlook, as Robert Southey notes, was the millenarian belief that "God was about to exercise judgment upon the nations, to decimate the earth, and chuse for himself a new people." These new people were to form "a college of Victims," who would form a secret society that consisted of an equal number of men and women. This so-called Society of Victims "were to be his [Jesus'] coadjutors in the great work of redemption." Hence, "when all was fulfilled, the Victims would constitute the sole body of the church during the reign of the Redeemer."[21] In other words, here was the work of a prophetess whose millenarian vision was remarkably similar to that promoted by the NIS; namely, it was framed around the belief that only a select society of the pious (of both sexes) would overcome the havoc that was soon to be wrought over the earth.

Golitsyn confesses that he was initially overwhelmed and confused by the group's reading and discussion of Brohon's hieroglyphical text. Yet this sense of bewilderment did not prevent him from being conscious that an attempt was being made to draw him into a select group: "I remained entirely ... convinced that *starik* Koshelev ... wished to pull me into some kind of unknown-to-me sect and that this evening served to turn my attention to further preparation." Indeed, Golitsyn added that "it even appeared clear to me then that they had their own ritualistic language and that evidently it was unintelligible to the uninitiated, because I understood nothing of it." That this assembly was much more than a mere reading group is also apparent in Golitsyn's observation that "this society . . . so noisily worshipped and during intervals they aspired to praise each other."[22] In other words, though these assemblies did not have any formal initiation rites, it is apparent that the invited participants had to absorb and accept the esoteric religious rituals performed at the meetings.

The path towards familiarisation and acceptance was not straightforward for Golitsyn. He confesses in his reminiscences that he was initially overcome by shyness when he participated in Pleshcheeva's salon, and that even after he had attended five or six assemblies, he still "constantly carried home" with him "a heart that was always uneasy," with his "reason troubled." But he never ceased to pray zealously and fervently during this trial, and God soon liberated him from "this difficult position."[23] During his time of tribulation, the group evidently continued to read Brohon's *Manuel*, and Golitsyn's religious awakening, when it came, was intrinsically linked to this text: "Well, suddenly and unexpectedly, to my greatest and most joyful amazement, I burst through the veil of my doubting ignorance. My heart began to beat faster with joy, became enflamed, and I began to freely, although still not entirely, to see and understand what the miraculous maiden Brohon wanted to say about her internal examination."[24] This description of religious awakening is fascinating in and of itself, but it also reveals the profound influence of Brohon on the millenarian sensibility of the Pleshcheeva salon around 1809 and 1810. It is also noteworthy that Krüdener was introduced to the works of Brohon by a "circle nourished" by Brohon's works in Strasbourg in 1811.[25] Krüdener's near contemporaneous interest in the prophetic works of Brohon would seem to have emerged independently of the Pleshcheeva salon. However, considering their shared religious trajectory, it is unsurprising that their paths were soon to cross, especially given Krüdener's ties to the Russian court.[26]

The Pleshcheeva salon in Petersburg seems to have enjoyed a remarkable longevity, despite the upheaval in Russia after 1810. In 1829 and 1830, for example, Golitsyn wrote a series of letters to F. K. von Berckheim (Krüdener's son-in-law), in which he reveals that meetings at Pleshcheeva's home were still a regular occurrence. Moreover, on March 7, 1829, Golitsyn wrote, "I am normally busy all morning in various committees and with the [State] Council until five, then I usually go to Madame Pleshcheeva's, where we read things, which compels us to forget worldly commotions."[27] The works discussed at Pleshcheeva's included the unpublished novel *Otil'da* by Krüdener.[28] In June 1833, Golitsyn replied to a letter from a relative and follower of Krüdener, A. S. Golitsyna, in which he assured her that "we will read [it] in the small society at Mme Pleshcheeva's." In a later letter to Golitsyna, dated March 20, 1834, Golitsyn confirmed that "we read *Otil'da* at Mme Pleshcheeva's."[29]

By the 1830s, both Lenivtsev and Koshelev were dead, but as the letters above testify, Golitsyn was still regularly attending the salon in Pleshcheeva's home. Lefort, the one-time chancellor of the NIS in Avignon, was still a regular attendee at Pleshcheeva's salon, up until at least December 1830.[30] The Pleshcheeva Circle was also bolstered by a younger generation of mystics, including, most notably, A. I. Koval'kov, the adopted son of I. V. Lopukhin.[31] Koval'kov was raised and educated by Lopukhin at the latter's country estates.[32] By the time of Lopukhin's death, in 1816, Koval'kov had already written and published a series of works of Christian theosophy that were heavily influenced by Lopukhin, Böhme, Eckhartshausen, and Jung-Stilling.[33] Before his death, Lopukhin had written to Golitsyn and asked him to take Koval'kov under his wing in Petersburg. On January 1, 1817, Koval'kov was appointed to the Ministry of People's Enlightenment under the directorship of Golitsyn.[34] At the same time as Koval'kov was beginning to enjoy Golitsyn's mentorship he was also becoming extremely close to Pleshcheeva. Koval'kov lived with Pleshcheeva into the 1840s, and sometime between 1817 and 1822, he married her charge Ekaterina Ivanovna Iakovleva.[35]

The millenarian doctrine of the NIS, first espoused by Grabianka and Pernety in 1780, encouraged members to actively seek out purported prophets and prophetesses in Europe who seemed to validate their own chiliastic beliefs. In the 1780s, for example, Grabianka sought out Rohoziński in Podolia, Samuel Best in England, and Cappelli in Italy. Moreover, in 1790, amid the revolutionary maelstrom in Paris, members of the society, including Gombault and Bousie, were among the first to promote the visionary gifts of Suzette Labrousse. We have no evidence that any self-declared prophet became associated with the society during the years it was based in Petersburg. But Grabianka's successful proselytising in the Russian capital between 1805 and 1807 was still based on a millenarian belief that certain individuals could be divinely inspired—that is, endowed by God with the gift of being able to proclaim his will and to foresee the consequences for humanity.

This mindset did not change when formal meetings of the society ceased after Grabianka's arrest and death in prison. It is thus in keeping with the tradition of the society that initiated members, such as Pleshcheeva and Lenivtsev, and like-minded friends (Koshelev) took such intense interest in the prophetic utterances of Brohon, and entirely unsurprising that members of the Pleshcheeva Circle came to form an intimate bond with Krüdener, the most famous prophetess of the Napoleonic era.

The close relationship between Golitsyn and Krüdener, which began in 1813, has been well examined by a number of historians.[36] Far less well-known is the close, even tender, relationship between members of the Pleshcheeva and Krüdener circles. It is not exactly clear when the links were forged, but ties had almost certainly been cemented by 1821–1822, when Krüdener lived with A. S. Golitsyna at her dacha near Petersburg, so that she could tend to her sick son-in-law. As one of Krüdener's biographers wrote, "The salon of the Princess Anna Galitzin . . . was daily besieged by a crowd of the most distinguished and elegant people in Russian court circles."[37] It seems almost certain that the members of the Pleshcheeva Circle were among these visitors. Moreover, in December 1822, Golitsyn recollected in a letter to Krüdener that Ekaterina Koval'kova, the one-time ward of Pleshcheeva and wife of Koval'kov, had dedicated herself to the Lord's service in the presence of the renowned prophetess in his private domestic chapel. What is more, he mentions that Koval'kova made a "miraculous recovery" after Pleshcheeva brought "benefactions" that had been suggested by Krüdener.[38]

By 1822, when Krüdener returned to her family estate, Kosse, in present-day Estonia, she had already established a very warm bond with the core members of the Pleshcheeva Circle. In his correspondence with Krüdener between September 1822 and January 1824, Golitsyn frequently refers to Pleshcheeva, Koval'kov, and Koval'kova. On September 5, 1822, for example, Golitsyn wrote that "Pleshcheeva was so enraptured, as was Koval'kov" with the news conveyed to them about Krüdener's activities in Kosse.[39] In subsequent correspondence to Krüdener, Golitsyn attached letters from Pleshcheeva, who, he notes, "loves her very much," and at one point says that she "listened to your letter in ecstasy."[40] Indeed, Golitsyn's correspondence with Krüdener from May 1823 indicates that Pleshcheeva, Koval'kov, and Koval'kova were planning to visit Kosse sometime after Whitsun.[41]

The surviving correspondence between Golitsyn and Krüdener, from 1822 until Krüdener's death in 1824, provides abundant evidence of the esteem in which she was held by Pleshcheeva and her circle, and of their intimate links with the prophetess. That such a bond existed between Krüdener and the Pleshcheeva Circle in the 1820s is unsurprising, considering the continued millenarian fervour of both parties. Krüdener's son-in-law, Berckheim expressed his mother in law's eschatological frame of mind in a letter to the Marquis de Langallerie in February 1820: "It has been revealed to my mother-in-law that the time has come when the various mysteries of the Christian Church . . . are to appear in a more living and active form."[42] The Pleshcheeva Circle's enduring belief in the imminence of the millennium is evident in a letter Golitsyn wrote to Berckheim in September 1834, in which he exclaims, "Evidently everything is heading towards collapse prior to the second coming of the Lord."[43]

Much has been written about the Krüdener's influence (or lack of it) on Emperor Alexander and his forming of the Holy Alliance, in September 1815, after the pair had met in Heilbonn, Germany, in June of that year.[44] Irrespective of her specific input on this mystical treaty, it is commonly agreed that the emperor came into the ambit of the prophetess because of the combined influence of Koshelev and Golitsyn.[45] Their devotion to Krüdener, in turn, stemmed from their own millenarian beliefs, which had been cultivated by Pleshcheeva and Lenivtsev in the years immediately following the disintegration of the NIS in Petersburg in 1807. The emperor remained favourably inclined towards Krüdener (with Golitsyn and Koshelev often acting as willing intermediaries between them) until at least the Congress of Laibach in 1821, from where he asked Golitsyn to "tell her a thousand affectionate things" in Petersburg.[46]

Yet any favour Krüdener had once enjoyed with the emperor had waned by the time the baroness retreated to Kosse in poor health, in 1822. In the spring of 1824, she, along with her daughter, son-in-law, and A. S. Golitsyna, set out to establish a religious colony in the Crimea, where she died in December of the same year.[47] The emperor's severing of ties with Krüdener seems to have played a part in emboldening those in the Orthodox Church who detested any form of ecumenicalism and deviation from the traditional doctrines upheld by the Russian clergy. The most forthright exposition of this stance at the time was delivered by Archimandrite Fotii. To be sure, Fotii did not limit his attack to a denunciation of the influence of prophetesses. Instead, he lambasted the entire "sect of illuminati . . . otherwise known under the name of true Christians," whom he labelled "evil schismatics" and a "society of Antichrists." However, a specific focus of Fotii's attack was on the doctrine of millenarianism, as espoused by the Pietist Johann Bengel, who predicted that the second coming of Christ would occur in 1836, immediately prior to the advent of the millennium.[48] Fotii undertook his own mathematical calculations in 1824 in order to reveal the folly of those who believed in Bengel's prediction, foremost among whom he names as Golitsyn and Koshelev and the evangelical pastor Johannes Gossner, who began to preach in Russia in 1812.[49]

Fotii was not reticent in admonishing individuals for their heretical views. However, he also directed his wrath at a state-approved institution—the RBS—which he regarded as a diabolical and malevolent hive of heresy. According to Fotii, this organisation did not simply promote the wider circulation and use of the scriptures in the Russian language— it was nothing less than the principal association of the "sect of illuminati." With this in mind, it is worthwhile examining whether the society, which was established in January 1813, did indeed have any links to the Russian *illuminés* who were drawn to the millenarian light exuded by Grabianka.

The first meeting of the RBS took place at the residence of Golitsyn on January 23, 1813. Golitsyn was elected president of the society, and Koshelev became one of six vice presidents.[50] Neither had been members of the NIS between 1805 and 1807, but as has been noted, both were subsequently heavily influenced by the millenarian doctrine espoused by former members of the group. Among the former members of the NIS who played leading roles in the RBS were M. I. Donaurov, Pleshcheeva's brother-in-law, who was elected a vice-president; A. F. Labzin, who in 1814 became the head of the Petersburg Committee of the RBS; and A. A. Lenivstev.[51]

It is significant that Pozdeev complained that Lenvitsev and other *Avin'ontsevy* had succeeded in firmly establishing roots in the Russian capital at precisely the time the RBS was first established. In other words, the *Avin'ontsevy* had not only succeeded in bringing firmly into their ambit Golitsyn and Koshelev, who both enjoyed direct access to, and influence on, the emperor, but, in Pozdeev's mind, had also established an official association to promote their millenarian doctrine. Pozdeev's tirade against Lenivtsev and the *Avin'ontsevy* does not explicitly reference either the emperor or the RBS, but the timing of his letter is highly suggestive.

A more overt attack on the RBS, sent directly to the emperor, was produced in February 1813—that is, only a few weeks after the first meeting of the RBS. It was written by an anonymous official in the capital and was sent to the emperor in the form of a gossipy report of "St. Petersburg rumours, news and anecdotes." The tsar was in Poland at the time, at the head of the Russian Army as it chased Napoleon's Grand Army westwards, and therefore removed from the everyday goings-on of his nobility. The writer of the despatch deemed it appropriate to comment on the public's negative reaction to the RBS. Despite presumably being aware that the emperor had officially sanctioned the society in December 1812, the official seems to relish this task:

> The public are roused against the Bible Society; some say that under this pretence the Martinists were united; others that it will create a heresy, and a third (group) that it is a polite manner to swindle money . . . This has reached the members who have lost heart a little. Labzin, gifted with a firm spirit, disregards the gossip and tries to inspire the same heroic spirit in others. But Aleksandr Alekseevich Lenivtsev, cannot attain this loftiness, he is not happy that he got caught among their ranks and is ready, if only he could find a suitable pretext to sign himself out [from the RBS].[52]

In all likelihood, the author purposefully exaggerated the extent of the ill will towards the RBS among the Petersburg educated elite. Yet the fears revealed by the reporter, who was prepared to relay such sentiments to the emperor, suggest that significant opposition to the ecumenical group existed from its very founding. The accusation that the RBS was nothing more than a front to unite the so-called Martinists—a broad label used in Russia since the 1780s to refer not only to followers of Saint-Martin but to all societies and individuals harbouring theosophical worldviews—is particularly pertinent. After all, the RBS not only included former members of the NIS, but the two leading lights in the society—Golitsyn and Koshelev—had drawn extremely close to senior *Avin'ontsevy* in the recent past, the latter also being a well-known personal acquaintance of Saint-Martin. Furthermore, the RBS included a significant number of Rosicrucian members based in the capital.[53]

This coalition of "Martinists" clearly appalled the author of the report, and may well have worried Pozdeev, who wanted nothing to do with the *Avin'ontsevy*. Another noteworthy feature of the report is that the author identifies only two individuals by name—Labzin and Lenivtsev—who had the distinction of being the only members of the RBS to have been initiated into both the NIS and Rosicrucianism. Fears about the pernicious motives of the RBS as a trojan horse, used by former *Avin'ontsevy* and other assorted Martinists to exert influence on the emperor and the nobility, did not dissipate over the course of a decade.

The year 1822 marks a watershed moment in the emperor's relationship to those who advocated a millenarian doctrine, first espoused in an associational setting by Grabianka's NIS in 1805. The tsar distanced himself from Krüdener, and banned Freemasonry and other secret societies.[54] The RBS was allowed to continue, but by 1824, the likes of Fotii and A. A. Arakcheev were openly labelling the group heretical; they succeeded in persuading the emperor to remove Golitsyn from all of his official roles (apart from director of the postal system) and pressured him to resign as president of the RBS.

The ascendancy in 1824 of supporters of a traditional form of Orthodox doctrine, such as Fotii and Arakcheev, over the likes of Golitsyn and Koshelev, who harboured a conservative millenarian worldview, proved to be long-lasting. This is not to say that the Pleshcheeva Circle, which included Golitsyn and Koshelev, abandoned their chiliastic beliefs. Instead, as Golitsyn noted in 1829, the salon meetings at Pleshcheeva's home offered a sanctuary in which they could forget worldly commotions. These meetings also allowed the group, which still included Lefort, to continue to share their faith in the imminent arrival of Christ's Second Coming. Indeed, in the case of the former chancellor of the NIS, this belief had endured for nearly half a century. But long gone were the days when they could unashamedly promote their distinctive religious vision directly to the Russian sovereign and among the Petersburg nobility.

NOTES

1. O. A. Pozdeev to P. S. [Likhonin], Jan. 1813. Cited in Pypin, "Materialy," 201.

2. Pozdeev to M. Iu. Viel'gorskii, Jan. 10, 1814, RGB, Fond 147. Ed. Kh. 83, 43r–45v.

3. Pozdeev to L. K. Razumovskii, Jan. 21, 1817, RGB, Fond 13, K. 34. Ed. Kh. 8, 11r.

4. Pozdeev to A. E. Miasoevdov, Feb. 27, 1807, RGB, Fond N. P. Kiselyova, 128, carton 22, 93–4.

5. On the influence of Pietism on Pestalozzi, see Michel Soëtard, *Pestalozzi ou la naissance de l'éducateur* (Berne: Peter D. Lang, 1981), 42–6. On visitors to Pestalozzi's institute, see Daniel Tröhler, *Pestalozzi and the Educationalization of the World* (Basingstoke: Palgrave Macmillan, 2013), 86–7.

6. N. F. Khitrovo and C. A. von Stackelberg were also in the party. Koshelev and Khitrovo (a cousin of A. N. Golitsyn) both met Pestalozzi in 1803 (Sept. 6 and Sept. 20 respectively). See ZBS, Pestalozzinachlass, künftig = Z Mappe 5 XI 201, Bl. 20/21 (Sept. 6, 1803); Z 53, 231 (Sept. 20, 1803). For more on these visits, see Herbert Schönebaum, "Pestalozzi und das zeitgenössische Russland," *Jahrbücher für Geschichte Osteuropas* (1941), 495.

7. "Briefe über Pestalozzische Institut," *Miscellen für die neueste Weltkunde*, no. 46, June 10, 1807, 183.

8. On Dec. 10, 1806, Grabianka wrote that Pleshcheeva and Lefort were being accompanied to Switzerland by "one of the closest and strongest of my friends." See Grabianka to Leyman, Dec. 10, 1806, RGIA, Fond 1163, op. 1, d. 16b, 85v–86r.

9. The young Russian was buried in a black marble tombstone in front of the Catholic church in the village of Assens, near Lausanne. Interestingly, the interior of the apse, reserved for Catholics, also features an inscription in memory of Mariia. It not only honours her pious qualities but also records that her mother promised to donate two thousand Swiss francs to the church every Easter Monday, as long as a solemn service was held in which two children, aged between 8 and 10 and distinguished by their piety, were each awarded half that sum. For details of Mariia Pleshcheeva's grave and the accompanying inscription inside the church, see, R. P. J.-J. Berthier, *La Baronne d'Holca Restauratrice de la Paroisse Catholique de Lausanne* (Fribourg: Imprimerie Catholique Suisse, 1894), 150–2. For Pleshcheeva's donation, see "Acte de donation, par madame la Générale veuve de Plescheyeff, née de Weriguine, de Saint Pétersbourg, domiciliée à Lausanne, en faveur de la paroisse d'Assens," ACV, SB 104/22 "Fondations."

10. On the Réveil movement in the Vaud Canton of Switzerland, see Timothy C. F. Stunt, "The *Réveil* in the Canton of Vaud," in *From Awakening to Secession: Radical Evangelicals in Switzerland and Britain, 1815–1835* (Edinburgh: T&T Clark, 2000), 51–74.

11. Iu. N. Bartenev, "Razskazy kniazia Aleksandra Nikolaevicha Golitsyna. Iz zapisok Iu. N. Barteneva," *Russkii arkhiv* 7 (1886): 309. Golitsyn also hung portraits of his brother and sister, as well as depictions of V. A. Murav'eva, Potemkina, V. A. Trubetskaia, Juliette Berckheim (née Krüdener), G. P. Shumlianskaia, and Martin Michel, a German peasant who worked closely with Alexander Hohenlohe-Waldenburg to supposedly bring about the miraculous cure of the latter's sister. On Hohenlohe-Waldenburg and Michel, see S. Baring Gould, "The Wonder-Working Prince Hohenlohe," *Gentlemen's Magazine*, vol. 260 (1886): 536–47.

12. On the Holy Alliance, Emperor Alexander, and the influence of Krüdener, see, for example, A. L. Zorin, "'Star of the East': The Holy Alliance and European Mysticism," *Kritika: Explorations in Russian and Eurasian History* 4:2 (2003): 313–42; Philipp Menger, *Die Helige Allianz: Religion und Politik bei Alexander I (1801–1825)* (Stuttgart: Steiner, 2014); Andrej Andrejev, "'Anbetung der drei Könige': Alexander I. und seine Idee der Heiligen Allianz," in *Die Heilige Allianz: Entstehung-Wirkung-Rezeption*, ed. Anselm Schubert and Wolfram Pyta (Stuttgart: Kohlhammer, 2018), 19–32.

13. Bartenev, "Razskazy," 79.

14. Bartenev, "Razskazy," 79.

15. Bartenev, "Razskazy," 80.

16. Bartenev, "Razskazy," 80–1.

17. Pleshcheeva graduated in 1791 from the prestigious Smol'nyi Institute for Noble Maidens in St. Petersburg. See N. P. Cherepin, *Imperatorskoe vospitatel'noe obshchetvo blagorodnykh devits*, vol. 1 (St. Petersburg: Gosudarstvennaia Tipografiia, 1914), 286.

18. Steven Kale, *French Salons: High Society and Political Stability from the Old Regime to the Revolution of 1848* (Baltimore: Johns Hopkins University Press, 2004), 21–2.

19. Bartenev, "Razskazy," 81.

20. Also see *Instructions édifiantes sur le jeûne de Jésus-Christ au desert* (Paris: L'imprimerie de Didot L'Aine, 1791); *Réflexions édifiantes* (Paris: L'imprimerie de Didot L'Aine, 1791). On Brohon, see Henri Grégoire, *Histoire des sects réligieuses*, vol. 2 (Paris: Potey, 1814), 1–16; Hannah Adams, *A Dictionary of All Religions and Religious Denominations* (New York: James Eastburn & Company, 1817), 270–3; Alfred Maury, "Des hallucinations de mysticisme chrétien," *Revue des deux mondes*, 2nd ser., 8 (1854): 454–82; Viatte, "Une visionnaire," 336–44; Catherine Maire, "L'abbé Grégoire devant les prophetesses," *Rivista di Storia del Cristianesimo* 4:2 (2007): 411–29; Marc Kolakowski and Francesca Prescendi, "En guise d'introduction 'Victim': un aperçu historique des significations du mot," in *Victimes au féminin*, ed. Francesca Prescendi and Agnes A. Nagy (Geneva: Georg, 2011), 31–3.

21. Robert Southey, "Review of Gregoire's *Histoire des sectes réligieuses*," *Quarterly Review*, 28 (1822): 28–9.

22. Bartenev, "Razskazy," 81–2.

23. Bartenev, "Razskazy," 82.

24. Bartenev, "Razskazy," 82.

25. Charles Eynard, *Vie de Madame de Krudener*, vol. 1 (Paris: Cherbuliez, 1849), 244.

26. Baroness Krüdener (née Vietinghoff, married the Russian diplomat Baron Bourkhardt-Alexis-Constantine Krüdener, of Livonian descent, in 1782. See Eynard, *Vie*, vol. 1, 8–23.

27. Golitsyn to F. K. von Berckheim, Mar. 7, 1829, in "Kniaz' A. N. Golitsyn (v ego pis'makh)," *Russkii arkhiv* 3 (1905): 431.

28. For mention of this unpublished work, see Abram Efros, "Iuliia Kriudener i frantsuzskie pisateli," *Literaturnoe nasledstvo* 33–34 (1939): 118.

29. See the letters from A. N. Golitsyn to A. S. Golitsyna from June 7, 1833, and Mar. 20, 1834, respectively, "Kniaz' A. N. Golitsyn," 412, 415.

30. Golitsyn mentions Lefort in several letters to Berckheim, and it is clear from this correspondence that all are very close. In one letter, dated Nov. 12, 1825, Golitsyn attached a letter to Berckheim from Lefort. Lefort is also mentioned as being in Pleshcheeva's company in letters to Berckheim dated Oct. 11, 1829, and Dec. 1830, in which Lefort is included among the tight-knit circle of Pleshcheeva and Goitsyn. See "Kniaz' A. N. Golitsyn," 428, 436–7.

31. P. D. Markelov was also a regular attendee at Pleshcheeva's salon at this time. He was a member of the Dying Sphinx Lodge and a close confidante of Golitsyn. See Kondakov, *Rozenkreitsery*, 406–16.

32. On Lopukhin's country homes of Savinskoe and Retiazhi, near Moscow and Orel respectively, as literary and philosophical inspirations for both him and Koval'kov, see T. Dragaikina, "Usad'ba kak filosofskii tekst: imeniia I. V. Lopukhina savinskoe i retiazhi," *Kul'tura i tekst* 11 (2008): 234–44.

33. Five books in Koval'kov's name were published between 1811 and 1815: *Plod serdtsa poliubivshego istinu, ili Sobranie kratkikh rassuzhdenii o ee sushchnost, napisannykh plamennoiu k nei liuboviiu* (Moscow: Univ.Tip., 1811); *Iisus pastyr' dobryi svoego stada, svet i kamen', glava, zhrets i zhertva svoei tserkvi* (Orel: Gubern. Tip., 1815); *Mysli o mistike i pisateliakh ee* (Orel: Gubern. Tip., 1815); *Misticheskie tvoreniia Aleksandra Koval'kova*, 3 vols. (Orel: Gubern. Tip, 1815); *Sozdanie tserkvi vnutrennei i tsarstva sveta Vozhiia: Dukhovnye otryvki* (Orel: Gubern. Tip, 1815).

34. See "Posluzhnye spiski po osoboi kantseliarii pri glavnoupravliaiushchem pochtovym departmentom," RGIA, Fond 1074, op. 1, d. 14, 6r.

35. The fact that Pleshcheeva and the Koval'kovs were buried together in the Lazarev Cemetery in St. Petersburg testifies to their extraordinarily close bond. See *Peterburgskii nekropol'*, vol. 2 (St. Petersburg: Tipografiia M. M. Stasiulevicha, 1912), 412. On the close relationship between Pleshcheeva and Koval'kov, see N. K. Shil'der, "Dva donosa v 1831 godu. Vsepoddanneishiia pis'ma M. Magnitskago imperatoru Nikolaiu ob illiuminatakh," *Russkaia starina*, no. 2 (1899), 301.

36. See Francis Ley, *Madame de Krüdener, 1764–1824: Romantisme et Sainte-Alliance* (Paris: Champion, 1994); Debora Sommer, *Eine Baltisch-adlige Missionarin bewegt Europa: Barbara Juliane v. Krüdener* (Göttingen: V&R Unipress, 2013); N. I. Sidorova, "Mistitsizm v russkoi religioznoi kul'ture pervoi chetverti XIX veka" (Kandidatskaia dissertation, Saratov State University 2010); Iu. E. Kondakov, *Kniaz' A. N. Golitsyn: Pridvornyi, chinovnik, khistianin* (St. Petersburg: ElekSis, 2014); E. Iu. Nazarenko, *Kniaz' A. N. Golitsyn v obshchestvenno-politicheskoi i religioznoi istorii rossii pervoi poloviny XIX veka* (Voronezh: Voronezhskii gosudarstvennyi universitet, 2014).

37. C. Ford, *The Life and Letters of Madame de Krudener* (London: Adam and Charles Black, 1893), 309.

38. Golitsyn to Krüdener, Dec. 1822, *Russkii arkhiv*, 388–9.

39. Golitsyn to Krüdener, Sept. 5, 1822, *Russkii arkhiv*, 384.

40. Golitsyn to Krüdener, Nov. 1, 1822, and Jan. 25, 1823, *Russkii arkhiv*, 387–8, 393–4.

41. Golitsyn to Krüdener, May, 30, 1823, *Russkii arkhiv*, 396. A subsequent letter from Golitsyn to Krüdener, written in Dec. 1823, strongly suggests that Koval'kov, at least, visited Kosse. See *Russkii arkhiv*, 399.

42. Ford, *Life and Letters*, 306.

43. Golitsyn to Berckheim, Sept. 10, 1834, *Russkii arkhiv*, 438.

44. For the meeting at Heibronn, see Francis Ley, "Le tsar Alexandre et Mme de Krüdener à Heilbronn, juin 1815," *Etudes Germaniques* 2 (1968): 232–6. For subsequent letters from Krüdener to Emperor Alexander, see Romanov, *Imperator*, vol. 2, 215–26.

45. For a reproduction of the extensive correspondence between Koshelev and Emperor Alexander between 1810 and 1818, see Romanov, *Imperator*, vol. 2, 1–78. On the correspondence between Golitsyn and Alexander between 1807 and 1825, see Romanov, *Imperator*, vol. 1, 527–75.

46. Emperor Alexander I to Golitsyn, Feb. 8, 1821. See N. M. Romanov, *Imperator Aleksandr I opyt istoricheskago* izsledovaniia, vol. 1 (St. Petersburg: Gosudarstvennaia bumaga, 1912), 542. The Emperor seems to have been in possession of Krüdener's copy of Brohon's *Manuel des victims*, which she had requested before her departure for Kosse in 1822. See Romanov, *Imperator*, vol. 1, 572.

47. On the establishment of this colony, see Tat'iana Fadeeva, *Iuzhnyi bereg russkoi aristokratii. Iz istorii osvoeniia krymskogo iuzhnoberezh'ia 1820–1830 gg.* (Moscow: Progress-Traditsiia, 2016).

48. On Bengel and his prediction, see M. D. Isaacs, "The End-Time Calculation of Johann Albrecht Bengel," *Journal of Unification Studies* 11 (2010): 137–66.

49. Fotii, "Avtobiografiia Iur'evskago Arkhimandrita Fotiia," *Russkaia starina*, No. 10 (1895), 196–9. On Gossner's religious mission in Russia, see Kondakov, *Rozenkreitsery*, 303–18.

50. For the minutes of the first meeting of the RBS, see "Zhurnal pervago general'nago sobraniia Sanktpeterburgskago Bibleiskago Obshchestva," RGIA, Fond 808, op. 1, d. no. 2.

51. On the RBS, see Raffaella Faggionato, "From a Society of the Enlightened to the Enlightenment of Society: The Russian Bible Society and Rosicrucianism in the Age of Alexander I," *Slavonic and East European Review* 79:3 (2001): 459–87; G. V. Velikanov, "Rossiiskoe Bibleiskoe Obshchestvo kak iavlenie dukhovnoi zhizni," *Gosudarstvo, religiia, tserkov' v Rossii i za rubezhom* 1:2 (2006): 108–44; Stephen K. Batalden, *Russian Bible Wars: Modern Scriptural Translation and Cultural Authority* (Cambridge: Cambridge University Press, 2013), 12–40.

52. "S.-Peterburgskie slukhi, izvestiia i anekdoty," in *Pis'ma glavneishikh deiatelei v tsarstvovanie Imperatora Aleksandra I (c 1807–1829 god)*, ed. N. Dubrovin (St. Petersburg: Imperial Academy of Sciences, 1883), 85–6. Dubrovin suggests that the writer was Jacques de Saint-Glin, the chief of the Secret Department of the Police.

53. V. K. Kochubei, A. K. Razumovskii, and Z. I. Karneev were all members of the RBS and the Rosicrucians. See Faggionato, "From a Society of the Enlightened," 462.

54. For the edict banning Freemasonry and "all secret societies," see *Polnoe sobranie zakonov Rossiiskoi Imperii*, vol. 38 (St. Petersburg: Tipografiia II Otdeleniia, 1830), 579–80.

8

The Prophetess Madame Bouche and the Triune of Emperor Alexander, A. N. Golitsyn, and R. A. Koshelev, 1810–1822

ON MARCH 21, 1817, a 57-year-old woman, Thérèse-Marguerite Bouche (1759–after 1822), who had been raised in Avignon and was living in Marseille at the time, penned a letter to Emperor Alexander I of Russia.[1] Bouche saw herself as a prophetess, and her letter to the Russian monarch sought to convey her grand plan to enable him to be "the instrument of Providence," which would "render immortal Y[our] I[mperial] M[ajesty]." She foresaw that Emperor Alexander, who possessed "heroic qualities" equal to Alexander the Great and Julius Caesar, was "the only one" able to "complete the happiness of France [and] establish calm and peace in Europe."[2] This flattering letter was followed by another, in which Bouche beseeched the emperor not to ignore her message. In her first epistle Bouche had called herself a "lowly individual," but now she added that "this is not the first time that weak creatures have served . . . to make His will known to men" and proclaimed that "the mission of the prophet should not be doubted unless one wants to close one's eyes entirely to the obvious." She then implores the emperor "not to reject the Lord's mission" as "the Almighty has cast his eyes on you to begin the reformation he wants to bring to the earth."[3]

It is entirely predictable that Emperor Alexander's triumphant vanquishing of Napoleon in 1814 and his subsequent espousal of the Holy Alliance in 1815 would have been keenly observed by a visionary such as Bouche. After all, Krüdener had gained considerable fame in 1815 by promoting her own vision of the Russian monarch's grand mission.[4] Moreover, in 1816 a humble farm labourer, Thomas Martin of Gallardon, had created a sensation in France with his prophecies regarding Louis XVIII, who granted him an audience.[5]

Initiating the Millennium. Robert Collis, and Natalie Bayer, Oxford University Press (2020) © Oxford University Press.
DOI: 10.1093/oso/9780190903374.001.0001

It is not known whether Emperor Alexander read these two extraordinary letters in 1817. However, by October 10, 1819, Bouche had set sail from Honfleur in Normandy destined for St. Petersburg. She and her travel companion, a cabinetmaker from Marseille named Dubié, had obtained passports, letters of recommendation, and 1200 francs in travel expenses from C. A. Pozzo di Borgo, the Russian ambassador in Paris. Bouche was to remain in the Russian capital for two years. During this time, she enjoyed the intimate confidence of a "holy triune"—Emperor Alexander, A. N. Golitsyn, and R. A. Koshelev—who, it seems, secretly kept her close at hand to be able to readily consult Heaven for divinely-inspired advice.[6]

We would probably know nothing about Bouche's career as a prophetess in France and Russia were it not for the extensive surveillance of her activities by the French authorities between 1819 and 1822. The sheer volume of documents contained in the dossier devoted to Bouche in the archive of the Police Générale in Paris—a veritable treasure trove—is testament to the significance attached to her activities at the time by the Ministry of the Interior.[7] Almost as stunning as the exploits of Bouche in France and Russia is our lack of awareness about this fascinating and consequential episode in European history. In the two centuries since Bouche arrived in St. Petersburg, the sum of historical writing about her life and influence effectively amounts to a two-page, unreferenced magazine article by G. de Bertier de Sauvigny, published in 1960.[8] As informative as the article is, it is high time a thorough study of this visionary was conducted, as she was arguably far more influential in shaping the religious imagination of Emperor Alexander than Krüdener or anyone else in the years after his triumphant victory over Napoleon.

In truth, the French authorities were caught unprepared in 1819. Their sudden burst of activity only occurred once Bouche had already set sail for Russia on October 10.[9] No doubt frustrated by Bouche being out of his grasp, the interior minister, Élie Decazes, ordered the collation of all prior documents related to the prophetess, as well as reports about her activities in Russia. Decazes's agents performed a hasty information-gathering exercise, which soon uncovered a lengthy paper trail. Unbeknownst to Decazes, it transpired that his ministry had been alerted about the activities of Bouche as recently as September 12 by Armand Jahan de Belleville, the newly appointed prefect of the Hautes-Pyrénées region.

In Jahan's despatch to Paris he describes in detail his two encounters with Bouche in his office in Tarbes. The first meeting took place at the end of April 1819, only a matter of weeks after Jahan had assumed office. On this occasion, Jahan seems to have taken Bouche for a local madwoman, as her husband was employed in the spa village of Barèges in the Pyrenees. He recounts verbatim Bouche's description of her spiritual awakening in a church in Marseille, when the "great secret was revealed" to her. According to Jahan, Bouche proclaimed to him that despite being a "weak and unworthy creature," she had been chosen by God to be the instigator of a concert of four rulers—Pope Pius VII; Charles IV, the former king of Spain; Louis XVIII; and the Russian Emperor—who will "save the world from the terrible danger that threatens it." Yet up until 1819 Bouche confessed that she felt like she had been "working in vain." Pius VII had been forewarned against her initiative during his exile in Savona between 1809 and 1812, and Charles IV had died and was "guilty of abandoning the throne." Moreover, the French king "did not believe and did not want to believe" in Bouche's mission. Bouche had therefore come to pin her hopes solely on the Russian emperor and informed Jahan that "the voice of God enjoins me to persevere."

Jahan may have been inclined to dismiss his initial meeting with Bouche in 1819 as an odd aberration in his normal business in Tarbes. However, such a feeling would have been misguided, as the prophetess visited him again on September 11 with bona fide proof of her links to and favour of the imperial court in St. Petersburg. On this second visit Bouche was accompanied by Dubié, who was in his thirties and whom she described as "the son of one of my friends in Avignon." According to Bouche, the elder Dubié was also able to hear the voice of Heaven, as she did.[10] Moreover, the prophetess also confided to Jahan that there was "a third person associated with this great mystery," who she reveals is none other than Joseph Ferrier, "an old Jesuit and very aged" who now lived in Marseille. The prefect provided no further information about Ferrier at this juncture. However, the French authorities did not overlook this link between Bouche and one of the former members of the Council of Seven of the Illuminés d'Avignon.

Indeed, an unnamed police lieutenant in Marseille compiled a report on Ferrier only four days after Jahan's despatch. The officer provides a brief biographical sketch of Ferrier, noting that he hailed from Arles and once belonged to the Jesuit order. The report also states that Ferrier taught a class in Latinity in Arles until "approximately ten years ago."[11] At this time, Ferrier was "noted for his exaggerated ideas on the subject of religion." More specifically, the lieutenant emphasizes that "he was distinguished by his preoccupation with the prophecies of St. Caesarius [of Arles] found in the archives of the Church of St. Trophime." This assertion is affirmed in a report marked "highly confidential," which was relayed to the prefect of the Bouches-Rhone region in Marseille on January 26, 1820. This despatch repeats that Ferrier was well known in Arles in the first decade of the nineteenth century for predictions and, crucially, "for finding an explication in the prophecies of St. Caesarius for all political events" that had recently occurred.

It would seem that Ferrier turned to the most revered Church Father of Arles for prophetic inspiration after the fall of Cappelli. This is easy to understand when one reads Caesarius's prophecies, several of which were published after the Bourbon Restoration in 1814. One prophecy, for example, seems to foresee the spoliation and chaos the beset France during the Revolution: "The administrators of this kingdom shall be so blinded, that they shall leave it without defenders. The hand of God shall extend itself over them, and over all the rich. All the nobles shall be deprived of their estates and their dignities."[12] Ferrier would surely have viewed Pope Pius VII's imprisonment by Napoleon in Savona, between 1809 and 1812, as further validation of the realisation of another of Caesarius's ancient prophecies: "Then all the churches will be defiled and profaned . . . There will be no king in France and no Pope in Rome. Whoever governs the whole church will change his seat . . . and eat the bread of pain in this valley of tears."[13]

The author of the report on Ferrier was in no doubt that Ferrier's enthusiastic espousal of Caesarius's prophecies was "the source of the revelations that Dame Bouche pretends to have received." This assertion was strengthened by evidence that had recently been obtained during an interrogation of a former acquaintance of Ferrier and Bouche in Marseille. In a report of this interrogation, a certain Monsieur Capure is cited as referring to Ferrier as "a man of genius, a profound meditator [and] a heroic character," who travelled to visit Pope Pius VII in Savona in around 1811, but had been arrested by the governor overseeing the pontiff's imprisonment in the Episcopal Palace. In a letter written shortly after his interrogation, Capure informed the authorities that Ferrier had undertaken his trip to Savona in order to "inform [the Pope] of Madame Bouche's visions." In both his interrogation and his subsequent letter, Capure also asserted that Ferrier made a trip to Rome on behalf of Bouche. This journey apparently had a dual purpose. First, Ferrier once again tried to secure an audience with the Pope. Once again, he did not succeed, but according to Capure, he did communicate his mission to Cardinal Ercole Gonsalvi, the pontiff's secretary. Second, Ferrier was charged with relaying Bouche's mission, based on her visions, to Charles IV, the former king of Spain, who settled in the Eternal City in 1812. Curiously, Charles IV and his wife had resided for the previous three years in Marseille. In his testimony, Capure claims that Bouche was a frequent visitor to the couple's home, where the king's wife, Maria Luisa of Parma, "especially honoured her with a particular benevolence."

We only have Capure's testimony in regard to whether Ferrier undertook a mission to Rome. However, the French authorities did unearth corroborating evidence to back up Capure's claim that Ferrier did indeed journey to Savona at the end of 1810. The paper trail discovered by the authorities led back to December 11, 1810, when the commissioner-general of police in Savona filed a report to his seniors in Marseille, regarding Ferrier's suspicious conduct in the city. Ferrier was asked directly whether he had seen the Pope, to which he replied negatively. In a second despatch, sent on January 23, 1811, the commissioner-general added extra detail. This included the fact that General César Berthier, the governor of the Episcopal Palace in Savona, had been the first to report Ferrier's suspicious activity in the vicinity of the pope's residence. Berthier deemed Ferrier sufficiently troublesome that he had him arrested and transported back to Marseille. Thus Capure's account from 1820 is entirely consistent with this official account from the time of Ferrier's brief stay in Savona.

On returning to Marseille, Ferrier was interrogated by the local police. When questioned about the reason for his eight-day stay in Savona, Ferrier protested that it was simply due to passport issues. He claimed that he intended to travel to Genoa to procure financial help from several notable families. This explanation was deemed satisfactory by the authorities in Marseille at the time. Although the police were unable to uncover any direct evidence that Ferrier had had an audience with the Pope, they were able to glean valuable biographical information during his cross-examination. Of particular interest was the fact that Ferrier had first become a resident in Marseille shortly after May 1810, when he retired from his post as a professor of Latinity at the *école secondaire* in Arles. The timing of his relocation to Marseille is significant, as it coincides with the dawn of Bouche's grand spiritual mission. In other words, this tallies with the opinion of the police lieutenant and Capure's testimony vis-à-vis Ferrier's pivotal role in encouraging Bouche's career as a prophetess.

Ferrier, a former lawyer, was able to successfully convince the authorities in Marseille, in 1811, that his journey to Savona was entirely innocent. In all likelihood, the police at the time were ignorant of his links to the prophetess Bouche and her grand mission. However, the authorities in Marseille conducted a much more thorough and informed background check of both Ferrier and Bouche in 1820. This was born of necessity as they scrambled to answer the urgent dispatches of their superiors in Paris following Bouche's arrival in Russia. Indeed, Decazes was furious and embarrassed at the incompetence of his officials, and he entrusted two of the finest bloodhounds in his ministry, *sieurs* Vincent and Darcourt, to gather up all morsels of information about the elusive prophetess. The documents and testimony they obtained in 1820 are extraordinary.

It soon came to light that, in 1813, Bouche was already well-known to the authorities in Paris and Marseille, owing to a series of letters she penned to Napoleon and A.-J. Savary, his interior minister. Her principal claim was that she had a project that, if executed, would render the emperor "seven times stronger than he had become by his conquests and of which I guarantee its success." Bouche's bold claims were met with scorn by Savary, who warned her that she would enjoy the emperor's hospitality in one of his notorious asylums if she did not desist in sending unsolicited epistles.

The police in Paris, Marseille, and Avignon also conducted a flurry of interviews with individuals they deemed to be in possession of valuable information concerning Bouche's activities. Many of those interrogated seem to have relished the chance to sully her reputation. Indeed, Capure confirmed that Bouche had many enemies in Marseille and Avignon. One such foe was a certain Monsieur Dandé, who claimed that Bouche was "at the head of a sect of *illuminés*." He had no qualms about telling the police a scurrilous anecdote about how Bouche had gathered her neophytes one night, and after the usual ceremonies, the male and female initiates retired into adjacent boudoirs to fulfil their carnal desires.

Dubié's uncle, J.-A Dubié, also seems to have had a vitriolic hatred of Bouche. According to him, Bouche had, over three decades earlier, been one of the first initiates into Grabianka's sect of *illuminés*. Dubié also claims that Bouche had collaborated with Dr. Bouge in Avignon to continue the sect after Grabianka's departure. Apart from emphasizing her links to the sect of *illuminés* in Avignon, J.-A. Dubié testified that Bouche left Avignon after the exiled Charles IV of Spain had taken up residence in Marseille at the end of 1808. According to him, Bouche "managed to insinuate herself at the king and queen's house," and she received three thousand francs to help her daughter.

Dubié Sr. labels Bouche "an intriguer," who "passes herself off as a saint," and who has "regular conversations with God and the Holy Virgin." If this was not damning enough he brands Bouche "a dangerous woman" who "must be locked up for life." He also paints an unflattering physical description of Bouche—a "big, fat" woman with "shady eyes."

Lastly, Agricol Moreau, the Jacobin *procureur général* in Avignon during the Terror, and later in the Vaucluse department, also asserted that Bouche was the head of an "association of *illuminés*" that was directly linked with Grabianka's earlier sect.[14] He attested that "nobody knows of [her] intriguing more than me, because at the time I was the public prosecutor in Vaucluse." Moreau goes so far as to suggest that "three-fifths of the inhabitants of Avignon" knew of her schemes. At this point, he brings up a personal rivalry with J.-M. Verger, a fellow lawyer, who did indeed have links with Grabianka at the turn of the nineteenth century (see chapter 5), whose embrace of the illuministic sect he claims to find revolting. As an example of his colleague's offensive conduct, he says that it was Verger who recommended Bouche to Charles IV in Marseille, which tallies with Dubié's testimony.

Is there any basis to these lurid accusations against Bouche, many of which concerned events nearly three decades in the past? Her name does not surface in the extant correspondence of known *illuminés* between 1787 and 1791. Furthermore, the cache of documents produced by the Russian authorities in 1807, after Grabianka's arrest of, do not contain any explicit references to Bouche. Nonetheless, a single baptismal record from the Saint-Agricol parish in Avignon, dated April 18, 1791, confirms the links between Bouche, Grabianka, and other *illuminés*. The previous morning Madame Bouche had given birth to a son, who was christened Thadée-Marie-Raphael-Gabriel Bouche. The choice of names is highly suggestive in itself, but the baptismal record also notes that the godfather was none other than "Thadée Leszczyc Grabianka . . . gouverneur de la province de Live," and the godmother is named as Charlotte Corberon. The document also contains the signatures of Baron Corberon and Bouge as witnesses.[15] Here we are presented with unquestionable proof that Bouche had established a close bond with Grabianka, Bouge, and the Corberons by April 1791, some twenty-eight years before her arrival in St. Petersburg.

A decade later Bouche is mentioned in flattering terms in a letter from Verger to J.-B. Willermoz, the famous illuminist-mason, in Lyon. One of Bouche's sons is travelling to Lyon for his health, and Verger is effectively providing an introduction for him to Willermoz. Bouche Jr. is described as the "son of one of our good friends." What is more, he hails from a family that "believes what you believe, who expects what you expect." In other words, Bouche and Willermoz share the same religious worldview. This is the same letter that mentions that Ferrier and Richardière are also journeying to Lyon with the young Bouche.[16] Verger wrote again to Willermoz on November 29, 1801. In this letter we learn that Bouche's son is being treated by Willermoz's nephew Dr. Pierre-Claude-Catherin Willermoz, who was not optimistic about his patient's chance of recovery. Verger goes on to inform Willermoz that Madame Bouche intended to be by her son's side in Lyon and that "she will have the advantage of seeing you." He adds "I am sure that if you needed a new reason to take an interest in her child, you would certainly find it in your knowledge of the mother."[17]

In other words, Moreau was not mistaken in linking Verger with Bouche and other *illuminés*. Moreover, this letter provides evidence of a continued illuministic milieu in Avignon at the turn of the nineteenth century, which included Bouche. She certainly maintained close to the schismatists Ferrier and Richardière into 1801, but it is not known whether she also retained links to Grabianka.

Whatever the case, by 1810 Bouche was effectively the heiress to the prophetic tradition championed by the *illuminés* in Berlin, Avignon, and St. Petersburg. It seems to have been around this time that she first began to articulate her grand vision of a concert of four rulers who would save the world from a terrible danger. Bouche also used her prophetic gift to communicate directly with the Sainte Parole, taking on the mantle bequeathed by the likes of Brumore, Bouge, and Cappelli.

This inheritance is on display in a series of questions posed to the Holy Word, alongside the corresponding responses. These documents, which date from 1817 and 1818, demonstrate that Bouche followed in Cappelli's footsteps, in terms of believing that she possessed an inspired ability to act as a conduit between the divine and earthly realms. In the summer of 1817, for example, she asked Sainte Parole a number of questions on behalf of individuals who wanted to know whether they had been "called to this holy union?" Two enquiries were transmitted on behalf of the Marquise de Lespinay, who was married to the *conseiller général* for the Vendée.[18] In August she also beseeched the Holy Word to "deign to give me instruction to inform me if M[onsieur] Blanchet is called to this holy union?"[19]

Bouche also entreated the Holy Word for advice for herself on various matters. On February 1, 1818, for example, she begged her "divine master, whilst prostrating herself before the Eucharist" how she should be reprimanded for an undisclosed misdemeanour. Bouche's priest confessor had apparently "suspended [her] from approaching the holy table." The response she received from the Holy Word, as with all the answers, are largely impenetrable and convoluted. The key message from the Holy Word on this occasion was to "obey the ministers of my church."[20]

Yet Bouche's role as a divinely inspired mediator between the faithful and the Holy Word in the 1810s, as well as her involvement in the Avignon Society in the 1790s and her continued links to Ferrier, do not explain how she entered into the orbit of Emperor Alexander I. Notwithstanding Ferrier's importance in promoting Bouche as a prophetess in the 1810s, he was not in a position to act as a conduit to the Russian Imperial court. This role was played by the dukes Eugen-Friedrich (1758–1822) and Ferdinand of Württemberg. The latter had been an ardent devotee of the Illuminés d'Avignon for a time between late 1788 and the end of 1790.[21] The brothers were the uncles of Emperor Alexander on his mother's side, and they enjoyed close ties with the imperial court in St. Petersburg.[22] Significantly, at the close of his dispatch of September 12, 1819, Jahan informed the interior minister that "Prince Eugène of Wurtemberg, the uncle, I think, of the Emperor of Russia" had written to Ferrier, whom he referred to as his "brother in J. C.," about Bouche's impending voyage. The prefect had also seen a letter from Bouche to the prince in which she also referred to him as a "brother in J. C." In other words, he was part of this "mystical association" uncovered by the French authorities.

The links between Bouche and the dukes of Württemberg had already been established by the summer of 1817, when both Bouche and Ferdinand were residing in Marseille.[23] This is confirmed by a fascinating question Bouche asked the Holy Word on August 2, 1817: "*Ste Parole*, deign to tell me if Duke Eugène of Württemberg, who received his brother's letter and replied to it and whose sentiments he is updating is designed to give us the assurance that this is a person who your divine providence was seeking in Carlsruhe in Prussian Silesia, near Rumslau on June 18, 1817." The response written down by Bouche is equally interesting:

> Do not doubt that Eugène, whose family was blessed by his brother's faith, whose delay caused by the common enemy made you miss this beloved one by a quarter of an hour in Marseille . . . I have the power to draw good from evil itself and this brother belongs to me and his brother by this circumstance will be instructed instead and will serve me even more to hasten what God wants in might.[24]

This communication with the Holy Word indicates that at Bouche's behest Ferdinand had written to his brother at his family estate of Carlsruhe in Silesia.[25] The response also suggests that Bouche, who moved to Barèges in the Hautes-Pyrénées around this time, was frustrated at not meeting Eugen-Friedrich prior to her departure and sought reassurance.

That Eugen-Friedrich would be drawn to a prophetess such as Bouche is entirely consistent with his long-held illuminist outlook. In 1784, for example, he published *Die Wichtigkeit der Christus-Religion*, which cites Lavater on the title page: "It is a great wisdom to see Christ in every blade of grass!"[26] In the same year he published a Masonic work in which, as Rudolf Schlögl has noted, Pietism and Rosicrucianism merged into a barely distinguishable single component.[27] Moreover, in July 1786 he responded to an essay published in the *Berlinische Monatsschrift* by Elisa von der Recke. It was the opening salvo of her attack on Count Cagliostro, whom she accused of being a charlatan. Among other things, she renounced the count's purported ability to conjure up spirits, which she had witnessed first-hand in Mitau in 1779.[28] In response, Eugen-Friedrich did not defend Cagliostro, but did affirm the existence of spirits. In arguing against Recke's critique of "mystics, enthusiasts and ghost seers," Eugen-Friedrich concluded his essay by citing Hamlet: "There are more things in heaven and earth . . . than are dreamt of in your philosophy."[29] The Comte de Mirabeau, who undertook a diplomatic mission to Berlin in 1786 and 1787, provides a striking portrait of Eugen-Friedrich at this time: "He has lived in Paris and plunged into the *baquet* of Mesmer. He afterwards professed to be a somnambulist . . . These different masquerades accompanied and concealed the real object of his ambition and his fervour, which is to give credit to the sect of *illuminés* of whom he is one of the most enthusiastic chiefs."[30] The passing of the years does not seem to have altered his worldview in any discernible manner.

Several other references to Eugen-Friedrich can be found in the early reports pertaining to Bouche, which were hastily compiled following Jahan's initial despatch.[31] Yet an initial despatch by the police deputies assigned by Decazes to investigate the Bouche affair, written on January 22, 1820, simply confirmed that Bouche had communicated with Emperor Alexander via "the intermediation of a prince of the House of Württemberg." In a despatch written on February 4, 1820, the prefect of Bouches-du-Rhône clarified that it was Ferdinand, not Eugen-Friedrich, who was a resident of Marseille.[32] Indeed, at the time this report was written, Ferdinand, a Protestant, was a notable participant in religious discussions in Marseille organised by the Catholic Missionaries of Provence.[33]

Ferdinand of Württemberg may have become disillusioned with the machinations of his fellow *illuminés* in Avignon by 1791. Nevertheless, nearly three decades later he evidently still retained a religious enthusiasm that was susceptible to the clarion calls of millenarian visionaries. Ferrier may well have played the role of spiritual mentor to Bouche in Marseille, but it was the aristocratic pedigree of Ferdinand and Eugen-Friedrich that unquestionably brought her to the attention of their nephew, the Russian emperor, in St. Petersburg.

At some point in the summer of 1819 Bouche received word that Alexander I was willing to accept her instruction in the Russian capital. By the time of her second meeting with Jahan in Tarbes, on September 11, 1819, all necessary arrangements had been made. In his report of the following day, Jahan informed his superiors in Paris that Bouche would be leaving for the capital in two days. Once in Paris, she was to receive all things necessary for her travel to St. Petersburg from Pozzo di Borgio, the Russian ambassador. This may well have seemed like an unlikely cock-and-bull story to Jahan had it not been for the fact that Bouche was able to corroborate her account by showing a letter from A. N. Golitsyn. A similar account is given by Capure in February 1820, who had known Bouche in Marseille. He recalled that in late September his wife had encountered Bouche by chance while strolling in the Tuileries Garden. At a subsequent dinner in the Capures' home, Bouche informed them that "an invisible voice . . . had recently instructed" her that Emperor Alexander was "destined to accomplish the work of the Lord."

On receiving Jahan's report, Decazes instructed the head of police in Paris to enquire whether Bouche and Dubié had indeed arrived in the capital, and whom they may have met. The police officials assigned to this task reported back that they had found no trace of Bouche and Dubié in the city. This dearth of evidence led Decazes to question Jahan about whether he had been duped. Faced with a sceptical boss and sensing a threat to his integrity, Jahan fired off three despatches in quick succession, on October 6, 12, and 16, which not only confirmed the veracity of his initial report, but also provided fresh details about their journey. However, by the time the interior minister in Paris received these reports, Bouche and Dubié were en route to St. Petersburg, having departed the capital on October 1.

Bouche and Dubié arrived in Petersburg on November 2, 1819. We know this as the dossier complied by the French police at the time contains a series of reports by Jahan, which he wrote between January and August 1820, as well as letters sent to him by Bouche. These reports and letters provide invaluable insights into Bouche's residence in Russia. Jahan's first report, written on January 9, was based on a letter Bouche wrote to him on November 20, 1819, that is, seventeen days after her arrival in Russia. We learn that Bouche and Dubié resided with Golitsyn after their arrival and that he gave them "a very good welcome" and put a carriage and servants at their disposal. Bouche also disclosed that she was first presented to Emperor Alexander on November 7, who accorded her an audience of two hours. The Russian sovereign apparently asked many good questions, but Bouche declared that she would not divulge the details of their spiritual conversation, which, nonetheless, had given her much satisfaction.

Jahan's second report, written on February 2, 1820, documents what appears to be a burgeoning relationship between Bouche and Emperor Alexander. He recounts Bouche's description of her last audience with the monarch, which apparently went from seven o'clock until eleven o'clock in the morning. At this meeting, the emperor insisted that Bouche sit on a canapé, whilst he sat on a simple chair, as she was his "spiritual superior and God commands me to treat you so." Bouche added that the emperor confided that he had had a revelation during a previous night. No detail is provided, other than that it had prompted the emperor to write to the French king.

Jahan penned two more reports in quick succession—on February 4 and 20, 1820—in response to two remarkable letters that Bouche had written to him at the end of 1819. In the first letter, written on December 29, 1819, Bouche confides in Jahan that she enjoys three or four audiences a week with the emperor and is ushered into his presence through a secret passageway. In the second (undated) letter, Bouche informs Jahan that she had relocated to a hotel, where she was graced with the company of Golitsyn and Koshelev for several hours each day. Her new abode—in the Hotel de Londres—was located at the corner of Nevskii Prospekt and Admiralty Square, that is, little more than a stone's throw from the Winter Palace.[34]

Both letters by Bouche were principally concerned with providing a detailed description of an extraordinary ceremony involving the emperor that took place after the celebration of three rites of Communion on December 25, 1819 (Christmas Day) in "one of the halls of the Imperial Palace."[35] All three masses were "celebrated in the greatest secrecy," the first two according to the Orthodox rite, and the last according to the Roman rite. Of the two Orthodox ceremonies, the emperor was the sole participant in one, and Golitsyn and Koshelev were the only worshippers in the other. Lastly, the Catholic rite was celebrated by Bouche and Dubié. Bouche wrote to Jahan that Orthodox theologians had been consulted and that they had deliberated and approved of her conducting the liturgical rites in place of a cleric.

Yet, these three exceptional masses were merely a preliminary to the main event: the emperor's formal acceptance of his "grand mission," whereby he would bring about the fulfilment of the divine command Bouche had received to unite the Christian flock in order to save the world from "frightful danger." The ceremony involved Bouche handing the emperor a small gold box, suspended by a metal chain, which apparently contained, or indeed constituted, the great secret. The emperor lowered himself onto his knees and took a candle in his hand. Then, Bouche "standing, and with the solemn attitude of a person charged with a grand mission, handed the little gold box to H[is] M[ajesty], who received it with an intoxication and a piety that is difficult to describe. His Majesty got up and kissed the hand of Madame Bouche." Jahan adds that Bouche herself wore one of these gold boxes on a chain around her neck, but hid it under her clothing.

In essence, Alexander's acceptance of the "grand mission" at the close of 1819 reflects his continued wish to realise the grandiose aims of the Holy Alliance of 1815. He saw himself as an agent who, as the sovereign of Russia, was able to usher in an era of peace and justice based on the sublime truths of the "Holy Religion of our Saviour."[36] However, the rather confusing legalese employed in the formal act of the Holy Alliance was clearly not inspired by celestial forces. Moreover, the Holy Alliance had been ridiculed by the British foreign secretary, Viscount Castlereagh, who referred to it as a "piece of sublime mysticism and nonsense."[37] Even Metternich, the Austrian foreign minister, whose sovereign did sign the treaty, dismissed its wording as "this loud sounding [of] nothing."[38] Such derogatory responses help to explain Alexander's willingness to believe in Bouche's mission, which seemingly offered divine confirmation of his special role via the direct intercession of a prophetic intermediary.

The earliest extant letter in the police dossier from Bouche in Petersburg to Jahan is dated January 31, 1820. As might be expected, the tone of the letter is decidedly mystical and cryptic. Bouche informs Jahan that she had been instructed by God to write to him to reveal that "the great man who made me come to him [i.e. Emperor Alexander] was not surprised when he had all the knowledge, since God made him march the same way" and that "all the operations were in harmony." Bouche does not divulge what this knowledge is, or anything about the nature of the harmonious operations, but she does disclose that "all we have left to do is to guard the secret of this great and important affair." Although Jahan was not yet privy to this secret knowledge, Bouche promised to instruct him "when our august sovereign is educated." Indeed, she hints that she has instructed two others in addition to the emperor, when she adds that "the three veritable friends . . . nominated by Heaven [have] the advantage of being a little more educated in his Holy Work." Evidently only the emperor, Golitsyn, and Koshelev, who referred to themselves as a triune, had been granted access to the secret knowledge possessed by Bouche.

Jahan issued a flurry of reports, in April 1820, based on letters sent by Madame Bouche in March to himself and to her husband. The French prophetess was at this time at the height of her powers among her trinity of devotees, seeing the emperor four times a week and Koshelev and Golitsyn, who "show her a lot of veneration," daily. In a letter to her husband, written on March 10, Bouche even explained that she had been commanded by Heaven to reprimand the emperor for an undisclosed misdemeanour. The sovereign granted her an audience and asked to drink a glass of rum before receiving his dressing down, which he apparently accepted with "humility and redoubled veneration." This letter also contains the first mention of two important and interrelated diplomatic initiatives, which were instigated as a direct result of Bouche's mission to instruct the emperor of his divine duty to fulfil his grand mission—namely, to achieve Christian unity among the sovereign heads of Europe's continental powers. First, Bouche relayed to her husband that she, Golitsyn, and Koshelev had decided in a conference to send Dubié on an important, but as yet unspecified, mission. Second, Bouche informed her husband that the emperor had written to the Duc de Richelieu, the French prime minister, in regard to "the accomplishment of the work of God," and that "His Majesty had received very satisfactory answers." Here we find the first references to practical initiatives being undertaken to realise the emperor's "grand mission."

It was at this time that the French ambassador in St. Petersburg, Auguste, Comte de La Ferronnays, sent a confidential despatch to Paris vis-à-vis the emperor's attraction to mysticism. He wrote that the emperor had been heavily influenced by Golitsyn and Koshelev since 1812. According to Ferronnays, the emperor's soul had been imbued with the spirit of liberalism and half-scepticism during his education. The events of 1812–1814 had jolted him from this state of mind, but neither Orthodoxy nor Catholicism was able to satisfy his spirit. Hence he found "in the doctrine of Mde de Krudener a religion according to his heart." No mention is made of Bouche, but Ferronnays describes the malevolent influence of Golitsyn and of Koshelev, who professed to receive visions from the Blessed Virgin. In one of these visions, according to Ferronnays, the Blessed Virgin proclaimed that Koshelev would soon receive 120,000 roubles from a young and handsome prince. Alexander apparently recognised himself in this portrait and duly fulfilled the prediction.[39]

Although Bouche believed that the Russian emperor had been chosen by God to accomplish great things, as we have already seen, she was not afraid to scold the monarch. This tendency is most starkly illustrated in a report produced by Jahan on June 6, based on a letter written by Bouche on April 24. Bouche describes experiencing two revelations that led her to reproach the emperor concerning recent domestic events: the expulsion of the Jesuits from the Russian Empire and the divorce of Grand Duke Konstantin, the emperor's brother.

On June 27, 1820, Jahan wrote yet another report based on two letters by Bouche, sent on May 6 and 18. His summary reveals a growing preoccupation with Dubié's upcoming mission. We learn, for example, that Bouche's companion was preparing to depart for "Berlin, Vienna and Paris, charged with a grand matter." Indeed, in recognition of the importance of this undertaking, Bouche envisaged Dubié presenting medals as a token of gratitude to all those who responded favourably to his message. These talismanic medals were the same as those apparently worn next to the heart by Alexander, Golitsyn, and

Koshelev. Bouche also underlines the seriousness of Dubié's mission by stressing that the three friends (Alexander, Golitsyn, and Koshelev) had prayed in the greatest secrecy for him "so that God and the Holy Mother may give him "strength to triumph over hell and the force to succeed in a matter that will secure peace on earth."

It would be another month before Dubié finally set out on his mission. His departure was confirmed by Bouche on June 18, 1820, in a letter to two confidantes in Tarbes. This letter was passed on to Jahan, who dutifully relayed its contents to the interior minister. Bouche wrote: "My son Dubié left yesterday, filled with the grace of Heaven, as well as from the three friends [Emperor Alexander, Golitsyn, and Koshelev], who saw him leave with the pain of pure friendship in God, but triumphant with hope for a reunion from his majestic voyage." Indeed, Bouche added that "the respectable friend who is aged 71 [Koshelev] had the goodness to delay his departure to the country by 28 days to be here for Dubié." Both Koshelev and Golitsyn are lavishly praised in this letter, as Bouche comments on the satisfaction, confidence, friendship, and veneration that she receives daily from "these virtuous personages." Judging by Bouche's letter, it appears that Koshelev and Golitsyn showered her with gifts, which they sent in a carriage, and provided her with domestic servants. The only inconvenience for Bouche in Petersburg at this time may well have been the continued insistence of her hosts that she remain incognito.

The first seven months of Bouche's residence in Petersburg, culminating in Dubié's departure, undoubtedly constitutes the period of her greatest influence over the Russian emperor. Shortly after Dubié embarked on his mission, the emperor also left Petersburg, only to return on May 24, 1821. Alexander's long sojourn outside Russia was primarily the result of his attending the Congress of Troppau (Ostrava), held between October and November 1820, and the Congress of Laibach (Ljubljana), which convened between January and May 1821. In her last letter to Jahan, which he documented in a report on August 29, 1820, Bouche wrote that the emperor's absence had led to "a suspension of affairs, which will resume on his return." She also wrote that she was still being treated with the same care and respect, and that she did not envisage leaving Russia before another year had passed. This prediction turned out to be true; she only left Petersburg in November 1821. However, there was to be no resumption of "affairs." Bouche was denied further audiences with the emperor on his return from Ljubljana.

It would seem the origins of the emperor's displeasure with Bouche can, in large measure, be traced to Dubié's secretive mission. According to a report by Jahan, written on October 29, 1820, Dubié's visit to Berlin had been a complete success, and he was en route to Paris, where he planned to meet Richelieu. Dubié's arrival in Paris in November was confirmed by the city police. However, by January 1821 Dubié had returned to Marseille, where he was soon interviewed by the police there. The resulting report indicated that Dubié claimed that he had communicated the details of the mission he had been entrusted with to K. A. von Hardenberg in Berlin and to Metternich in Vienna, as well as obtaining an audience with Richelieu in Paris. Official diplomatic records, perhaps unsurprisingly, contain no acknowledgement of any such meetings between the lowly Dubié and three of Europe's most powerful ministers.

We learn by far the most about Dubié's mission and Emperor Alexander's vexation at how he conducted himself in a long letter written by the Russian sovereign to Golitsyn in February 1821, written from the Congress of Laibach. Written over the course of a week, the emperor felt it necessary at this time to vent his deep sense of frustration and embarrassment at Dubié's conduct:

> When it came to sending Dubié to Berlin, you will remember how much I was against this trip: I felt inside me something that told me that it was not good. Finally, by deference to the opinions of M. Koshelev and yourself, I ended up no longer opposing this departure; however, I had demanded that there should be no mention of me in the negotiations that Dubié intended to conduct.[40]

The emperor describes trying to ease his doubts by reasoning that Dubié would succeed "if it is a work of God," in which case he would be "the first to admit" that his inner feelings had failed him. Initially, Alexander had been comforted by letters he received from Golitsyn, who informed him that Dubié had boasted of being very well received by the Prussian king "and of being very happy with the results of his conversations with him." The news had reassured Alexander, and he admits that he was "ready to believe myself guilty" of doubting Dubié when he arrived at Troppau in October 1820.[41]

This modicum of optimism regarding Dubie's mission was shattered, however, during Alexander's time in Troppau. For two weeks the Russian Emperor did not broach the subject with King Friedrich-Wilhelm III of Prussia, despite "finding myself almost daily with him alone and in very private conversations." He was clearly on tenterhooks waiting for the Prussian monarch to instigate a conversation on the matter, but he "did not hear him speak one word about Dubié and his interviews." Unsettled by this silence, Alexander described to Golitsyn how he "broke the ice myself" a few days before the king's departure and asked him outright about his interviews with Dubié. Friedrich-Wilhelm's reply left Alexander in no doubt that "Dubié had transgressed the first condition I had set at his departure by announcing himself to the king as sent to him by me." The Prussian king met Dubié, who could apparently not articulate anything to him, so he "considered him only an adventurer, who was not qualified to inspire confidence." Alexander also enquired about Dubié's mission to Vienna with Emperor Francis II, who, tellingly, responded by keeping his mouth shut. The Russian emperor took this as a sign "of the truth of my inner feeling"[42]—namely, that the Dubié mission had been a major error. The Russian emperor's negative pronouncements against Dubié may have disappointed his uncle Duke Ferdinand, who arrived in Troppau at the beginning of November to consult with his nephew.[43] After all, Ferdinand had played a pivotal role in facilitating the voyage of Bouche and Dubié to St. Petersburg in 1819.

Dubié's conduct in Berlin and Vienna was the principal focus of the emperor's ire in his letter to Golitsyn. However, he also expresses unmistakable frustration and scepticism about Bouche, who was still being lavishly hosted in St. Petersburg: "I will tell you about Mme. Bouche, that more than once I have been in the position to tell you in our conversations that I thought that sometimes a lot of the human entered into the words of Mme. Bouche."[44] Alexander also admonished Bouche for sending numerous letters in relation to Dubié's mission, which "have not produced anything other than a deleterious effect." Moreover, the emperor scolds Bouche for intervening in the affairs of Madame Zebrowsky, who was also a resident of the Hotel de Londres in Petersburg. For Alexander, this was more proof of Bouche's increasing (and unwanted) dalliances into earthly affairs that should not concern her.

Interestingly, in his reply to the emperor from Petersburg, written on March 4, 1821, Golitsyn seems to defend Bouche: "If the powers do not want this new order of things, then hell has permission to raise the peoples to take away their power." Here Golitsyn seems to insinuate that if the other sovereigns reject the overtures transmitted by Dubié, then they risked revolutionary upheaval. Moreover, he defends this stance in millenarian terms by pronouncing that "the march of the Elect is clear in these circumstances," according to the preaching of Bouche.[45] Golitsyn also defends Bouche by downplaying the overall significance of any human concerns apparent in her behaviour.

Golitsyn's letter also has a pleading tone. He reminds the emperor that "the commitment that we have taken all three in the face of the living God was not a pleasantry." He seems to be reminding the emperor here of the secret ceremony they had participated in on December 25, 1819, in which they had accepted their "grand mission." The following passage seems to imply that Golitsyn, because he had been placed at the summit of the "Triangle," felt that he had a duty to be frank and tell the emperor what thoughts were playing on his mind: "And he whom you placed at the top of Triangle, which was laborious for him and without having wanted this . . . does he not have a responsibility before the High *Tré-Un*, if he did not tell you what weighted on his heart?"[46]

Given the overt scepticism revealed in the emperor's letter to Golitsyn from Laibach, it is wholly unsurprising that he chose to distance himself from Bouche when he returned to St. Petersburg, in May 1821. Golitsyn's long and heartfelt plea in March seems to have fallen on deaf ears. We know very little about Bouche's final months in the Russian capital, apart from what appears to have been a last-ditch effort in October to preserve her privileged lifestyle. She approached Ferronnays for the first time at the beginning of the month, and was permitted five hours to unburden herself of her current frustrations at her diminished status.[47]

On October 18, 1821, on the eve of her departure from Petersburg, Bouche contacted the emperor for a final time whilst she was still in Russia. It is a letter that protests her innocence and reaffirms her veneration of the monarch. She begins by stressing that "by submitting to the higher wills . . . I must remain silent, no longer having freedom." It would seem that she had been instructed by Heaven to return to France. She, the "organ of God who never changes" and "who made me announce the truth . . . without disguise" had no other option than to submit. Yet, Bouche reveals that she is reluctant to leave, because "Your Majesty needs, more than ever, the voice of the Word," which only she, a "most unworthy servant of the Lord," was able to give to the emperor. She also discloses that she had received "orders not to write" down these divine messages. In concluding her farewell letter, Bouche proclaims that she will continue to pray unceasingly for the emperor.[48]

The next day Bouche asked the Holy Word to give her permission to react to the instructions she had received from Heaven the previous day. The response she obtained from the Holy Word, as with all the answers, is highly abstruse. It begins by proclaiming: "Why, my daughter, would I not want it because I am calling you to serve my purposes."[49] One possible conclusion from the reply of the Holy Word is that Bouche had been commanded to cease acting as a divine intermediary. At one point the Holy Word exclaims, "I have opened this door for you and I have the right to close it to anyone."[50] The Holy Word's answer concludes with a reference to Matthew 7:21–23, which states: "Many will say to me in that day, Lord, Lord, have we not prophesied in thy name? . . . And then will I profess unto them, I never knew you: depart from me, ye that work iniquity."[51] This appears to be a warning not to purposefully ignore the will of God.

Resigned to her fate, Bouche sent two brief messages to Golitsyn on October 21, 1821.[52] It is apparent from the first letter that Golitsyn and Koshelev (who is mentioned by name) were still favourably inclined towards Bouche and still willing to convey her messages to the emperor. Bouche mentions that "your visit would have calmed the humility of which I am blessed," indicating that she had recently seen Golitsyn, before seemingly lamenting that God's will "is not done."[53]

Bouche departed from St. Petersburg in early November and arrived in Paris on December 6, where she stayed in the Hotel de la Paix until January 22. By February 1822, in one more remarkable twist of fate, Bouche was staying in Chaillot, at the home of Paul Barras, the former executive leader of the Directory, between 1795 and 1799. As strange as it may seem, it is likely that Richelieu facilitated this arrangement. He had granted an audience to Dubié in 1820 and was regularly updated on matters pertaining to Bouche, both when she was in Russia and on her return in Paris. Barras, in his memoirs, recalled that Richelieu "sought me out in my retreat" at Chaillot in March 1822 and engaged "in a conversation which quickly became familiar."[54] The timing of the duke's first visit was surely not coincidental. Indeed, it is understandable that Richelieu's curiosity may have been piqued by over two years of surveillance reports updating him on the progress of Bouche and her grand mission. By April Bouche felt sufficiently confident to pen a personal letter to Richelieu. Therein, she requested his aid in persuading the Duc de Doudeauville, the new director-general of the post office, to secure employment for her husband as a postal worker in Paris.[55]

Bouche continued to write to the Russian emperor for a time from her new residence at Chaillot. However, by the time of the Congress of Verona, in October 1822,

Emperor Alexander wanted nothing whatsoever to do with Bouche. This sentiment is forcefully expressed in a letter he wrote to Golitsyn from the congress: "I thought I told you that I did not want to maintain any relations with Mme Bouche. So, I beg you to return the letter she sent me, warning her that if there will be others, they will all be returned." In connection with Bouche, he then emphasised to Golitsyn to "remember the medallions and how we left them!!!" This is quite possibly a reference to the medals that Bouche had presented to them in December 1819.[56] The emperor's decisive severing of all contact with Bouche did not occur out of the blue. Indeed, since at least February 1821, the Russian sovereign had been expressing a degree of scepticism vis-à-vis the authenticity of the prophetess's gift. It is not clear whether Golitsyn was still sympathetic to Bouche at this point, but one cannot blame her for attempting to rekindle her brilliant lifestyle as a feted visionary, housed in style within stone's throw of the Winter Palace.

Despite her dramatic fall from grace, Bouche's lengthy two-year residence in St. Petersburg is testament to the profound and consequential legacy of the NIS in Russia. The emperor's attraction to the supposed prophetic talents of Bouche did not occur in a vacuum. Indeed, it should also not be seen as a mere continuation of a proclivity for female visionaries, first evident when he became acquainted with Krüdener, in 1815. By this time Golitsyn and Koshelev had already succeeded in channeling his spiritual worldview towards those who espoused chiliastic doctrines. In turn, Golitsyn and Koshelev themselves had been profoundly influenced by a millenarian culture that burst to life in 1805 in the Russian capital, following Grabianka's arrival in the city.

NOTES

1. Thérèse-Marguerite Isnard was born in the parish of St. Agricol in Avignon on Dec. 24, 1759. Here father was Laurence Isnard and her mother Thérèse Clare. She married Jean-François Bouche, a merchant, in the parish of Saint-Agricol, on Feb. 3, 1778. See ADdV GG 16 St. Agricol Baptêmes 1748–1772, 221; GG 28 St. Agricol, Mariages, 1773–1791, 103.

2. Bouche to Emperor Alexander I, Mar. 21, 1817. BIdlA, Fonds Richelieu, MSRIC 99, 170r–171v.

3. Bouche to Emperor Alexander I, undated. BIdlA, Fonds Richelieu, MSRIC 99, 176–7.

4. For an encapsulation of Krüdener's vision of the Russian Emperor's prophetic role, see Barbara v. Krüdener, *Le Camp de Vertus* (Lyon: Guyot Frères, 1815).

5. On Martin, see Louis Silvy, *Relation concernant Les Évènemens qui sont arrives a Thomas Martin, Laboureur a Gallardon* (Paris: L.-F. Hivert, 1831); Vicomte de Larochefoucauld, *Memoires de M. Le Vicomte de Larochefoucauld*, vol. 5 (Paris: Allardin, 1837), 5–27; Paul Marin, *Thomas Martin de Gallardon* (Paris: G. Carré, 1892); Claude Guillet, *La rumeur de Dieu: Apparitions, prophéties et miracles sous la Restauration* (Paris: Imago, 1994).

6. Emperor Alexander used the phrase "Éclairer *le Tri-Un*" in several letters to A. N. Golitsyn. See, for examples the letters he wrote to Golitsyn on Sept. 22, 1820 and Jan. 8, 1821. See Romanov, *Imperator Aleksandr*, vol. 1, 540–1.

7. "Surveillance de Mme Bouche, née Isnard, intriguante devenue member de la secte des illumines (1810–1823), AN, F/7/6971, dossier no. 12785. Note that the documents in this dossier are all unnumbered. All subsequent citations in this chapter are from this dossier, unless otherwise stated.

8. G. de Bertier de Sauvigny, "L'extravagante équipée de la prophetésse marseillaise à la cour extravagante du tsar Alexandre I-er," *Le Figaro littéraire* (Dec. 10, 1960): 5–6.

9. AN, F/7/6971, dossier no. 12785.

10. Dubié was the nephew of Joseph-André Dubié, a well-known book publisher in Marseille. On J.-A. Dubié, see AN F/18/1866. The baptismal records of Saint-Marie-Madeleine Parish in Avignon for August 1787 record the birth of a Sebastian Dubié to Léonard and Francesca Dubié. He would have been thirty-two in September 1819. The birth of no other male Dubié is recorded in the parish records of Avignon for the period and hence it is likely that Sebastian Dubié is the identity of the cabinetmaker who accompanied Bouche to meet Jahan and later journeyed with her to Russia. See ADdV GG 112 La Madeleine Baptêmes, 1782–1790, 94.

11. A "citoyen Ferrier" is listed in 1804 as being Professor of Latin and French at the *École secondaire* in Arles. See F. Heurley-Chaunier, "L'instruction publique au XVIIIème siècle et plus précisément après 1789, à Arles," *Bulletin des Archives municipals d'Arles* 6 (1990–1), 79.

12. "An early French Prophecy," *Gentleman's Magazine*, vol. 84 (1814), 210.

13. *Prophétie, écrite en 540 par Césaire, Évêque d'Arles* (Paris: Chaumerot, Jeune, Libraire, 1815), 6.

14. Agricol Moreau was known as a militant revolutionary and corresponded with Robespierre. He was arrested and put on trial in 1797, but was acquitted after three months. He became *procureur general* of Vaucluse in 1799. See Joseph Décembre, *Dictionnaire de la Révolution Française*, vol. 2 (Paris: Librairie Décembre-Alonnier, 1866), 438.

15. ADdV, GG 37 St. Agricol, N. M. D. 1791–1792, 7.

16. J.-M. Verger to J.-B. Willermoz, Oct. 24, 1801. BMdL, MS. 5425, 32.

17. Verger to Willermoz, 8 Frimaire, An 10. BMdL, MS. 5425, 33.

18. BIdlA, Fonds Richelieu, MSRIC 99, 172–3, 174–5.

19. BIdlA, Fonds Richelieu, MSRIC 99, 180–1.

20. BIdlA, Fonds Richelieu, MSRIC 99, 182.

21. In September 1790, Tieman wrote to Lavater that Ferdinand "is always full of his friends in A[vignon]." It is also possible that Eugen-Friedrich was an initiate of the Avignon Society. According to R. A. Koshelev, the Duchess of Württemberg went to Avignon in January 1789 "with two of her sons in order to find sublimities." See R. A. Koshelev to J. C. Lavater, Mar. 22, 1789. ZBZ anL 516.86.

22. Their sister, Sophie-Dorothea (1759–1828), known in Russia as Mariia Fyodorovna, became Dowager Empress after the assassination of her husband, Paul Petrovich, in 1801. See Shumigorskii, *Imperatritsa*. Eugen-Friedrich's son, Friedrich-Eugen-Karl (1788–1857), served with distinction as a general in the Russian army in the War of 1812. See Freiherrn von Helldorff, *Aus dem Leben des kaiserlich Russischen Generals der Infanterie Prinzen Eugen von Württemberg*, 4 vols. (Berlin: Verlag von Gustav Hempel, 1862).

23. Indeed, it is possible that Bouche and Ferdinand, at least, first became acquainted at the turn of the 1790s in Avignon.

24. BIdlA, Fonds Richelieu, MSRIC 99, 178–9.

25. Now known as Pokój and located in Lower Silesia Province in Poland. For a history of the Württemberg family at Carlsruhe, see F.-C. Esbach, *Das herzogliche Haus Württemberg zu Carlsruhe in Schlesien* (Stuttgart: Verlag von W. Kohlhammer, 1906).

26. E. P. v. W., *Die Wichtigkeit der Christus Religion* (1784).

27. [Eugen Friedrich Heinrich, Prinz v. Württemberg], *Einige freymäurerische Versammlungsreden* (Frankfurt-Leipzig, 1784). For a brief discussion of Eugen-Friedrich and this text, see Rudolf Schlögl, "Alchemie und Avantgarde: Das Praktischwerden der Utopie bei Rosenkreuzern und Freimaurern," in *Die Politisierung des Utopischen im 18. Jahrhundert*, eds. Monika Neugebauer-Wölk and Richard Saage (Tübingen: Max Niemeyer, 1996), 134–5.

Eugen-Friedrich was a leading Freemason of various lodges in Prussia from 1778 until into the nineteenth century, as well as a so-called *Zirkel* director of the *Gold- und Rosenkreuzer-Orden* in Oels. On his active participation in Prussian Freemasonry, see Karlheinz Gerlach, *Die Freimaurer im Alten Preussen 1738–1806: Die Logen zwischen mittlerer Oder und Niederrhein* (Innsbruck: Studienverlag, 2007), 152, 186–7, 194–5, 209; Gerlach, *Die Freimaurer im Alten Preussen 1738–1806: Die Logen in Berlin* (Innsbruck: Studienverlag, 2014), 378. On Eugen-Friedrich and Rosicrucianism, see R. D. Geffarth, *Religion und arkane Hierarchie* (Leiden: Brill, 2007), 113–14, 121.

28. Elisa von der Recke, "Elisa an Preissler," *Berliner Monatsschrift* (May 1786): 385–98. Also see Elisa von der Recke, *Nachricht von des berüchtligten Cagliostro Aufenthalte in Mitau im Jahre 1779* (Berlin-Stettin: Friedrich Nicolai, 1787).

29. E. F. H. von Württemberg, "Über Elisens Aufsatz im Mai der Berliner Monatsschrift 1786," *Berliner Monatsschrift* (July 1786), 9. The Shakespeare citation is from *Hamlet*, act 1, scene 5, 159–67. On Eugen-Friedrich as the inspiration for the protagonist of Friedrich Schiller's *Ghost Seer* (1787–1789), see Adalbert von Hanstein, *Wie entstand Schillers Geisterseher?* (Berlin: Verlag von Alexander Duncker, 1903), 33–80.

30. Mirabeau, *Histoire Secrete de la cour de Berlin*, vol. 1, 105.

31. See, for example, a report to the prefect of Bouches-Rhone, dated Jan. 26, 1820. Also see the letter from Monsieur Capure, dated Feb. 8, 1820.

32. Ferdinand married Pauline von Metternich, the sister of Klemens, the foreign minister and chancellor of Austria, on Feb. 23, 1817, in Marseille. See Lorenz Sönke and Dieter Mertens, *Das Haus Württemberg: Ein biographisches Lexicon* (Kohlhammer: Volker Press, 1997), 297.

33. L. J. M. R., *Précis historique de la mission de Marseille, en janvier et février 1820* (Marseille: Masvert, Libraire, Sur Le Port, 1820), 17.

34. In a letter to Golitsyn, penned between Feb. 8 and 15, 1821, Emperor Alexander wrote that a certain Madame Zebrowsky lived in the Hotel de Londres and "therefore in the same premises as Mme Bouche." See Romanov, *Imperator Aleksandr*, vol. 1, 550. For a contemporary description of the Hotel de Londres, see P. L. Iakovlev, *Chuvstvitel'nye puteshestviia i progulki po Nevskomu prospektu* (St. Petersburg: Petropolis, 2009).

35. Most likely the Winter Palace (as the ceremonies took place in mid-winter, but possibly the Catherine Palace at Tsarskoe Selo.

36. For a translated reproduction of the text of the Holy Alliance treaty, see Edward Hertslet, ed., *The Map of Europe by Treaty*, vol. 1 (London: Butterworths, 1875), 317–19. For a recent article on Emperor Alexander's project for a Christian union of nations in Europe, see Svetoslav Manoilov, "Emperor Alexander I's Project for a United Christian Nation in Europe," CLIOHRES.net, vol. 5 (2010): 17–30. Also see Adrian Brisku, "The Holy Alliance as 'An Order of Things Conformable

to the Interests of Europe and to the Laws of Religion and Humanity,'" in *Paradoxes of Peace in Nineteenth-Century Europe*, ed. Thomas Hippler and Miloš Vec (Oxford: Oxford University Press, 2015), 153–69.

37. Castlereagh to Lord Liverpool, Sept. 28, 1815, cited in C. K. Webster, *British Diplomacy, 1813–15* (London: G. Bell and Sons, 1921), 383.

38. G. B. Malleson, *Life of Prince Metternich* (London: W. H. Allen & Co., 1888), 143.

39. Ferronnays to É.-D. Pasquier, April 15, 1820, AMAE, 112CP/160, 198, 199v.

40. Emperor Alexander to A. N. Golitsyn, Feb. 8–15, 1821, in Romanov, *Imperator Aleksandr*, vol. 1, 549.

41. Emperor Alexander to Golitsyn, in Romanov, *Imperator Aleksandr*, vol. 1, 549.

42. Emperor Alexander to Golitsyn, in Romanov, *Imperator Aleksandr*, vol. 1, 549.

43. Richard Metternich, ed., *Memoirs of Prince Metternich 1815–1829*, vol. 3 (New York: Charles Scribner's Sons, 1881), 400.

44. Emperor Alexander to Golitsyn, in Romanov, *Imperator Aleksandr*, vol. 1, 548.

45. A. N. Golitsyn to Emperor Alexander, Mar. 4, 1821, in Romanov, *Imperator Aleksandr*, vol. 1, 554.

46. Golitsyn to Emperor Alexander, in Romanov, *Imperator Aleksandr*, vol. 1, 553.

47. Bertier de Sauvigny, "Une Marseillaise," 6.

48. Bouche to Emperor Alexander, Oct. 18, 1821. BIdlA, Fonds Richelieu, MSRIC 99, 196–7.

49. Bouche to "Saint Parole," Oct. 19, 1821. BIdlA, Fonds Richelieu, MSRIC 99, 198.

50. BIdlA, Fonds Richelieu, MSRIC 99, 201.

51. BIdlA, Fonds Richelieu, MSRIC 99, 201–2.

52. Bouche to A. N. Golitsyn, Oct. 21, 1821, BIdlA, Fonds Richelieu, MSRIC 99, 204–6.

53. Bouche to A. N. Golitsyn, Oct. 21, 1821, BIdlA, Fonds Richelieu, MSRIC 99, 204.

54. Paul Barras, *Memoirs of Barras: Member of the Directorate*, vol. 4, ed. George Duruy (New York: Harper & Brothers, 1896), 467–8.

55. Bouche to the Duc de Richelieu, April 8, 1822. MSRIC 84, 136r–136v.

56. Emperor Alexander to A. N. Golitsyn, Oct. 28, 1822, in Romanov, *Imperator Aleksandr*, vol. 1, 560.

Conclusion

ALTHOUGH MADAME BOUCHE fell out of favour with Emperor Alexander I in 1821, the fact that she and Dubié were invited to St. Petersburg by the sovereign in the first place is staggering. More remarkable still is the knowledge that Bouche's two-year residence in Russia cannot be regarded as a fleeting affair or a passing whim of the emperor. Indeed, after Bouche was effectively ostracised by Alexander I, she seems to have retained the confidence and affection of A. N. Golitsyn and, most likely, Koshelev. One other fascinating aspect of Bouche's time in St. Petersburg is that Emperor Alexander, Golitsyn, and Koshelev seem to have been very successful in concealing her presence at court and influence on their triumvirate. No contemporary Russian sources, at any rate, contain any mention of Bouche.

To keep Bouche's presence in St. Petersburg utterly secret was surely a calculated decision by Golitsyn, Koshelev, and the emperor. Knowledge of her intimate access to Alexander would have shocked and appalled a great many civil and church officials. After all, we must remember the harsh treatment Grabianka, who enjoyed no such direct access to the emperor at the time, received in 1807. In his official opinion of the entire interrogation process of Grabianka, between May and July 1807, Péchard-Deschamps was adamant that the leader of the NIS and his acolytes were a clear and present danger to the religious and civil pillars of Russian society:

> Russia is now the only country in Europe where religion is still a means of government for the Sovereign and a restraint on the people. The New Israel sect has dogmas that are so much opposed to the Greek religion, that it appears that any sectarian ... is constituted in revolt against his legitimate sovereign and against the religion of his fathers. Indeed, a sectarian swears allegiance and obedience to Count

Initiating the Millennium. Robert Collis, and Natalie Bayer, Oxford University Press (2020) © Oxford University Press.
DOI: 10.1093/oso/9780190903374.001.0001

Grabianka. He swears to obey the divine oracles and the royal and pontifical ordinances; he submits to two jurisdictions—civil and an ecclesiastical—and finally he changes the communion of his religious belief.[1]

Both Golitsyn and Koshelev would have been well aware of the hostility towards Grabianka and the NIS among powerful cliques in Russia in 1807, such as the Moscow Rosicrucians, led by Pozdeev, and the conservative Orthodoxy clergy and their supporters in the emperor's government. Indeed, Muromstov testified that Golitsyn tried (and failed) to secure Grabianka's release from prison.[2] Yet, as we documented in chapter 7, Golitsyn and Koshelev formed a circle of like-minded chiliasts with Pleshcheeva and Lenivtsev, the foremost Russian members of the NIS in St. Petersburg, not long after Grabianka's death.

To be sure, the Russian authorities were not alone in viewing the NIS in a wholly negative hue. For them they were a heretical sect intent on destabilising the religious foundations of the countries in which they were active. The officials' sense of paranoia vis-à-vis the perceived nefarious ambitions of the society was exacerbated by the war against Napoleon. It was also easy to latch onto the conspiratorial theories advanced by Barruel, which found a receptive audience in Russia after 1805. Furthermore, the arrest by the British government of Richard Brothers in 1795, for the supposedly treasonable crime of imagining the regicide of the sovereign, provided a legal precedent in the wake of the execution of Louis XVI.

Grabianka's arrest in 1807 occurred some twenty-one years after a number of *illuminés* in Avignon had suffered a police raid by the papal authorities, who were highly suspicious of the heretical aspects of the group's religious practises. The revolutionary leaders in Avignon also arrested several *illuminés* in 1793, although this had less to do with heresy and more to do with potential links to counter-revolutionary forces. The *illuminés* in Avignon also aroused the indignation of other sects and seemingly like-minded prophets. As mentioned in chapter 3, Benedict Chastanier, a former *illuminé* himself, labelled the group "lying prophets."[3] The English prophetess Sarah Flaxmer went even further in 1795, when she wrote that "Satan knowing that the kingdom of Christ was now at hand [had] established a synagogue at Avignon." These satanic "angels" had been "dispersed into all nations . . . to deceive the elect of God."[4] Former devotees, such as Tieman, Reuterholm, and Ferdinand of Württemberg, quickly abandoned the society once they realised they had been duped. This was especially the case after Cappelli's arrest in Rome in 1790. For Tieman, Cappelli was now nothing more than an "an adventurer, [an] imbecilic man, so vain and stupid"; for Reuterholm the entire society in Avignon had been "completely unmasked" as "spiritual deceivers."[5] In 1792, Ferdinand, too, confessed to being profoundly humiliated by his initial faith in the "cunning trickster" Cappelli.[6]

Yet twenty-seven years later, Ferdinand fell under the sway of Madame Bouche in Marseilles. Had he not taken on board the lessons of 1790? In May 1790, he had proclaimed to Lavater that "the time is short, the end approaches, the bow is bent, and the angel (Michael) is about to descend."[7] Crucially, it would seem that the bitter disappointment Ferdinand felt about Cappelli's charlatanism did not extinguish his millenarian worldview. As he wrote to Reuterholm in 1792, "God alone knows the purity of my intentions."[8] Consequently, though he was never reconciled with the *illuminés* in Avignon or the NIS in St. Petersburg, he maintained his profound sense of millenarian expectancy.

In essence, Madame Bouche reimagined the vehicle by which the church would be restored to its original purity, with, it would seem, the aid of Joseph Ferrier. No longer was this vision tied to a society of consecrates, as had been the case up until the death of Grabianka. By 1810, she had begun to articulate a prophetic vision that foresaw sovereigns and the pope, that is, counter-revolutionary leaders, as the means by which an earthly millennium would be accomplished. She was to be rebuffed by the pope, as well as Charles IV of Spain and Louis XVIII of France. However, Emperor Alexander proved to be much more amenable to her grand vision, as well as to the similar utterances of Krüdener, after his triumphant victory over Napoleon in 1814–1815. And it would seem that Ferdinand, as the emperor's uncle, was more than willing to imagine his nephew in such a consequential role for humanity. Alongside his brother, Eugen-Friedrich, therefore, Ferdinand was eager to ensure that Bouche was able to be at the emperor's side to guide him via the pronouncements of the Holy Word. Thus, there was far from a descent into a chiliasm of despair after the disintegration of the NIS in 1807. Bouche, in particular, imagined a new path to the realisation of New Jerusalem on earth. However, after this *route de la vérité* was permanently blocked by Emperor Alexander himself in 1822, Bouche was forced to retreat to France to live out the rest of her life in obscurity. What is more, her followers in Russia, Golitsyn and Koshelev, soon ceased to play such an active and intimate role as the emperor's spiritual advisers. Although they did not despair, they seemingly resigned themselves to expressing their chiliastic visions among a small circle of peers in St. Petersburg.

NOTES

1. RGIA, Fond 1163, op. 1, d. 16a, 188r.

2. Muromtsov, "Razkaz," 19–20.

3. Chastanier, *Word of Advice*, 38.

4. Sarah Flaxmer, *Satan Revealed; or the Dragon Overcome* (London, 1795), 9.

5. Tieman to the Duchess of Württemberg, Nov. 29, 1791, HSAS, G237 Bü 23; Reuterholm to Duke Karl of Södermanland, Dec. 5, 1791, RA, Ädelgrenska samlingen, 720742, vol. 35.

6. Ferdinand of Württemberg to Reuterholm, Jan. 23, 1792, RA Reuterholmska samlingen, 720741, vol. E5122.

7. Ferdinand of Württemberg to Lavater, May 13, 1790, cited in Viatte, *Les Sources Occultes*, vol. 1, p. 96.

8. Ferdinand to Reuterholm, Jan. 23, 1792, RA Reuterholmska samlingen, 720741, vol. E5122.

Appendix

INITIATES AND CLOSE ASSOCIATES OF THE ILLUMINÉS
D'AVIGNON/NIS, 1779–1807

I. BERLIN-RHEINSBERG-PODOLIA PERIOD (1779–1783)

Name	Number (if known)	Consecration Date (if known)
1. Tadeusz Grabianka	139A	April, 20, 1779
2. Antoine-Joseph Pernety	135A	April 22, 1779
3. Louis-Joseph-Bernard-Philbert Guyton de Morveau (Brumore)	579A	April 22, 1779
4. Mademoiselle Bruchié	579B	April 22, 1779
5.Charles-Pierre de Morinval	246A	April 26, 1779
6. Anna Grabianka	139C	June 22, 1779
7. Martyna Stadnicka	357A	June 24, 1779
8. Teresa Grabianka	137A	July 14, 1779
9. Jan Amor Tarnowski	357B	August 4, 1779
10. Tekla Tarnowska	579C	August 11, 1779
11. Michał Aleksander Ronikier	379A	c. October 1780
12. Teresa Ronikier	137B	c. October 1780
13. Jean-Alexis Borrelly	767	c. December 1780
14. Marie-Jeanne Borrelly	123A	c. December 1780
15. Prince Heinrich of Prussia	999	c. December 1780
16. Catherine Baley	135E	c. April 1782
17. Józefa Ronikier		c. April 1782
18. Franciszek Leyman		c. August 1782

Individuals who consulted the Holy Word (without seemingly being consecrated)

Name	Dates
1. Claude-Etienne Le Bauld de Nans	February 20–21, 1779
2. Pierre-Jean-Fromentin de Blainville	December 24, 1779
3. Alexandre de Baligand Ferrières	September 6–26, 1780

2. FIRST AVIGNON PERIOD (1785–1790)

Name	Number (if known)	Consecration Date (if known)
1. François-Louis Bourgeois de la Richardière	915	March 20, 1785
2. Antoine-Étienne Bouge	219A	March 23, 1785
3. Claude-François Delhomme		c. May 1785
4. Thomas-Nicolas-Jean de Rozières		c. 1785
5. Joseph Ferrier	369B	c. 1786
6. Jean-Agricol Leblond		c. 1786
7. Ottavio Cappelli	111	1787 or earlier
8. Jacques-Maurice Pernety	135F	June 16, 1787
9. Honoré-Louise Pernety		
10. François-Hippolyte Barthélémon		c. 1787
11. Françoise Pernety	389	before March 1788
12. William Bousie		1788 or earlier
13. Mary Bousie		1788 or earlier
14. Robert Bousie		1788 or earlier
15. Alexander Mackglashan		1788 or earlier
16. Chevalier John MacGregor		1788 or earlier
17. Benedict Chastanier		1788 or earlier
18. Guillaume de Paul		earlier than July 1788
19. Chiara Cappelli		
20. Cerbonio Cappelli		
21. Marie-Daniel Bourrée de Corberon		1788 or earlier
22. Charlotte de Corberon		1788 or earlier
23. Louis-Michel Gombault	123E	
24. Thomas Spence Duché		1788
25. Marcus Lemort de Métigny		1788 or earlier
26. Madame de Métigny		1788 or earlier
27. Comte Marie-Antone Bouët de Martange		1788 or earlier
28. Baron de Seiffert (Saiffert)		1788 or earlier
29. Chevalier C.-M. de Roqueville		1788 or earlier
30. Vineau		1788 or earlier
31. Marquis René de Thomé		1788 or earlier

Name	Number (if known)	Consecration Date (if known)
32. Bellery		1788 or earlier
33. Joseph-Pascal Parraud		1788 or earlier
34. Sergei Ivanovich Pleshcheev	973	November 19, 1788
35. Deravine		November 20, 1788
36. Duchess Friederike Sophia of Württemberg		c. November 1788
37. Duke Ferdinand of Württemberg		c. November 1788
38. William Bryan	147	1789 or earlier
39. John Wright	123	April 1, 1789
40. Louis Dagobert Lefort		1789 or earlier
41. Peter Woulfe		1789 or earlier
42. Abbé Barozzi		1789 or earlier
43. François Picot		1789 or earlier
44. Marie-Elisabeth Colas		1789 or earlier
45. Jean-François Nicolas		1789 or earlier
46. Sophie Rivoire		1789 or earlier
47. Anne-Marie-Olympe de Fumel		1789 or earlier
48. Baroness Finnely?		1789 or earlier
49. Anne-Claudia Le Maire d'Attigny		c. November 1789
50. Gustaf Adolf Reuterholm	373A	December 9, 1789
51. Carl Göran Silfverhielm	357D	December 10, 1789
52. Louis-Marie-François de la Forest Divonne	579G	December 19, 1789

Individuals who sought initiation

1. Carl Friedrich Tieman	October 1787-1789
2. François-Marie de Chefdebien	July 1788
3. Alexandre Louis Thiroux de Mondésir	August 1789

Possible link	**Period of Involvement**
1. Charles Rainsford	1788–

3. SECOND AVIGNON PERIOD (1791–1802)

Name	Consecration
1. Thérèse Bouche	1791 or earlier
2. Jean-François Bouche	1791 or earlier
3. Jean-Baptiste Allier	
4. Nicolas Simonin	1796/1797
5. Parmentier	
6. Muratori	

Name	Consecration
Close Association	**Period of Involvement**
1. Klemens Liberadzki	1795–1797
2. Joseph-Marie Verger	1801 or earlier
3. Ange-Charles Gabriel de Saint-Charles	c. 1802

4. GALICIA, VOLHYNIA, AND PODOLIA (1803–1805)

Name	Consecration
1. Elżbieta Izabela Lubomirska	c. 1803–1804
2. Józef August Iliński	c. 1803–1804
3. Stanisław Szczęsny Potocki	c. 1804–1805
4. Michał Jerzy Wandalin Mniszech	c. 1804–1805

New Israel Society Membership List (1805–1806)

Name	Number	Consecration Date
1. Aleksandr Alekseevich Lenivtsev	731	September 14, 1805
2. Mikhail Alekseevich Lenivstev	527	October 1, 1805
3. Ivan Andreevich Petrov	121	October 20, 1805
4. Pyotr Iakovlevich Il'in	222a	October 20, 1805
5. Anton Ivanov	234a	October 20, 1805
6. Pyotr Ivavovich Timofeev	271	October 20, 1805
7. Vasilii Fyodorovich Malinovskii	413	October 20, 1805
8. Natal'ia Fedotovna Pleshcheeva	341	November 19, 1805
9. John Grieve	523	December, 6, 1805
10. Hélène Laurent (?)	191	February 7, 1806
11. Tat'iana Timofeeva	334	February 14, 1806
12. Ekaterina Danilovna Volkova	122A	April 11, 1806
13. Praskov'ia Aleksandrovna Volkova	244	April 11, 1806
14. Elizaveta Aleksandrovna Volkova	112A	April 11, 1806
15. Aleksandr Aleksandrovich Volkov	365	May 8, 1806
16. Agrippina Petrova	357	May 8, 1806
17. Sof'ia Andreevna Malinovskaia	133	May 8, 1806
18. Sof'ia Aleksandrovna Volkova	111	May 26, 1806
19. Josephine Cuënod	332	May 26, 1806
20. Tat'iana Petrovna Timofeeva	532	May 28, 1806
21. Agrippina Petrovna Petrova (née Timofeeva)	842	May 28, 1806
22. Mariia Petrovna Timofeeva	392	May 28, 1806
23. Pyotr Petrovich Timofeev	412	May 28, 1806
24. Natal'ia Petrovna Timofeeva	123	May 28, 1806

Name	Number	Consecration Date
25. Varvara Ivanova	139	May 30, 1806
26. Evdokhiia Ivanova	818	May 30, 1806
27. Vladimir Lukich Borovikovskii	432	June 4, 1806
28. Aleksei Efimovich Miasoedov	234B	June 16, 1806
29. Vladimir Vasil'evich Nekliudov	343	June 16, 1806
30. Pavel Alekseevich Lenivtsev	231	July 7, 1806
31. Anton Jeletzky	912	July 25, 1806
32. Liubov Petrovna Il'ina	134	July 30, 1806
33. Sof'ia Petrovna Il'ina	132	July 30, 1806
34. Grigorii Maksimovich Pokhodiashin	113	July 31, 1806
35. Egor Mikhailovich Riabinin	313	July 31, 1806
36. Iakov Alekseevich Il'in	122B	July 31, 1806
37. Pyotr Ivanovich Ozerov	112B	August 5, 1806
38. Mariia Aleksandrovna Ozerova	142	August 5, 1806
39. Mariia Ivanovna Ozerova	573	August 5, 1806
40. Mikhail Ivanovich Donaurov	363	August 6, 1806
41. Mariia Fedotovna Donaurova	222B	August 6, 1806
42. Agrippina Riabinina	767	August 10, 1806
43. Sasha Salamatin	111	August 21, 1806
44. Gavriil Sterliadev	244	September 6, 1806
45. Vasilii Fyodorovich Nalimov	637	September 8, 1806
46. Andrei Ivanovich Kovalevskii	121	September 12, 1806
47. Aleksandr Fyodorovich Labzin	138	December 9, 1806
48. Aleksandr Grigor'evich Cherevin	341	December 9, 1806
49. Iosif Adamovich Turchilo	322	December 9, 1806
50. Dmitrii Grigor'evich Levitskii	119	December 9, 1806
51. Pyotr Ivanovich Rusanovskii	121	December 9, 1806
52. Anna Evdokimovna Labzina	313	December 9, 1806
53. Georg Ewald Hermann von Hoyningen-Huene	975	December 30, 1806
54. Nadezhda Fyodorovna Mikulina	467	December 30, 1806
55. Elena Ivanova	353	December 30, 1806
56. Elizaveta Vasil'evna Malinovskaia	159	December 30, 1806
57. Christine Wenigge	517	December 30, 1806
58. Christine Krollé	538	December 30, 1806
59. Anastasiia Iakovleva Levitskaia	564	December 30, 1806
60. Agaf'ia Andreeva	642	December 30, 1806

Additional Members Consecrated in Early 1807

61. Sof'ia Alekseevna Mudrova
62. Matvei Matveevich Muromtsev

SELECT BIBLIOGRAPHY

Amblard, Léon. "Tardivon (Jacques de), dernier Abbé de la Congrégation de St-Ruf et la Société académique de Valence." *Bulletin de la Société Départementale d'Archéologie et de Statistique de la Drome* 27 (1893): 69–81.

Anderberg, Göran. "Till frågan om Reuterholmska arkivets mystiska papper." *Historisk Tidskrift för Finland* 1 (2003): 1–23.

Anderberg, Göran. "Gustaf Adolf Reuterholms vallfart till revolutionens Frankrike och Italien." *Historisk Tidskrift för Finland* 3 (2005): 305–39.

Aulard, F.-A. *Recueil des Actes du Comité de Salut Public.* 28 vols. Paris: Imprimerie Nationale, 1893–1951.

Barrell, John. *Imagining the King's Death: Figurative Treason, Fantasies of Regicide, 1793–1796.* Oxford: Oxford University Press, 2000.

Barruel, Augustin. *Memoirs: Illustrating the History of Jacobinism.* Translated by Robert Clifford. 4 vols. London: T. Burton, 1797–1798.

Bartenev, Iu. N. "Razskazy kniazia Aleksandra Nikolaevicha Golitsyna. Iz zapisok Iu. N. Barteneva." *Russkii arkhiv* 8 (1886): 305–33.

Berbiguier, A.-V.-C. *Les Farfadets, ou tous les démons ne sont pas de l'autre monde.* 3 vols. Paris: P. Gueffier, 1821.

Bernard, Thalès. "L'Alchimie." *L'Europe Littéraire* (January 10–February 28, 1863): 181–4, 212–14, 264–6, 295–9.

Bernard, Thalès. "Notes sur Samuel Best, serviteur de dieu." *L'Europe Littéraire* (January 24, 1863): 219–20.

Bertier de Sauvigny, G. de. "L'extravagante équipée de la prophetésse marseillaise à la cour extravagante du tsar Alexandre I-er." *Le Figaro littéraire* (December 10, 1960): 5–6.

Breymayer, Reinhard. "Elie Artiste: Johann Daniel Müller de Wissenbach/Nassau (1716 jusqu'a après 1785), un aventurier entre le piétisme radicale et l'illuminisme." In *Lumières et illuminisme: Actes du colloque international (Cortona, 3–6 octobre 1983)*, edited by Mario Matucci, 65–84. Pisa: Pacini, 1984.

Breymayer, Reinhard. "Elias Artista: Johann Daniel Müller aus Wissenbach/Nassau, ein kritischer freund Swedenborgs, und seine wirkung auf die schwäbischen pietisten F. C." In *Literatur und Kultur im deutschen Südwesten zwischen Renaissance und Aufkläkrung: neue Studien*, edited by Wilhelm Kühlmann, 329–72. Amsterdam: Rodopi, 1995.

Bricaud, Joanny. *Les Illuminés d'Avignon: Étude sur Dom Pernety et son groupe.* Paris: Amici Librorum, 1927.

Brownbill, Elizabeth. *A Short Account of the Personal Appearance of Jesus Christ to Eliz. Brownbill.* Liverpool: R. Ferguson, 1788.

Brumore, M. de. *Drames Nouveaux: Les Calas, en trois actes et en prose. Les Salver, ou la faute réparée.* Berlin: George-Jacques Decker, 1778.

Brumore, M. de. *La Vie privée d'un Prince Célèbre, ou details des loisirs du Prince Henri de Prusse.* Veropolis [Berlin]: 1784.

Brumore, M. de. "Lettre à M. le marquis de Thomé." *Journal encyclopédique* (December 1785): 285–97.

Bryan, William. *A Testimony of the Spirit of Truth, concerning Richard Brothers.* London: J. Wright, 1795.

B[ulgakov], A. *Biografiia Aleksandra Aleksandrovicha Volkova.* Moscow: Tipografiia Avgusta Cemena, 1833.

Caillet, Serge. "Des Illuminés d'Avignon à la Fraternitié Polaire: Deux Oracles Numériques aux XVIII^c et XX^c siècles." *Politica Hermetica* 21 (2007): 26–47.

Chastanier, Benedict. *A Word of Advice to a Benighted World.* London, 1795.

Collis, Robert, and Bayer, Natalie. "Light from the North: Tadeusz Grabianka, the New Israel Society and Millenarian Sentiment among the Russian Nobility, 1788–1807." In *A Century Mad and Wise: Russia in the Age of the Enlightenment*, edited by Emmanuel Waegemans et al., 353–68. Groningen, The Netherlands: Russia Centre, 2015.

Colonjon, Henry de. "Société Académique et Patriotique de Valence." *Bulletin de la Société Départementale d'Archéologie et de Statistique de la Drome*, vol. 1 (1866): 90–99.

Dampmartin, A. H. *Événemens qui se sont passes sous mes yeux pendant la Révolution Française.* 2 vols. Berlin, 1799.

Danilewicz, M. L. "'The King of the New Israel': Thaddeus Grabianka (1740–1807)." *Oxford Slavonic Papers*, n.s., 1 (1968): 49–73.

Daudet, Ernest. *Histoire de l'émigration pendant la Révolution française: Du 18 fructidor au 18 brumaire.* 2 vols. Paris: Librairie Hachette, 1905.

Dobbs, Francis. *A Concise View from History and Prophecy, of the Great Predictions in the Sacred Writings.* Dublin: John Jones, 1800.

Drzewiecki, Józef. *Pamiętniki Józefa Drzewieckiego spisane przez niego samego (1772–1802).* Vinius: Nakładem i Drukiem Józefa Zawadzkiego, 1858.

Edelstein, Dan, ed. *The Super-Enlightenment: Daring to Know Too Much.* Oxford: Voltaire Foundation, 2010.

Eynard, Charles. *Vie de Madame de Krudener.* 2 vols. Paris: Cherbuliez, 1849.

Fabre, P.-J. *L'Alchimiste chrétien.* Edited and translated by Frank Greiner. Milan: Arché, 2001.

Faivre, Antoine. "Un Familier des Sociétés Ésotériques au Dix-Huitième Siècle: Bourrée de Corberon." *Revue des Sciences Humaines* 126 (1967): 259–87.

Faivre, Antoine. *Eckartshausen et la théosophie chrétienne.* 2nd ed. Hyères: La Pierre Philosophale, 2016.

Faivre, Antoine. *De Londres à Saint-Pétersbourg: Carl Friedrich Tieman (1743–1802) aux carrefours des courants illuministes et maçonniques.* Milan: Arché, 2018.

Felice, Renzo de. *Note e Ricerche Sugli "Illuminati" e il Misticismo Rivoluzionario (1789–1800).* Rome: Edizioni di Storia e Letteratura, 1960.

Garrett, Clarke. *Respectable Folly: Millenarians and the French Revolution in France and England.* Baltimore: Johns Hopkins University Press, 1975.

Garrett, Clarke. "Swedenborg and the Mystical Enlightenment in Late Eighteenth-Century England." *Journal of the History of Ideas* 45:1 (1984): 67–81.

Golitsyn, A. N. "Kniaz' A. N. Golitsyn (v ego pis'makh)." *Russkii arkhiv* 3 (1905): 360–455.

Goriaïnow, Serge. "Paul Ier et Stanislas Auguste. Leurs entretiens en 1797 à Peterhof, Gatchina et St.-Pétersbourg." *Revue contemporaine* 33 (1911): 44–52, 161–83.

Gosse, Pierre Frédéric. *Portefeuille d'un ancien Typographie ou recueil de lettres.* The Hague: n. p., 1824.

Grégoire, Henri. *Histoire des Sectes Religieuses.* 2 vols. Paris: Potey, Egron, Foucault, 1810–1811.

Hamilton, Andrew. *Rheinsberg: Memorials of Frederick the Great and Prince Henry of Prussia.* 2 vols. London: John Murray, 1880.

Hindmarsh, Robert. *Rise and Progress of the New Jerusalem Church, in England, America and other parts.* Edited by Rev. Edward Madeley. London: Hodson & Son, 1861.

Holmberg, Linn. *The Forgotten Encyclopedia: The Maurists' Dictionary of Arts, Crafts, and Sciences, the Unrealized Rival of the Encyclopédie of Diderot and d'Alembert.* Umeå, Sweden: Umeå University Press, 2014.

Joly, Alice. "Le Sainte-Parole des illuminés d'Avignon." *Cahiers de la tour Saint-Jacques* 2–4 (1960): 98–116.

Jones, John Paul. *Memoirs of Rear-Admiral Paul Jones.* 2 vols. Edinburgh: Oliver and Boyd, 1830.

Kondakov, Iurii. *Orden zolotogo i rozovogo kresta v Rossii. Teoreticheskii gradus solomonvykh nauk.* St. Petersburg: Asterion, 2012.

Kondakov, Iurii. *Rozenkreitsery, martinisty i "vnutrennie khristiane" v Rossii kontsa XVIII-pervoi chetverti XIX veka.* St. Petersburg: RGPU im. A. I. Gertsena, 2012.

Kondakov, Iurii. *Kniaz' A. N. Golitsyn: pridvornyi, chinovnik, khristianin.* St. Petersburg: ElekSis, 2014.

Kruglikov, A. P. *Moi vospominaniia.* Iaroslavl': Avers Plius, 2006.

Laikevich, S. A. *Vospominaniia Sof'i Alekseevny Laikevich.* St. Petersburg: Tip. M. P. S., 1905.

Le Forestier, René. *La Franc-Maçonnerie templière et occultiste aux XVIIIe XIXe siècles.* Paris: Aubier-Montaigne, 1970.

Lekeby, Kjell. *Gustaviansk Mystik.* Sala/Södermalm: Vertigo Förlag, 2010.

Lekeby, Kjell. *Gustaf Adolf Reuterholms hemliga arkiv från 1780-talet.* Stockholm: Pleiaderna, 2011.

Lekeby, Kjell *Esoterica i Svenska Frimuraordens arkiv 1776–1803.* Stockholm: Pleiaderna, 2011.

Lineham, Peter. "The Origins of the New Jerusalem Church in the 1780s." *Bulletin of the John Rylands Library* 70:3 (1988): 109–22.

Longinov, Mikhail. "Odin iz magikov XVIII veka." *Russkii vestnik* 28 (1860): 579–603.

Lubianovskii, F. P. *Vospominaniia Feodora Petrovicha Lubianovskago, 1777–1834.* Moscow: Tipografiia Gracheva, 1872.

Luchet, J.-P.-L. de. *Essai sur la secte des Illuminés.* Paris: n. p., 1789.

Marcel, Adrien. "Quatre Maisons des Illuminés d'Avignon." *Mémoires de l'Académie de Vaucluse* (1922): 85–101.

Marker, Gary. "The Enlightenment of Anna Labzina: Gender, Faith and Public Life in Catherinian and Alexandrian Russia." *Slavic Review* 59:2 (2000): 369–90.

Martin, John. *Imposture Detected: Or Thoughts on a Pretended Prophet and on the Prevalence of His Impositions.* London: W. Smith, 1787.

Meillassoux-Le Cerf, Micheline. *Dom Pernety et les Illuminés d'Avignon.* Milan: Arché, 1992.

Mesliand, Claude. "Franc-Maçonnerie et religion à Avignon au XVIIIᵉ siècle." *Annales historiques de la Révolution française* 197 (1969): 447–68.

Mesliand, Claude. "Renaissance de la franc-maçonnerie Avignonnaise a la fin de l'ancien regime (1774–1789)." *Bulletin d'Histoire Économique et Sociale de la Révolution Française. Année 1970* (1972): 23–82.

Mirabeau, H.-G. Riqueti de. *Lettre du Comte de Mirabeau à M. . . . sur M. M. de Cagliostro et Lavater.* Berlin: François de Lagarde, 1786.

Morveau, Abbé de. *L'Inoculation par aspiration: Épitre présentée a la reine.* Paris: Musier, 1774.

Morveau, Abbé de. *Le Triomphe de la religion, où le sacrifice de Madame Louise de France.* Paris: Musier fils, 1774.

Muromtsov, M. M. "Razkaz ochevidtsa o grafe Grabianke." *Sovremennaia letopis' russkago vestnika* 13 (1860): 19–21.

Odhner, C. T. *Annals of the New Church.* Philadelphia: Academy of the New Church, 1898.

Önnerfors, Andreas. "'Envoyées des Glaces du Nord Jusque dans ces Climats': Swedish Encounters with *Les Illuminés d'Avignon* at the End of the Eighteenth Century." In *Diffusions et circulations des pratiques maçonniques XVIIIᵉ–XXᵉ siècle,* edited by Pierre-Yves Beaurepaire et al., 167–94. Paris: Classiques Garnier, 2012.

Pernety, Antoine-Joseph. *Les Vertus, le pouvoir, la clémence et la gloire de Marie, Mere de Dieu.* Paris: n.p., 1790.

Porset, Charles. *Les Philalèthes et les convents de Paris.* Paris: Honoré Champion, 1996.

Pypin, Aleksandr. "Materialy dlia istorii masonskikh lozh." *Vestnik Evropy* 1 (1872): 174–214, 561–603.

Rolle, Antoni Józef. *Tadeusz Leszczyc Grabianka Starosta Liwski i Teresa z Stadnickich Jego Małżonka.* Lviv: We Lwowie Winiarz, 1875.

Romanov, N. M. *Imperator Aleksandr I. Opyt istoricheskago izsledovaniia.* 2 vols. St. Petersburg: Gosudarstvennaia bumaga, 1912.

Romme, Gilbert. *Correspondance 1779–1786,* vol. 2, tome 1. Edited by Anne-Marie Bourdin et al. Clermont Ferrand: Presses Universitaires Blaise-Pascal, 2014.

Saint-Martin, Louis-Claude de. *Mon Portrait Historique: 1789–1803.* Edited by Robert Amadou. Paris: R. Juilliard, 1961.

Schinkel, B. von. *Minnen ur Sveriges Nyare Historia. Andra Delen. Gustaf III och hans tid (1788–1792).* Stockholm: P. A. Norstedt, 1852.

Serkov, Andrei. *Istoriia russkogo masonstva XIX veka.* St. Petersburg: Izdatel'stvo imeni N. I. Novikova, 2000.

Serkov, Andrei. *Russkoe masonstvo 1731–2000. Entsiklopedicheskii islovar'*. Moscow: ROSSPEN, 2001.

Shumigorskii, E. S. *Imperatritsa Mariia Fyodorovna (1759–1828)*. 2 vols. St. Petersburg: Tipografiia I. N. Skorokhodov, 1892.

Snoek, Jan. "Illuminés d'Avignon." In *Dictionary of Gnosis and Western Esotericism*, edited by Wouter J. Hanegraaff, 597–600. Leiden: Brill, 2006.

Sturzen-Becker, O.-P. *Reuterholm efter hans egna memoirer*. Stockholm-Copenhagen: S. Trier, 1862.

Swedenborg, Emanuel. *Les Merveilles du ciel et de l'enfer et des terres planétaires et astrales*. Translated by A.-J. Pernety. Berlin: George-Jacques Decker, 1782.

Swedenborg, Emanuel. *Traité curieux des charmes de l'amour conjugal dans ce monde et dans l'autre*. Translated by M. de Brumore. Berlin and Basle: George-Jacques and J. Henri Decker, 1784.

Swedenborg, Emanuel. *La Sagesse Angélique sur l'Amour Divin, et sur la Sagesse Divine*. Translated by A.-J. Pernety. 2 vols. Lyon: les frères Périsse, 1786.

Ujejski, Józef. *Król Nowego Izraela*. Warsaw: Kasa im. J. Mianowskiego, Instytut Popierania Polskiej Twórczości Naukowej, 1924.

Viatte, Auguste. *Les Sources Occultes du Romantisme. Illuminisme: Théosophie 1770–1820*. 2 vols. Paris: Honoré Champion, 1965.

Vissac, Marc de. "Dom Pernety et les Illuminés d'Avignon." *Mémoires de l'Académie de Vaucluse* 6 (1906): 219–38.

Worrall, David. "William Bryan, Another Anti-Swedenborgian Visionary Engraver of 1789." *Blake: An Illustrated Quarterly* 34:1 (Summer 2000): 14–22.

Wright, John. *A Revealed Knowledge of Some Things that will speedily be fulfilled in the World*. London, 1794.

Zarcone, Thierry. "Francs-Maçons et illuminés face à l'inquisition dans l'Avignon pontificale (1737–1792)." *Politica Hermetica* 32 (2018): 83–111.

INDEX

241